Corporate Governance in India

An Evaluation

Fifth Edition

Subhash Chandra Das
Management Consultant
Former Visiting Faculty
Indian Institute of Social Welfare and Business Management
University of Calcutta
and
Former Director (Finance), HPC Ltd.

PHI Learning Private Limited
Delhi-110092
2024

₹925.00

CORPORATE GOVERNANCE IN INDIA: An Evaluation, Fifth Edition
Subhash Chandra Das

ISBN-978-93-91818-06-7 (Print Book)
ISBN-978-93-91818-11-1 (e-Book)

Published by Asoke K. Ghosh, PHI Learning Private Limited, Rimjhim House, 111, Patparganj Industrial Estate, Delhi-110092 and Printed by Syndicate Binders, A-20, Hosiery Complex, Noida, Phase-II Extension, Noida-201305 (N.C.R. Delhi).

Dedicated to

My Parents

Contents

Foreword

Good governance is not just good management. It is something which is much broader, and includes fair, efficient and transparent administration designed to meet certain well-defined objectives in an organization. The essence of good corporate governance is a framework which ensures effective accountability of management towards all its stakeholders. Good governance ensures that all the stakeholders, be they shareholders, employees, customers and suppliers, government and the community, all get fair and adequate attention to meet their justified requirements. It also involves the corporate to ensure that environmental and societal requirements of the community in which it operates are adequately addressed.

Good governance demands that a corporate house must have a responsibility to set exemplary standards of ethical behaviours in its internal and external relationships, thereby achieving 'value addition' in terms of stability and growth, confidence and long-term sustenance of stakeholder relationships, brand equity and excellent governance credentials. The economic policy adopted by the Government of India consequent to liberalization of the economy post 1991 necessitated a demand for introduction and implementation of a proper corporate governance policy in the day-to-day management of companies, both in the interests of stakeholders as also for the development of the economy. The need of the hour is a total shift towards 'shareholder approval and disclosure based regime' from the erstwhile 'government approval based regime' on the issue of company affairs.

I have read with interest the book *Corporate Governance in India: An Evaluation* authored by Prof. Subhash Chandra Das, based on his research project on the same theme.

I had a close association with Prof. Das during his tenure in 'Tata Steel' for over a decade. He, in his distinguished career, has vast work experience for more than 30 years during which he has served the country's most renowned companies, initially as an executive and later on as Director (Finance). A person of his calibre in my opinion, is best suited to author a book on this subject.

Professor Das has arranged his study in a commendable style. The whole book is explorative, conceptual and empirical in nature. The *explorative* study makes the journey towards the evolution of corporate governance system in India. From *conceptual* point of view the study has dealt critically, the purpose of corporate governance, its core principles, cornerstones of corporate governance philosophy and the factors influencing the quality of governance. From *empirical* perspective, the study examined the corporate governance system in the industrialized countries of the world and the trend of corporate governance code world over recommended by the internationally renowned committees. Prof. Das has also analyzed the corporate governance system in India with reference to the corporate governance system in industrialized countries in order to assess the state and trend of governance system in India as compared to the outside world. The existing gap and anomalies between country's various regulations and enactments with respect to corporate governance have also been identified in this study.

For *analytical* purpose, Prof. Das took the samples of all companies under BSE Sensex and NSE Nifty, and analyzed their annual reports critically, to review the current status and standards of the corporate governance system and reporting of governance practices by Indian corporate houses. The study has been concluded with his in-depth and valued suggestions and recommendations on the subject.

In my opinion, this book is the first of its kind in this country to highlight the existing gap and anomalies between various enactments and regulations made by the regulatory bodies. He has also brought together, all suggestions and recommendations of various international and national committees under a common platform for adequate evaluation. This exercise could lead to the setting up of a comprehensive and standard code of corporate governance applicable to the Indian corporate houses. From this perspective, Prof. Das deserves the gratitude not only of the contemporary researchers, students of postgraduate courses and general readers, but also of the professional community (i.e., senior executives, board members of corporate houses, industry associations, policy makers and regulatory authorities) who are seriously involved in improving the quality and standard of corporate governance in India.

Jamshed J. Irani

Jamshed J. Irani
Director
Tata Sons Limited

Preface

As we are aware that a sea change was made in the legislations and provisions of the corporate laws by the Statutory Authorities with the introduction of Indian Companies Act, 2013, and Rules, 2014. Thereafter, several doses of amendments to this Act and Rules were made in between the years 2015 and 2019. Similarly, SEBI also made several amendments within these years in regard to SEBI Listing Regulations in order to align and ensure compatibility with the Company Law as amended.

Having felt the need to incorporate all these amendments, this book has been thoroughly revised to enable the readers to get an updated knowledge and information relevant to corporate governance.

Besides, a Case Study of selected listed large companies on their corporate governance practices in India for the Financial Year 2015–2016 already given in Chapter 11, 13 more Live Case Studies have also been provided in different chapters of this new edition to facilitate readers in conceptualising the present-day corporate governance issues in vogue in India. Also, each chapter includes a last section 'Test Your Knowledge' for self-evaluation and assessment. The new edition comes with an accompanying website https://www.phindia.com/corporate_governance_india_by_das to provide *Learning Resources* for students to practice objective questions and prepare them for various competitive exams and interviews. *Glossary* has been provided towards end of the book.

I sincerely hope this book, in its revised form, will be more useful to the readers, especially the students of commerce, law and management. Any constructive suggestion is most welcome for further improvement of the book.

Subhash Chandra Das

Preface to the First Edition

A good corporate governance recognizes the diverse interests of shareholders, lenders, employees, government, etc. It is expected that shareholders would increasingly assert their rights than ever before. The financial institutions would, similarly, demand effective and efficient corporate governance in order to justify their performance for borrowing in a market-driven economy. Foreign institutional investors would also demand greater transparency and internationally recognized and sound corporate practices. The new concept of governance to bring about quality corporate governance is not only a necessity to serve the divergent corporate interests, but also is a key requirement in the best interests of the corporates themselves and the economy. In the industrially developed countries, the corporate system and structure is characterized by well-spread out ownership and shareholding among the general public. They have a well-developed capital market with active shareholders' participation. The companies are liable to strict disclosure norms and investors' protection under the 'code of best practices'.

In India, hitherto, pre-liberalization period in particular, the so-called governance process in most Indian companies, run by the leading business families, had hardly ensured that the companies would be managed in a manner that would meet stakeholders' aspirations, interests, and social expectations. The lack of 'trusteeship', 'transparency', 'empowerment', 'accountability', and 'control' led to the ultimate corruption in the management and mismanagement in the affairs of many such companies.

The question of corporate governance in India has come mainly in the wake of economic liberalization, deregulation of industry and business as also the demand for a new corporate ethos and stricter compliance with the legislation. The new economic policy adopted by the Government of India since 1991 has necessitated the demand for introduction and implementation of a proper corporate governance policy in management of companies, not only in the interests of their stakeholders, but also for development of the economy.

The theme of this book is essentially, based on my research project 'Corporate Governance in India: An Evaluation'. The *main objective* of the book is to critically examine the governance system prevailing in the Indian corporate sector in light of the notable international practices with a view to suggesting ways and means for its improvement to serve the needs of the stakeholders within the regulatory framework in a best possible manner.

At this juncture, I would like to record my sincere gratitude to my research guide, Dr. Bhabatosh Banerjee, Professor of Commerce, University of Calcutta, former Dean of the faculty of Commerce, Social Welfare and Business Management, University of Calcutta, former Visiting Professor of Accountancy, Rutgers University, New Brunswick, USA, President, IAA Research Foundation, for helping me meticulously at every step of my work and instilling confidence and optimism in me. Without his helpful guidance, I could not have dreamt of completing this work at the advanced age of mine.

Unlimited is my gratitude to the authors of books and various research publications whose works have been consulted by me in course of my endeavour. I am grateful to the learned faculty members in the Department of Commerce, University of Calcutta, for their valuable advice and sincere help.

Thanks are also due to the Librarians of Indian Institute of Management, Calcutta, Indian Institute of Social Welfare & Business Management, Calcutta, The Institute of Chartered Accountants of India, and the University of Calcutta for permitting me to use their libraries. I am also thankful to all of my colleagues, friends, and well-wishers who always inspired me in completing the work.

I am also grateful to Mr. Rahul Roy, Former President of The Institute of Chartered Accountants of India, Partner, S.R. Batliboi and Co., Chartered Accountants and Director Ernest and Young, Management Consultants, Professor Sunil Shah, Associate Dean, ICFAI National College, Dr. P.K. Ghosh, former vice-chancellor, North Bengal University and Sri Siddhartha Sen, senior Director Research and Journal, The Institute of Cost and Works Accountants of India and Editor, The Management Accountant, for their constant encouragement and help.

I would also like to record my deep sense of gratitude to my parents, late Sri Nalini Ranjan Das and Srimati Hiran Prava Das, who were my constant source of inspiration. I shall fail in my duties if I do not admit of the support provided to me by my wife, Anjana Das, who relentlessly created a congenial atmosphere at home and relieved me totally of the household work. My two loving daughters, Aparajita and Animita, not only sacrificed with a smiling face, their precious hours of association with me, but also did their best to keep me smiling in times of my feeling out of sorts. For completion of my work, the untiring help from my elder daughter Aparajita in providing me continuous computer support, deserves special acknowledgement.

Subhash Chandra Das

List of Abbreviations

ABI	:	Association of British Insurers
ADR	:	American Depository Receipt
AG	:	Aktiengelleschaft; lit (Share Company)
AGM	:	Annual General Meeting
ALM	:	Asset Liability Management
AMC	:	Asset Management Company
AS	:	Accounting Standard
ASSOCHAM	:	Associated Chamber of Commerce and Industry
BOD	:	Board of Directors
BSE	:	Bombay Stock Exchange
CBI	:	Confederation of British Industry
CBI	:	Central Bureau of Investigation
CCAB	:	Consultative Committee of Accountancy Bodies
CCI	:	Controller of Capital Issues
CEO	:	Chief Executive Officer
CFO	:	Chief Finance Officer
CGR	:	Corporate Governance Rating
CIA	:	Chief Internal Auditor
CII	:	Confederation of Indian Industry
CLB	:	Company Law Board
CMD	:	Chairman cum Managing Director
COO	:	Chief Operating Officer
CRISIL	:	Credit Rating Information Services of India Limited
CS	:	Company Secretary
CSR	:	Corporate Social Responsibility
D&O	:	Directors and Officers
DCA	:	Department of Company Affairs
DFIs	:	Development Financial Institutions
DIN	:	Director Identification Number

DPE	:	Department of Public Enterprises
DPs	:	Depository Participants
DRS	:	Directors' Responsibility Statement
DSVR	:	Deposited Share Voting Rights
ED	:	Executive Director
EGM	:	Extraordinary General Meeting
EHS	:	Environment, Health and Safety
EIA	:	Environmental Impact Assessment
EIC	:	East India Company
ESOS	:	Employee Stock Option Scheme
ESPS	:	Employee Stock Purchase Scheme
FERA	:	Foreign Exchange Regulation Act
FI	:	Financial Institution
FICCI	:	Federation of Indian Chamber of Commerce and Industry
FII	:	Foreign Institutional Investor
GAAP	:	Generally Accepted Accounting Principles
GAAS	:	Generally Accepted Auditing Standards
GDP	:	Gross Domestic Product
GDR	:	Global Depository Receipt
GmbH	:	Gesellschaft mit beschrankte Haftung; lit (Company with limited liability)
GNP	:	Gross National Product
GOI	:	Government of India
GVCR	:	Governance and Value Creation Rating
HRD	:	Human Resource Development
ICAI	:	Institute of Chartered Accountants of India
ICRA	:	Investment Information and Credit Rating Agency of India
ICSI	:	Institute of Company Secretaries of India
ID	:	Independent Director
II	:	Institutional Investor
ILPIC	:	Industrial Licensing Policy Inquiry Committee
IMF	:	International Monetary Fund
IOD	:	Institute of Directors
IPO	:	Initial Public Offer
IR	:	Industrial Relation
IT	:	Information Technology
JJI	:	J.J. Irani Committee
KMB	:	Kumar Mangalam Birla Committee
KMP	:	Key Managerial Personnel
KRAs	:	Key Result Areas

LSE	:	London Stock Exchange
MCA	:	Ministry of Corporate Affairs
MD	:	Managing Director
MDA	:	Management Discussion and Analysis
MFs	:	Mutual Funds
MNC	:	Multinational Company
MRTPC	:	Monopolies and Restrictive Trade Practices Commission
NASD	:	National Association of Securities Dealers
NAPF	:	National Association of Pension Funds
NCC	:	Naresh Chandra Committee
NED	:	Non-Executive Director
NEP	:	New Economic Policy
NMC	:	Narayana Murthy Committee
NSE Nifty	:	National Stock Exchange Fifty Companies
NYSE	:	New York Stock Exchange
OHSAS	:	Occupational Health and Safety Assessment Series
OECD	:	Organization for Economic Co-operation and Development
PRONED	:	Promotion of Non-Executive Directors (a British head hunting firm established in 1982 to provide boards with qualified, independent, non-executive directors)
PSB	:	Public Sector Bank
PSU/E	:	Public Sector Undertaking/Enterprise
RBI	:	Reserve Bank of India
ROC	:	Registrar of Companies
SAARC	:	South Asian Association for Regional Co-operation
SCRA	:	Securities Contracts Regulation Act
SEBI	:	Securities and Exchange Board of India
SEC	:	Securities and Exchange Commission
SENSEX	:	Sensitive Index
SHE	:	Safety, Health and Environment
UPSC	:	Union Public Service Commission
UTI	:	Unit Trust of India
VCFs	:	Venture Capital Funds
WTO	:	World Trade Organization

CHAPTER 1 Introduction

Learning Objectives	Key Words
After reading this chapter, the readers will be able to understand:	Corporate Governance
The nature of the study of Corporate Governance	Code of Conduct
The objectives of the study of Corporate Governance	Stakeholders
The issues examined concerning the Corporate Governance	Accountability
The methodology of the study of Corporate Governance	Value Addition
	Collective Vision
	Tick boxes

1.1 NATURE OF THE STUDY

Corporate governance is a system of structuring, operating, and controlling a company with a view to achieving long-term strategic goals to satisfy its shareholders, creditors, employees, customers and suppliers. It aims to comply with the legal and regulatory requirements, besides meeting the environmental and local community needs. It includes the policies and procedures adopted by a company to achieve its objectives in relation to its shareholders, employees, customers suppliers, regulatory authorities and the community at large. It prescribes a Code of Corporate Conduct in relation to all the stakeholders. Therefore, a framework of effective accountability to the stakeholders is the essence of corporate governance.

In India, the question of corporate governance has come up mainly in the wake of economic liberalization and deregulation of industry and business as well as the demand for a new corporate ethos and stricter compliance with the legislation. In this context, where the financial institutions hold substantial stakes in companies, the accountability of all the directors, including ex-officios/independent and nominees, has come into sharp focus. Therefore, a good governance demands that a company must have a responsibility to set exemplary standards of ethical behaviour, both within the organization and in their external relationships, by virtue of which the company can achieve 'value addition' in terms of stability and growth, confidence, reduction of perceived risks, reduction of cost of capital, stability and long-term sustenance of stakeholders relationship, position of pride and exemplary governance credentials. The new economic policy adopted by the Government of India consequent to liberalization and opening up of the economy since 1991, has necessitated the demand for introduction and implementation of a proper corporate governance policy in the day-to-day management of the companies, not only in the interest of their stakeholders but also for the development of the economy.

Corporate governance reforms in India have evolved a wide range of institutional and corporate initiatives that include (a) improving the functioning of capital markets, (b) ensuring more effective protection of minority investors through promoting greater transparency of operations and higher standards of information disclosure, (c) reforming company board structure and operational systems to make the board of directors more accountable to the shareholders, (d) reforming governance mechanisms of financial institutions, etc. The corporate governance initiatives have come from (a) the Government through government legislations involving several amendments to the Companies Act, 1956; (b) the organizations, regulating capital market, especially the Securities and Exchange Board of India (SEBI) in the form of statutory regulations; and (c) through self-disciplining and voluntary initiatives taken by the industry, chambers of commerce and business associations, professional bodies and the company themselves. Various committees have been formed by the Government of India, SEBI and industry associations and their recommendations for implementation of corporate governance norms in Indian corporate houses have been submitted during the period 1998–2016.

In the recent times, the roles, responsibilities and expectations of a board has undergone considerable change. An effective board needs to stay abreast of a wide array of issues pertaining to a company. The board must provide its collective vision as to how a company should conduct its business and it needs to define a framework of prudent and effective controls which will enable risk to be assessed and managed. More importantly, an effective board must demonstrate and promote ethical leadership throughout the company.

The board of directors represents the interests of the company's stakeholders in optimizing long-term value by way of providing the management with guidance and strategic direction on their behalf. The board's mandate is to oversee the company's strategic direction, review corporate performance, assess the adequacy of risk management and mitigation measures, authorize and monitor strategic investments, ensure regulatory compliance and safeguard interests of all stakeholders.

The board is now taking cognizance of the new evolving corporate governance framework in India. It takes a holistic view and remains committed towards ensuring that the spirit and code of governance-related practices will always be upheld. The board stands resolute that it will not subscribe to governance *tick boxes* and will continue to build on its founding principles of fairness, kindness, efficiency and effectiveness.

Corporate Governance has received tremendous boost all over the world, India in particular, by the induction of independent directors in the board of directors of public companies all over the world in recent times. The status of independent directors and their contribution to the board functioning are supposed to gain adequate importance in managing the business of the corporate houses. It has also received momentum due to inclusion of women directors in the board activities by way of enactment of the law in all developed and developing countries in order to ensure gender diversity and appropriate balance in the corporate board structure.

1.2 OBJECTIVES OF THE STUDY

The present study critically examines the governance prevailing in the corporate sector in India in the light of notable international practices with a view to suggesting ways and means for its improvement to serve the needs, as best as possible, of the stakeholders within the regulatory framework. A good governance is likely to lead to growth and prosperity of not only of the corporate sector but also of the economy as a whole. On the contrary, bad governance may bring in disaster to the stakeholders and the economy. Thus, the *specific objectives* of the study have been identified as follows:

(a) To examine the evolution of corporate governance in India.

(b) To find out the purpose of corporate governance and its core principles.

(c) To examine the cornerstones of corporate governance philosophy and the factors influencing quality of governance.

(d) To spell out in detail the structures and processes in corporate governance generally envisaged for implementation as a concept.

(e) To assess the trend of corporate governance code world over.

(f) To find out what are the structures and processes for corporate governance followed by the Indian corporate houses.

(g) To analyze the corporate governance system in India with reference to the corporate governance system in some industrialized countries of the world with a view to finding out,

 (i) whether and to what extent Indian corporates are lagging behind.

 (ii) whether the existing codes of corporate governance and guidelines are adequate, etc.

(h) To examine and analyze the provisions of the new company law and rules enacted and enforced by the Government of India with effect from 1st April 2014, on directors of companies.

(i) To examine the requirement of newly revised Clause 49 of the Listing Agreement introduced by SEBI with effect from 1st October 2014, and SEBI (Listing Obligations and Disclosure Requirements) Regulations, 2015 concerning corporate directors.

(j) To examine whether the requirement of SEBI Listing Regulations, 2015 and the Companies Act, 2013 concerning the corporate directors have been broadly complied with by the companies.

(k) To identify the areas wherein further improvement in terms of corporate governance is necessary.

(l) To find out the existing gap and anomalies, if any, between the various regulations and enactments made on corporate governance and suggest improvement in this regard.

(m) To suggest for setting up, if possible, a comprehensive and standard code of corporate governance—(i) compulsory, and (ii) voluntary.

(n) To formulate a standard code of governance practices and comprehensive disclosure norms on (i) social responsibility of business, (ii) business ethics and (iii) environmental issues.

(o) To evolve a policy for customization and code servicing for corporate governance.

1.3 ISSUES EXAMINED

We have examined a large number of issues concerning the corporate governance in our study. Some of the principal ones may be stated as follows:

(a) What were the characteristics of governance under the Managing Agency System, the Promoter System and the Anglo-American System? And how these were practised?

(b) How were the economic responsibilities of corporate governance discharged under these systems? Was there any concept of shareholders' right, control and maximizing shareholders' value at that time?

(c) What was the Government policy in the pre-independence and post-independence period towards Indian industry? Was it really effective against economic concentration under these systems?

(d) What regulatory measures have been taken by the Government in 1990s for the promotion of more responsible corporate governance practices in India?

(e) What are the philosophy, objectives, purposes, and cornerstones/core principles of corporate governance? How do these factors influence quality of governance?

(f) What are the expectations of various stakeholders from a company?

(g) What is the relationship between governance and performance and development of the economy at macro and micro levels?

(h) Is there any relationship between business ethics and corporate governance? If so, how do business ethics influence governance process in a company?

(i) What is meant by the term 'corporate social responsibility' (CSR)? Is there any relationship or congruence between corporate governance and corporate social responsibility? Why the corporate social responsibility has been given substantial importance in the corporate functioning nowadays? Can corporate profitability and CSR co-exist?

(j) What are the 'environmental issues and concerns' for the society? Is there any influence of such issues on corporate governance?

(k) What is corporate sustainability? How does it help the companies in enhancing their development?

(l) What are the various structures and processes for corporate governance in vogue in various countries?

(m) What are the salient features of recommendations of the six most renowned Committees (viz. Cadbury, Greenbury, Hampel, LSE Combined Code, OECD, and Blue Ribbon) on corporate governance principles, guidelines and best practices?

(n) What are the main features of corporate governance system in India and how is it compared with the corporate governance systems in the industrialized countries, viz. the USA, the UK, Germany, and Japan to find out whether and to what extent Indian companies are lagging behind, and whether the existing codes of corporate governance and guidelines are adequate?

(o) Are there any developments on corporate governance reforms in the post-liberalization era? If so, what are they?

(p) What are the existing gaps and anomalies between the various regulations and enactments made in the Companies Act, and those in the SEBI Act on corporate governance?

(q) What are the areas wherein further improvement in terms of governance is necessary and what are the suggestions for improvement therein?

(r) What are the structure, strength, and size of the company's board of directors? Has the requirement of SEBI Listing Regulations in respect of independent directors in the boards been maintained?

(s) Is there any need for gender diversity through quota system by enactment of law for inclusion of women directors in the corporate boards? Has the gender diversity been practised and followed by other countries? What are the rules made by the Companies Act, 2013 and requirements made by the SEBI Guidelines in favour of the gender diversity?

(t) What is the position of chairman and CEO in companies? Is the post of chairman separated from the post of CEO/MD? How many companies appoint a lead independent director in their boards?

(u) Did the companies disclose the retirement policy of directors including their tenure and age limit in the annual report? If so, whether it is in line with the provisions of SEBI Listing Regulations?

(v) How many companies have defined 'independent directors', 'financial expert', and disclosed the selection criterion of board directors including independent directors?

(w) Are the disclosures of board procedure and information placed before the board? Is there a regular post-meeting follow-up system and compliance reporting to the board?

(x) Are there adequate disclosures of remuneration policy and remuneration of directors in the annual report? Do they fully comply with the provisions of SEBI Listing Regulations?

(y) Do the companies disclose information about formation of statutory board committees? Is the minimum requirement of the number of independent directors and the number of audit committee meetings maintained? Is there any disclosure regarding 'charters' of these committees and the roles played by them? Is there adequate information of nature of shareholders' complaints and queries received and disposed—itemwise, in the annual report?

(z) How many companies have set up non-mandatory board committees? Are there adequate disclosures of minimum requirement of the non-executive directors in remuneration committee, independent director as chairman of remuneration committee? Is there disclosure of nomination committee charter and report of nomination committee in the annual report?

(aa) Do the companies comply with all disclosure norms (both statutory and non-mandatory) as required by SEBI Listing Regulations as also by the Companies Act?

(bb) Are there adequate disclosure regarding stakeholders' interests and the policies on (i) Environment, Health and Safety (EHS), (ii) Human Resource Development (HRD), (iii) Corporate Social Responsibility (CSR), (iv) Corporate Sustainability and (v) Industrial Relation (IR)?

1.4 METHODOLOGY

The present study is explorative, conceptual and empirical in nature.

The *explorative part* makes the journey towards the evolution of corporate governance system in India. Broadly speaking, the corporate governance practices, which had been in vogue at different points in time has been examined in this study. From *conceptual viewpoint*, the study has examined in detail, the purpose of corporate governance, its core principles, the cornerstones of corporate governance philosophy and the factors influencing quality of governance. It also spelt out in detail, the structures and processes for corporate governance generally envisaged for implementation as a concept.

Empirically, the study has examined the corporate governance system in the industrialized countries of the world. It has also examined the trend of corporate governance code world over recommended by the various world-renowned Committees. An analysis has also been made on corporate governance system in India with reference to the corporate governance system in some industrialized countries in order to assess the state and trend of governance system in India as compared to others. The existing gap and anomalies between the various regulations and enactments with respect to corporate governance have also been identified and suggestions made thereon.

For *analytical* purpose, i.e., for reviewing the current status and standards of corporate governance system in vogue and the reporting in corporate governance practices by Indian companies, we have relied on the published annual reports for the year 2015–2016 of the selected companies. Our sample comprised all the 30 companies that were considered for computing the Bombay Stock Exchange (BSE) Sensex as well as 50 companies considered for computing the National Stock Exchange (NSE) Nifty. A good number of the units are of course common, i.e., finding place in both the cases. These companies have been selected on the ground that their scrips dominate and influence the stock market movement of the country and they also represent different major industries. The period of study covers the financial year, 2015–2016.

1.5 CONCLUSION

In this introductory chapter we have endeavoured to understand what is called corporate governance and its nature. The objectives of our study and the issues involved on corporate governance have also been pin-pointed. In the next chapter and onwards we shall discuss in detail more about corporate governance prevalent in our country and evaluate its status in the perspective of corporate governance practised in other countries.

Test Your Knowledge

1. What do you mean by Corporate Governance? Describe when and how corporate governance practices came up and introduced in India.
2. Discuss the nature of the study of Corporate Governance.
3. What are the objectives of Corporate Governance?
4. Discuss the issues to be examined in regard to Corporate Governance.
5. What methodology has been applied in the current study of Corporate Governance?

CHAPTER 2 Evolution of Corporate Governance in India

Learning Objectives	Key Words
After reading this chapter, the readers will be able to understand: • The evaluation of Corporate Governance in India and its various Reforms processes • The Managing Agency System (1850–1955) in India and its Reforms process • The Promoter System (1956–1991) in India and its Reforms process • The Anglo-American System (1992 and Onwards) and its Reforms process • The Recent Developments and Measures taken by Regulatory Authorities in India in improving the standard of Corporate Governance	• Entrepreneurs • Inter-locking Directorships • Intercorporate Investments • Economic Concentration • Financial Irregularities • Liberalisation

2.1 SYSTEMS OF CORPORATE GOVERNANCE IN INDIA

Looking at the history, it can be said that a good corporate governance has always been an issue since the companies started using stock market to meet their financing needs. The history of East India Company (EIC) suggests how the first publicly listed company's indulgence in trade and accounting malpractices led to the widespread public protests and demand for reform. A unique similarity of such corruptive practices has been observed even after 400 years and repeated in modern corporates like Enron and WorldCom.

Executive greed, rampant corruption, insider trading and appalling corporate governance practices were all there. It is sheer irony that East India Company, where the seeds of the modern-day board were first sown, faired miserably on corporate governance front. Even then, the importance of practicing corporate governance principles was not played down.

In India, every segment attached to the corporates has unanimously accepted the proposition that there is a need for practicing the corporate governance principles. Let us now look through various systems of corporate governance in India.

India has a very long history of commercial activity and has always been a major source of many of the world's most sought-after products. It is, therefore, natural that the corporate India has a long history of its corporate governance systems. With this perspective, it is considered prudent to make a journey in this chapter towards the evolution of corporate governance systems in India. Broadly speaking, the corporate governance practices in vogue at different points in time may be studied under three groups viz.

1. The Managing Agency System (1850–1955)
2. The Promoter System (1956–1991)
3. The Anglo-American System (1992 and onwards)

The rationale behind division of the systems into three groups is that the Managing Agency System was an age-old system, which began in 1850. In the year 1956, i.e. after independence, many developments took place as the Government of India, in order to restrict the abuse of powers and ill-effects caused by the managing agents, adopted many corrective measures and provisions in the Companies Act, 1956. Therefore, with the introduction of the Act of 1956, the importance of the managing agency system almost diminished. A new system in the form of Promoter System emerged from the year 1956 was characterized by these developments. In the year 1991, the Government of India opted for economic liberalization in her mission to become an active player in the global economy. Radical changes in the economy started taking place since then. The corporate sector being one of the components of the economy also followed suit. Consequently, influences from outside, characterized by the changes in corporate governance in many developed economy, were not few and far between. Therefore, the Promoter System was expectedly replaced by the Anglo-American System since 1991. In the matter of corporate governance, many changes have already taken place in India in tune with the changes in the more developed economy and many more are no doubt in the offing.

2.1.1 The Managing Agency System (1850–1955)

A major contribution to the rise of the modern corporates in India was the institution of the Managing Agency System. This system rather unique to India, not only spurred the growth of modern corporations of India, but with the control it exercised over the companies that it 'managed', also served as the basic mechanism of the corporate governance.

The first Managing Agency System was introduced way back in 1809. During the same period, further development took place in legal front, resulting in the enactment of the first Indian Companies Act of 1850, followed by an amendment in 1857 providing for limited liability. In fact, spreading of the Managing Agency System got momentum by these developments.

The first managing agents in this country were the British merchants as the initial entrepreneurs who brought necessary financial and managerial resources together in a bid to make very high profits. They served *three basic functions*: *First*, they started or promoted new companies. When these companies became successful, they sold most of their shareholdings. *Second*, since they were having managerial expertise to run the companies, they were appointed to manage and control the existing companies based on managing agency contract. *Third*, they provided important financial functions as managing agents, due to their ability to attract new investors to secure bank loans etc. This made the Managing Agency System attractive to the investors in joint stock companies, especially at the time when the credit system was not fully developed and the money and capital markets were virtually non-existent.

Gradually, in line with the British managing agencies in and around Bengal, Indian Managing Agency System began to emerge on the West Coast of India in and around Bombay and Ahmedabad. These agencies, mostly merchant families (e.g. Parsees and Gujaratis), focused on cotton and textile industries and reaped high profits through managing agency contracts. Some of these entrepreneurs also ventured out in the new areas like iron and steel. Most notable in this regard was J.N. Tata, the first Indian industrialist and the founder of the Tata Group—largest business house in India. Between 1920s and 1930s, this group took up industrial production. The most significant development took place with the emergence of the *Marwari* community in the 1930s. Other significant entrepreneurial communities which came to adopt the Managing Agency System and move into industrial production were the *Chettiars* in Tamil Nadu, the *Banias* in U.P., Haryana and Delhi, the *Khatris* in Punjab and the *Syrian Christians* in Kerala.

In the pre-independence period, the Managing Agency System played a key role in the industrialization of India, although the major Indian business houses developed and consolidated the empires through this system.

The characteristics of governance under the Managing Agency System are twofold. First, the formal mechanism of control through the managing agency contract; second, the macro-economic situations of control and governance. It is this agency contracts through which the managing agents were able to exercise control over the 'managed' companies. In fact, variety of binding provisions in the contract, such as unlimited terms of tenure, heavy penalties for dismissal of the agency, did ensure the inability of the shareholders to remove them. These agents used to exercise the function of corporate governance along with their wide powers towards investment decisions, appointment of directors, etc. Under their stewardship, many companies did not even have boards or did have the 'puppet' boards to their advantage. That was how this Managing Agency System became dominant and increased its strength from 75% in 1936 to 95% in 1955 of the industrial firms in India.

The undeveloped macro-economic situation and unorganized capital and money markets, absence of stock exchanges etc. gave the managing agents great opportunity to step in to fill the void. The second contributing factor was a weak credit system, which gave them the opportunity to play a key role in securing working capital for managing companies. Absence of government regulations against abuse of these powers was the third factor. On the contrary, the Government policy systematically favoured Europeans and Indian entrepreneurs. However, the fact remains that it was ultimately ownership of the managing agency that enabled them to maintain a control over managed firms. This ownership was in the nature of partnerships predominantly restricted to family relations. It was not unusual for a family business house dominated by a 'Karta' to be in control of several managing agencies, each of which used to manage several joint stock companies.

The other mechanisms adopted by these agents to ensure corporate control over the managed companies were discouraging shareholder activism, and continued practice of multiple directorships within the companies (Table 2.1), to mention a few. Needless to mention, these managing agents consolidated their empires by taking over existing firms or floating new firms with a minimum contribution of their own capital.

TABLE 2.1 Multiple Directorships Held by Leading Indian Industrialists

Name	No. of companies in which directorships held
F.E. Dinshaw	65
Sir P.D. Thakurdas	42
Sir P.C. Sethna	34
N.B. Saklatwala	29
Sir F.C. Ebrahimbhoy	26
Sir L. Samal Das	26
H.P. Mody	14

Source: Reed, D., "Three Historical Models of Corporate Governance: An Examination of Corporate Economic Responsibilities", Indian Institute of Management Calcutta, 1998.

Was the role of the Managing Agency System undisputed? One school of thought argued that this system should not be seen as inherently flawed. Rather, it arose as a historical necessity and made a significant contribution to the economic development of the country at a stage when investment potential was very low and the capital markets undeveloped. Another school, however, felt that the system was abused and its significance lost.

Two important changes for promoting industrialization took place within a couple of years. They are as follows:

- *Industrial Policy Resolution, 1948:* The Government announced its first major policy statement called Industrial Policy Resolution,1948. The policy statement affirmed the complementary roles of both 'state' and the 'private sector' for development of the economy.
- *Industries (Development and Regulation) Act, 1951:* This Act was one of the most significant of all legislations of the Government, providing for the legal basis for industrial licensing scheme.

Let the Managing Agency System be evaluated with respect to the economic responsibilities of the corporate enterprises—(a) shareholder rights, shareholder control, and maximization of shareholder value, and (b) market competition.

(a) Shareholder rights–Shareholder control–Maximizing shareholder value

The critics of the system were of the opinion that these agents did not respect the basic rights of the shareholders. In order to minimize shareholders' participation, they established the firms, sold them to new shareholders but retained management control through various means, viz. interlocking directorships, inter-corporate investments, stringent stipulations in the managing agency contract making virtually impossible for shareholders to remove them, offering deferred shares, limiting public distribution of shares, calling annual general meeting at very short notice and at inconvenient times etc. These managing agents never bothered themselves in maximizing shareholder value. They used to remunerate themselves at a very high percentage of the profits of the firm, leading to an inherent conflict of interests between the managing agents and shareholders. A study conducted by the Reserve Bank of India (RBI) disclosed that the average rate of compensation for them in the year 1950–1952 was 27.7% of the net profits. Moreover, they used to extract huge funds from the companies as 'perks' in the form of hefty office allowances.

Another area of abuse involved financial irregularities in running the companies. The Vivian Bose Commission (GOI,1963), while investigating the activities of Dalmia-Jain during the 1950s, found the complete range of all possible irregularities in the system, viz. (i) improper inter-corporate transfers at the cost of shareholders, (ii) advancing companies' fund elsewhere as unsecured loans, (iii) investing funds of listed companies including banks and insurance companies to acquire controlling interests in other firms with high liquid assets, (iv) transferring the assets of public companies to closely held companies and then converting them into private companies and thereafter the private companies into liquidation, (v) intentional non-declaring of dividends of the companies genuinely making profits and forcing the other shareholders to sell their shares at falling share price and then again cornering and buying those shares for declaring huge dividends thereafter, (vi) operating in the black economy (vii) appointing sole purchasing agents and (viii) various other speculative activities etc.

Even the renowned business houses like Tata Sons and Birla Brothers also used their power to bring more number of firms under their fold. Nevertheless, the groups like Tatas and Bird & Company did attempt to cultivate a reputation for honest business practices and sought to protect the interests of their shareholders. However, these are only a few exceptions to prove the prevalent practices.

In most of the cases, there was lack of professional management, absence of professional education and technical training in this system. In fact, in many managing agencies, especially those controlled by family business houses, it was almost invariably family ties, not professional competence that determined who could manage the firm, with a few exception like J.R.D. Tata who was among the first to appoint professional managers and directors from outside into the boards of managed companies.

(b) Market competition

Did the Managing Agency System encourage behaviours opposed to the logic of fair market competition? The activities of firms contributed to economic concentration, which is evident from the pattern of management and directorships of firms. A study in 1950–1951 indicated that nine leading Indian industrial families held nearly six hundred directorships or partnerships in Indian industry, with Dalmias' and Singhanias' alone holding two hundred of these positions. One hundred individuals were found to hold one thousand seven hundred directorships in the corporate sector, thirty of them holding eight hundred sixty directorships including top ten of them holding four hundred directorships. Six hundred industrial concerns were controlled and managed by thirty-six managing agency houses, of which only two hundred fifty companies were controlled by nine leading British agency houses (Table 2.2).

TABLE 2.2 Number of Companies Managed by Leading British Managing Agencies

Name	No. of companies in which directorships held
Andrew Yule	50
Mcleod	40
Martin Burn	26
Duncans	26
Octavious Steel	24
Martin Burn	21
Jardines Henderson	20
Gillanders Arbuthnot	20
British India Corporation	20
Total	**247**

Source: Reed, D., "Three Historical Models of Corporate Governance: An Examination of Corporate Economic Responsibilities", Indian Institute of Management Calcutta, 1998.

Despite the stated objective of government policy to build a much wider economic base, economic concentration had continued to increase in this period. During the period 1951–1958 the gross capital stock of companies controlled by the top four industrial 'complexes' (Tata, Birla, Martin Burn and Dalmia-Jain) increased by 100%, and 31% of the funds to these companies were distributed by the financial institutions and banks, in which large business houses were well represented on the boards of these institutions. This situation was ratified by the RBI report (1962) as also by the report of the Committee on Distribution of Income and Level of Living, known as Mahalanobis Committee report (1963).

2.1.2 The Promoter System (1956–1991)

The basic form of the post independence economy was characterized by many factors; such as:

(a) restrictions on importing consumer and capital goods;
(b) restrictions on dealing in foreign exchange;
(c) a policy of mixed economy;
(d) economic planning and a wide range of government support programmes in the area of industrial financing.

The Government passed a new Companies Act with the intention to:

(i) eliminate the institution of managing agency,
(ii) safeguard the shareholder rights, and
(iii) protect the common interests in a more effective way.

All these factors were responsible for setting up the new form of corporate governance, which we shall refer to as the Promoter System.

After independence the leading Indian managing agents began to actively promote new business by contributing a certain amount of equity capital with the balance capital to be raised through public offers or from financial institutions. Eventually, the notion of a promoter was extended further for controlling individual or group in a company. Before we discuss the form of corporate governance that emerged under the Promoter System in the post independence period, it is prudent to mention the changes that took place in the economy after independence.

A. Industrial Policy Resolution, 1956

In pursuit of a socialist pattern of society as the principal objective of all economic and social policy, the government adopted a new industrial policy resolution in 1956, whereby all economic activities were divided into three categories. Industries in 'Schedule A' like defence, atomic energy etc. were to be the exclusive responsibility of the state. Industries in 'Schedule B' like aluminium, other minerals and ferro-alloys, drugs and fertilizers, were to be progressively taken over by the state with the private sector. The third category consisted of all remaining industries which were open for private sector.

B. The Companies Act, 1956

In order to stop abuses to shareholders and the common public prevailing in the Managing Agency System and in order to lay the basis for a socialist pattern of society, the government introduced a new Companies Act in the year 1956. The Act provided for several different management options/recognitions for companies, e.g. (a) secretaries and treasurers, (b) board of directors [Section 2 (13)], (c) a manager [Section 2 (24)], and (d) a managing director/whole time director [Section 2 (26)]. Since secretaries and treasurers were functioning practically as the managing agents, the Companies (Amendment) Act, 1969, ultimately abolished it based on the recommendation of the I.G. Patel Committee. Despite various options prescribed by the Act, vast majority (98%) of the new companies after 1956 registered themselves as 'board managed companies' headed by a managing director/whole time director (Table 2.3).

TABLE 2.3 Distribution of New Companies According to Their Forms of Management

Management form/year	Managing agents	Managers	Sect. and treasurers	Managing directors	Board of directors	Total	% (MD+BOD)
1956–57	14	2	1	197	634	848	98
1957–58	15	1	1	227	717	961	98
1958–59	7	1	7	250	830	1095	99
1959–60	14	3	3	508	924	1452	99
1960–61	21	3	1	596	1062	1683	98
Total	**71**	**10**	**13**	**1778**	**4167**	**6039**	**98**

Source: Reed, D., "Three Historical Models of Corporate Governance: An Examination of Corporate Economic Responsibilities", Indian Institute of Management Calcutta, 1998.

Securities Contracts (Regulation) Act, 1956 (SCRA)

The Government enacted this Act with a view to regulating the transactions in securities and checking speculation in the securities.

Characteristics of the governance under the Promoter System can be explained in two ways. With the Promoter System there was a transformation in the formal mechanism of governance from the managing agency contract to the board of directors, based on the provisions of the Companies Act, 1956 which discouraged strongly the earlier system of managing agency and thereby intended to bring the management under the control of BOD. The Act also contained some more important issues, e.g. disclosure norms, AGM rules, maintenance of records, maximum limit of an individual's directorship, appointment, salary and removal of directors etc. which served to protect shareholder interests. Another significant formal mechanism of control came in the form of induction of nominee directors by the banks/financial institutions (FIs), based on the recommendations of the report of the Industrial Licensing Policy Inquiry Committee (ILPIC), commonly known as Dutt Committee. The main purposes of induction of nominee directors into the board of private sector companies were to help prevent economic concentration and to ensure public interest in the functioning of the corporate management. Between 1981 and 1983 companies of all sizes had nominee directors on their boards of which 87% of the largest companies had nominee directors (Table 2.4).

TABLE 2.4 Listed Companies with Nominee Directors (1981–1983)

Size/Class of companies as per paid-up capital (₹ Million)	Number of companies	% of companies having nominee directors
Below 2.5	73	32.9
2.5–below 5.0	87	52.9
5.0–below 10.0	69	44.9
10.0–below 30.0	115	61.7
30.0–below 100.0	76	67.1
100.0–and over	24	87.5
Total	**444**	**55.0**

Source: Reed, D., "Three Historical Models of Corporate Governance: An Examination of Corporate Economic Responsibilities", Indian Institute of Management Calcutta, 1998.

In regard to the macro-economic situation, it was observed that since 1950s and onwards, the commercial banks including the State Bank of India (SBI) began to play a major role in the field of industrial finance. In addition, the government at the central and state level, fostered financial institutions, viz. State Financial Corporation (SFCs), State Industrial Development Corporations (SIDCs), The Industrial Finance Corporation of India (IFCI–1948), The Industrial Credit & Investment Corporation of India (ICICI–1951), The Industrial Development Bank of India (IDBI–1964), with the intention of financing and developing industries. The Government also sponsored investment institutions, viz. Life Insurance Corporation of India (LICI), The Unit Trust of India (UTI) and the General Insurance Corporation (GIC), which came to dominate industrial financing during the promoter period. Despite all these programmes and efforts of the government, capital market could not be strengthened because all these institutions were interested mainly to provide easy access to credit under soft conditions. Even the institution of the Controller of Capital Issues (CCI–1947) could not improve the condition of capital market.

The second major factor defining the circumstance of control and governance was the Government restrictions and intervention in market competition through import restriction, export promotion, financing infrastructure and R&D projects etc. with a view to promoting economic development. The Monopolies & Restrictive Trade Practices Act (MRTP Act) was also introduced with the similar objectives.

With respect to the locus of control of corporate management, it was observed that both Indian companies (i.e. mostly family business houses) and foreign firms (i.e. subsidiaries of MNCs) were controlled through minority ownership in most cases. In the case of MNCs, minority ownership (i.e. holding up to 40%) was forced upon by the Foreign Exchange Regulation Act (FERA–1973). In the case of Indian firms, the minority ownership of group companies was either direct ownership by family members or through an apex company controlled by family members.

In regard to other mechanisms of control, the same two mechanisms (practised by the Managing Agency System) viz. interlocking of directorships and inter-corporate investments continued to be the significant methods used by the controlling groups to maintain their power over managed firms. It was observed that seven leading industrial families held 303 directorships, of which Bangurs and Goenkas held 136 directorships in companies. A study by Company Law Board (CLB) indicated that more than 20% of the directors held more than 10 directorships each, which was considered to be substantially higher than in the USA and the UK at that time.

In regard to the inter-corporate investments this trend continued up to the early 1970s. The share of the top two business houses, viz. Tatas and Birlas in the net worth of the private companies increased from 11.94% in 1961–62 to 14.74% in 1972–73 (Table 2.5).

TABLE 2.5 House-wise Control of Companies Through Inter-Corporate Investments during 1972–1973

Business houses	Control through inter-corporate investments (%)		
	of paid up capital	of net worth	of gross capital employed
Birla	44.39	54.43	47.37
Tata	25.18	18.88	23.90
Mafatlal	38.17	45.53	44.83
Martin Burn	13.60	1.63	8.25
Bangur	53.00	57.97	58.27
Thapar	87.43	95.93	85.68
Shriram	18.59	10.75	9.00
J.K. Singhania	53.62	40.40	45.79
Walchand	57.53	60.32	60.85
Kirloskar	16.86	12.03	18.72
Mahindra	20.82	9.77	15.36
Parry	12.54	19.30	23.41
TVS Iyengar	72.41	75.32	62.49

(Contd..)

(*Contd.*)

Business houses	Control through inter-corporate investments (%)		
	of paid up capital	of net worth	of gross capital employed
Jardine Henderson	44.28	46.91	37.55
Modi	1.32	0.42	1.44
Andrew Yule	54.99	62.81	48.49
Rallis	40.24	30.39	23.28
Shaw Wallace	45.58	25.95	20.18

Source: Reed, D., "Three Historical Models of Corporate Governance: An Examination of Corporate Economic Responsibilities", Indian Institute of Management Calcutta, 1998.

We may now examine two economic responsibilities of corporate governance under the Promoter System to assess how far these responsibilities were fulfilled by the system.

(a) Shareholder rights – Shareholder control – Maximizing shareholder value

With the shift of system from the managing agency to the Promoter System, a variety of changes were made by the company law with a view to promoting shareholder right to exercise control over the corporates. These included: (i) disclosure norms, (ii) AGM rules, (iii) standard for maintenance of record (iv) maximum limit on the number of directorships for an individual, (v) restriction on family members serving on a board, (vi) the power to remove directors etc. In reality, however, there was hardly any change with respect to the power of private investors to exercise control over the firms. All through 1960s a large percentage of companies continued to have 'dummy boards' full of promoters' friends and relatives. It was observed that 66% of the companies had directors belonging to the same families (Table 2.6), of which 33% of the companies had 100% directors belonging to the same families.

TABLE 2.6 Size of Boards and No. of Companies having Directors Belonging to the Same Family

Size of board	No. of companies examined	No. of companies having directors belonging to the same family
3	13	2 (15%)
4	18	12 (67%)
5	12	9 (75%)
6	5	4 (80%)
7	8	8 (100%)
8	2	1 (50%)
9	2	2 (100%)
10	3	3 (100%)
11	1	1 (100%)
Total	**64**	**42 (66%)**

Source: Reed, D., "Three Historical Models of Corporate Governance: An Examination of Corporate Economic Responsibilities", Indian Institute of Management Calcutta, 1998.

Due to the dispersion of shareholdings the shareholders had no effective voice in the company management. Despite major shareholdings by the financial institutions during these periods, the situation could not improve, as these institutions were largely passive shareholders. It was only after implementation of the recommendations of the Dutt Committee these institutions became more active demanding board representation on the companies in which they held equity. Even the induct of nominee directors could not improve shareholder control because of the fact that these directors were initially confused about the roles and responsibilities as board members and at the same time they were in a minority position on the boards controlled by the promoters.

Under the Promoter System, the Government took two basic measures in order to maximize shareholder value. The first measure was legislative action by the Companies Act, 1956, setting the limits on directors' remuneration. Further, administrative guidelines were issued in 1969 setting absolute ceilings on remuneration, commission, perquisites of the directors. In 1978, a substantial cut on the maximum levels of remuneration was imposed by another administrative guidelines. Despite all these efforts, major shortcomings remained in regulating the same. Since these restrictions were not applicable on the 'executives', many board members chose to resign, and designated themselves as senior executives (e.g. president, vice-presidents), and at the same time controlled the company affairs through dummy boards. Moreover, as this restriction on remuneration was not applicable to the privately held companies, the family members of the promoters could easily circumvent the regulations by receiving bulk of their salaries from their closely held apex companies.

Financial irregularities continued unabated during the Promoter System as the promoters continued to increase inter-corporate investment, promoting new firms, siphoning off funds etc. to secure their hold over the group firms. Besides, some unique corrupt practices were adopted by the promoters by way of making the companies sick by taking sums of debts and transferring the funds through inter-corporate loans and investments, depriving dividends to the shareholders due to deliberate sickness, and after receiving new injection of capital from the Government to revive the sick companies and thereafter, again diverting the funds out of the company.

A variety of other abuses of shareholder rights during the promoter period were (i) operating in the black economy, (ii) issuing consultancy services to the friends and family members, (iii) lack of professional management, education, training, (iv) non-adherence to the codes of professional conducts and ethics and social responsibility etc.

(b) Market competition—Economic concentration

After independence, the government took various measures against economic concentration by a few large industry groups like (i) abolishing the Managing Agency System, (ii) promotion of state sector, (iii) development of small and medium industries, (iv) restriction on the activities of large corporations, (v) establishment of Monopolies & Restrictive Trade Practices Commission (MRTPC) etc. Despite all these, economic concentration could not be minimized due to (a) concentration of management control by the industry groups, (b) product-wise concentration, (c) skewed distribution of privately held shares, (d) continued inter-corporate investment, (e) substantial percentage of assets held by a few largest business groups. All these factors, which started from the Managing Agency System, had continued even throughout the 1970s and 1980s. The net result was that there was hardly any competition in the market.

In the post independence period the government developed an extensive network of financial institutions, viz. ICICI, IFCI, IDBI, investment institutions, viz. LICI, UTI, GIC and nationalized commercial banks to help promote its various goals of economic and social development. But the benefits were received by the large industrial groups from these institutions in the form of loans and equity participations. Borrowings were as huge as 77% of the total financing of large corporate sector during the period 1960–1961 to 1976–1977. The shareholdings of these institutions were substantial in those companies (44%) in 1981–1990. There were instances where unjustifiable corporate governance practices by the promoters contributed to the skewed distribution of public financing in favour of large firms. The promoters adopted various tactics to get the funds out of these governmental systems of funding, e.g. (i) influencing financial institutions and bureaucrats to finance their takeover bids, (ii) non-repayment of the loans, (iii) lobbying with the Government officials to get disproportionately high share of licenses with limited number of application etc. Various chambers of commerce also lobbied in the corridor of power in favour of these promoter groups and influenced the Government to promote policies, which could be actively in the interest of industry. All such practices were responsible for increasing economic concentration at that time.

2.1.3 The Anglo-American System (1992 and Onwards)

The 1980s was the era of radical economic liberation. The USA under Reagan and the UK under Margaret Thatcher paved the path of global trend in economic liberalization and introduced several programmes. The fiscal crisis of 1991 and the resultant need to approach the International Monetary Fund (IMF) forced India to move in the same direction. This movement also implied a change in the system of corporate governance. Associated with these reform policies, of course, was the Anglo-American System featured by a strong reliance on capital markets as a disciplinary tool and a single-tier board structure in which representation is limited to directors elected by the shareholders.

While the latest system of corporate governance practices is still emerging in India, however, this can be characterized as an Anglo-American System. With respect to formal mechanism of control and governance, the Government has already passed sufficient provisions in the new Companies (Amendment) Acts right from 1998 up to 2002. Another dose of amendment in the Act is likely to occur soon. The amended Acts have allowed the standard Anglo-American option of a single tier board composed of a mix of inside and outside directors including a managing director/CEO who tends to occupy the position of chairman. Under this system, the board is increasingly having responsibility to 'govern' while the executive to whom it appoints, viz. manager/ managing director, is responsible for the day-to-day 'management' of the firm.

The one area concerning the formal mechanism of control in which significant change has taken place is the role of independent/non-executive directors and the nominee directors. The new provisions have given these directors a significant voice in affairs of many large publicly held companies in order to ensure maximum shareholders' value and stakeholders' expectations. On the other hand, the key institutional players and regulatory authorities, viz. SEBI, FIs etc. are placing primary emphasis on the role of capital markets in disciplining the companies.

The second defining characteristics of corporate governance practices comprise the circumstances of governance. Here, significant policy changes have taken place in a number of different areas, e.g. (a) capital market, (b) banking industry, (c) industrial policy, and (d) foreign trade and foreign exchange.

So far as the locus of power is concerned, it has been observed that the liberalization of the Government's foreign investment policy has attracted many foreign parent companies to gain a majority interests in their existing subsidiaries and to establish new wholly owned subsidiaries. In the case of Indian family business groups, liberalization has induced inter group mergers with a combination of minority/majority holdings and strategic control through managerial control by the business family of the apex company. Apart from this, the traditional methods of other mechanisms of control used by the family controlled business houses, viz. extensive cross holdings and interlocking of directorships continued.

Let us now examine two economic responsibilities of corporate governance under the Anglo-American System to evaluate how far the corporate governance practices were met by the system.

(a) Shareholder rights–Shareholder control–Maximizing shareholder value

In principle, a number of provisions in the 1997 Company Bill, which, was incorporated in the Companies (Amendment) Act during the period 1998–2002 could help to improve ability of shareholders to participate in control of the companies. There have been, however, some criticisms from the experts who felt that many of these provisions are largely cosmetic in appearance. For instance, the increased number of issues to be approved by shareholders really has no effect, given that shareholder democracy is largely a myth. A number of provisions, in fact, will have an adverse effect on the quality of corporate governance. These include: (i) provision for buy-back of shares, (ii) an increase in the age limit for managing directors and directors, (iii) relaxation of curbs on inter-corporate loans and investments etc. Besides, the amended provisions have failed to take action in a number of key areas which could have improved corporate governance by altering the balance of power between management and dominant shareholders, on the one hand, and small shareholders and other stakeholders on the other. One of the provisions, i.e. allowing the companies to issue equity shares with differential voting rights (non-voting deferred shares) has gone strongly against the rights of shareholders to control the firm, as this would allow groups with 10% of the shares to control 50% or more of the voting power of the firm.

The right of maximizing shareholder value implies that there will be no financial irregularities and there will be professional managements. It has been observed that with the relaxation of the restrictions on remuneration established in the Companies Act, 1956, managerial remuneration has increased manifold over the years, which, as per shareholders, are disproportionately high as compared to the performance of the companies. Moreover, taking advantage of the de-regulated capital market the dominant group in Indian and foreign companies earned thousands of millions of rupees by 'preferential share options' during the period 1992–1994, thereby abusing the rights of minority shareholders. However, this abuse was curtailed in 1994 when the Security and Exchange Board of India (SEBI) ruled that the price of preferential offerings must not be below the average share price of the previous six months. Other abuses on the minority shareholders include: (a) imposing significant royalty charges on subsidiaries for use of brand names of the parent companies, (b) payment for services to closely held private companies, (c) practice of establishing wholly owned subsidiaries and transferring more profitable operations of the MNC's minority owned subsidiaries to these subsidiaries, (d) unfair re-distribution of assets among group companies due to fear of hostile takeover, (e) lack of professional management, education and training, (f) encouraging the practice of hereditary management in the Indian family run business groups, (g) non-adherence to the codes of professional conduct, ethics and social responsibilities etc., however, with a few exceptions of large companies like Tata groups, Infosys and a few others.

(b) Market competition

Liberalization has served an important function by subjecting Indian companies to the long-needed competitive pressures. Indian firms have been forced to adopt strategies in the new liberalizing economy, viz. (i) expeditious decision to quit the market, (ii) focus on core competencies, (iii) hiving off less profitable ventures, (iv) maintaining healthy debt-equity ratio and rate of return on capital employed (ROCE), (v) adoption of new techniques of management practices, e.g. benchmarking, Total Quality Management (TQM), Business Process Re-engineering (BPR), supply chain management etc. In the short run, the major winners have been middle class consumers purchasing new and better products. In the medium and long term, however, the prospects may be different. If firms are successful in evading the discipline of the market, then oligopolistic market segmentation is likely to occur. Indian companies have also been trying to defend themselves by limiting market pressures through mergers and acquisitions and by lobbying the Government to limit foreign competition, the MNCs have followed the routes of joint venture opportunities and more conventional acquisition procedures.

2.2 REFORM PROCESSES

2.2.1 Reforms of the Managing Agency System

Major abuses of the system first began to emerge with the entry of the people of questionable reputation into industrial promotion during the economic upswing of the early 1870s. In Bombay, such abuses not only led to outcry by shareholders and the newspaper editorials but also resulted in shareholders' direct action to remove managing agencies by taking recourse to the courts. In Calcutta, the public outcry was mute because the shareholding pattern was different. In Ahmedabad newspaper went against the abuses of the shareholders' rights. The combined effects of all these reactions ultimately called for reforms of the system.

The first reform came along with the English Companies (Consolidated) Act, 1908. The Government decided to introduce a new Companies Bill in 1913 with the intention of addressing the issue of managing agents. However, it was only with the Companies (Amendment) Act, 1936 that the Managing Agency System was actually acknowledged in company law and the problems related to it were addressed. The key provisions included in the Act were: (i) limitation on the tenure of a managing agent up to 20 years and the rights of shareholders to remove them in case of a non-bailable offence, (ii) no provisions for compensation except in the case of termination of contract due to liquidation of a firm where no negligence of duty of the agents noticed, (iii) abolition of the power of the agents to transfer agreements, (iv) acknowledgement of three distinct sources of remuneration of agents (viz. commission, office allowance and payment for other sources) only as a percentage of the net profit, (v) restriction to appoint more than one-third of the directors, (vi) prohibition on guarantying loans and investments in companies in which they had an interest, without board's approval, (vii) prohibition on loans to themselves, and (viii) prohibition on agents engaging in business in competition with their managed firms.

Despite all these restrictions/prohibitions, Companies (Amendment) Act suffered a set back due to its failure to address many other vital issues, viz. (a) to set a limit on the number of managed firms under their control, (b) to establish a reasonable formula for remuneration of managing agents, (c) to provide for the power of removal of these agents in the event of fraud, breach of trust, gross negligence, secret profits etc., (d) to provide for administrative machinery to enforce its provisions. The net effect of these shortcomings was that the abuses of the system not only continued unabated, but even increased. Eventually, such practices evoked a sharp response from the shareholder groups, viz. Bombay Shareholders Association, which, in its memorandum issued in 1949, a list of wide ranges of abuses by the agents and suggested for reforms.

In 1950, a company law committee known as Bhaba Committee was established to submit recommendations for a new draft of the Act. After submission of the said report by the Committee in 1952, a new Companies Act came into effect on 1st April 1956. This new Act contained 52 provisions restricting the activities of the managing agents, some of which are: (a) limitations relating to term of office, (b) elimination of compensation for termination of office due to resignation, suspension or removal from office, (c) prohibition on transfer of office, (d) ceiling on remuneration of 10% on net profits and no commission on sales and purchases, (e) restrictions on the power to enter into contracts with managed companies, (f) prohibitions on loans to the agents or inter-corporate loans and investments, (g) limiting the number of companies under control up to 10, (h) greater control by the board over them etc.

The introduction of the new Companies Act, 1956 reflected a doubt as to the future of the Managing Agency System, which was evident in the sharp decline in the number of firms managed by them in the subsequent years (Table 2.7).

Ultimately, on the recommendation of the Managing Agency Enquiry Committee, known as I.G. Patel Committee, the Companies (Amendment) Act, 1969 abolished the continuance of the managing agency system with effect from 3rd April 1970.

2.2.2 Reforms of the Promoter System

During the 1950s and major part of 1960s, the Indian economy had achieved impressive rates of growth. However, from the late 1960s up to 1980s the growth stagnated. The major impact of this stagnation was a decline in the purchasing power of the middle class citizens of the country, causing a continuous contraction of the domestic market on which the business was particularly dependent for its profitability. The

TABLE 2.7 Decline in Number of Managed Companies and their Paid-up Capital

Year	No. of companies & (paid-up capital)		No. of companies managed & (paid-up capital)		% of managed companies & (paid-up capital)	
1954–55	9178	(616.6)	4091	(439.0)	44.6	(71.2)
1960–61	5688	(826.0)	1049	(391.7)	18.4	(47.4)
1962–63	5477	(1076.1)	1149	(391.7)	21.0	(38.1)
1963–64	5607	(1187.1)	1121	(523.9)	20.0	(44.1)
1964–65	5639	(1236.3)	1090	(509.4)	19.3	(41.2)
1965–66	5606	(1255.0)	800	(487.5)	14.3	(38.8)
1966–67	5543	(1309.4)	683	(493.4)	12.3	(37.7)
1967–68	5452	(1375.4)	642	(584.8)	11.7	(42.5)
1968–69	5432	(1402.3)	568	(57.5)	10.4	(4.1)

Source: Reed, D., "Three Historical Models of Corporate Governance: An Examination of Corporate Economic Responsibilities", Indian Institute of Management Calcutta, 1998.

Government was facing a fiscal crisis due to a combination of factors, e.g. declining tax revenues, sick industries and the increased use of borrowing funds to finance defence and civil administration expenses. In addition, the crisis of debt servicing and the falling maturity period of loans had induced capital flight since 1989. For example, the capital flight amounted to USD 102 million in October 1990, went down to USD 11 million only in February 1991. Foreign exchange reserves dropped to an all time low and inflation crossed double digits at that time, resulting in a substantial reduction in India's credit rating.

In the Promoter System the Government was under great pressure to address the issues of corporate governance. It took many steps to promote responsible business practices. The Government introduced the Companies Act, 1956 to safeguard shareholders' rights and placed stricter limits on the activities of the promoters, e.g. limits on remuneration, inter-corporate loans, family members appointment into the boards etc. The Governments also introduced a range of economic policies, e.g. restrictions on the fields of activity of large firms, promotion of small-scale and medium-sized industries etc. Besides, the Government also provided for enforcement mechanisms, e.g. the Company Law Board, the MRTPC etc. Despite greater attention given, systematic abuses of corporate power continued due to (i) blunt nature of the Government policy instruments used, (ii) ambiguities and loopholes in the policies, (iii) lack of proper motivation to the business, (iv) bureaucratic inefficiency, and (v) lack of enforcement of the policy.

The above developments along with the changes in the international economy led both the Government and the big business houses to favour a programme of liberalization. It was in this context that the then Congress Government undertook a New Economic Policy (NEP) in mid 1980s. The Government turned to the IMF for a loan in 1991. The conditionality of the IMF loan required a serious structural adjustment of the Indian economy, of which economic liberalization was an integral part.

2.2.3 Reforms of the Anglo-American System

The process of liberalization and globalization opened new and exciting opportunities. The winds of liberalization blowing through the country had irreversibly changed the course of the business of the Indian corporates both in domestic as well as in the international market. Indian companies began to form strategic alliances with the foreign counterparts. Mergers, amalgamations, takeovers have become the order of the day.

Perceptions of Multinational Corporations (MNCs) towards Indian market have changed tremendously. With the advent of MNCs, Indian corporates are facing global competition. They have started to expand their business beyond the domestic territory. As a result, Indian corporates have been venturing into overseas locations to reap the benefits of concessions available in the changing global economic scenario. Thus, a new breed of Indian multinationals has emerged slowly. Quite a large number of companies have spread their wings across the border and have set up joint ventures, and acquired companies abroad.

The changes initiated during the last decade in terms of deregulations, simplification and harmonization of laws and procedures and the changes proposed to be effected in the Companies Act have clearly indicated the shift in government attitude to allow the corporates for self-regulation of their affairs. The changing business environment and activities have necessitated the need for reinstating the principles of corporate governance and professionalization of corporate management.

The programmes of economic liberalization implied the need for change in the entire range of economic policy issues. The most significant with regard to our concern with corporate governance and the emergence of an Anglo-American System are company law and the capital market. We shall now refer to the key changes made in these areas and elaborate further on the significance of changes in these areas or promotion of more responsible corporate governance practices in India.

The Securities and Exchange Board of India (SEBI)

With the abolition of the office of the Controller of Capital Issues, the Securities and Exchange Board of India (SEBI) was constituted. It was established originally in 1988 but was only given statutory power with the enactment of the SEBI Act in January 1992. The SEBI did not obtain complete autonomy and authority to pursue its twin goals of investor protection and market development. The authority in key areas remained with the Department of Company Affairs (DCA). Gradually, its powers were expanded, but not to the extent enjoyed by the Securities and Exchange Commission (SEC of the USA). The statutory and regulatory powers to SEBI have been given by the Government with the mission to move from control regime to prudential regulation. SEBI was empowered to regulate the working of the stock exchanges, monitoring the members of the stock exchanges and all the players of the capital market including all listed companies. The bankers and registrars to the issue, merchant bankers, underwriters, portfolio managers, credit rating agencies, Foreign Institutional Investors (FIIs), venture capital funds, mutual funds and Asset Management Companies (AMCs) also came within the purview of SEBI operations.

SEBI, thereafter, formulated various rules and regulations for the purpose of regulating the operations of the players of the capital market, which were aimed at promotion of more responsible corporate governance. A list of important SEBI regulations is given in Appendix 4.

In principle, all these regulations should help to promote more responsible corporate governance by:

(a) providing investors with greater information to make informed choices;
(b) curbing insider trading and manipulations on the one hand and ensuring transparency and fair play, integrity and confidence of the investors on the other;
(c) providing investors with more effective means of redress in cases of abuse;
(d) providing equality of treatment and opportunities to minority shareholders, protection of the interest of minority shareholders, free and full disclosure of all material facts by the acquirers;
(e) preventing the actions that do not respect the interest of the shareholders, viz. manipulation of stock exchanges including price rigging and artificially increasing/ decreasing share prices; and
(f) ensuring greater transparency in the market for corporate control and facilitating the process for replacement of under-performing management through takeovers.

Depositories Act, 1996

The concept of holding equity shares into electronic form was introduced with the introduction of the Depositories Act, 1996. This enactment further established the confidence into true ownership of shareholding without any fear of being declared as *benami*, bogus or tainted securities in future. This step has improved the capital market scenario and has helped the management in serving and protecting shareholders' interest.

Companies Act and the Companies Amendment Bill, 1997

Another key action of the liberalization programme has been the revision of the Companies Act. To this end, a working committee was established in 1996. The Committee made many recommendations for updating the proposed corporate legislation in consonance with the international standard. The Government introduced the Companies Bill, 1997 in both Houses of Parliament in 1997. The new Bill proposed a wide range of changes. The important of these changes pertaining to corporate governance were: (i) the requirement that all large companies with a paid-up capital of more than ₹50 million, have an audit committee—2/3rds of whose members to be Non-executive Directors (NEDs), (ii) increase in the number of issues requiring special approval by the shareholders (e.g. buy-back of shares, issue of shares at premium, loans to directors etc.), (iii) increase in the financial disclosure requirements, (iv) increase in the compensation to Non-executive Directors (NEDs), (v) provision of postal ballots, (vi) greater role for proxies, including the right to speak at Annual General Meetings (AGMs) etc.

However, the Bill did not come up for consideration before the Parliament at that time. Later on, the new government announced its intention of forming a new committee to reappraise the draft bill before it gets reintroduced into the Parliament. Subsequently, some of the provisions contained in the Companies Bill, 1997 were enacted by the Companies (Amendment) Act, 1999 and Companies (Amendment) Act, 2000.

Recent developments and measures taken during the period 1998–2015

(a) *CII Code of Desirable Corporate Governance (1998):* In India, the history of corporate governance got real momentum from the year 1998 and onwards, when the Confederation of Indian Industry (CII) framed a voluntary code of corporate governance for listed companies, named as CII Code of Desirable Corporate Governance. The CII Code recommended: (i) key information to be reported, (ii) listed companies to have audit committees, (iii) corporates to give a statement on value addition, (iv) consolidation of accounts to be optional etc.

(b) *SEBI norms based on Kumar Mangalam Birla Committee recommendations on corporate governance (2000):* Another code of corporate governance was followed by the recommendations of the Kumar Mangalam Birla Committee (2000) set up by SEBI. This culminated in the introduction of Clause 49 of the standard Listing Agreement to be complied with by all listed companies in stipulated phases. Birla Committee recommended: (i) board to set up qualified and independent audit committee to enhance credibility of financial disclosures and to promote transparency, (ii) corporates to provide consolidated statements in respect of all its subsidiaries having a shareholding of 51% or more of the share capital, (iii) shareholders to exhibit greater degree of interest and involvement in the appointment of directors and auditors etc.

(c) *Companies (Amendment) Act, 2000:* In order to hasten the process of bringing improvement in the companies' functioning, the government amended the Companies Act in 2000. Various provisions concerning corporate governance included in this Amendment Act were: (i) board to report in cases where buy-back not completed within the time specified [Section 77 (4)], (ii) providing for directors' responsibility statement [Section 217 (2AA)], (iii) small shareholders' representation in the board through a director (Section 252), (iv) limitations in directorships in companies (Sections 274 & 275), (v) constitution of audit committees [Section 292 (A)], (vi) provisions for higher penalties for offences in various sections of the Companies Act etc.

The Amendment Act of 2000, thus increased manifold the duties and responsibilities of the directors in the companies to improve corporate governance.

(d) *Insertion of New Clause 49 of the Listing Agreement by SEBI (2000):* Immediately after the provisions of the Companies (Amendment) Act, 2000 came into force, SEBI in its meeting held on 25th January 2000, decided to make amendments to the Listing Agreement by inserting a new Clause 49 and published it through a circular no. SMDRP/Policy/Cir-10/2000 dated 21st February 2000. The new Clause 49 dealt with corporate governance and included the aspects, viz. (i) providing for appointment of optimum number of executive, non-executive/ independent directors, (ii) appointment of audit committee, (iii) remuneration of directors and its disclosure, (iv) board procedures and meetings, (v) management report, (vi) report on corporate governance.

In brief, many of the matters covered by Clause 49 were repetition of what was provided by the Companies (Amendment) Act, 2000.

(e) *Reserve Bank of India (RBI) Report of the Advisory Group on Corporate Governance (2001):* A standing committee under the chairmanship of Dr. Y.V.

Reddy, the then Deputy Governor of RBI was set up by the then Governor of the Reserve Bank of India (RBI) on 8th December 1999. The standing committee in its first meeting on 13th January 2000, constituted non-official advisory groups in ten major subject areas, of which 'corporate governance' was identified as one of the areas. Accordingly, an advisory group on corporate governance under the chairmanship of Dr. R.H. Patil, Managing Director, National Stock Exchange (NSE), Mumbai was constituted on 8th February 2000. They submitted report on 24th March 2001. The report contained several recommendations on corporate governance.

(f) *Companies (Amendment) Act, 2002 and Companies (Second Amendment) Act 2002:* Subsequent to the passing of the Companies (Amendment) Act, 2000, these two Amendment Acts were passed. These Acts have also dealt with some aspects of corporate governance.

(g) *Naresh Chandra Committee's (First) Report on Corporate Audit and Governance (2002):* Consequent to the Enron debacle in 2001 followed by the scams in WorldCom, Qwest, Global Crossing, Xerox, all corporate giants in the USA, involving the hand-in-glove relationship between the auditors and corporate clients as well as the subsequent enactment of the stringent Sarbanes Oxley Act in the USA, the Government of India promptly appointed the Naresh Chandra Committee in 2002 to examine and recommend drastic amendments to the law pertaining to auditor-client relationships and the role of the independent directors. The Committee's recommendations included: (i) audit partner to rotate every 5 years instead of audit firm's rotation, (ii) audit committee to be set up with all independent directors, (iii) companies to have at least 50% independent directors, (iv) certain professional assignments not to be undertaken by the company auditors etc.

(h) *N.R. Narayana Murthy Committee Report on Corporate Governance (2003):* In 2002, SEBI, while analysing the status of compliance with Clause 49 by the listed companies, felt a need to look beyond mere systems and procedures in order to make the corporate governance more effective in protecting the interest of investors. SEBI, therefore, constituted a committee under the chairmanship of N.R. Narayana Murthy, chairman and mentor of Infosys, and mandated the Committee to review the performance of corporate governance in India and make appropriate recommendations. The Committee submitted its report on 8th February 2003.

(i) *Companies (Amendment) Bill, 2003:* The Companies (Amendment) Bill, 2003 was introduced in the upper house of the Parliament on 7th May 2003. The introduction of this Bill indicated the seriousness of the Government to reform once again the Companies Act, 1956, which had undergone piecemeal amendments since the year 1998 till 2000. The statement of objects and reasons to the Bill of 2003 stated that the said Bill included: (i) certain provisions of the Companies Bill, 1997 still relevant today with or without modifications, (ii) recommendations of the Naresh Chandra Committee Report regarding (a) prohibition of relationships between the auditor and his clients, (b) prohibition of certain non-audit services by the auditors, (c) appointment of independent directors and women directors on the Board of Directors (BODs) and (iii) recommendations of the Joint Parliamentary Committee (JPC) relating to (a) restrictions on inter-corporate loans made to share broking companies, (b) prevention of vanishing companies by proper identification of the directors at the time of incorporation of companies etc.

The Companies (Amendment) Bill, 2003 proposed drastic changes in the provisions of the Companies Act pertaining to corporate governance which included: (i) accounting standard, (ii) chief accounts officer, (iii) independent director, (iv) liability for non/insufficient disclosure, (v) no gift in addition to dividends, (vi) consolidated accounts etc., (vii) segment reporting, (viii) protection of environments, (ix) appointment of auditors, (x) resolution for removal of auditors, (xi) disqualification of auditor, (xii) prohibition of services other than audit, (xiii) auditors report, (xiv) special audit, (xv) penalty for non-compliance by auditor, (xvi) information regarding persons having interest, (xvii) maximum and minimum number of directors, (xviii) number of directorships not more than 15, (xix) retiring age of directors, (xx) board meetings, (xxi) notice of board meetings, (xxii) audit committee, (xxiii) restriction of appointment of Managing Director or whole time Director.

In totality, 174 sections have been affected for proposed new insertions, amendments, substitutions, modifications in this Bill. This Amendment Bill was sharply criticised by the industry group, chambers of commerce and some anomalies were also pointed out by the experts in the field. As a result, the Companies (Amendment) Bill 2003 was withdrawn by the government for further review, rectifications or amendment by the Department of Company Affairs (DCA), Government of India.

(j) *Revision of Clause 49 of the Listing Agreement by SEBI (2003 and 2004):* In exercise of the powers conferred by Section II (1) of the SEBI Act, 1992 read with Section 10 of the SCRA (1956), SEBI revised Clause 49 of the Listing Agreement. Accordingly, all stock exchanges were directed vide Circular No. SEBI/MRD/SE/31/2003/26/08 dated 26th August 2003, to immediately replace the existing Clause 49 of the Listing Agreement by the revised Clause 49. This revision was brought by SEBI in order to ensure better corporate governance practices in the companies.

However, the above circular was deferred for implementation due to its controversial and debatable provisions and subsequently replaced by a new SEBI Circular No. SEBI/CFD/DIL/CG/1/2004/12/10 dated 29th October 2004 after complete overhaul of Clause 49 (new Clause 49), superseding all previous circulars issued by the SEBI in this regard.

(k) *Naresh Chandra Committee's (Second) Report on Amendment of Penal Provision for Independent and Non-executive Directors (2003):* The Naresh Chandra Committee in its second report submitted in 2003 to the government had suggested radical changes in the penal provisions of the Companies Act. The Committee recommended *inter alia*, exemption of independent and non-executive directors from civil and criminal liability.

(l) *Concept Paper on Company Law (2004):* The Ministry of Company Affairs, Government of India has taken another special initiative after having failed in three major attempts during all these years to re-write the company law, which has undergone amendments 24 times and released 'concept paper' containing a model codified company law and invited suggestions and critical comments before finalising the Bill.

(m) *Expert Committee (Dr. J.J. Irani Committee) Report on Company Law (2005):* After release of concept paper, an Expert Committee (consisting of 13 members and 6 special invitees) under the chairmanship of Dr. J.J. Irani was constituted by the Ministry on 2nd December, 2004 to evaluate the comments and suggestions received on concept paper and provide recommendations to the government in making a simplified modern company law. The Committee has submitted its report to the Government on May 31, 2005, which is under consideration. It is expected that corporate India will soon receive a simplified, updated, sleek, and user-friendly version of the company law with rules and regulations and effective monitoring mechanism for attaining world-class governance standards.

(n) *New Companies Act, 2013 and the Company Rules, 2014*: India took up its economic reforms programme in 1990s. Again, a need was felt for a comprehensive review of the Companies Act, 1956, which had become the bulkiest and archaic. Three unsuccessful attempts were made in the years 1993, 1997 and 2003 to rewrite the company law. Thereafter, in the year 2013, the Government of India (GOI) introduced a new and revised Companies Act, 2013 and the Rules, 2014. The Act is now sleek and thoroughly overhauled and revised with 470 sections and 7 schedules. The new Act has been enforced with effect from 1st April 2014. Many provisions of the erstwhile Act have been omitted, many existing provisions revised, merged, extended and re-written, and many provisions have been newly introduced as per the requirement of the current conditions and reality. It is the first time in the history of company law that the corporate directors have been recognized and classified as executive directors, non-executive directors and independent directors in the new Companies Act, 2013.

(o) *New Clause 49 of the Listing Agreement, 2014 by SEBI*: With the enactment of New Companies Act, 2013 and the Company Rules, 2014, SEBI also decided to review the provisions of the Listing Agreement, with the objective to align with the provisions of the Companies Act, 2013, adopt best practices on corporate governance and to make the governance framework more effective. Accordingly, SEBI issued a new Circular (no. CIR/CFD/POLICY CELL/2014) on 17th April 2014, superseding all other earlier circulars issued by SEBI on Clause 35B (provision of e-voting facility to the shareholders) and Clause 49 of the Equity Listing Agreement.

(p) *Securities and Exchange Board of India (Listing Obligations and Disclosure Requirements) Regulations, 2015*: Further, SEBI has introduced SEBI (Listing Obligations and Disclosure Requirements) Regulations, 2015 on 2nd September 2015, replacing the new Clause 49 of the Listing Agreement, 2014 with effect from 1st December 2015, with the view to consolidate and streamline the provisions of earlier Listing Agreement. These regulations have incorporated the principles for corporate governance in line with the Organization for Economic Co-operation and Development (OECD) principles and the International Organization of Securities Commissions (IOSCO) principles.

In addition to all the above developments affecting the company law and capital markets, economic liberalization had also affected a number of other policy areas pertaining to the corporate governance practices. Most significant areas have been: (i) changes to the banking sector, (ii) industrial policy, especially the abolition of license permit raj, (iii) trade and foreign exchange liberalization.

2.3 SUMMARY AND CONCLUDING OBSERVATION

Under the **Managing Agency System**, most of the companies acted in the ways contrary to shareholder rights and the spirit of fair market competition. As a policy, the system was problematic in the sense that by allowing systematic abuses of shareholder rights and practices, the policy was not compatible with common interests. We have seen how the managing agency contract was used by the agents to ensure virtual permanent control over the firms, to extract unjustifiable levels of remuneration, to siphon off funds etc. With respect to the competitive market practices, we have seen how these agents were able to utilize the resources of the managed firms to create new firms and resulted in increased economic concentration.

These agents utilized the resources to avoid the discipline of the market and also to influence the policy of the state. In fact, the British managing agents, through the help of Bengal Chamber of Commerce, were successful in such tactics to favour their own interests. The Indian managing agents, through FICCI, did follow the same tactics to influence political parties to favour their own interests. The combined result was that the system was not effectively reformed and economic concentration continued. Besides, the prevalent laws could not motivate these agents to conform to their economic responsibilities. The net result was that their structural power enabled them to circumvent these laws with impunity.

Under the **Promoter System**, it is observed that the Government was under much greater pressure to address the issues of corporate governance. It took many steps intended to promote more responsible business practices. Still however, the promoter groups regularly continued to act in ways inconsistent with the desired standards of behaviour. The Government introduced the Companies Act, 1956, which in principle, safeguarded shareholder's rights and placed stricter limits on the activities of the promoters. The Government also introduced a range of economic policies, which would have had its favourable effect if successfully implemented through the enforcement mechanisms. But government policy was proved to be quite ineffective. Despite greater attention, systematic abuses of corporate power continued.

Again the structural power of big business promoters helped them to apply for and secure a disproportionate share of industrial licenses and also enabled them a disproportionate share of public financial support. They took advantage of the market restrictions, which effectively protected them from foreign competition. That is how their structural power did undercut the formal intention of the Government policies involved and violated their economic responsibilities.

Under the Promoter System, the policies failed to provide, by and large, with the pragmatic motivation necessary to enable them to live up to their economic responsibilities, but of course, with a few exceptions. Some prominent business leaders like J.R.D. Tata criticized the abuses perpetrated by members of the business community and advocated for a much more transparent approach to business-government relationships.

With liberalization and the switch to an **Anglo-American System** of corporate governance, a substantial shift in emphasis has occurred in the approach to policy as it relates to the goal of encouraging firms to live up to their economic responsibilities. We have discussed variety of measures taken by the Government that are designed to achieve basic purposes, which should contribute to firms living up to their economic responsibilities. It has been observed that the Indian business groups have used their structural power to pressurize the Government to liberalize the economy but they have been rather selective in their approach to liberalization. They still want the Government support to reduce their costs as well as to protect them from foreign competition. While Indian firms do exert pressure on the Government to restrict activities of foreign companies, they make no argument to address the issue of concentration. On the other hand, the Government has provided Indian firms with more tools to defend themselves from foreign encroachment, e.g. buy-back of shares, non-voting shares etc. Practically, there has been no policy till date, which could provide business firms with pragmatic reasons for competing purely on the basis of 'innovation'.

Unfortunately, despite several measures taken so far, the corporate governance practices by the Indian corporates have remained more in paper and almost negligible in real practice. In examining the evolution of corporate governance in India, the following facts have emerged:

(i) The Advisory Group of RBI observed: "a distinguishing feature of the Indian Diaspora is the implicit acceptance that corporate entities belong to founding families". ".......... In the Indian scenario, the promoters dominate governance in every possible way".

(ii) The security scams of 2002 following the same modus operandi as the scam of 1992 have exposed the hollowness of the surveillance and enforcement of the Companies Act and Clause 49 of the Listing Agreement.

(iii) The total amount of money duped by the vanishing companies has been calculated to be about ₹ 669 billion.

(iv) Non-performing Assets (NPAs) of scheduled commercial banks has reached to the tune of ₹ 1423 billion (gross value) and ₹ 650 billion (net value) as on 31st March 2012.

(v) As per the Transparency International Corruption Perception Index, 2016, India's position is 76th out of 168 countries with a score of 38 out of 100.

In spite of many developments that have taken place in the corporate sector in recent years, the Anglo-American System does not appear to be very successful in generating and enforcing policies that could provide Indian business with sufficient pragmatic motivation to consistently live up to their economic responsibilities. However, it is also a fact that Indian firms have suffered from a comparative disadvantage not entirely created by them. This has happened due to the previous systems, which did not encourage them to develop competitive advantages.

Test Your Knowledge

1. Describe in brief, the Evolution of Corporate Governance in India?
2. Explain briefly the corporate governance practices in vogue in India at different points in time.
3. Discuss the Managing Agency System prevalent in India with respect to the economic responsibilities of the corporate enterprises (a) shareholder rights, shareholder control and maximisation of shareholder value, and (b) market competition.
4. Explain the reforms process undertaken for the 'Managing Agency System' in India.
5. What are the changes that took place in the Indian economy in the year 1956?
6. Evaluate 'Promoter System' (1956–1991) in India with respect to the economic responsibilities of the corporate enterprises (a) shareholder rights, shareholder control and maximisation of shareholder value, and (b) market competition.
7. Explain the reforms process undertaken for the 'Promoter System' in India.
8. Evaluate 'Anglo-American System' (1992-Onwards) in India with respect to the economic responsibilities of the corporate enterprises (a) shareholder rights, shareholder control and maximisation of shareholder value, and (b) market competition.
9. Explain the reforms process undertaken for the 'Anglo-American System' in India.
10. Explain the recent developments and measures taken by the Govt. of India, Regulatory Authorities, Industry Associations etc. during the period 1998–2015 to enhance corporate governance system in India.

CHAPTER 3
Corporate Governance: The Conceptual Issues

Learning Objectives	Key Words
After reading this chapter, the readers will be able to understand: ☛ The philosophy, objectives and purposes of Corporate Governance ☛ The concept of Corporate Governance, and its various factors, the cornerstones/principles, and theories of Corporate Governance and underlying conflict areas ☛ Corporate Governance and Value Creation ☛ Governance, Performance and Development at the macro and micro levels ☛ Business Ethics and Corporate Governance ☛ Corporate Social Responsibility (CSR) and Corporate Governance ☛ Environmental Issues and Corporate Governance ☛ Corporate Sustainability and Corporate Governance ☛ Structures and Processes for Governance in the Corporates	☛ Board of Directors ☛ Integrity ☛ Transparency ☛ Disclosures ☛ Statutory Liabilities ☛ Evaluation ☛ Value Creation ☛ Ethical Values

3.1 INTRODUCTION

We have discussed at length the evolution of corporate governance in India in Chapter 2. We now address, in this chapter, a few conceptual issues concerning corporate governance. Our objectives are to:

(a) examine the cornerstones of corporate governance philosophy and the factors influencing quality of governance;

(b) find out the purpose of corporate governance and its core principles;

(c) spell out in detail, the structures and processes for corporate governance generally envisaged for implementation as a concept.

In this chapter, we examine, in general, the various conceptual issues concerning corporate governance to analyze the effect of such issues on governance system, prevailing all over the world.

The contents of this chapter have been divided into the following sections:

- Philosophy, objectives and purposes of corporate governance
- Concept of Corporate Governance, and its various factors, the cornerstones/ principles, and theories of Corporate Governance and underlying conflict areas
- Corporate governance and value creation
- Governance, performance and development at the macro level
- Business ethics and corporate governance
- Corporate social responsibility (CSR) and corporate governance
- Environmental issues and corporate governance
- Corporate sustainability and corporate governance
- Structures and processes for corporate governance in the corporates

3.2 PHILOSOPHY, OBJECTIVES AND PURPOSES OF CORPORATE GOVERNANCE

The core objectives of any business firm are: (a) survival, (b) profitability, and (c) growth. The success or failure of a company's objectives depends on the effective application of essential aspects of its corporate philosophy, viz. 'freedom', 'reach', and 'uncertainty'. In the changing environment of business consequent to the globalization, new strategies have to be developed and implemented by the corporates. They must be consistent with the core objectives of a corporate in a market driven economy. Greater 'freedom' and its value help the organization to promote growth and profitability in the long run. Greater 'reach' leads to a systematic search for friends and foes in business and helps to protect profits in the short period. Greater 'uncertainty' results in a strategy of systems thinking and helps a company to strive for survival.

Ten to fifteen years ago, interest in the field of corporate governance was concentrated to legislators, company lawyers and the commentators who were concerned with accountability and financial disclosure of the company. More recently, interest has been escalated and widened, which automatically ask the vital question: why do we need corporate governance?

The following reasons may be listed as of particular significance: (a) the increasing scale, complexity and international activities of major corporate groups, (b) greater power and activities of institutional investors, (c) hostile activities of predator companies, (d) renewed responsibilities and powers of the regulatory authorities due to company law amendment and new securities trading regulations in various parts of the world, (e) recent disclosures and rethinking on insider trading, (f) demand for more checks and balances at board level and demand for separation of CEO's function from that of the chairman of the board, (g) calls for greater accountability by companies and their boards, (h) changes in the world of international audit profession, (i) developments in accounting standards and corporate regulation, (j) emergence of newly corporatized and privatized corporate entities, and (k) an increasingly litigious environment.

As a corporate governance philosophy, social responsibility should be an outcome of business strategy. Social responsibility has three major dimensions, viz. (a) the quality of a company's engagement in dealing with its employees, shareholders, others stakeholders, and society at large, (b) systems thinking leading towards going beyond the pursuit of pure profits in a corporation's engagement with society, and (c) managing a broader portfolio of assets including social investments in areas like education, health, community development and conservation of environments.

A company has to keep a balance between short-term profitability and long-run social development, which involves going beyond meeting the minimum regulatory standards of pollution control or energy conservation.

However, in a rapidly changing today's business environment and consequent to the market-friendly economic reforms, the dominance of the Government has been reduced considerably. It has affected the social sector services, which used to be provided by the Government at zero or subsidized costs. In turn, the pressure to provide such services have been shifted to the companies as the society expects companies to carry some of the social responsibilities of government. On the one hand, the social needs and expectations for responsible corporate citizenship have been substantially growing as a consequence of market-friendly reforms. On the other hand, the corporates are caught by the forces of global fierce competition, threatening their survival resulting in continuous pressure to find adequate profitability by any means.

In today's corporate world, no company can afford to ignore and abstain itself from discharging its social obligations emanating from the trust and faith that society at large and stakeholders in particular, have reposed on it. Fortunately, the new organizations, which are growing at a faster pace in the era of economic reforms, have started reaching out in the areas of 'education', 'creation of human capability' and 'upliftment of the society'. It has definitely reflected a new image of self, a new evaluation of responsibilities, and a new realization of the fact that social commitment need not necessarily go against creating 'profitability' in the long-run.

3.3 CONCEPT OF CORPORATE GOVERNANCE AND ITS FACTORS

All societies run by human beings need to be properly governed. Wherever power is exercised to direct, control and regulate activities that affect people's legitimate interests, governance is necessary. The question comes: What is Corporate Governance? Why is it necessary and how can it be focused, practised or implemented?

Corporate governance is concerned with the process by which corporate entities, particularly limited liability companies, are governed with the exercise of power over the direction of the enterprise, the supervision of executive actions, the acceptance of a duty to be accountable and the regulation of the company within the jurisdiction of the country where it operates.

In many countries, corporate governance is rooted in western practices, culture, and ideologies. In most cases, it has followed the tradition of Anglo-American common law (e.g. Australia, Canada, Hong Kong, India, Malaysia, New Zealand, Philippines, South Africa, Singapore, the USA and the UK. The approaches to corporate governance are less similar in the West European countries where tradition of Roman law is followed and quite dissimilar in Eastern Europe, Russia, China etc.

Primarily, corporate governance is concerned with the functioning of Board of Directors (BODs)–its structure, style, processes, their relationships and roles, activities etc. It is also concerned with the roles of company stakeholders—shareholders, institutional investors or large shareholders, auditors, banks and others. The practice of corporate governance varies across firms due to a number of factors, the first category of which is the 'formal mechanism of governance'. It includes a *single-tier* board structure, election of directors by the shareholders, various shareholders' rights and restrictions (example, the Anglo-American model) [Figure 3.1].

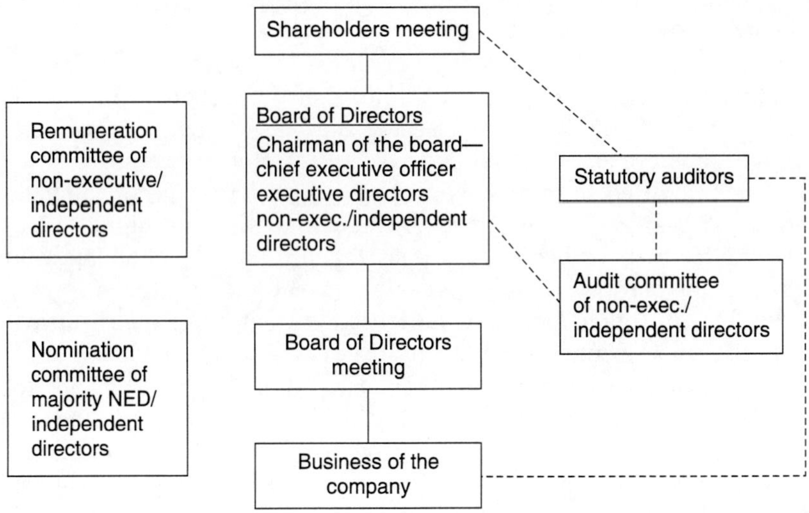

Figure 3.1 Single-tier Board Structure (Anglo-American Model).

On the contrary, there is a *two-tier* board system consisting of a supervisory board and a management board. In the supervisory board workers are allocated 50% of the seats and the major banks, financial institutions are also represented there (example, the German model) [Figure 3.2(a) and 3.2(b)].

The second category of factors is the 'regulatory and macro-economic circumstance' under which governance is exercised. For example, capital markets, in the case of Anglo-American model, tend to be a strong factor that readily allow for mergers and acquisitions, and hostile takeovers. But in the German model, capital markets have tended to be relatively weak and hostile takeovers are, in fact, unheard of. Other significant areas of difference effecting on the governance of the firms include the credit system, tax policy, macro-stabilization policy and industrial planning.

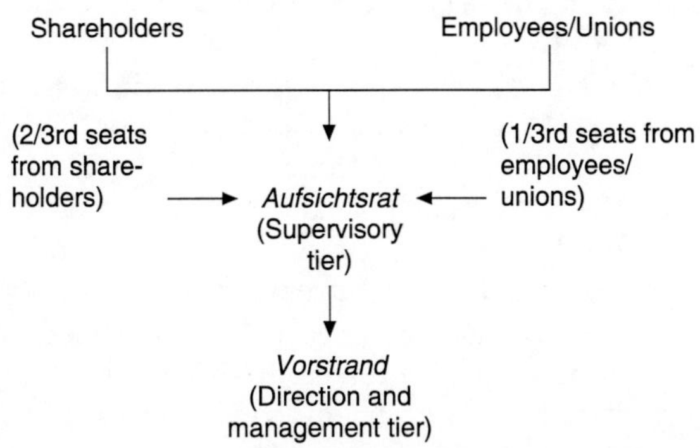

Figure 3.2(a) Two-tier Board Structure (German Model: GmbH Co.).

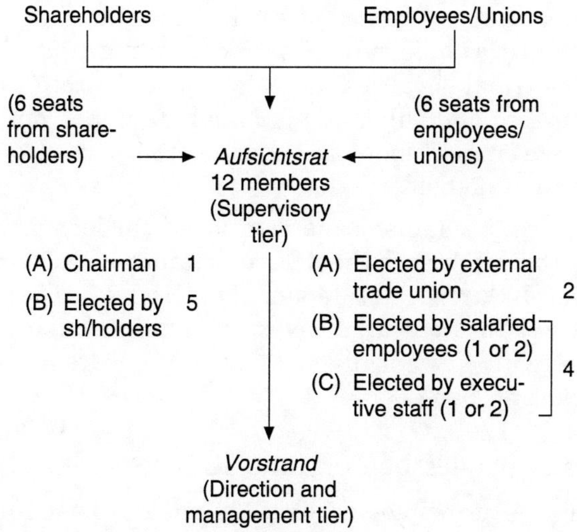

Figure 3.2(b) Two-tier Board Structure (German Model: AG Co.).

The research studies on corporate power and corporate governance suggest two basic categories most significant to understand these variations. These are: (i) the locus of control in corporation and (ii) the mechanisms for attaining and maintaining control. There are only two or three groups potentially capable of exercising such control on the basis of different sources of power. They are owners (exercising control on the basis of their shareholdings), management (exercising control on the basis of their strategic location), and the lenders (exercising control based on their financial clout). Of these three bases for exercising control, it is the only 'ownership', which is legally recognized as the source of control. The main criterion in establishing which of these groups actually controls the company, depends on who has the ability to appoint and replace top executives. These groups use to attain and maintain control over the formal mechanisms of control like hostile takeover, friendly takeover and mergers, cross-holdings, interlocking directorships, various anti-takeover bid methods, e.g. poison pills, golden parachutes, green mail etc., discouraging shareholders participation and so on.

Therefore, it can be said that there can be no one universally acceptable model of the corporate governance. Whatever may be the model followed, there are three different forms of corporate responsibilities which all models of corporate governance do respect. They are: (i) the political responsibilities, (ii) the social responsibilities, and (iii) the economic responsibilities. The basic political obligations are: (a) abiding by legitimate law, (b) respect for the system of rights and the principles of constitutional state. The basic social obligations of the corporation are the corporate ethical responsibilities, which the company understands and promotes either as a community with shared values or as a part of larger community (e.g. neighbourhood, city, state, nations) with shared values. The basic economic obligations of companies are: (i) acting in accordance with the logic of competitive markets to earn profits on the basis of innovation, and (ii) respect for the rights/ democracy of the shareholders which can be expressed in terms of managements' obligation as "maximizing shareholders value".

The history of corporate governance has pointed out four key causes of governance problems in the past, e.g. (a) a culture of secrecy leading to governance by discretion rather than rules, (b) tribal loyalties causing unusual protection for the directors, (c) legislative weaknesses, and (d) lack of commitment not only on the part of the board and the corporate management but also on the part of owners (shareholders), large shareholders, and stakeholders.

Corporate governance mechanisms, as mentioned earlier, vary a great deal around the world. Firms in the USA and the UK substantially rely on legal protection of investors. In continental Europe and Japan, there is less reliance on elaborate legal protections and more reliance on large investors and banks. In the rest of the world including India, ownership is typically heavily concentrated in families with a few large outside investors and banks.

3.3.1 Cornerstones/Principles of Corporate Governance

The corporate governance principles revolve around the basic interrelated segments. These are: (i) integrity and fairness, (ii) transparency and disclosures, and (iii) accountability and responsibility. Written down legislation and regulation are essential to introduce a framework of good corporate governance practices no doubt, but in addition, the voluntary codes are also essential to make the practices commensurate with principles.

Integrity and fairness

Integrity and fairness occupy a central position in the studies and research in corporate governance. The understanding and practice of ethics and the related value system lie at the heart of this element. The top management has to inculcate a culture of ethical practices, which will be demonstrated and percolated to the other levels within the organization to create a culture, which would reflect ethics, fair play and integrity par excellence. In this context, there is a need for a 'code of conduct' for the Board of Directors (BODs) and senior management. The code should be so designed to reflect the intention of highest standards of integrity to be followed in practice. The boards are required to discharge fiduciary responsibilities as they act as the trustees of shareholders and other stakeholders. The foundation of trusteeship concept is integrity, fairness and ethical standards of the highest order.

Transparency and disclosures

The elements of transparency and disclosures in corporate governance are equally important. The board of directors and its committees are expected to work in a harmonious manner to review all the activities and results on a periodic basis. The effectiveness, however, would depend upon strong management information system, active role of audit committee, proper internal control, systems and procedures and the vigilant monitoring and supervisory role of the boards. An important requisite in this regard would be to step up a well-developed and interactive websites by the corporates for transmission of all information relating to business and its performance on a real time basis.

Accountability and responsibility

Accountability and responsibility function as the third pillar in the principles of good corporate governance. A company, which follows high ethical standards and discloses more than what is required would always, has the courage to be accountable to all stakeholders for any act of omission and commission. A company of high standards of integrity and with good performance record would generally have concerns for the society, which would be visible from the discharge of duties on social responsibility.

3.3.2 Theories of Corporate Governance

The two basic theories of corporate governance are: (i) Stewardship Theory and (ii) Agency Theory. The original corporate concept enshrined a philosophical assumption about the nature of man, one that has been reflected in the Stewardship Theory, which assumes that man is essentially trustworthy, able to act in good faith in the interest of others with integrity and honesty. This is implicit in the fiduciary relationship required of directors. The theoretical underpinning is normative, based on the belief that stewardship will be exercised by the directors to whom the shareholders have delegated responsibility and authority, while requiring appropriate accountability. The Stewardship Theory of corporate governance is an adjunct of classical management theories. However, one of the earliest studies in the field of corporate governance, by Berle and Means in 1932 had challenged the conventional assumptions of the Stewardship Theory. They pointed out that ownership in large public companies had been separated from management. The shareholders were no longer able to monitor the affairs of the business in which they had invested. Therefore, they surrendered their control to management. But the interests of owners and management were divergent—the owners asking for increased corporate worth in terms of share price and dividend, whereas the managers asking for job security, reward and incentive package and other personal benefits. Such a perception has practically underpinned the agency theory. The view on directors taken by agency theory is that they cannot be trusted to act in the public welfare in general and in the interest of shareholders in particular. In fact, they need to be monitored and controlled to ensure compliance. Obviously, such checks and balance mechanisms incur agency costs. Examples of such agency costs being incurred in practice in a company are reflected in board structures by way of inclusion of outside independent directors, board committees comprising independent directors to be concerned with 'audit', top management 'remuneration', 'nomination' of new directors and the 'separation' of the roles of Chairman and CEO.

3.3.3 Underlying Conflicts

While going through the literature and the research studies undertaken so far on the subject of corporate governance, it is observed that there are a few underlying conflicts which form the basis for corporate governance issues. Three distinct areas of conflicts have been noticed, viz. (i) narrow vs. broad-based analysis of corporate governance, (ii) governance vs. management, and (iii) separation of ownership and control.

Narrow vs. broad-based analysis of corporate governance

Corporate governance can be studied for different purposes and from different perspectives and approaches, e.g. the positive, normative and the strategic approaches.

The 'positive' analysis demonstrates the manner in which governance is exercised in the corporates. The 'normative' analysis shows the manner in which the companies should be governed. The 'strategic' analysis points out the manner how the corporates can attain their goals.

The 'narrowest' concepts of corporate governance restrict the understanding of governance limited to the activities and fiduciary obligations of the directors only to the shareholders of the large companies, thereby ignoring the effects on other stakeholders. On the contrary, the 'broader' concepts extend the narrowest understanding in much more broad-based manner in the sense that these concepts do examine the impact of corporate decision-making on all other stakeholder groups as well under different models of corporate governance. Therefore, unlike the broad-based analysis, the narrowest approach is not very effective in analyzing the governance systems across the companies in various countries of the world.

But in understanding the effectiveness of these two concepts, we also observe some counter-arguments in favour of so called the 'narrowest' concept over the 'broad-based' concept. **Firstly**, it is no denying the fact that the shareholders are the true owners of the company. It is natural that the primary tasks of the directors should be to satisfy the owners and maximize their value in terms of 'return' on risk investment made by them as also increased 'market capitalization' of investment. Hence, it is neither unfair at all nor should it be considered as holding narrowest conception of corporate governance. **Secondly**, it seems improper to hold the view that expectations of other stakeholders are ignored if the fiduciary obligations are concentrated only to the shareholders. On the contrary, it is observed that maximization of shareholders' value generally have a favourable impact on the other stakeholders also. A progressive company with its good governance practices and policies is expected to take care as much of the expectations of the other stakeholders as it would do for its owners. **Thirdly**, there may, of course, arise a conflict of interests among the shareholders and other stakeholders in time of crisis when a company has no other alternative but to take certain drastic and justified action (say, cost cutting measures including reduction of employee cost etc.) for its survival. This may cause hardship not only for the stakeholders (employees in this case) but for the shareholders as well. If the company, after all, does not survive, not only the interest of the shareholders but also the interest of all other stakeholders will be in jeopardy. In such a situation, can a company management be blamed as holding 'narrow' concept of corporate governance? Therefore, there should not be any such interpretation of corporate governance concepts as 'narrow'/'broad', as the managerial action of a company depends mostly on circumstance of the case. Even if it is done, attempts must be there to draw a balance between the narrow and broad-based concept of corporate governance so that a win-win situation arises between shareholders and other stakeholders.

Governance vs. management

Corporate governance and corporate management are defined in the context of legal doctrines and regulatory activities which elaborate the rights and responsibilities in the two-dimensional relationship between the boards (acting as the agents of shareholders) and the senior management. The fundamental distinctions are as follows:

(a) managers operate within the hierarchy of the delegated responsibility and authority. But all board members are jointly and individually responsible and they have equal rights and duties;

(b) the responsibility of the board is to govern the company while the managers' task is to run its business;

(c) governance has an external focus whereas management has an internal focus;

(d) governance assumes an open system while management assumes a closed system;

(e) governance is strategy-oriented, whereas management is task-oriented;

(f) governance is concerned with 'where the company is going' and management is concerned with 'getting the company there'.

The process of corporate governance essentially has four principal activities, viz. (i) direction, (ii) executive action, (iii) supervision, and (iv) accountability. However, in a unitary board system, the activities and processes of governance and management get overlapping unlike the two-tier board system where these are totally compartmentalized [Figures 3.3(a) and 3.3(b)].

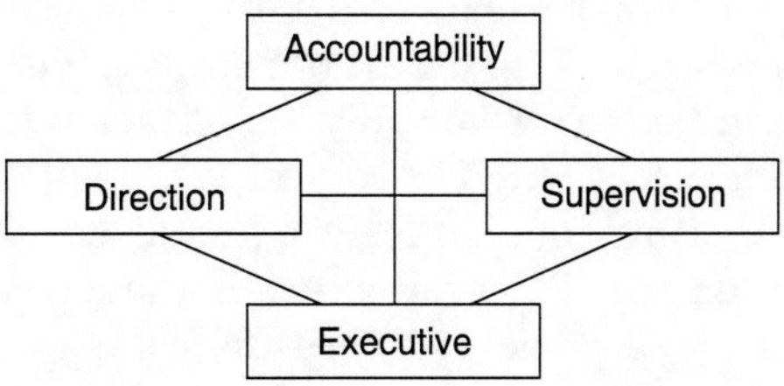

Figure 3.3(a) Processes and Activities of Corporate Governance.

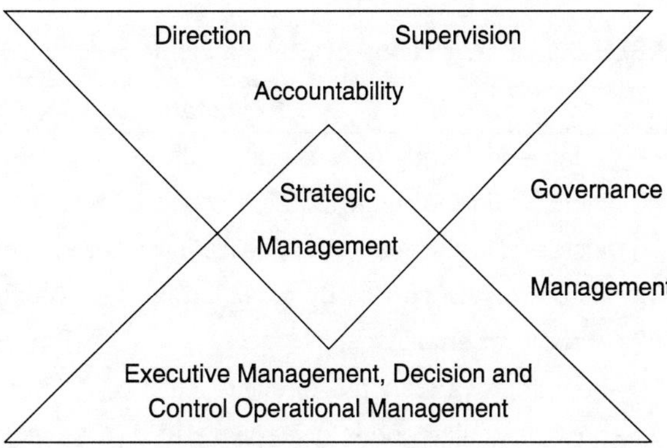

Figure 3.3(b) Processes and Activities of Governance and Management Compared.

Separation of ownership and control

While applying the concept of corporate governance to reality, the issues are surfaced in the separation of ownership and control. In fact, the governance issues begin to form with the question of 'control'. On the one hand, there are proponents like

Nader, Green and Seligman who argue that management makes its decision in its own self-interest and needs only to appease shareholders. The board is a buffer, which serves management interests and deflects shareholders demands as ownership is so widely dispersed that the shareholders can hardly influence the managements' use of corporate assets. On the other hand, there are proponents like Baysinger and Butler who argue that shareholders do maintain control over the use of corporate assets through their behaviour in financial markets. The buying and selling of stock as a reflection of shareholder control cannot be minimized. Management that makes decisions detrimental to shareholder interests is penalised through the market, and therefore, risks its position in management. The boards that ignore shareholders' interests are similarly prone to penalties of the market. However, this separation of ownership and control has been a rule in corporate philosophy and this actually lies at the root of the origin of corporate governance.

3.4 CORPORATE GOVERNANCE AND VALUE CREATION

The need for setting up of a foundation of value creation drive has been felt as a prime point on top of the corporate agenda. Governing companies in an effective manner, should ultimately result in transparency and best practices on the one hand, and a healthy bottom line on consistent basis for all the stakeholders on the other. The global debate now is increasing in favour of not only the ethics but also creation of value in a transparent manner. Therefore, higher volume of long-term value creation for all stakeholders should be the prime concern for the board. To adopt transparent practices in the companies and to ensure a better value management we have to know the stakeholders' expectations, as also the ability of the companies to satisfy expectations.

The expectations of various stakeholders (including shareholders) from the corporates can be listed as follows (Table 3.1).

TABLE 3.1 Expectations of Stakeholders/Shareholders

Stakeholders		Expectations
(a) Shareholders	(i)	a fair and steady rate of return (dividend) on investment;
	(ii)	increase in the future earning of the company;
	(iii)	increase in the market capitalization of investment.
(b) Employees	(i)	recognition of service by providing fair remuneration as also incentives;
	(ii)	stability of employment;
	(iii)	help improve standard of living.
(c) Customers	(i)	provide quality goods or services at a fair price and on fair terms;
	(ii)	restraint from restrictive practices or unfair practices.
(d) Competitors	(i)	restraint from adopting any strategy to elbow competitors out with unfair or restrictive practices or through violation of competition law norms.
(e) Creditors	(i)	ability to pay the principal and interest as per contractual obligations.

(Contd.)

(*Contd.*)

Stakeholders		Expectations
(f) Government	(i)	behave as a responsible and good corporate citizen;
	(ii)	non-evasion of taxes and dues to the Government;
	(iii)	involvement in social cause, e.g. charities, donations etc.
(g) Community	(i)	growth in employment generation to secure good local employment;
	(ii)	protection of environment.
(h) Public at large	(i)	To hold the board accountable for—
		(a) limiting senior executives' compensation;
		(b) full environmental protection;
		(c) avoidance of fraud within the company;
		(d) caring for employees.

In an open economy, it is extremely important how the strategies are made by a company. The main strategies adopted by a company may be: (a) business portfolio strategy, (b) vertical integration, (c) horizontal integration, and (d) financial holding strategy. The core of all the strategies is to deliver the best value for the stakeholders. The ultimate test is to see whether the company has generated wealth and has earned future earning capabilities as to ensure increased market capitalization. However, the fact remains that a company is responsible to the stakeholders for value creation on a continuous basis, and hence, the focus should be to find out the gap and the cause thereof.

3.5 GOVERNANCE, PERFORMANCE AND DEVELOPMENT AT MACRO AND MICRO LEVELS

The concept of 'development', as we have seen, had emerged and became popular since the post-Second World War era. It was closely identified with the 'economic development', which in turn was related to the level of industrialization. So the main focus of development had been the development of industrial economy. In the process, other aspects of development, viz. socio-cultural, political etc. were treated as secondary because the economic development was considered to be the only basis for sustained development. Therefore, the economic growth measured in terms of per capita GNP remained the dominant criterion for development. However, over the last couple of decades the term 'development' has been reconceptualized and extended further to bring socio-cultural, political dimensions and related concerns, viz. impact of environment and future generations etc. under the fold of 'development'. These new concepts of development have raised the normative issues about the justice of the universal distribution of resources, opportunities and the priorities of development efforts.

The companies can contribute to 'development' through the above three-dimensional concepts in terms of positive, normative and strategic analyses and this development is possible only through 'good governance'. It is the responsibility of the board of directors of companies to ensure that the companies are directed and governed well according to the policies framed and strategies adopted. At the same time, the chief executives and senior managers are to ensure that the companies are run and administered well and thereby performance achieved against the targets set. All of these can be ensured if the companies are steered with a good governance system. There should not be any doubt that good governance practice imbibes good habit and discipline and encourages the 'personnel' to perform at every level of the organization, which ultimately results in a better performance at individual level as well as in a group level. This again pushes up the growth—quantitative and quality-wise for the companies in terms of better profitability and better return on investment, which ultimately brings improved return to the shareholders in the form of increased dividend and capital appreciation of their holdings. At the same time, the stakeholders are also benefitted by the improved performance of the company. For example, the employees get increased remuneration and higher incentives, the creditors by the prompt payment of their dues, the customers by quality goods at reasonable price, the government by increased taxes and duties in its exchequer, the community and public at large by way of growth in employment generation and environment protection. Finally, the net effect of the better performance and growth of the corporate sector leads towards all round economic growth of the country in terms of GDP.

The companies, through their governance policies and practices, can have development impact on economic, socio-cultural and political dimensions of development. The companies can promote development in maximizing shareholder value. While developing the strategies they can bring development impact in their business activities in terms of plant location, choice of technology, selection of products etc. which ultimately result in income and employment generation, development of rural/backward areas, utilization of local resources etc. As part of the strategy this may also include business-government relationship in terms of lobbying practices, political donation and other influences on the Government and other non-business activities, viz. corporate social responsibility etc. All the above development activities of the companies having impact on economic, socio-cultural and political dimensions finally result in the impact on their performance as also on the overall performance of the economy in the long run.

3.6 BUSINESS ETHICS AND CORPORATE GOVERNANCE

The word 'ethics' owes its origin to Greek word 'ethos' which means a system of moral principles, the basis for deciding right and wrong actions, and implies customs, habits, noble traits in character, discipline, culture and disposition. The ethical principles are the rules of conduct that are derived from ethical values, known as six pillars, viz. trustworthiness, respect, responsibility, fairness, caring and citizenship. These values are inseparable from one another and are closely interwoven and interlinked with each other.

It is now established that a high sense of professional morality must comprise one of the core values of corporate governance for long term as also short-term success of a company. The ethical values nowadays, are not looked upon any longer, as costs imposed on the industry or a check on efficiency and profit maximization, but are regarded as imperatives for sustainable corporate growth and competitive edge. A highly developed sense of ethics enables corporate governance to build a trusting, long-term relationship with consumers.

The ethical values in relation with 'competitors' explore the issue of how far a business should go in trying to beat a competitor. The ethical values in relation to 'employment' raise question on whether an employer owes any special duties to employees beyond legal ones. The ethical values in relation to 'customers' explore the extent to which ethical considerations restrict the traditional attitude of caveat emptor in this area. The ethical values in relation to 'society' consider whether business owes any duty to society other than profit-making.

The following factors, by and large, influence the ethical environment in an organization:

(a) ethical vision of management which may need a review;
(b) holistic human values the organization has developed;
(c) ethical code acquired within the organization;
(d) source of individual inspiration;
(e) managerial character and ethical dedication;
(f) workplace environment and compulsion to follow the ethical norms.

A company is characterized by its ethical culture, which remains paramount in its daily operations. Good corporate governance is an integral part of business ethics. When a company's board of directors adopts ethics and declares it as its credo, to its management group, its executives and employees, ethics would automatically pervade the organization and build a fair amount of goodwill for the business. Many good organizations, in order to upheld and ensure ethical practices within the organization and outside have developed a 'code of conduct' for their employees. There also exists another form of document called a 'code of ethics'. These codes do help to make the employees and executives sensitive to their own behaviour and ethical implications.

The convergence of the roles and responsibilities of directors—both executive and non-executive, auditors, and shareholders is pre-requisite for achieving the targeted mission of a modern corporate governance and excellence. Certain core values—desirable and auditable values are to be in-built in the system of governance so that boundaries for performance for each player are well defined. This facilitates in laying down the responsibility and accountability in ensuring proper governance. Corporate governance, after all, is a system embedded with confirmation of values and ethics towards making the companies "good corporate citizen".

3.7 CORPORATE SOCIAL RESPONSIBILITY (CSR) AND CORPORATE GOVERNANCE

Corporate social responsibility (CSR) is essentially a concept whereby companies integrate social and environmental concerns in their business operations and in the interaction with their stakeholders on a voluntary basis. Through voluntary commitment to CSR, companies send a positive signal of their behaviour to their various stakeholders, viz. shareholders, employees, investors, creditors, suppliers, customers, regulators, government, and the society at large. In doing so, they make an investment towards future and increase their profitability. In fact, corporate governance and corporate responsibility towards society are inextricably interlinked, intertwined and inseparable from each other. If a corporate house is expected to provide good governance to its stakeholders and society at large, it is because it enjoys so much facilities from the society (in terms of developed infrastructure, trained workforce, peaceful environment, law and order etc.) that it is only appropriate that the company gives back to the society at least something in return in the form of good governance. Therefore, it is a well-conceived fact that good corporate governance itself is part and parcel of corporate responsibility towards society.

There are many factors that have compelled the corporates to recognize and attach tremendous importance to CSR in discharging their day to day activities. Some of these are:

(a) New concerns and expectations from various stakeholders in the context of large-scale industrial change due to globalization;
(b) Increased influence of social criteria on the investment decisions of individuals and institutions, both as consumers and as investors;
(c) Increased concern about the damage to the environment caused by economic activities;
(d) Transparency of business activities brought about by the modern information and communication technologies.

In the present era of intense competition, it is imperative for the corporates to generate and sustain 'goodwill' among their stakeholders and the community at large. Therefore, active participation in various social welfare projects is surely going to improve the corporates' visibility and place them on a pedestal of high public esteem. The business firms should understand the fact that economic goals and social responsibility objectives need not be contradictory to each other rather both can co-exist and both can be achieved simultaneously.

Corporate Social Responsibility is discussed in detail in Chapter 12.

3.8 ENVIRONMENTAL ISSUES AND CORPORATE GOVERNANCE

It is a well-known fact that the present environmental problems are serious. In recent years, the environmental degradation due to different types of pollution occurring in air, water, soil and the biosphere have grown to an alarming level. Much of the blame has been laid at the doorstep of industry. The big companies have been targeted as the main culprits and enemies of the environment. The problems like global warming, depletion of ozone layer, increased instances of health problems etc. have arisen due to rapid industrialization without any consideration for environment protection. Industry can no longer survive with the 'damaging image' of being responsible for environmental damage. Therefore, companies have to re-examine and refurbish their activities right from the nature of products they produce, technology they employ, raw materials they use and the way they market their products.

The environment protection and pollution prevention have been recognized as the essentials for good corporate governance practices. In fact, many international committees on corporate governance have required the companies to publish a detailed report on the measures taken by them in preventing pollution and environment protection in their annual reports. As recommended by these committees, many well-governed companies have developed their 'environmental policy' and disclosed the same in the annual report.

In the near future, companies that refuse to "go green" will definitely perish in an environmentally conscious society. Therefore, corporate leaders should essentially learn to promote resource preservation by reducing waste and maximizing resources while improving profitability. The time is ripe for all companies to take a fresh look into environmental issues. The attempts to improve environmental performance should be considered as an opportunity to innovate and not as a burden. Environmental audits can provide an in-depth review of the company processes and progress in realizing long-term strategic goals.

3.9 CORPORATE SUSTAINABILITY AND CORPORATE GOVERNANCE

Corporate sustainability is a business approach that creates long-term consumer and employee value by creating a *green* strategy aimed towards the natural environment and taking into consideration every dimension of how a business operates in the social, cultural, and economic environment. It also formulates strategies to build a company that fosters longevity through transparency and proper employee development. Corporate sustainability can be measured through composite indicators, which include environmental, social, corporate governance and economic measures. It increases corporate revenues and productivity of employees, and reduces energy expenses, wastes, material costs, hiring costs, and operational risks. Corporate sustainability can be regarded as the response of corporate to sustainable development represented by the strategies and practices that address the key issues for the world's sustainable development.

In other words, we can say that corporate sustainability is a business approach that creates long-term shareholder value by embracing opportunities and managing risks deriving from economic, environmental and social developments. The main focus on corporate sustainability is based on the following two guiding principles:

(a) Sustainable business practices are critical to the creation of long-term shareholder value in an increasingly resource-constrained world, and
(b) Sustainability factors represent opportunities and risks that competitive companies must address.

Sustainability requires a company to look internally and externally to understand its environmental and social impacts. This requires the engagement of stakeholders to understand impacts and concerns. A business can address sustainability internally by educating employees and seeking to reduce impacts through waste reduction, energy efficiency, etc. As a company looks externally, stakeholders include customers, suppliers, community, and non-government organizations. Corporate sustainability is a long-term challenge, which creates new opportunities and risks the companies must address today to remain competitive tomorrow. The companies that anticipate and manage current and future economic, environmental and social opportunities and risks by focusing on quality, innovation and productivity will emerge as leaders and are more likely to create a competitive advantage and long-term stakeholder value.

A review of the literature suggests that the concept of corporate sustainability borrows elements from four more established concepts: (a) sustainable development, (b) corporate social responsibility, (c) stakeholder theory, and (d) corporate accountability theory. These concepts are considered part and parcel of good governance. Therefore, the concept of corporate sustainability is synonymous to the concept of corporate governance. A company cannot be called a good governed organization unless it has established and well-practised the concepts of sustainable development, corporate social responsibility, stakeholders' value and corporate accountability in its organization.

3.10 STRUCTURES AND PROCESSES FOR CORPORATE GOVERNANCE

The structures and processes of corporate governance are not universally same in all countries. The different countries have adopted different structures and processes in governing their companies depending on suitability of their social culture, economic environment, government policy, capital and money market systems etc. Whatever the structures of corporate governance adopted, one thing is common that the board of directors has been recognized as the heart of the structure of corporate governance and the board processes have been accepted as the most important processes of governance. It has also been recognized that along with the board of directors, the other participants, viz. shareholders including institutional investors or large shareholders, other stakeholders, banks and auditors etc. do have significant roles in the governance structures and their commitments in the processes of corporate governance. Therefore, while discussing the various structures and processes of corporate governance, it will be prudent to touch upon the roles and commitments of these participants simultaneously, without which the discussion on governance structures and processes remains incomplete.

3.10.1 Directors—Board of Directors (BOD)

The main responsibility of governing a company is upon the Board of Directors (BODs). Directors are appointed by the shareholders of the company and the board appoints one or more of them as managing director/whole time directors/executive directors to be approved by the shareholders. The roles of the board and the shareholders are interactive and, therefore, the quality of governance depends upon the level of interface set up by them. Ideally, the board should be the heart and soul of a company. Whether or not, the company grows or declines, depends mostly upon the sense of purpose and direction, the values, the will to generate stakeholders' satisfaction and the drive to achieve them. The boards are accountable in many ways to the shareholders and stakeholders in a company. The directors are required to achieve a balance between competing interests of shareholders, customers, lenders, promoters and directors.

Challenges to the board

The challenges to the board are how to govern the companies effectively. Many reasons can be cited: (a) aggressive competition, (b) adverse/volatile economic and political conditions, (c) technological change, (d) expansion of global financial markets and sophisticated financing methods, etc.—all of these are making the task of directors of identifying and holding strategic business advantage increasingly difficult. Moreover, many companies operate within group ownership and board structures, which have become more complex, with subsidiaries, joint ventures, complex cross-holdings and inter-trading, causing more complication in the matter of corporate direction and control.

Besides, the threat of predators launching hostile bids has added another dimension to the board level concerns in the listed companies. Moreover, the regulatory climate all over the world surrounding companies and their boards has also been intensified. Finally, there has been growing realization of the personal exposure of the board and individual members to the threat of legal action for infringements of specific legislation or legal action claiming damages for alleged negligence and other misdemeanor in running their company's affairs.

The focus has, therefore, been on board processes, alternative board structures and styles, and the board relationships with the existing and potential shareholders, with top management and with stakeholders, including regulators, customers, employees, suppliers, and other claimants.

Management of the board

In most free enterprise countries, there is a broad agreement that the *following areas of concern* are important in management of the board. They are:

1. The board must agree how it will manage itself. This will include its composition, agenda, process and performance.
2. It will have a clear understanding of directors' terms of tenure and how new appointees are nominated and chosen.
3. There will be a process to monitor the chief executive and his senior colleagues that will involve the chairman and non-executive outside directors alone.
4. The chairman will ensure that there is a periodic opportunity to review the functioning of the board.
5. There must be freedom for the outside/independent directors to meet with inside/executive directors individually or collectively. This will include information-seeking, individual discussion on a topic of interest or socially to build up the two-way benefits of networking.
6. There must be an appropriate opportunity either through committees or direct involvement to review compensation plans, succession plans, strategy and issues of internal control.

Board activities

There are *four components* of the board activities, viz. (a) strategy formulation, (b) policy making, (c) monitoring and supervision of executive management, and (d) providing accountability to the stakeholder groups. These are shown in Figure 3.4.

Figure 3.4 shows, on one hand, the board's involvement in contributing to the company's performance by way of strategy formulation and policy making, and on the other hand, in ensuring conformance to the required results by way of maintaining accountability to the shareholders and others having legitimate interests in the company.

Strategy Formulation: Strategy formulation is the process through which each member of the board appreciates the competitive situation in which the business exists and

External	**Accountability** Reporting to shareholders Ensuring regulatory compliance Reviewing audit reports	**Strategy formulation** Reviewing and initiating strategic analysis Formulating strategy Setting corporate direction
	Appointment and rewarding CEO/Managing director	
Internal	**Supervision** Reviewing key executing performance Reviewing business results Monitoring budgetary control and taking corrective action Short term	**Corporate policy making** Approving budgets Determination of remuneration policy for senior executives Creating corporate culture Long term

Figure 3.4 Board Activities.

moves towards a shared vision of the future that the board holds for the company. The strategy should include:

(a) areas in which the company will be competitive;

(b) strengths of the company vis-à-vis its competitors in the current and desired areas;

(c) financial parameters in which the board exists;

(d) determination of appropriate balance of size, growth, risk, return, etc.

However, every board member should have the potential to add to the review, provide additional information, and ask inherent assumptions. He should be a part of creative process through which the entire board comes to share the strategic intent for the business. There is a common practice of holding strategy seminars for two or three days or review meetings for the board of directors in large companies.

Policy Making: Policy making by the board is the natural extension of the strategy formulation process. Specific proposals such as capital investment projects, acquisition, merger, de-merger, divestment opportunities, financing alternatives, crucial management and organization development policies, regular annual budget plans and crisis planning come before the board for consideration.

Monitoring and Supervision: Monitoring and supervision of performance of executive management is another element in the activities of the board of directors. The key to successful management supervision lies in a reliable and timely measurement of performance system. This involves regular comparisons of attained levels of revenues and costs with budgets, profit performance and returns on assets and shareholders' funds. Special emphasis is needed for the performance in the areas of market development, market share, product development and research, management development, labour relations, productivity and technological development, stock market position, market capitalization, and social responsibility of business. Proper balance is desirable between long-term growth of the business and short-term measures of success.

The inter-connections of components of the board activities are shown in Figure 3.5.

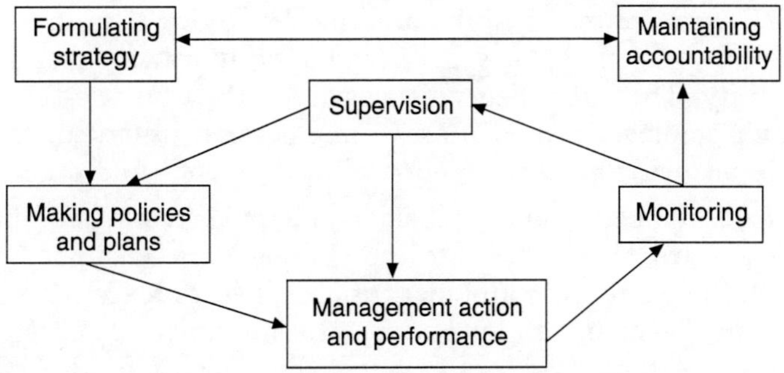

Figure 3.5 Components of Board Activities and Their Interrelationships.

In the course of monitoring and supervision of the performance of management, the board oversees the full cycle of management activities that include:

1. Approval of corporate philosophy;
2. Annual review and approval of the corporate strategy;
3. Review and approval of company's capital allocations;
4. Review and approval of the corporate's long range goals;
5. Review and approval of the company's financial standards, policies, and plans;
6. Review of results compared with (a) corporate philosophy, (b) goals, and (c) competition;
7. Annual appraisal of the performance of the board and taking steps to improve its performance;
8. Ensuring that the status of organizational strength and manpower planning is equal to the requirements of the long-range goals;
9. Ensuring that management succession is being properly provided;
10. Election of top management;
11. Appraisal of top management.

The board's relationship to the management process is shown in Figure 3.6.

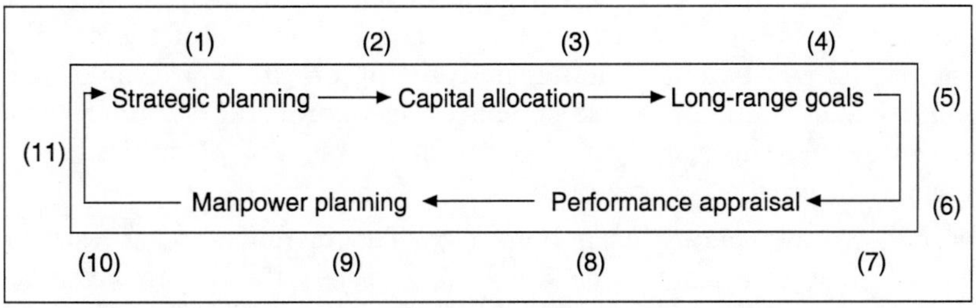

Figure 3.6 Board's Relationship to the Management Process.

Accountability: Essentially, the duty of the corporate board of directors is to provide accountability to the shareholders, as it has become tremendously important in recent years due to separation between management and ownership. The board should be accountable to the shareholders for the efficiency of company's operations and profitability. The low return to the equity and the slow growth in industrial productivity in the recent years suggest that there is a need for greater awareness of the importance of this accountability. The supervisory board, as part of the two-tier form of control, which could include employee representatives and possibly others, may well be the most effective means of ensuring greater accountability for profit and other responsibilities.

The annual general meeting of shareholders, periodic meetings at different locations with stakeholders, board presentation to the shareholders, customers, and employees and dialogues with financial press and institutional investors are the vehicles for better communication with the members and financial community. Besides, a wide range of stakeholders like regulators, creditors and lenders banks, etc. also look to the board to provide information about the company's standing.

Composition of board

The principal issues involved in respect of board composition are: (a) proportion of directors—inside vs. outside directors, (b) size, structure and style of the board, and (c) the age of the board members.

Board structure is a foundation for an effective board, focusing on the background interests, affiliations and positions of board members. It is concerned with the balances of power, and it is at the heart of board's performance and accountability. Board style describes the way in which the members of the board work together, both inside and outside the boardroom. Boards differ considerably in the style they adopt. There may be opportunities to develop styles that are more appropriate to the company's changing corporate and strategic situation. However, the success of a board of directors lies in the specific contribution that each member of the board makes, given the group dynamics and the leadership style that exists.

The board structure distinguishes between those directors who hold management positions in the company and those who do not. Those who occupy management positions are referred to as the executive directors and those who do not, are called the non-executive directors. Two variants of the non-executive directors do exist—one, who are genuinely independent of the company's affairs, other than holding their board appointment and receiving sitting fees only. On the other hand, there are the non-executive directors in the board, whose positions might bring their objectivity and independence into questions. For example, a retired executive of the company (who is receiving company's retirement benefits) now sitting on the board, as a director being the representative of a major block of shares, a significant supplier, customer etc. These directors are not independent from the point of view of accountability because of their sectional interests.

The board does not operate as a hierarchy. The members must work together as equals. Each member bears the same duties and responsibilities in law irrespective of their positions as executive, non-executive, independent or nominee. If we analyze the board structures, we find four types of structures prevailing: (a) all-executive board, (b) majority executive board, (c) majority outside board, and (d) two-tier supervisory board. The board structures can be shown in Figures 3.7(a), 3.7(b), 3.7(c), 3.7(d), 3.7(e), and 3.7(f).

In the all-executive board there is really no separation between ownership and management as the management is dominated by the owners/promoters of the business. Before the corporate governance came into prominence, most of the boards in the countries like, the UK, India used to be all-executive boards [Figure 3.7(b)]. In the majority executive board, the non-executive directors are appointed in small proportions, say, 2 or 3 in the board. Generally in such a board, there is a danger of domination of board affairs by the executive members but they may find difficulty in exercising genuine independence of opinion when their boss, CEO, is also a board member. Most of the boards in the UK and India are the majority executive boards [Figure 3.7(c)].

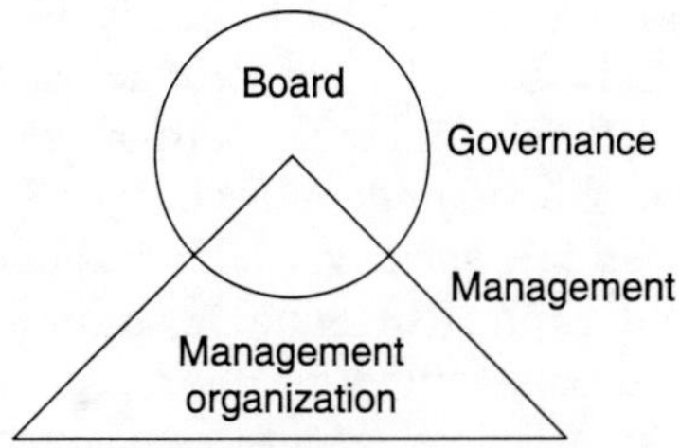

Figure 3.7(a) Board Structure.

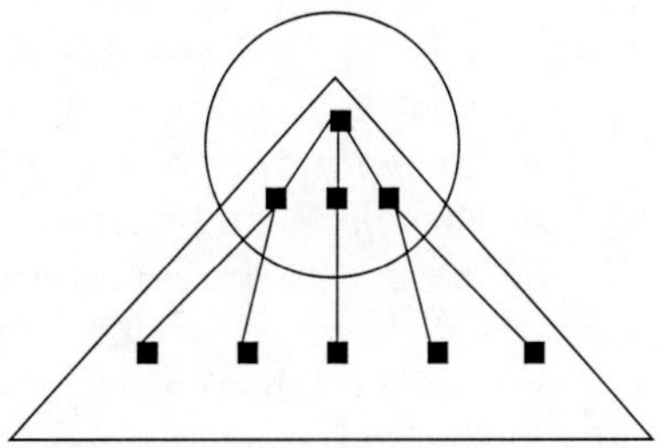

Figure 3.7(b) The All-executive Board.

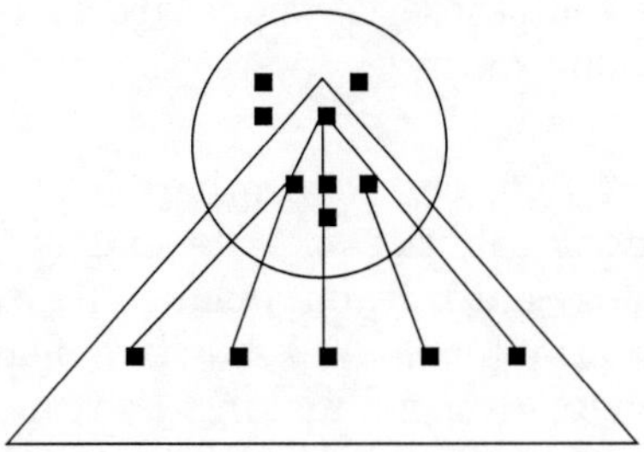

Figure 3.7(c) The Majority Executive Board.

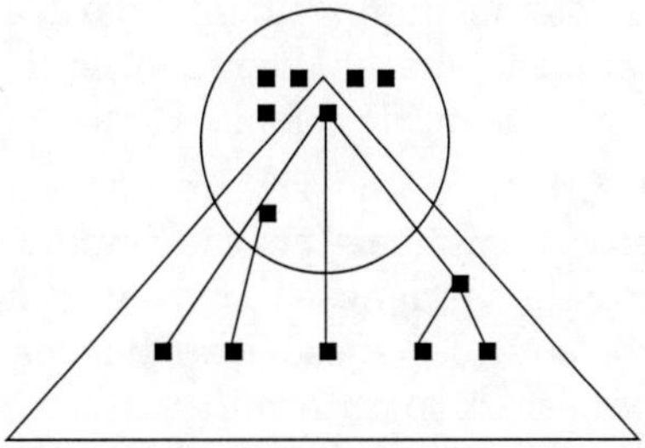

Figure 3.7(d) The Majority Outside Board.

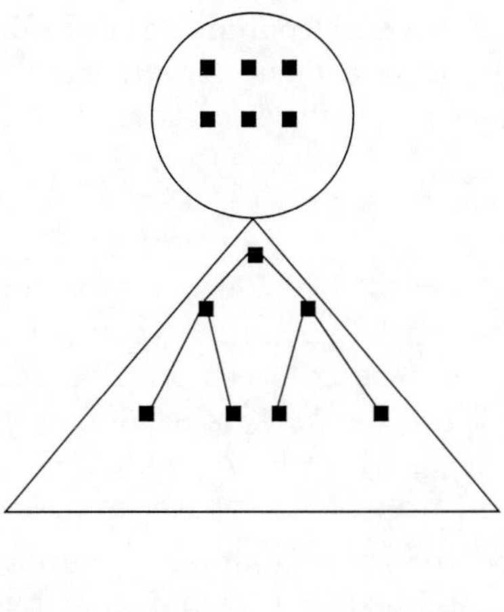

Figure 3.7(e) The Two-tier Supervisory Board.

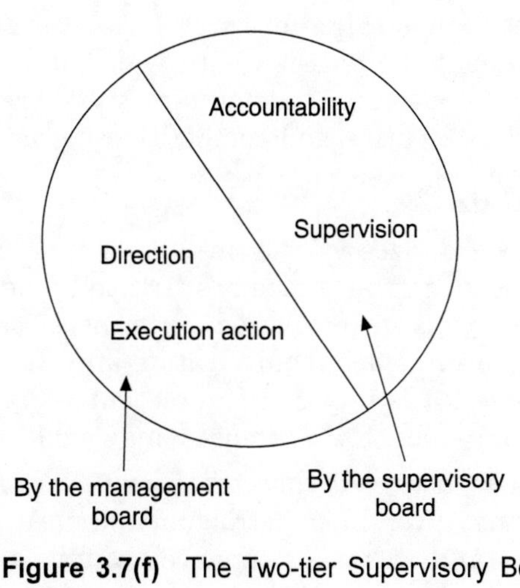

Figure 3.7(f) The Two-tier Supervisory Board.

In the majority outside board where non-executive directors form the majority on the board, particularly the independent majority, such board as exists in the USA and Australia, can emphasize checks and balances, and keep close supervision of management performance [Figure 3.7(d)]. In fact, the reliance on independent outside directors in the unitary board to provide a separation of function and check on management has been reflected much in the corporate world in the growing use of audit committee, nomination committee and remuneration committee of the main board.

However, the ultimate separation of the executive management from the non-executive direction is found in the two-tier supervisory board [Figure 3.7(e) and 3.7(f)]. Most boards in the continental European countries, particularly Germany, do have such type of boards. In Germany, the 'supervisory boards' (aufsichtsrat) has no common membership with the 'executive board' (vorstand). The supervisory board's role is to oversee the plans and performance of the management board. Its primary power lies in the ability to hire and fire the chief executive. The members of the German supervisory board represent labour and capital in equal numbers, with the employees appointing the labour members and the shareholders their representatives. One advantage of the more formalized German structure of separate management and supervisory boards is that it recognises the difference in the position of executive and non-executive directors. As stated before that the supervisory board can monitor the decisions of the management board and ensure that these decisions are in the best interests of the shareholders, without requiring non-executives to accept responsibility for executive-level decisions.

The structure and size of Japanese boards is different from others. Contrary to the western emphasis on the importance of the contribution of independent outside directors, the Japanese board is made up almost entirely on inside all executive directors. The Japanese board is essentially hierarchical. A distinctive feature of the Japanese corporate culture is the approach to decision-making by 'consensus'. Decisions are reached after a lengthy process of discussion, involving the roots of the organization. Negotiation, rethinking and influencing take place throughout the organization until a consensus gradually emerges which makes the top management ratification straightforward. It leaves an enthusiastic and committed workforce to implement the decision with which they are totally in agreement. Therefore, there is neither a need for outside directors nor there is a natural place for them within the board's executive and competitive hierarchy.

Board size

The board sizes vary from 2 or 3 up to large boards of 20 members or even more as laid down in the company's Articles. The board size can be partially explained by the company's size (measured in terms of sales volume), need to access capital markets (measured as debt/equity ratio), and whether or not the company is locally regulated. However, it is important to recognize that there is no one board size, which is best for all companies. Each company may well have different needs with respect to board size.

It is observed that the board size of the large Indian companies in automobile, banking, diversified, petroleum and natural gas, cement, textile, iron and steel, telecom, paints and chemicals, finance, mining and metals, power and IT sectors is generally broad-based (around 10 to 17 board members). On the other hand, almost all FMCG and pharmaceutical companies' boards are small, ranging between 8 to 9 members. The analyses of companies listed under BSE Sensex and NSE Nifty reveal that 13% of such companies have single digit board size, ranging from 8 to 9 board members, whereas the rest 87% of the companies have double digit board size varying from 10 to 17 members. It is also observed that the board size of the public sector undertakings (PSUs) and the public sector banks (PSBs) is large as compared to that of most of the private sector companies in India.

Board style

Similarly, the board style also varies from companies to companies depending on board expectations and leadership. Partly, it is the result of power base and the role of the board and partly it is the function of the company's history, its culture, value and belief systems and the norms of the industry. But basically the board style evolves under the leadership of the particular chairman and the chemistry of the board members at the time. Figure 3.8 depicts two determinants of the board style.

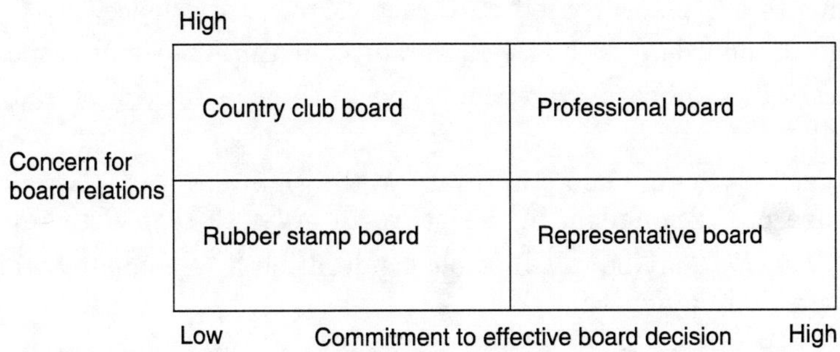

Figure 3.8 Board Style.

Figure 3.8 is the two-by-two matrix that shows the *following cases*:

(a) Boards which are low on both counts and consequently acting as rubber stamp to the decisions elsewhere—1st case;

(b) Boards which are high in their concern for the decisions but low, even adversarial, in board climate, being concerned with representative interests—3rd case;

(c) Boards which are high on interpersonal concern but low on decision content, with a comfortable club atmosphere—2nd case;

(d) Boards which score high on both counts and which might be classified as professional boards—4th case.

It has been observed that in some cases, the board acts like a formal 'rubber stamp' for proposals from management. This is appropriate in the owner-managed business where the board is needed for statutory compliance, as the management decisions are taken by the person who is both owner and director. A similar situation arises in the case of a wholly owned subsidiary company in which the management control is exercised through the group management and organization systems.

Sometimes, a board may be treated as a forum that serves the interests of the parties represented by various nominees of the board. Although according to company law, all directors are supposed to act in the interests of the company as a whole, if there is a predominance of nominee members in the board, it is likely that board deliberations will reflect the concerns of those interest groups.

At times, the culture of boards may lead to a self-supportive and comfortable club-like atmosphere, wherein maintaining the group norms and supporting pleasant inter-personal relations become more important than anything else.

But, there are boards which are professional in that they are able to balance the need to move towards consensus, avoiding destructive adversarial relationships, with the ability to take tough decisions. An effective professional board can offer the following *benefits* to its style of functioning:

(i) A proper balance can be ensured for moving through the agenda in a timely manner while allowing fuller discussion on important items.
(ii) Contributions from all directors are treated respectfully and valued.
(iii) Conflicts and tensions in the meetings are handled constructively for the purpose of making better decisions. Criticisms do not become personal while arguments are placed based on directors' own experience.
(iv) Ethical standards are clearly understood, maintained and respected.
(v) Directors in the board are encouraged to think as directors and as customers as well.

However, each style may be appropriate in the right situation. Attempts should be made to increase professionalism in the board in order to reap high rewards.

Following *checklist* may be taken into consideration by a company while examining its size and style of functioning:

1. Is the maximum and minimum size of board laid down in the Articles of the company? Is there a need for change in size?
2. Given the style of board functioning, is the current size of the board O.K. in view of the work to be performed?
3. Is the current board membership the best? Is there a necessity for change?
4. Has there been a succession plan for the board?
5. Is the balance between executive and non-executive board members appropriate? Does the current board function well together and in the professional manner?
6. Is the present board structure appropriate considering the balance of interests of the shareholders?
7. Is there a need for change is board membership to reflect the interests of any other significant stakeholders?
8. Recognising the importance of outside professional contributions, is there a need for change is non-executive board membership with a view to contributing towards corporate performance and ensuring executive conformance to plans?
9. Are there adequate numbers of the non-executive directors who are genuinely independent of the company and having no relationship with the business or the officers of the company that could affect the exercise of independent judgement?

10. Is the board a comfortable club of like interests, or a rubber stamp for decisions of dominant individuals, or an association for the members being loyal to the sectional interests?
11. Is it a professional board that is capable of reaching consensus after tough-minded, penetrating exploration of issues reached without adversarial discussion?
12. Is there a separation between chairman and chief executive officer/managing director? Given the present and future circumstance, is this situation most desirable?
13. Has the issue of duality of interests between loyalties to the individual company and to the group been resolved with companies within a group?
14. What are the views of members of the board regarding the present board structure and style of functioning?
15. Is the present board competent and committed to provide appropriate directives to the company in future in line with the current strategy adopted by the company?

Age and tenure of directors

Another issue comes up simultaneously, i.e. Does the age of directors matter? Does directors' age have any effect on corporate performance? Practically speaking, the age of the board members is not an important criterion so long as each individual is able to perform his or her functions diligently and honestly for the interest of the company. However, there may be justification for a relatively diverse board with age difference. As such a board may have a better perspective than a board consisting of members of the same generation or age group.

A study on the Indian companies listed under BSE Sensex and NSE Nifty reveals that only 10% of such companies have clearly disclosed their policy in regard to age limit and tenure of directors. In almost all private sector companies, the tenure of service of directors is contractual ranging from 2 to 5 years although there is no age limit. The age limit and tenure of directors in PSUs and PSBs are governed by the government (Department of Public Enterprises DPE) guidelines. However, for discharging of corporate governance functions effectively and particularly for the efficient functioning of the board, the companies should declare a retirement policy of directors and fix up the retirement age maximum at 75 years.

The deliberation so far has considered the key question of what the most appropriate structure for a board of directors is. The boards can differ considerably in structure, relative emphasis on performance versus conformance, and on the style by which boards conduct their affairs. Therefore, understanding the existing situation, analyzing the relevant circumstances, reviewing and evaluating alternatives and choosing a structure and style appropriate to the reality of the corporate situation are crucial issues for every board.

Information for the board

Recently, there has been a considerable concentration on effective information flows to the boards. The directors are increasingly required to understand not only their own organization but also its industry, its competitive environment, prospective management successions, and its short, medium and long-term strategies. Moreover, there are increasing legal obligations on directors. Therefore, getting possessions of appropriate information is an absolute necessity. Largely, it is the management that provides such information to the directors. There are *five basic areas* about which the boards are mostly concerned such as

(i) maximizing shareholder value;
(ii) financial results of the company;
(iii) management succession;
(iv) strategic planning; and
(v) long-term survival of the organization.

An important development, consistent with the current trend, is the provision of both current operating financial data and material that deal with company's strategic plans. There is also a trend towards provision of board papers. Another development is the trend towards provision of competitor analyses. Boards are being presented with comparisons of their companies' current performance with those of their competitors. Besides, there is also a trend towards provision of CEO's formal report to the board members in which the CEO expresses his views on a range of issues and engages with non-executive independent directors in a suggestion-and-question session.

There is also an increasing trend to put independent and outside directors on a 'briefing programme', which involves taking the new directors around major company facilities, meeting departmental managers, getting brief on the industry and competition, and the environment surrounding the company.

Roles of directors

There is a global consensus on the objective of 'good' governance: 'maximizing long-term shareholders value'. Fulfillment of this objective is the responsibility of the corporate directors. Broadly, the roles of directors are separated into two categories:

(a) *The performance roles*, in which the board focuses on strategic and policy issues for the future, sets the corporate direction and contributes to the performance of the business; and
(b) *The conformance roles*, in which the board ensures that the company is conforming to the policies, procedures and plans laid down by the board and being properly accountable for its activities.

The *performance roles* of directors include the following:

(i) Contributing know-how, expertise and external information
(ii) Role of specialist
(iii) Role of window of the world
(iv) Role of contact person
(v) Role of figure-head
(vi) Role of status provider

On the other, *conformance roles* of directors include:

(i) Role of marking their own exam papers
(ii) Role of the judge

(iii) Role of the catalyst
(iv) Role of the watchdog
(v) Role of the confidante
(vi) Role of the safety valve

But, overall emphasis that the directors are expected to provide is the emphasis on external issues, i.e., direction and accountability, and on internal issues, i.e., executive management and supervision—all towards satisfying the needs of the business as well as shareholders' and stakeholders' interests, as shown in Figure 3.9. However, the fact remains that the roles and responsibilities of the board are measured by the degree of involvement of the directors in their functioning of strategic management.

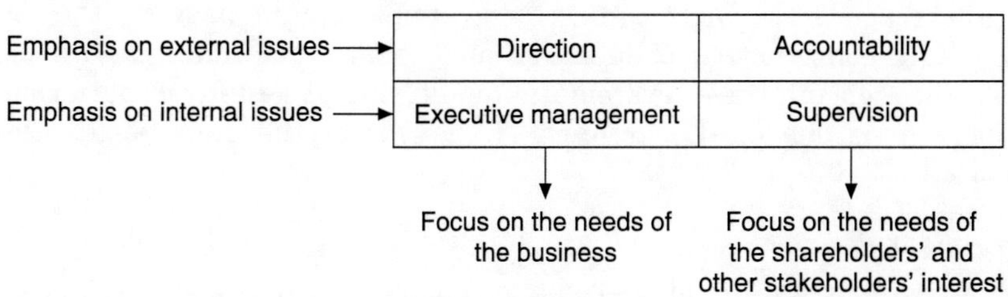

Figure 3.9 A Conceptual Model of the Activities of Corporate Governance.

Independent director

A significant trend that has characterized the boards over the last 20 years has been the rise of the independent outside directors, particularly after the happenings of corporate scandals that had shaken the corporate world. Enron, WorldCom, AOL, Time-Warner, Xerox, Global Crossing etc. in the USA. In order to be 'independent', a director must be independent and he will have no material or pecuniary relationship with the company in which board he sits, either directly or indirectly. In the USA, while the independent directors are called outside directors, in the UK they are broadly termed as Non-executive Directors (NEDs). The role of non-executive/outside directors is to act as fully participating members of the board for performance of its duty: (i) to direct the company as well as to bring wider experience, technical expertise, independent judgement and new ideas to its discussion, (ii) to monitor and challenge the performance of executive directors and management, and (iii) to ensure that there are adequate control systems in place to protect the company's interests as also the interests of the shareholders and stakeholders as they enjoy the investors' confidence.

The non-executive directors have fiduciary duties, as the law does not distinguish between executive and non-executive directors, which mean the non-executive directors have similar and equal responsibilities as that of executive directors in the eyes of law. In discharging all these responsibilities, the non-executive directors/outside directors, being equal members of the boards have the power to: (i) demand information from the management, and (ii) exercise their votes based on their independent judgement.

The Cadbury report highlights a monitoring responsibility for independent directors, stating that non-executive directors are in the best position to monitor performance of the board and the CEO. There is a possible danger in that the executive board members might come to see the monitoring role as purely a job of their independent colleagues. Further, this may lead to weakening of the notion that the board is such a team whose every member shares equal responsibility. The great threat here is the possible outbreak of battles between the executives and independent directors. Therefore, the central issue is: whether independent directors are supposed to be monitors only or should draw their skills and backgrounds towards progress of the company. Assuming that independent directors will increasingly be chosen for the breadth of experience and skills, which they can bring to a board, then there is a question about appropriateness of limiting their contribution to that of a monitoring role. To deny such directors the opportunity to exploit their backgrounds by contributing to setting the policy framework would be rather self-defeating.

While the responsible outside directors cannot remain passive, their monitoring need not impair constructive collegiality on the board. Finding a way to make a contribution through informed, systematic monitoring of long-term performance, while avoiding friction, is one of the greatest challenges of the outside directors in their board service.

Lead independent director

Another question arises: Should there be an appointment of lead independent director in the corporate board? If so, what should be his role in the board functioning?

The international standard of corporate governance recommends good governance practice which says that irrespective of whether the posts of chairman and CEO are held by different persons or by same individual, there should be a strong and independent non-executive element on the board as lead independent director (other than the chairman), to whom concerns can be conveyed. It will be the responsibility of lead independent director to act as a spokesperson for independent directors as a group, work closely with the chairman/CEO, and take a lead role in the board evaluation process, apart from other important board functions. A lead independent director should be identified in the annual report. In order to meet this standard, the majority of companies in the world have initiated the appointment of lead independent directors in their boards. However, corporate India's position is dismal in this regard. Only 8% of the listed companies have appointed lead independent directors in their boards. Therefore, there is an urgent need to improve the standard of corporate governance in India in this regard.

Responsibilities of directors

There are *two basic responsibilities* of directors in companies, viz.

(a) responsibilities to the shareholders; and
(b) obligation to honesty and integrity.

As we know, the corporate directors are appointed by the shareholders as members of the company. Therefore, the basic responsibility of a director is to the shareholders. The boards need to provide strategic direction for the business, set relevant policies, and supervise the activities of top management. The boards are required to be accountable to the members, and also required to present regular reports and accounts duly audited in most cases, in the statutory form.

A company director is expected to act with honesty, integrity and candour towards the company, especially its members. Therefore, decisions must be taken in good faith for the common good. In other words, the primary duty of a director is to act honestly in good faith, giving all shareholders equal, sufficient and accurate information on all issues that could affect their interests. Consequently, a director must not make a secret profit out of dealings with the company. His duty is to disclose any such interests to the board and to abide by their decision as to what is in the company's best interests. Insider trading, i.e., dealing in the shares of a quoted company, based on privileged, price-sensitive information is considered a criminal offence, which a director shall not do.

Liabilities of directors

The next question comes: What are the liabilities of directors in law? Can the directors be held responsible in a court of law for non-compliance of various laws, procedures and regulations?

Directors have, at various occasions, been described as the agents, trustees or managing partners. Therefore, they stand in a fiduciary position towards the company in respect of their powers and capital under their control. Besides, directors are also treated as officers of the company for certain matters and are placed with the similar position of manager, secretary, etc. as 'officer in default'. Directors are, therefore, liable for negligence, breach of trust and misfeasance in either of their capacities as agents or trustees or as both.

Broadly, apart from various statutory liabilities, the courts have determined the broad areas of duty of directors:

(a) the fiduciary duty of loyalty and good faith; and
(b) the duties of care and skill.

The fiduciary duty of loyalty and good faith emphasises that a director must demonstrate unyielding loyalty to the company's shareholders. He must act in what he believes to be the best interests of the company. He must avoid conflicts between his duty to the company and his personal interests. He must not make a secret profit by virtue of his dealings with the company. It is his duty to disclose all such interests. He must not reveal confidential information, obtained through board service, to outsiders.

The duties of care and skill emphasise that a director must exercise his due diligence in making decisions. He must gather as much information as possible on the question at issue and be able to exhibit that while coming to a decision, he has considered all reasonable alternatives. He is expected to bring to bear that degree of skill and care to the affairs of the company, which might reasonably be expected from a person of his knowledge and experience.

Directors' handling of business risks and financial risks

While discharging the various roles, the directors should also address key *business risks and financial risks* of the company. Following questions may be addressed by them while dealing with these risks:

Board and organization structure:

(i) Is the operation of the board open and frank or is there a risk that senior executives could be playing down some issues of real concern?

(ii) Does the board have a clear strategy for the company?

(iii) Does the whole board receive sufficient information to be aware of business and financial risks on a timely basis?

(iv) Does financial information coming to the board appear to be reliable?

(v) Does the board have sufficient information from operating subsidiaries, especially overseas?

Accountability:

(i) Does the board understand and accept its responsibilities towards the investing public?

(ii) Are there areas such as executive terms of employment, where shareholders might feel that they have cause to complain?

Control environment:

(i) Has the board adequately communicated its policies on key risks and its attitude to control failure or illegal or unethical behaviour?

(ii) Are there lessons to be learnt from past control failures in relation to both specific risks and general attitudes within the organization to control?

(iii) Are mechanisms for monitoring the quality of controls adequate?

(iv) Do incentive schemes encourage management to ensure effective compliance and control?

(v) Do personnel policies limit the risk of employing dishonest or insufficiently competent staff?

(vi) Are authority levels of senior executives clearly agreed?

(vii) Do significant transactions and commitments require specified high level authorizations?

Company assets:

(i) Does the company have sufficient assets that are susceptible to theft, deterioration, wide fluctuations in value or obsolescence?

(ii) Are highly liquid assets properly safeguarded including separation of responsibilities in relation to handling the assets and authorizing transactions?

(iii) Are there particular physical dangers associated with company operations?

(iv) Are there adequate disaster recovery plans?

Products, services and markets:

(i) Are the company's markets facing particularly difficult conditions, e.g. from changes in customer demand or levels of competition?

(ii) Is the company heavily reliant on a small number of customers or types of customers?

(iii) Are there substantial risks of being sued by customers, employees, or others, e.g. for product liability?
(iv) What are the risks associated with faulty goods or services?
(v) Is there a risk of infringing patent rights?
(vi) Does the supply of raw materials, skilled labour, or capital employment pose difficulties?
(vii) Are there risks associated with the way the company promotes and markets its goods or services?
(viii) Where the company uses agents, sub-contractors, or representatives, do they pose a financial or reputational threat to the company?

Regulatory environment:

(i) Are there regulations (including taxation) to which the business is subject where failure could lead to serious difficulties for the business, e.g. through fines, loss of goodwill, or loss of licenses?
(ii) Is the company in a fiduciary position in relation to other parties?
(iii) Are there significant environmental concerns?
(iv) Are there major litigation problems?

Change:

(i) Is there rapid or substantial change or uncertainty in the business or its environment?
(ii) Is there new legislation expected which will have a major impact on the business?
(iii) Is the business keeping pace with technological change?
(iv) Are acquisitions properly controlled?

Financial risks:

(i) Is the company highly geared or heavily reliant on short-term sources of finance?
(ii) Is there a risk that the company might be in breach of loan covenants or borrowing limits?
(iii) Is the company financially exposed, e.g. to interest rate, or currency fluctuations?
(iv) How effective are banking relationships?
(v) Are there major commitments or contingent liabilities?
(vi) Does the company have highly complex financial dealings?
(vii) Is cost and other management information reliable as a basis for strategic business decisions?
(viii) Is cash forecasting effective?
(ix) Does the company have any unusual or aggressive accounting policies or any figures in internal or external account which are highly subjective?
(x) Does the company have significant loss making activities?
(xi) Is there any question over going concern status of the business?
(xii) Is the finance function adequately qualified and resourced?

Board leadership

The next question arises: Who provides board leadership? What should be the working relationship between the chairman and the CEO when both these positions are separated?

In most countries, the appointment and role of the board chairman is not determined by statute, but left to the company articles or rules, which typically require the board to appoint one of its members to take the chair in board meetings. In major public companies, where the roles of the chairman and the CEO are separated, studies have shown that the chairman faces an important and growing set of responsibilities. These include management of the board, maintaining a close relationship with the CEO, stimulating the development of the strategic vision and direction of the company, and acting as the 'public face' of the company in the public arena, thus allowing the CEO to focus on the operational management of the company.

Effective board leadership involves the creation and maintenance of a dynamic and innovative board of directors. One of the key roles of the chairman is the process of building and managing the board. The *key foundations* for strategic board leadership are:

- (i) a soundly built and effective board of directors;
- (ii) a shared strategic direction and commitment to pursue it; and
- (iii) strong processes to effect strategic management.

A soundly built and effective board of directors: In examining the issue of building an effective board, the following key competencies of directors may be highlighted:

- (a) Strategic perception and decision-making;
- (b) Analytical understanding;
- (c) Skill in communication;
- (d) Effective interaction with others;
- (e) Ability to plan, delegate, appraise, and develop others;
- (f) Focus on achievement through risk taking;
- (g) Resilience;
- (h) Integrity;
- (i) Independence (especially for non-executive directors).

The real need in this respect is to have a board which can cover the field and a chairman who can ensure that these competencies are brought to bear on issues when needed. A key part of the process of building an effective board is to subject it to review at regular intervals, which should bring out criticisms of the board's performance by individual directors and also enable those who work with the board to air their views.

A shared strategic direction: Setting the strategic direction of the company and controlling progress towards it are the prime tasks of a board. Without a clear sense of direction, the managers of the business cannot produce the results expected by the board from them. Leadership comes from the board in establishing a vision and values which set the target and tone of the company. The board has to decide how the resources needed to deliver the strategy will be provided.

Strategic management processes: Though the boards of directors do not manage their companies, yet they need to be sure that their strategies are effectively delivered. Leadership to achieve this is generally provided through a strategic management process, in which the board sets the strategic direction of the company and the business units contribute their plans and strategies. The process of developing strategies must be balanced by the processes to monitor their implementation and to react to the emergent opportunities and threats. After all, the board is responsible for creation and maintenance of the processes to achieve effective strategic management.

Chairman of the board

As mentioned before, the appointment and role of board chairman is not determined by the statute, but is left to the company articles or rules, which typically require the board to appoint one of its members to take the chair in board meetings. The chairman is the leader of the board, and therefore, must set the standards required for board colleagues. He must provide the required leadership by following an appropriate agenda. After all, the contribution of the chairman ultimately determines the effectiveness of the board.

Externally, the chairman is often seen as the responsible person who ensures that appropriate standards are in place. He is accountable publicly in the event of a failure. It is the irony that in the case of a failure down the executive line, it is the chairman who is held publicly accountable. As the chairman is also the link between board and shareholders, he needs to be satisfied with the corporate reporting to them. This will include the interim and annual results, annual report, annual general meeting, and periodic reports on special occasions such as during merger, takeover, etc. Reporting of results to the market analysts and financial institutions is also an important event in which the presence and involvement of the chairman is expected. A chairman must therefore:

- be a strong leader
- have the intellectual capacity to deal with complexity and multi-dimensional issues
- be a capable communicator
- have both the energy and the time to get around the company and see the key executives in action on their own field.

Chairman and CEO duality

Quite often, an argument is put forward by the proponents of agency theory that the roles of CEO and chairman of the board should be separated as it adds to the essential checks and balances at board level over the exercise of the executive function and reduces the risk of domination by a powerful CEO to achieve self-interest rather than the interests of various stakeholders. Pucky, Brown as well as the contemporary researchers, viz. Tricker, Monks, Minow, Bain, and Band clearly opined in favour of separation of the role of chairman from CEO in the interests of providing checks and balances. They argue that a person in the position of chairman and CEO is subject to an inherent conflict of interest, which the shareholders can no longer afford. This conflict results from the obvious concentration of power and the lack of accountability that results from combining the two positions. Separation of the functions of the chairman and the CEO has been widely advocated by regulatory bodies and financial commentators in all commercially advanced countries around the world.

There is no denial of the fact that the conflict of functions on a unitary board may be increased where the roles of chief executive and chairman are combined. The individual who holds both offices is subject to a measure of conflict between his commitment to management and the need for a balanced view of the interests of shareholders. There is a danger that the interests of shareholders will be subordinated to the priorities of management. In such case, the shareholders are deprived of a safeguard in that one of the functions of the chairman is to dismiss the chief executive should that become necessary. The removal of the chief executive becomes considerably more difficult if the office is combined with the chairmanship of the company. Therefore, wherever there is a combined chief executive/chairman, the need for strongly independent non-executive directors is even more pressing.

The counter argument is that though separation of roles can enhance conformity, however, one person as CEO and chairman encourages performance, provides single-minded leadership, which is needed for a company in the present-day complex and competitive conditions. Some highly successful companies in North America, Europe, and Australia have been led decisively by one man over a considerable period. Whatever may be the divergent opinion on the issue of 'duality', majority have opined clearly in favour of separation of these two roles.

In India, 50% of the listed companies examined do have chairmen/CMDs in the helm of affairs as executive chairmen/CMDs. The rest 50% of the companies do have non-executive chairmen in their boards and are run by the managing directors/ CEOs. It also reveals that the position of chairman and CEO/managing director has been segregated in a majority of private sector companies, whereas by contrast, the incidence of chairman-CEO duality remains wholly intact (100%) in the PSUs due to the government policy.

Recently, the new government in the centre has initiated another dose of banking reforms, whereby the posts of chairman and managing director in the public sector banks except SBI would be separated in view of several financial irregularities noticed in the banks' functioning. The government has decided to separate and fill up the post of chairmen through non-executive directors in Bank of Baroda, United Bank of India and several other PSBs. The post of managing directors in these banks would be filled up by the executive directors. However, this change will not be applicable for SBI because the (executive) chairman of SBI is assisted by four other managing directors of the bank in the functioning of SBI.

Chairman and CEO/managing director relationship

Then, the next question arises: What should be the relationship between a chairman and the CEO when both the posts are separated?

The *working relationship* between them should be:

(i) complementing;

(ii) directing;

(iii) consulting and coaching;

(iv) reviewing and controlling; and

(v) restricting the power of CEO through rules and procedure.

From the above discussion, it is clear that the division of labour between a chairman and a CEO varies from company to company. So also their relative functions, which depend on the organization structure and the personalities involved.

Board Effectiveness

The next question crops up: How the effectiveness of the board can be reviewed and improved and what strategy should be adopted for development?

Three issues are frequently raised in the pursuit of board level efficiency and effectiveness such as

(a) whether directors can ever have sufficient information;

(b) whether they can devote enough time to do justice to their jobs as directors; and

(c) whether most suitable people can be persuaded to become and to remain directors and how they can be adequately compensated.

A board review involves a comprehensive look at the board and its activities. The aim is to explore board processes, structure and style in the light of corporate needs, to highlight potential problems for the future and to provide the basis for measuring effectiveness. The review needs to be set in the context of the governance power base. It raises a *few questions*:

(a) What business and other results, is it seeking to achieve directionally and by when?

(b) What risks is it prepared to take?

(c) How has the company performed in comparison to other major firms?

(d) How is the company performing in the global competitive scenario?

There are many *opportunities* for improving board effectiveness. These include:

(i) better use of board time;

(ii) proper delegation to board committees; and

(iii) obtaining better board level information.

In addition, the board processes and the style that the board has adopted can be reviewed—rubber stamp, representative forum, comfortable club, or more professional direction. The agenda of the board meetings, reports and minutes can provide information on the focus and concentration of board time and effort.

Some *warning signals* that the board is not being effective are mentioned hereunder.

(a) A number of important decisions coming late for approval, and then being handled through short-cut route rather than proper board processes;

(b) Information gaps or errors in board papers coming to notice after a period of poor performance or when tough decisions are on the table;

(c) Reporting and accounting standards being adopted to present a better picture of performance than would otherwise be the case, particularly, when the change in approach has not been made explicit;
(d) Technical breaches of processes or reporting requirements being ignored;
(e) Reluctance to undertake rigorous review exercise of past decisions;
(f) Sign of managerial conflict, conflicts and tensions in the board meetings and criticisms becoming personal;
(g) Inadequate depth of management and too much reliance on the chief executive;
(h) Time wasted in the board meetings on trivial issues and failing to discuss major issues in depth, etc.

Assessment of board in terms of corporate strategy

The next critical process is to assess the board in terms of corporate strategy. If the business strategy shows significant developments in the size, products and markets, technology or financing, then the following questions arise:

(i) Will the present structure, membership and methods of the board still be appropriate?
(ii) Is there a necessity for the introduction of new members or the development of existing members or changing board processes to reflect the potential new situation in the business?
(iii) Is the size of the board OK?
(iv) Is the present balance between executive and non-executive appropriate?
(v) Is it necessary to separate the role of chairman-cum CEO?

Is the board process and style professional or a rubber stamp, comfortable club?

Evaluation of board's performance

One of the most essential issues in governance is the effectiveness and efficiency in the functioning of a corporate board. Therefore, it is imperative that board must ensure that it is acting efficiently and effectively. So, it is necessary that the board has in place, appropriate accountability mechanisms. One such method as could be considered for adoption is 'evaluation of board's performance'. Evaluation should be considered as an integral part of the overall board's planning process and it should be non-confrontational. Performance evaluation, in fact, is a flexible dynamic process, which includes the act of setting goals and standards of performance. Then, goals need to be measurable and achievable. The system should allow regular evaluation of these criteria for each director and the board as a whole.

There should be a formal appraisal process to review the board's workings. Directors are required to be satisfied that there are clearer objectives and procedures for the board. They need a process to measure their own performance as the performance of board of directors is under severe public scrutiny nowadays. This public scrutiny and critical analysis of board's performance has taken place because investors and other shareholders are of the opinion that some companies could have been operated more effectively and that there are reasons for failure which could be prevented. By and large, it is true that only a few people focus on board's performance until there is a crisis and a few directors and even fewer boards address the issue of performance evaluation. There is evidence to suggest that current board practice usually does not include any form of evaluation whether it is of individual directors or the board as a whole. Evaluation may occur on an adhoc individual basis.

According to Zander, a board that evaluates its performance and changes its objectives, methods, or both, is engaged in a feedback cycle. In this connection, a diagrammatic form of feedback cycle in a governing board is shown in Figure 3.10.

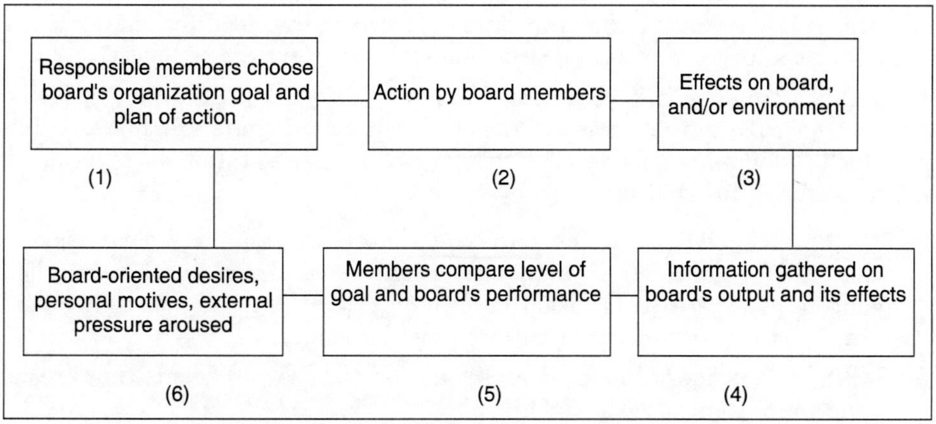

Figure 3.10 Feedback Cycle in a Governing Board.

Source: Zander, A., *Making Boards Effective,* Jossey-Bass, 1993.

The first three stages in Figure 3.10 are self-explanatory. Stage 4 shows members observing any deviations between the original goal and the board's performance through gathering of information. Stage 5 involves comparing and reflecting. Stage 6 shows that if the deviation between the board's level of attainment is larger than what is tolerable to members, the board members take steps to reduce the discrepancy, either by way of changing the board's actions in the future or by changing the group's goal. This link goes back to stage 1 signifying that feedback is an ongoing process.

Both Demb and Neubauer opined that evaluation of board's performance is done in terms of its inputs, outputs and the quality of the process. They suggested a diagrammatic form of elements of board's performance shown in Figure 3.11.

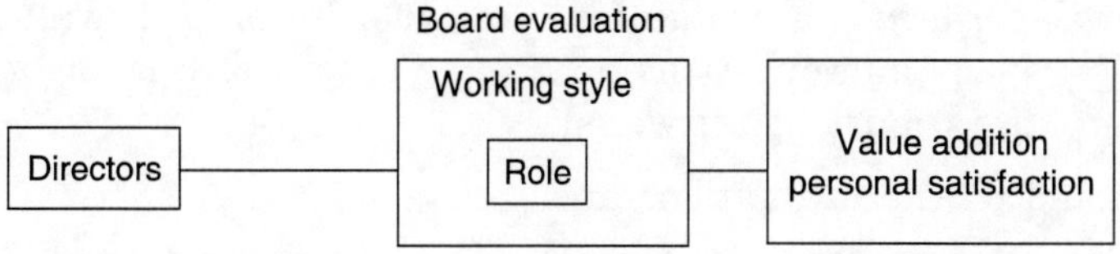

Figure 3.11 Elements of Board Performance.

Source: Demb, A. and Neubauer, F.F., *The Corporate Board: Confronting The Paradoxes,* OUP, 1992.

Figure 3.11 suggests that the evaluation of board's performance can relate to the type of output that it is relevant to measure. The aim of the board should be to add value to the company, and at the same time, gain personal satisfaction through the intrinsic value of being on a board and doing a good job.

Process of implementing evaluation: There must be a change in the philosophy, structure, and culture of the board so that there is a consensus that evaluation of performance is necessary and is possible in a manner that suits the board as a whole. Since the chairman is the leader of the board, and has the authority to manage change in the board, it is imperative that the chairman drives the need for change. It is also necessary that the process of developing the evaluation system is objective.

The actual sequence of events for implementation depends on the individual company, the board, and the drivers of the change process. There are, of course, certain aspects which should be considered if success of implementation is to be achieved. These are briefly mentioned below:

(i) *Vision:* The chairman, being the key driver, must have a clear vision as to what will be gained from implementation of evaluation and how the board is going to get there. This vision must be articulated to all board members and they must understand the reasoning of the leader.

(ii) *Timing:* Consideration must be given to the issues and events that are current while implementing evaluation.

(iii) *Planning:* The chairman must plan the process of change, including input from the rest of the board. The plan must be flexible so that any necessary amendments can be incorporated. The chairman should perceive and anticipate any implementation difficulties that may arise. Planning involves setting of the objectives which stem from the agreed performance standards and provide for ease of performance measurement.

(iv) *Organizational design:* It is essential to ensure that the structure of the board and even the organization is conducive to accepting and responding positively to the proposed changes.

(v) *Ownership:* It is essential that the key affected players have ownership of the plan.

(vi) *Communication:* A well-functioning board should have clear and effective internal and external communication at all times.

Conducting board's performance evaluation: In order to conduct evaluation of board's performance, the criteria and questions need to be specified. But, before this exercise, *two important questions* must be answered:

(a) Who should do the evaluation? and

(b) When should it be done?

The *criteria for evaluation* can be grouped into following three categories:

(i) the directors themselves;

(ii) the role of directors; and

(iii) the board's working style.

The main points of these categories are summerized below:

(i) The directors themselves
   (a) Intent, especially of CEO/chairman of the board;
   (b) Selection, nomination, and departure of directors; and
   (c) Composition and balance of the board.

(ii) The role of directors
   (a) Agreeing on a board's mission;
   (b) Defining the portfolio and identifying the areas of value addition by the board;
   (c) Setting priorities depending on the company and its size;
   (d) The board-management balance;
   (e) Involvement for the board—setting the vision, analyzing options, implementing strategy, monitoring progress, and evaluating outcomes;
   (f) Legal requirements setting minimum standards;
   (g) Conditions in the company's business environment; and
   (h) Status of the company development reflecting the level of board involvement.

(iii) The board's working style
   (a) Size, structure, committees of the board;
   (b) Board meeting schedule;
   (c) Timely, adequate and correct information to the board; and
   (d) Climate of board proceedings supporting constructive criticism.

When all these points are accepted as positive standards, then only the evaluation by way of measurement of performance in relation to these standards should start.

Evaluation of the board as a whole

Evaluation of the board is the responsibility of the chairman. It is carried out by the whole board. In an ideal situation where the board is functioning well, there may be no need for formal evaluation as the efficiently performing boards review their practices and outcomes on regular basis, and make changes wherever required. This is regarded as an interactive and dynamic informal evaluation process.

Unfortunately, we do not find many boards functioning so well. Therefore, in majority of cases, it is necessary for the boards to have a formalized system. In order to test and evaluate the effectiveness in the performance of the board, the *following questions* may be honestly answered:

1. Has the board devoted significant time and deliberated seriously on the company's longer term objectives and has given serious thought to the strategic options for achieving them? Have these been put in writing?
2. Has the board consciously thought about and reached formal conclusions on its basic corporate philosophy, i.e., its value system, its ethical and social responsibilities, its desired image and goodwill, etc. embodied in explicit statement of policy?

3. Does the board periodically review the organization structure of the company?
4. Does the board regularly receive all the information required to ensure that it is in effective control of the company and its management?
5. Does the board require the managing director to present his annual plans and budgets for its review and approval?
6. Does the board monitor the performance of the managing director and his immediate subordinate managers in terms of actual results achieved against plans and budgets?
7. Does the board spend sufficient time and has adequate knowledge to take major decisions, rather than finding itself overtaken by events, and in effect, obliged to rubber stamp decisions already taken or commitments already made?
8. Are the board meetings confusing or do they clarify issues? Are discussions dominated by one or two members of the board or do all participants get the opportunity to have input?
9. Given the acceptance that it is for the directors to direct and for managers to manage, what proportion of the board's time and attention as a board is devoted to the kinds of issues raised in the foregoing questions, and how much to immediate issues of day-to-day management?

From the above list of questions, it is quite clear that the chairman should lead the board to focus on long-term vision of the company, and the structure within which the company operates. He should put more emphasis on review of all that a board governs and ensure that the board gets adequate information to make well-informed decisions.

Evaluation of individual directors

Evaluation of individual directors may require to be considered into two streams: (a) evaluation of non-executive directors; and (b) evaluation of executive directors.

In many countries, a committee of the board called the remuneration committee is set up to evaluate the executive directors. Evaluation of individual non-executive directors is the responsibility of the chairman. The chairman and the board have to decide which evaluation system will work best for them.

One of the most difficult tasks is the evaluation of individual director's contribution. Generally, evaluation of executive directors is a part of the board's overall assessment of company's performance. Discussions with individual directors should be held at least once a year, but review of board, directors, and CEO's performance should be held on regular basis. The chairman should find out whether individual members are happy with the way the board is functioning and with other individuals' contributions to the board.

Criteria for evaluation of a director's own performance: Evaluation of directors should be conducted by the chairman who should seek an emphasis on the director's contribution individually and to the group. Following criteria should be set for evaluating director's performance:

(i) *Independence:* Confidence, courage, avoiding conflict of interest, free thinker, etc.

(ii) *Preparedness:* Briefing self thoroughly, spending extra time when required, knowing key officers, respecting confidentiality, knowing organization and the industry, understanding statutory and fiduciary roles, etc.

(iii) *Practice as director:* Thoroughly prepared, doing necessary homework, asking probing questions, insisting on getting all necessary information, participating on committee meetings, etc.

(iv) *Committee activity*: Exhibiting ideas, enthusiasm, understanding the process of committee work, relationship with management, etc.

(v) *Development of the organization*: Making concrete suggestions on innovations, strategic direction and planning, understanding the impact of productivity, helping to win the support of investors, customers, peers, suppliers, etc.

There is a mix of both *formal and informal* sections of the evaluation. Formal section constitutes a written agreed set of objectives which are fixed at a specified time each year. The individual meetings for evaluation should be non-confrontational, objective and informal. There are several *steps* that are useful for individual's evaluation in the meeting, as mentioned below:

(a) The chairman should establish an open, and two-way communication system.

(b) He should start review of the tasks that had been set. Assessment of the tasks should be essentially objective that will reduce the involvement of egos.

(c) An atmosphere of problem solving should be created in order to reduce defensiveness on the part of the director.

(d) There should be discussion and evaluation of behavioural issues, and the planning emphasis should be focused.

(e) At the end of the meeting, the director and the chairman should write up the individual objectives for the coming year.

Evaluation of individual directors in an informal way is often more comfortable for both the chairman and the director as the discussion generally is non-confrontational. An ideally functioning board ensures regular dynamic evaluation and assessment against standards that the individual director and the chairman have already agreed at the beginning of the year.

Evaluation of the chairman

As we know, chairman is the heart of the board. He is the person with final responsibility for his company's governance. Therefore, it is imperative that the chairman functions in that role efficiently. The board, usually decides on evaluation criteria for the chairman. All objectives and criteria for chairman's performance should be linked to the (a) strategy of the company, (b) performance of the company, (c) performance of the board, and (d) his own contribution.

The board should have structure such that any dissatisfaction among the board in regard to the chairman can be ventilated easily and addressed as an important issue. A time may be formally allocated to discuss the performance of the chairman, followed by an informal discussion among directors, and arrangement of meetings outside the boardroom. Any issues arising should be taken up to the next board meeting for discussion and resolution. A director should be allocated the responsibility to make it an agenda item for the meeting.

Evaluation of CEO

The evaluation of CEO is one of many important duties undertaken by the board. The evaluation process should be positive and a part of the regular planning function. It should provide the CEO and the board with a better understanding of how the organization is functioning in relation to the implementation of its strategies.

The evaluation of CEO should be carried out on the *following lines*:

1. *Establish standards for tasks:*
   (a) Standards should be fixed through (i) the CEO's work contract, (ii) the annual work plan, and (iii) quantitative performance standards.
   (b) The contract should specify outcomes or actions for the CEO and progress against these should be assessed.
   (c) The work plan, being the annual implementation plan for the company's strategies should be developed against a set of standards and quantifiable objectives.

   All these objectives become the criteria against which the CEO's performance should be evaluated. The financial ratios, data from peer companies, etc. can be used for the purpose of assessment.

2. *Establish functional standards:* It is supposed to be a very difficult and subjective area of CEO's evaluation as it involves how the CEO should perform. The behavioural criteria like communication skills, financial management, etc. should be identified by the board so that the value can be added. The board should:
   (a) identify 5/10 criteria that it considers essential to the performance of the CEO.
   (b) define these criteria in relation with the organization. The criteria should be specific and clear.
   (c) define the optimum performance level and the range of possible performance levels for the CEO to attain in order to measure his actual performance against these levels.

3. *Conduct the evaluation:*
   (a) The board should meet, without the CEO, to discuss and reach agreement on its assessment of the CEO's performance against the quantitative criteria.
   (b) The full board, excluding executive directors, should participate in the evaluation meeting with the CEO. The meeting should be open and involve free and frank discussion.
   (c) Review of the evaluation of CEO's tasks should be completed.
   (d) The focus of discussion should be positive and should concentrate on what needs to be done and how that can be achieved rather than accusations as to why something was not done.
   (e) Behavioural issues should then be discussed. Here also, the focus of discussion should concentrate on planning, rather than attaching blame.

There is no doubt that performance evaluation is a real difficult process to install into board practice. Nevertheless, it is essential to the long-term successful performance of a board of directors, especially in a complicated business climate of today.

Board development

Effective corporate governance largely depends on the effective board development, which requires consideration of various *steps*, viz.

(i) the implications of the corporate business strategy at the board level;
(ii) the overall governance situation;
(iii) external situation affecting corporate governance matters;
(iv) review of board structure in the context of the company's present and future needs;
(v) consideration of board style;
(vi) succession planning;
(vii) training and development of directors in an organized and systematic way;
(viii) providing opportunities for achieving greater board efficiency and effectiveness; and
(ix) development of an agreed strategy for board development

A strategy for development of the board must be set in the context of overall business strategy. If the company is developing new strategies for products, markets, or technology, or is entering into new areas of financial or acquisition strategy, or is planning new industrial relations, management or organizational strategies, it is imperative that the board of directors of the company must be capable of monitoring and supervising executive management in the changed situation.

Expectations of a board and its directors

There are diverse expectations of a board and its directors that are held by different groups in society.

First, the *shareholders* expect the board to act in their best interests, provide acceptable total shareholder returns when compared with peer groups or competitors for shareholders' money.

Second, the *employees* expect the board to meet their claims for improved pay and service conditions of their employment.

Third, the *customers and suppliers* have increasingly moved towards partnership relationship that provides new challenges for a board's freedom of action.

Fourth, governments have an expectation that companies should provide welfare services as part of their 'good citizenship' or at least they can be forced to undertake duties on government's behalf without too much of a backlash.

Fifth, the *community at large* has an economic interest in a company's operation by way of (i) employment created at affordable rate of pay, (ii) services used, and funds made available through state government or community involvement. Increasingly, there is an added expectation that especially the local management of the company will be more greatly involved in local affairs such as charities, various welfare societies, etc.

Finally, the *public at large* has a wide variety of items to hold the board accountable for. These are generally well publicized by the media and include:

(a) limiting senior executives' compensation;
(b) full environmental protection;
(c) avoidance of fraud within the company;
(d) hiring and firing key executives; and
(e) caring for employees.

Non-executive directors

Before initiating discussion on various board committees, it is felt prudent to deliberate on the roles and importance of non-executive directors. The *roles* of non-executive directors are to act as fully participating members of the board in the performance of its duties to direct the company as well as to bring wider experience and novel ideas to its discussions, monitor and challenge the performance of executive directors and management, and also ensure that there are adequate control systems in place to protect the company's interests. Non-executive directors have a duty to be independent, challenging and watchful of the personal agendas of their executive colleagues and they need to generate creative tension, not harmony, in board deliberations.

For the non-executive director to be perceived as competent in any particular boardroom, it is imperative for him to maintain an adequate level of relationship with all his fellow directors. This will ensure that the board is able to operate smoothly and the directors will be able to work together easily.

The non-executive director must be amicable and able to communicate easily. He must present an appearance of getting on with his colleagues for the decision-making process to operate smoothly. He must use tact and diplomacy in order to present his questions, suggestions, or disagreements without giving offence to his colleagues. He must acquire the common language of his board and become integrated into the existing structure, before he is able to perform his role adequately.

In regard to his relations with the executive directors, it is important for the non-executive director to have good relations with all the executive directors for various reasons. The board must be able to operate smoothly in a procedural sense. Also, the executive directors will often represent an essential source of information to the non-executive director, who, due to time constraints, may be less well-informed about certain aspects of company affairs. It is also necessary for him to be perceived as competent by the executive directors in order for them to be prepared to implement decisions wholeheartedly, which the non-executive director has been instrumental in making.

Many non-executive directors perceive a close relationship with their chairman, and also with the chief executive where the roles are separate, as being especially important for competent role performance. The contribution made by a non-executive director is seen by some other non-executive directors as proportionate to the closeness of the relationship. If a non-executive director does not have the ear for the chairman, it may be difficult for him to achieve anything.

A non-executive director, even more than the executive director, stands on his track record. Therefore, he cannot afford this record to be of continual or serious errors of judgement. He needs to be very confident that his view is the correct one before he is prepared to enter into an open disagreement with his board because his position depends on maintaining his credibility. There can be occasions the exercise of these skills is not sufficient, where disagreements are expressed in the context of the board meeting. The theory of power of the non-executive director would suggest that such confrontations are amicable, that the ability to disagree amicably is important to the role performance, since this is seen as a more effective way of securing agreement.

In the past, it was observed that non-executive directors had too often been beholden to the chairman or managing director and only a few could successfully challenge the abusive management. It was this situation in part which led to the various committees on corporate governance to place greater emphasis on the appointment of non-executive directors through open processes and on their effective use when appointed.

Non-executive directors have often been the representatives of special interests on the board. Major shareholders such as institutional investors have appointed directors as per terms of the agreement with the companies. This conflicts with the legal duty of the board to act in the interest of all shareholders.

Another issue which needs to be addressed is the practice of appointing executive directors of other companies as non-executive directors. It has definite disadvantage in the sense that the executive directors often find difficulty in giving sufficient time and attention to external appointments, and in some cases, their involvement may raise conflicts of interest. Another aspect of the use of outside executive directors as non-executive members of the board is the tendency for remuneration committees to act as a ratchet to drive up remuneration packages through intercompany comparisons. It is difficult for those concerned not to establish benchmarks, which may be used by their own remuneration committees in reviewing their packages.

Another questionable practice is that of appointing erstwhile executive directors to be non-executive directors. It not only carries the risk of perpetuating influence from the past but also negates the independence and fresh outlook required for non-executive directors. Fortunately, the new codes of corporate governance and current regulations all over the world have provided for creation of lead independent director in cases where the roles of chairman and CEO are exercised by one person.

With the opening up of market economy and greater demand for company performance, it is expected that the value of good non-executives will grow. As the companies are required to come to terms with new markets, new competitors, new challenges and new cultures, they will value the experience and contacts of people who are at home in a wider world and who may have gone through similar challenges. Such people will need to include women directors and a spectrum of different nationalities, races and ages to reflect the company's varied stakeholders, rather than the clones of the chairman which most non-executive directors still remain. While dealing with a growing number of stakeholders and constituencies, the company needs whole new areas of competencies and understanding. In this endeavour, the non-executive directors may be much valuable to the company in facilitating some of those relationships.

It is interesting to go through certain appendices at the end of the book for better understanding of the structures and processes of corporate governance. Appendix 1 provides guideline or self-test of effectiveness of a director in the board. Appendix 2 provides 25 questions for diagnosing a board. Appendix 3 provides some sample diagnostic questions for analyzing the board of directors.

Board of directors in foreign subsidiaries

While discussing the roles and responsibilities of directors of companies, quite often, a few more questions are confronted with in regard to board of directors in foreign subsidiaries such as:

(i) What role does the board of directors discharge in foreign subsidiaries of MNCs?

(ii) What potential factors can be considered to determine the structure, role and effectiveness of the board?

(iii) How well the subsidiary board performs a given role assigned to it?

There are *three main roles* of the board in foreign subsidiaries, viz.

(a) External roles—External relations and advisory;

(b) Internal roles—Control and monitoring, coordination and integration, and strategy formulation; and

(c) Legal role.

Some of the roles performed by the board occur simultaneously, but it has been observed that different roles have been emphasized by different MNCs. The variations observed between the MNCs can be hypothesized to be determined by *four factors* which were identified by the research study, viz.

(i) Organizational interdependency and complexity;

(ii) Intensity of competition;

(iii) Dependence on the host country and government; and

(iv) Design and functioning of the administrative systems.

It has been observed that the active forms of the external and internal roles can easily come in conflict with each other in terms of actual decision-making.

The role of the local board tends to become a function of (a) the specific environmental demands facing the company, (b) corporate strategy, and (c) the structural, administrative, and operating characteristics of the MNC.

Most of the variations in effectiveness and roles of the board within each MNC are due to the factors, viz. (i) ownership structure; (ii) strategic importance of the subsidiary for the MNC as a whole; and (iii) the attitude of the subsidiary head.

From the managerial perspective, an MNC that wishes to assign any specific role to its subsidiary board should analyze and evaluate the relevant environment and company-specific characteristics, since these may influence the suitability of selecting any particular role for the board. Besides, the composition and responsibility of the subsidiary board are required to be matched and consistent with the role assigned to it. The procedures followed by the subsidiary board are also important for continued board effectiveness over the time.

3.10.2 Board Committees

The corporate failure in the past have in fact led to emphasize the need for increasing the effectiveness of the board through the use of the board committees. In order to ensure greater depth of understanding, committees of the board are an effective way to raise standards, provide the required level of reassurance and obtain greater coverage by directors. The most important *six committees*, which are normally constituted, are as follows:

(a) Audit committee;
(b) Remuneration committee;
(c) Nomination committee;
(d) Stakeholders' relationship committee;
(e) Corporate social responsibility committee; and
(f) Risk management committee

The next question comes: How do these board committees function? What are their utilities in the governing process?

Audit committee

An audit committee is formally set up by the board, usually consisting of independent board members and reporting to the board. It acts as a link between the board and the outside auditors. The members of the committee discuss the scope of the audit, explore matter that the auditors raise about management systems and controls, and are involved in resolving any disagreements that might occur on the form and content of the published financial accounts. The audit committee makes recommendations on audit fees and/or the reappointment or change of auditors.

This is one of the most important committees for providing checks against the executives with the ability to review systems and internal control, and particularly, to review objectively the progress made. In fact, the existence of a strong, independent audit committee avoids any possibility of domination by top executive management of the board's links with the auditors. It ensures that the board as a whole becomes aware of all the issues raised by the auditors and any significant problems in financial reporting, including disagreements on accounting matters such as balance sheet valuations, charges against profits and the presentation of accounts. Audit committees are not new although they are largely Anglo-Saxon. In Australia and Canada, all listed companies are required by law to have audit committees. Other countries such as the USA, the UK and India make this a listing requirement of their stock exchanges. The need to prevent fraud, cognitive omissions and management error were the prime reasons for their creation.

The most important *functions* of audit committees are to:

(i) discuss with independent auditors any problems and experience in completion of audit;
(ii) discuss scope and timing of independent audit work;
(iii) discuss effectiveness of internal controls;
(iv) discuss meaning and significance of audited figures and notes thereto;
(v) approve and nominate independent auditors;
(vi) discuss adequacy of staffing for internal audit;
(vii) discuss findings and recommendations of internal audit;
(viii) discuss organization and independence of internal auditors;

(ix) discuss plans for internal audit functions;

(x) review accounting principles and practices followed by the company;

(xi) discuss effectiveness of procedures to prevent conflicts of interest, improper payments, etc.

(xii) review financial data before submission to the board and regulatory bodies and release financial data to the press and distribution to the shareholders.

Sometimes, a question arises: Are audit committees successful in practice?

There are critics of audit committees who argue that audit committees are ineffective and unnecessary in many cases, particularly in companies where good controls already exist. Moreover, many members of the audit committees are not properly prepared for their role because they do not have adequate time and formal training, knowledge and required experience on the principles of accounting or accounting standards.

The success of the audit committee largely depends on its chairman, who chooses the agenda and keeps the discussion and conclusion of the meeting constructive. Therefore, a high level of interpersonal skills is needed to organize, control, elicit diverse views and deal with conflicts constructively. In fact, the informed chairman is required to build up direct relationship with the audit partner, internal auditor, and finance director. In practice, this investment of time is not always made, which often leads to the reduced effectiveness of the audit committee.

There may be a possibility of conflict arising between the various interests, viz. management, independent auditors, outside/independent directors, internal auditors, etc. due to the activities of the audit committee. However, it is felt that the potential for conflict can be reduced once the audit committee gains more experience, particularly if adequate care is taken on defining their duties, selecting the members involved, and emphasizing communication between the parties.

Though the audit committee has become vital, there are outstanding questions on its composition, particularly what constitutes real independence and on its constitution: Is it appointed by the chairman and CEO? Is its role to be an independent check on management? What is the balance between being management's ally or its adversary? Are they really cost-effective?

Let us not forget the fact that the rationale for the appointment of audit committee is *two-fold*, i.e.

1. To provide authority for the non-executive/independent directors; and
2. To preserve independence for the auditors.

The main *advantage* of having audit committee of the board is that the disputes and difficulties in financial reporting and criticism of management can be resolved or reported to the shareholders wherever necessary. The audit committee provides an unfettered channel between non-executive/independent directors and the auditors.

The *other benefits* include:

(a) The effectiveness and efficiency of the entire board may be improved by way of delegation of relevant tasks.

(b) The talents, knowledge and experience of the independent directors can be better utilized.

(c) Audit committee members are provided the opportunity to know more about the business of the company.

(d) Communication between statutory auditors and the client company is improved.

(e) Management of the company may be stimulated by independent assessment in addition to that of the auditors.

(f) The independence of the auditors can be, and seen to be, maintained.

Given the active support of the chairman, the cooperation of the entire board, and high-calibre independent directors to serve, there is no doubt that an audit committee can make useful contributions to the company as well as to its shareholders. In India, the detailed provisions regarding formation of the audit committees and their requirements have been spelt out in Regulation 18 read with Schedule II, Part C of SEBI (Listing Obligations and Disclosure Requirements) Regulations, 2015 as well as enacted in Section 177 of the new Companies Act, 2013 (effective from 1st April 2014).

A number of corporate houses in India have set up audit committees in their organizations as disclosed in their corporate governance report, but many of them have failed to comply with the full requirements of Listing Regulations due to non-disclosure of information about (a) literacy and expertise of the members of the committee in finance, accounts and law, (b) participation of head of finance, statutory and internal auditors in the committee, (c) audit committee charter and terms of reference, (d) audit committee reports, etc. in the annual reports of the companies.

Remuneration committee

Good governance has a major role to play. It is largely exercised through the remuneration committee, which needs to be, and seen to be, independent and professional. The committee is made up of independent members as the experience of the outside independent directors regarding compensation trends in other industries and companies would be valuable. The most important role of the remuneration committee is to have an appropriate reward policy that can attract, retain, and motivate directors to achieve the long-term goals of the company. Committee members will, of course, need to be sensitive to wider community concerns. It is, therefore, essential that:

(a) the committee is, and is seen to be, independent with access to its own external advice;

(b) it has a clear policy on remuneration that is well understood and has the support of the shareholders;

(c) performance packages are aligned with long-term shareholder interests and have challenging targets;

(d) reporting is clear, concise and gives the reader of the annual report a bird's eye view of payment policy and the rationale behind it.

In India, formation of remuneration or compensation committee has been a mandatory requirement as per Regulation 19 read with Schedule II, Part D of SEBI (Listing Obligations and Disclosure Requirements) Regulations, 2015. It is also a mandatory requirement for the companies to appoint remuneration committee according to Section 178 of the new Companies Act, 2013. However, no government companies are interested to form such committee, as it is argued that the remuneration of directors and officers is determined by the GOI. Therefore, there is no need to constitute remuneration committees in these companies.

Nomination committee

This is the third most important committee of the board, which is made up of outside independent directors. It is usually chaired by the company's chairman and is the vehicle by which new non-executive directors are brought for selection. Generally, they discuss and agree the brief, choose the search firms, agree the short list and interview final candidates.

It is a fact that often appointments are made more from within the circle of the chairman to offer him support, especially if times turned difficult. However, this practice is changing and financial institutions and more active shareholders have started to exert their views vigorously rather than just rubber-stamping a new appointment in the next AGM. They want to restrict on the number of non-executive appointments that a director can hold and abandon the system of cross-board appointments.

It is, however, observed that in most cases, the members of the nomination committee receive inadequate preparation for the new role and insufficient induction to the specific company. Increasingly, non-executive members of the committee need to spend more time on their roles. The companies, on the other hand, must ensure that they are rewarded adequately for discharging their roles as members of the nomination committee.

In India, formation of nomination and remuneration committee has been a mandatory requirement as per Regulation 19 read with Schedule II, Part D of SEBI (Listing Obligations and Disclosure Requirements) Regulations, 2015. It is also a mandatory requirement for the companies to appoint nomination committee according to Section 178 of the new Companies Act, 2013.

Stakeholders' relationship committee

Keeping in view the growing importance of the stakeholders' interests, the corporates in many countries have formed stakeholders' relationship committees as a mark of good governance. In India, hitherto, there was hardly any existence of such committee in Indian companies although there were shareholders' grievance committees in such companies. Now, formation of stakeholders' relationship committee has been a mandatory requirement as per Regulation 20 read with Schedule II, Part D of SEBI (Listing Obligations and Disclosure Requirements) Regulations, 2015. The companies are now required to form such committee under the chairmanship of a non-executive director and such other members to specifically look into redressal of grievances of shareholders, debenture holders, and security holders. It appears that the erstwhile shareholders' grievance committee has been renamed as stakeholders' relationship committee with wider activities to cater to the interests of other stakeholders as well.

Corporate social responsibility committee

Majority of the companies in the western world have already formed corporate social responsibility committees in their companies as part of their policy for good governance. In India, it is for the first time in the history of Indian company law that formation of such committee has been mandated in corporate houses with effect from 1st April 2014. Accordingly, Section 135 of the Companies Act, 2013, CSR Policy 2014, and

Schedule VII have been introduced requiring the companies to form corporate social responsibility committees to discharge various responsibilities of the corporates for the society. The details of these provisions are available in Chapter 9 of this book.

Risk management committee

In the era of globalization, all corporate houses are now getting the heat of fierce competition. They have become subjected to various kinds of risks in doing business. Therefore, it is imperative at present for the management to manage risks successfully in order to survive and sustain profitability in the competitive market. All listed companies have formed risk management committee as a mark of good governance system. In India, such committee has been a mandatory requirement as per Regulation 21 of SEBI (Listing Obligations and Disclosure Requirements) Regulations, 2015.

3.10.3 Board Governance and Ethical Values

Governance adds real value to an organization, and that for it to be effective, the standards laid down must be practised in spirit and be a part and parcel of the ethos of the concerned body. All senior managers and directors of the company need to have standards that must be compatible with the values of the company. They must be satisfied that their own reputation is enhanced rather than diminished in their work setting. They must protect their reputation by holding appropriate ethical and professional values. At the board level, directors need to feel that they are satisfied with the overall governance environment, including the provision of appropriate information.

In this connection, we provide some *sample questions* about the organization's ethical values in Figure 3.12.

3.10.4 Shareholders

What roles should the shareholders play as owners in ensuring proper corporate governance?

The shareholders are the true owners of the company. But, since shareholders are a body of individuals who are scattered over and not communicating with each other, real control lies with promoter group holding substantial or majority stake and with certain organized shareholders like financial institutions.

The proper corporate governance requires that voting majority should approve transactions or appoint directors and auditors only after properly evaluating them. However, in reality, it hardly allows such things to happen. Due to the voting power of the controlling group, all transactions go through and all appointments are made only as per the desire of the controlling group. The only way the shareholders can fight against unscrupulous promoters is by voicing their grievances at the AGM in sufficient number and making it a public issue through the shareholders' committee so that the promoters/controlling groups do not get away with what they want. The shareholders should also exercise their rights in demanding full particulars and disclosures in matters from the board at the time of AGM. The board will be fully responsible for placing all facts and figures before the general meeting on all business to be conducted in the meeting. The shareholders must ensure that the auditors discharge their duty properly and shall take active part in AGM where they are supposed to express their views freely.

(To be addressed by directors and the board; those marked * may need to be discussed without the directors who are also members of management)

For the individual director on a continuing basis

- Am I personally comfortable with the organization's mission, vision and strategy? And with its actions, proposals and values? Are they consistent with my own sense of what is right?
- Do I ensure I get all the information I need to exercise my judgement?
- Have I identified and disclosed conflicts of interest?
- Is the CEO responding in a forthright manner to board questions?*
- Does the conduct of the CEO and other senior management personnel, inside and outside the organization, set an appropriate example?*

For the board's consideration

- Has the board approved a suitable code of conduct for the organization? Does the board monitor the implementation of the code and the need for updating it in light of changes in the organization's activities and society's expectations?
- Is the board's own conduct consistent with that code?
- Does the board take the time to consider whether proposals presented for approval are right for the organization and consistent with its ethical values?
- Does the board act in the best interest of the organization, whether this interest conflicts or coincides with the best interest of a particular shareholder?
- Does the board receive appropriate reports from management on matters relating to ethical conduct such as environmental protection, employees' health and safety, human rights, improper payments and conflicts of interest?
- Does the board receive from management a report on the results of monitoring compliance with the organization's code of conduct?
- Has the board asked the internal and external auditors to bring to its attention any proposal or action of which they are aware that they believe is inconsistent with the organization's code of conduct?
- Can the board trust the CEO and other senior management personnel to act with integrity?*

Figure 3.12 Sample Questions about Organization's Ethical Values.

Source: Canadian Institute of Chartered Accountants, *Governance Processes for Control,* November 1995.

As stated earlier, due to a large number of shareholders in a listed company being scattered all over the country, it becomes impossible, but for a small number of shareholders, to attend AGM and vote. Therefore, another solution suggested by various committees for introduction of 'postal ballots' as well as 'e-voting' by the shareholders has received wider acceptance throughout the corporate world.

The new Indian Companies Act, 2013 has also made provision (Section 110) and requires the listed companies to send postal ballots to all the shareholders so that even if a shareholder is not able to personally attend and vote, he can exercise his voting right by postal ballot. In this manner, small investors would feel that they do participate in the annual affair of the company by expressing their opinion through vote.

The governance requires that small shareholders' representative should also be a member of the board of directors to protect their interest. Many countries, including

India, have now kept a provision (under Sections 149 and 151 of the new Companies Act, 2013) for minority shareholders' representation in the board of the listed companies. However, the fact remains that if the board and the independent directors are vigilant enough and follow corporate governance code, then the interest of shareholders can be protected and their investments can be preserved and well rewarded.

3.10.5 Institutional Investors (IIs)/Large Shareholders

What roles should the institutional investors (IIs)/large shareholders discharge actively in monitoring and improving the governance practices in portfolio companies?

Rise of big institutional investors (IIs) was one main reason why the corporate governance became a burning topic for debate in 1990s. Over the past fifty years, the share market has witnessed a shift towards increased institutional ownership. From a relatively low point in the late 1940s, we have come to a position in the early 21st century, in which institutional funds do control almost a majority of the shares held in major companies. In the USA, institutional holdings of US corporations has grown from 40% of common stock in 1949 to over 50% in many industries today. Growth of institutional investors has been spectacular in the UK also. In 1963, individuals held 54% of the corporate equity and institutional investors 29%. In 1994, the proportions were increased at 20% and 60% respectively. In Germany and Japan, on the other hand, banks and inter-corporate investments continue to dominant equity holdings and institutional investors do not matter there.

Institutional investors is a broad umbrella which covers mutual funds, unit trusts, investment trusts, foundations, endowments, trustee departments of banks, insurance companies and private as well as public pension funds. All these bodies invest funds on behalf of others and so have a fiduciary role. It is no denying fact that the institutional investors should play an active role in monitoring portfolio companies. The voting rights should be viewed as an asset, the use of which is of legitimate interest to those on whose behalf the institutional investors invest.

The studies have shown that there are broadly two views on institutional investing. The first view is that institutional investors should have a firm and lasting relationship with the managements of companies in which they have a large interest. They are, however, not expected to tell the management how to run their daily business, but if a company's actions are likely to jeopardize the interests of shareholders, a constructive intervention is preferable to disposing of a holding. Therefore, institutional investors should take a long-term view of performance and try not to be deflected by short-term considerations. The other view is that it is not sensible to expect institutional investors to step in and sort out management problems except as the very last resort. More importantly, their overriding responsibility is to their clients who judge them on the investment results achieved each year. Therefore, the institutional investors of the first view believe in: (a) concentration of the portfolio on fewer stocks, (b) larger stakes in individual companies, (c) close communication with the companies in which such investments are held, (d) high loyalty factor to these companies, and (e) a general interest in corporate governance matters. On the contrary, institutional investors holding the second view believe in: (a) wide diversification of portfolios and small stakes in each company, short-run profits, dividends and share prices, (b) superficial communication with companies mainly on short-term influence on the price, (c) loyalty factor, frequent dealings and interest in corporate governance non-existent. In any case, the institutional investors of the first view assert that close association between an institutional investor and a portfolio company can result in a stable relationship which gives freedom to management to be innovative and to take up long-term investment projects. This is the secret behind the strong, learning organizations in Germany and Japan. Such a relationship can reduce agency costs considerably and strike at the very root of the corporate governance problem.

It is time that the institutional investors should set on formulating corporate governance policies for their portfolio companies. Many public financial institutions have appointed nominee directors to a large number of companies. These directors have started becoming active and interfering on the major issues concerning corporate governance adherence. What is needed is a much more continuous and constructive ownership pressure from institutional investors to their portfolio companies, which will encourage and support a long-term approach to the direction of the companies' business.

3.10.6 Other Stakeholders

What are the contributions of other stakeholders in setting up of internal disciplines on the companies?

Often it has been observed that there is a conflicting interest among the shareholders and different stakeholders who make conflicting claims on the company. For example, the expectations of the shareholders may clash with those of the employees, particularly when there is need for companies to lower costs in order to sustain in the competition and retain the bottom line for payment of continued dividends, which ultimately may lead to severe 'downsizing' and 'loss of jobs'. Many more examples may be cited. However, these conflicting claims demonstrate that not all stakeholders are equal and that their relative power may change with events. Stakeholders interact within a system, which has ever-widening boundaries, due to complexity and globalization.

As we approach the 21st century, we can feel the intensity of the global competition for key stakeholders. While capital remains a necessary ingredient, access to specialized talents (labour) and to a specialized supplier infrastructure (including technology) have become much more important factors in the companies' ability to compete in increasingly sophisticated and global consumer markets. The services of the stakeholder groups such as consumers, employees and suppliers now each deserve to be regarded as trading in a separate 'market' in its own right, each having its own distinct characteristics and internal dynamics. These key stakeholders also impose a unique set of internal disciplines on the companies.

Therefore, the corporate governance is not simply a matter of giving investors more control over top management. The real governance crisis is an internal crisis due to failure of top management to address simultaneously the performance, adaptability and opportunity gaps. To add value, the top management must consistently balance the demands of the disciplines of four distinct markets–product markets (consumers), labour markets (specialized employees), the technology market (suppliers), and capital markets (investors).

3.10.7 Auditors

What roles and responsibilities do the auditors discharge to ensure improvement in the standard of corporate governance?

The statutory auditors of the company are appointed by the shareholders in annual general meeting every year to audit the accounts and financial statements and express their opinion on them, which are placed before the members in annual general meeting. Since the voting power is concentrated in hands of large shareholders or promoters, in reality, they appoint auditors of their choice and consequently, auditors also come into close contact with management and promoters during the conduct of their audit. Because of this proximity, sometimes the public and minority shareholders suspect whether auditors are discharging their duty properly or not. Let us not forget that audit is a noble profession and the auditors are not supposed to be committed to any group or a company. An independent auditor can excel in the field of his reporting requirements and in compliance with the conditions of the corporate governance. The end result of independence and excellence is the reposing of faith on the sincerity and integrity of the auditing profession.

The responsibilities of the auditing profession are increasing in many spheres day by day. The auditors are now supposed to certify on the compliance by the board on the code of corporate governance since it has become mandatory by the Companies Act as also by the Listing Agreements, on the companies for compliance all over the corporate world. An independent audit and a system of reporting to the shareholders has been part of the corporate laws all over the world. The professional skill and independence of the auditors are of equal importance. The audit firms have very strong commercial reasons for preserving an unblemished reputation for independence. But there may be a temptation to compromise on independence where an audit firm depends for a significant proportion of its income on a single audit client. The Hampel Committee suggested that the bodies concerned should examine whether, in the existing professional guidance, the 10% limit on total income from one listed or other public interest client should be reduced. The recommendatory ceiling, however, fixed in this regard by the ICAI is 40% from a single group.

A moot question may arise as to whether an auditor is primarily responsible for ensuring compliance of corporate governance? Though a direct answer to this question cannot be so emphatic and affirmative, the reports on various aspects of corporate governance have mainly highlighted the importance of financial statements, disclosures, transparency, responsibilities and accountability on the part of board as well as auditors.

Another issue, in the growing expectation gap on the role of auditors, is that whether the prime responsibility for prevention and detection of fraud is of the auditors or the fiduciary responsibility of the board. These are not easy questions, which can be answered straightway. The answer lies in the support systems that the company has created by way of internal control and systems, constitution of independent audit committee etc. In this respect, the setting up of the Serious Fraud Office (SFO), by the Government should help in detecting the frauds in a big way.

To enhance the independence of auditors, a 'surveillance mechanism' with necessary checks and balances must be put in place. There is a need to define 'independence' objectively and to prepare a checklist in which the Do's and Don'ts should be clearly spelt out. There is also a need to adopt 'internal code of conduct and ethics' and form a peer group for internal control.

3.10.8 Banks

What major roles the banks play in the implementation of corporate governance systems?

Banks have played a major role in the implementation of corporate governance systems in various corporates throughout the world. However, the roles of the banking system have been different in different countries depending upon corporate governance system adopted by the companies. In Germany and Japan, banks have historically played a larger part in financing industrial investment than in countries with relatively well-developed capital markets such as, Britain and United States. In Britain, banks are an important source of finance for industry, particularly for small and medium sized companies. However, they do not seek to become involved directly in the provision of long-term capital. They have not accepted a commitment to provide long-term finance as in Germany and Japan nor have they become involved in management problems through representations on company boards.

Unlike British banks, the German banking system has participated in long-term lending to industry and has some equity holdings. In addition, German banks hold bearer shares, which are deposited with them on behalf of shareholders and can exercise proxy votes at company meetings. They provide a wide range of financial services to companies and frequently hold the chairmanship or deputy chairmanship of the 'supervisory board' of major companies. It is observed that external pressures can be brought more readily on companies in the more bank-dependent systems of Germany and Japan than in the more market-oriented British and US systems. In Britain large financial institutions, despite their growing preponderance in share ownership, have not sought to intervene in the running of companies. In the USA, where a large proportion of shares are held by households than by financial institutions, it may be more difficult to exert external influences on company boards.

3.11 CONCLUDING REMARKS

Primarily, governance structures and processes in companies are concerned with the functioning of Board of Directors (BODs)—its structures, styles, processes, their relationships and roles etc. It is also concerned with the roles of other participants, viz. shareholders, institutional investors, large shareholders, other stakeholders, banks, auditors etc. As a natural consequence, the structures, roles and commitments of all these participants have been discussed simultaneously while delving on the issues.

The meaning of corporate social responsibility and corporate sustainability and their relationship or congruence with corporate governance has been explained. It has been highlighted that both corporate governance and corporate social responsibility can coexist and they can be achieved simultaneously. Various concerns for environment degradation and pollution created by the big companies and its adverse effect on the society have been discussed. It is observed that environmental protection and pollution prevention have been recognized as the essentials for good corporate governance practices.

CASE STUDY
Board of Directors of Unilever

INTRODUCTION

In 2012, with sales of USD 251 billion, Unilever was one of the largest packaged consumer goods companies in the world. It had over 700 brands in its portfolio. Headquartered at London and Rotterdam, Unilever operated in over 150 countries around the world. It was owned by the Netherlands–based Unilever NV and UK–based Unilever PLC. Since 1930 when the Unilever group was formed, NV and PLC together with their group companies had operated and worked as a single entity. They had the same directors, adopted the same accounting principles.

Unilever group had diversified into various businesses over a period of time. The major business segments were Foods, Home and Personal care. Unilever marketed different types of food products. These included savoury and dressings, spreads and cooking products, ice cream and frozen foods, health and wellness and beverages. Unilever was the market leader in margarine. The most important brands included Becel in the Netherlands, Flora in the UK, d'Or in France, Rama in Germany, Country and Take Control in the US.

BOARD STRUCTURE

Unilever reviewed its governance structure in the light of developments in the UK and the USA. The boards had direct responsibility for decision making in case of the following:

- Agreement of quarterly results announcements
- Approval of the annual report and accounts
- Declaration of dividends
- Convening of shareholders' meetings
- Approval of corporate strategy
- Authorisation of major transactions

The other matters were delegated to committees whose actions were reported to and monitored by the boards. The board meetings were held in London and Rotterdam and presided over by the chairman.

Directors were elected by the shareholders at the annual general meeting to hold office until the end of next annual general meeting. All directors submitted themselves for re-election each year and retired by the age of 62 years. Executive officers were appointed for an indefinite period. None of the directors or executive officers were elected or appointed under any arrangement or understanding.

Advisory Directors

Advisory (now Independent) directors were chosen for their broad experience, international outlook and independence. They were appointed by resolutions of the boards, normally for an initial term of 3 to 4 years. Thereafter their term could be extended for next 3 years. Their terms of appointment, role, powers and remuneration were specified in the resolutions of the boards. All appointments and re-appointments were based on the recommendations of the *Nomination committee.* All the advisory directors were considered to be independent of Unilever. They gave advice to the boards and to the executive committee on business, social and economic issues. They were expected to ensure that Unilever's corporate governance provisions were adequate and reflected the best practices. Advisory directors were not entitled to vote at meetings of the boards and bore no legal responsibility for the boards' actions.

Board Committees

The directors had set up various committees for effective governance. These were: the Executive Committee, Audit Committee, Corporate Risk Committee, External Affairs and Corporate Relations Committee, Nomination Committee, Remuneration Committee and Routine Business Committee.

Audit committee consisted of 3 advisory directors. The committee assisted the board in reviewing the risk management and control environment, financial reporting arrangements and standards of business conduct. It also provided independent monitoring of internal control arrangements. The chief auditor ensured that the committee was supplied with necessary information. The committee had historically met 3 times a year and in accordance with its new charter plans to meet 5 times a year from the year 2003. The committee meetings were attended by the finance director, general counsel, controller, chief auditor, and external auditors. Both the chief auditor and external auditors had direct access to the audit committee.

Corporate risk committee consisted of the finance directors, foods director, home and personal care director, personnel director, general counsel, chief auditor, and the controller. This committee assisted the board in carrying out their responsibilities to ensure effective risk management and systems of internal control. It reported to the boards, the executive committee, and to the audit committee. This committee held 2 meetings in the year 2012.

External affairs and corporate relations committee consisted of advisory directors. It oversaw the code of business principles and advised the board on external matters relevant to the business including issues like corporate social responsibility and reviewed corporate relations strategy. It met 4 times in the year 2012.

Remuneration committee consisted of 4 advisory directors. It reviewed the executive directors' remuneration and was responsible for the executive share-based incentive plans. The committee determined specific remuneration packages for each of the directors.

Nomination committee consisted of 3 advisory directors and the chairman of the company. It recommended to the board candidates, for the positions director, advisory director and executive committee member.

Routine business committees were set up to conduct routine business as and when they were necessary. It comprised of 2 directors and certain senior executives and officers of the company. It administered certain matters agreed by the boards or the executive committee. Joint secretaries were responsible for the operation of this committee.

Members of the audit, remuneration and nomination committees presented themselves to answer questions at the annual general meetings of the company.

Questions for Discussion

1. What were the direct responsibilities of directors for decision making?
2. What were the functions of different board committees?

Test Your Knowledge

1. Describe in brief, the philosophy, objectives and purposes of corporate governance.
2. Explain the concept of corporate governance with reference to its various factors.
3. Explain the cornerstones/principles of corporate governance?
4. What are the distinct areas of 'underlying conflicts' which form the basis for corporate governance issues?
5. What is value creation? How is it related to corporate governance?
6. Explain the expectations of various stakeholders from the corporates.
7. Explain the relationship between governance, performance and development at micro and macro levels.
8. What do you mean by business ethics? How is it related to corporate governance?
9. "Corporate Governance" is a system embedded with confirmation of values and ethics towards making the companies "good corporate citizen". — Discuss.
10. What is corporate social responsibility (CSR)? How is it related to corporate governance?
11. Explain how environmental issues are connected with corporate governance.
12. What are the different structures of the board of directors in companies?
13. Discuss the various components of the board activities.
14. Explain the principal issues involved in respect of board composition.
15. Explain the roles and responsibilities of directors in companies.
16. What are the questions to be confronted by the corporate directors while dealing with business risks and financial risks?
17. Explain how the Board's performance as a whole can be evaluated.
18. Explain how the performance of individual directors can be evaluated.
19. Explain how the performance of a corporate-CEO can be evaluated.
20. Explain how the effectiveness of the board can be reviewed and improved. What strategy should be adopted for board development?
21. What roles should the shareholders play as owners in ensuring proper corporate governance?
22. What is meant by "maximizing shareholders' value"? How this can be achieved by the corporates through corporate governance?
23. What roles should the institutional investors/large shareholders discharge actively in monitoring and improving the governance practices in portfolio companies?
24. What roles and responsibilities should the auditors discharge to ensure improvement in the standard of corporate governance?

25. Write short notes on:
    (a) Theories of corporate governance
    (b) Underlying conflicts of corporate governance
    (c) Corporate sustainability and corporate governance
    (d) Roles and responsibilities of directors
    (e) Liabilities of directors
    (f) Chairman and CEO duality
    (g) Non-executive directors
    (h) Independent directors
    (i) Board committees

CHAPTER 4

Board's Corporate Policies for Good Governance

Learning Objectives	Key Words
After reading this chapter, the readers will be able to understand: ☛ The meaning of Policy and its importance ☛ The Mandatory/Compulsory Corporate Policies as per the Companies Act, 2013 and SEBI Listing Agreement, 2014 ☛ The Essential Corporate Policies ☛ Corporate Policies for best practices	☛ Corporate Policy ☛ Best Practices ☛ Succession

4.1 INTRODUCTION

Corporate policies, as we all know, are framed and put into practice by the board of directors in companies for good governance. They lay down the guiding principles and procedures on the basis of which the companies do function. The Companies Act, 2013 and the new SEBI Listing Regulations have introduced various provisions to require significant changes in the corporate policies. There are some provisions which have mandated some policies specifically, whereas various other provisions have discussed about certain important matters and advised the corporate boards to frame policy documents.

This chapter identifies and discusses such board's corporate policies which are driven and guided by the regulatory framework directly and indirectly to be documented and implemented in order to ensure enhanced corporate governance.

4.2 MEANING OF POLICY AND ITS IMPORTANCE

A 'policy' is defined as a course or principle of action adopted or proposed by an individual or an organization. From the corporate point of view, it is an articulated document prepared and adopted by the board that is of utmost importance for its implementation by the corporate management.

The importance of policy documents is immense. They translate the corporate vision, mission and goals in writing and set parameters for governing the course of conduct of business. The policies, when implemented, do introduce the best practices that are followed by the corporates all over the world. Moreover, the written policy documents reduce the chance of misinterpretation, and at the same time, bring in uniformity throughout the organization.

4.3 CLASSIFICATION OF CORPORATE POLICIES

On a closer look at the Companies Act, 2013 and the new SEBI Listing Agreement, 2014, we could identify a total of 30 corporate policies which are classified in the following manner:

(a) Mandatory/Compulsory corporate policies;
(b) Essential policies; and
(c) Policies for best practices.

Let us discuss about these policies in detail.

4.3.1 Mandatory Corporate Policies

We have observed 7 compulsory policies, of which 3 policies have been mandated both by the Companies Act, 2013 and the new SEBI Listing Requirements, 2015, 2 have been mandated by the SEBI Listing Requirements, 2015 and 2 by the Companies Act, 2013 exclusively. These are discussed below:

Risk management policy (Section 134 of the Companies Act, 2013 and Regulation 21 of SEBI Listing Requirements, 2015)

It is no denying the fact that managing business risks is one of the most critical and challenging tasks of the corporate management for achieving positive results for the company. Risk management oversees and ensures the integrity of the process with which the business risks are undertaken.

The *main purpose* of this policy is to:

(a) connect risk management with business performance of the company;
(b) establish risk management process over all business units and critical support functions; and
(c) make every concerned employee responsible for ensuring risk management effective.

Nomination and remuneration policy (Section 178 of the Companies Act, 2013 and Regulation 19 of SEBI Listing Requirements, 2015)

Nomination and remuneration policy ensures that remuneration arrangements are in alignment with the strategic objectives of the business. It enables the recruitment, motivation and retention of senior executives, satisfies the expectations of stakeholders and remains consistent with the expectations of the employees.

The *main purpose* of this policy is to:

(a) lay down the criteria for appointment, renewal, removal of directors and key managerial personnel and evaluation of their performance; and

(b) determine remuneration/compensation based on the financial position of the company, trends and practices on remuneration prevailing in peers in the industry.

Board diversity policy (Section 149 of the Companies Act, 2013 and Regulation 17 of SEBI Listing Requirements, 2015)

Diversity of the directors' background, experience, qualifications, skills and perspectives are the essential ingredients of an effective board. Diversity leads to more innovation, diverse thinking, diverse culture, better governance and decision-making resulting in comprehensive, holistic and inclusive board effectiveness. The *main purpose* of this policy is to set out the approach to achieve diversity on the board towards the success of the company.

Corporate social responsibility policy (Section 135 and Schedule VII to the Companies Act, 2013)

Introduction of the mandatory CSR activities to be undertaken by the corporates on the basis of certain specified monetary threshold is one of the major steps taken by the Companies Act, 2013, with a view to making companies socially responsible. The *main purpose* of this policy is to identify the areas where the companies need to undertake such activities.

Code for independent director [Section 149(8) and Schedule IV to the Companies Act, 2013]

This provision makes it compulsory for the company and the independent directors to follow the stated requirements in the code. The detailed codes appearing in Schedule IV provide guidelines for professional conduct of independent directors. The *main purpose* of this provision is to foster the confidence of the investment community and other stakeholders.

Material subsidiary policy [Clause 49(V)(D and E) of the Listing Agreement, 2014]

This provision is applicable to all listed companies having share capital of more than ₹10 crore and net worth exceeding ₹25 crore. The *purpose* of this policy is to lay down the criteria for ascertaining material subsidiaries of the company and also for providing the governance framework for such subsidiaries.

Code of conduct for board members and senior management personnel [Regulation 26 (3) read with Schedule V, Part D of SEBI Listing Requirements, 2015]

This provision lays down the compulsory code of conduct for all board members and senior management of the company. The *main purpose* of this provision is to have a transparent conduct in order to retain the confidence of various stakeholders.

4.3.2 Essential Corporate Policies

There are various provisions under the Companies Act, 2013 and SEBI new Listing Requirements, 2015 which have pointed out numerous important and essential issues on which there is a need for framing board policies and implementing the same for smooth running of business as well as for better governance. Each of these essential policies deals with matters that lay down certain conditions to be fulfilled by the corporates.

We have identified 9 essential policies, of which the matters of 2 policies have been discussed both by the Companies Act, 2013 and the new SEBI Listing Requirements, 2015, 5 have been discussed by the Companies Act, 2013 and 2 by the SEBI Listing Requirements, 2015 exclusively. These are discussed below:

Policy on related party transactions (Section 188 of the Companies Act, 2013 and Regulation 23 of SEBI Listing Requirements, 2015)

The corporates must ensure that certain specified related party transactions are dealt and disclosed as per strict legal and accounting requirements to which the companies are subject to for the best interests of their stakeholders.

The *purpose* of this policy is to ensure due and timely identification, approval, disclosure, reporting and transparency of specified transactions between a company and any of its related party in compliance with the applicable rules and regulations.

Policy on remuneration and benefits [Section 325 of the Companies Act, 2013 and Regulation 19(4) read with Schedule II, Part D of SEBI Listing Requirements, 2015]

This is one of the essential policies of the corporates. It includes the board policies relating to salary administration, compensation, benefits and perks. Compensation includes all direct and indirect benefits the employees (including directors) are awarded with.

The purpose of this policy is to:

(a) ensure that all employees' dues are paid promptly and on time;
(b) ensure no over or under payment is made to the employees;
(c) ensure that long-term, short-term and terminal benefits are in line with the statutory requirements and accounting standards; and
(d) facilitate smooth functioning of the processes by setting up positive environment and contended workforce.

A well-set policy helps a company to remain competitive and ensure sustainability in future.

Loan policy (Section 67 and Section 185 of the Companies Act, 2013)

The companies should set out the guiding principles, general approach and fundamental considerations for lending activities by way of framing a loan policy. This policy aims at facilitating the credit dispensing functions, thereby creating a desired loan portfolio.

The *main purpose* of this policy is to:

(a) set up authority, rules and framework to operate and administer the loan portfolio effectively;
(b) assist in defining the extent of funding, eligibility criteria, tenure of loan, procedure for disbursement, etc. in compliance with the applicable regulations;
(c) ensure sufficient underwriting practices and loan documentation/records; and
(d) control lending risk and ensure the company's stability and soundness.

Investment policy (Section 68 of the Companies Act, 2013)

A company needs to articulate a policy document on investment to formalize the process of additional investible cash management, investment assets, various options of parking idle funds, etc.

The *main purpose* of this policy is to:

(a) identify investment goals and objectives;
(b) set up guidelines for investment activities;
(c) establish a basis for evaluating investment results;
(d) outline responsibilities for investment management;
(e) set out a clear process on hedging foreign risk exposure; and
(f) give a clear understanding to the personnel involved in investment objectives, various asset classes, asset allocation, acceptable risks, total long-term return, etc.

Recruitment and selection policy (Section 139 of the Companies Act, 2013)

A company needs to have a clear recruitment and selection policy to guide its talent search team to understand the mission, vision, goals and objectives of the company in order to identify the best-suited match for selection and recruitment of personnel. The policy ensures that the company selects the best possible candidate for the job based on the relevant merits and abilities measured against the job requirements.

The *purpose* of this policy is to:

(a) ensure that a professional approach is taken towards personnel selection and recruitment;
(b) ensure that proper skills, both technical and non-technical are taken into consideration while meeting strategic and operational requirements; and
(c) ensure that talented personnel are recruited based on merit, potential and ability.

Policy for prohibition of insider trading (Section 195 of the Companies Act, 2013)

With a view to curbing malpractices by the corporate insiders, i.e., directors, officers and employees having direct access to the company's critical and sensitive information and for the purpose of protecting the interest of investors and other stakeholders against such practices, it is imperative for the company's board to frame and implement a policy for prohibition of insider trading.

The *main purpose* for this policy is to:

(a) protect the interest of investors;
(b) bring in fairness and transparency in dealing with the stakeholders;
(c) ensure strict confidentiality of all price-sensitive information and to prevent misuse of such information; and
(d) comply with the rules and regulations in regard to prohibition of insider trading.

Non-disclosure agreement policy (Section 457 of the Companies Act, 2013)

A non-disclosure agreement is a signed formal agreement in which one party agrees to provide other party's confidential information and data about its business or products and the other party agrees not to share the same information with anyone else based on the terms and conditions as stated in the agreement.

The *main purpose* of this policy is to:

(a) list out possible parties who are required to execute this agreement;
(b) state in clear terms and conditions as to what information is private and confidential;
(c) set out the classes of data and level of security to be assigned to each class of data; and
(d) make out format of non-disclosure agreement.

Policy for succession [Clause 49 (II) (D) of the Listing Agreement, 2014]

In the era of competition, the corporate dynamics have changed considerably, thereby necessitating the companies to develop and nurture their human capital in order to ensure that the key positions are filled up with personnel who are capable of shouldering responsibilities effectively when the current key personnel retire from the companies, thus enabling smooth, transparent and effective transition of role and related handover as succession.

Therefore, succession planning is designed to establish the practice of identifying, evaluating and developing candidates for key posts and providing assurance to the stakeholders regarding continuity and growth prospects of the company. With a view to achieving this, the companies should have a formal succession plan policy, which also includes the process of a systematic succession planning activities with well-defined roles, responsibilities and time schedule.

Whistle blower policy (Regulation 22 of the Listing Requirements, 2015)

The companies are required to frame a whistle blower policy in order to set up a vigil mechanism for their directors and employees to report concerns about unethical behaviour, actual or suspected fraud or violation of the companies' code of conduct or ethics policy.

This policy should also provide for adequate safeguards against victimization of directors/employees as well as direct access to the top official of the companies in exceptional circumstance. The details of this policy should be disclosed on the companies' website and in the board report.

The policies bearing relevant provisions in Regulation 22 of the SEBI Listing Requirements are applicable to the listed companies only. The details of provisions are available in Chapters 9 and 10.

4.3.3 Policies for Best Practices

Besides the mandatory policies and essential corporate policies which are directly driven by the regulatory framework, there are various other important issues or matters that require for having policy documents in place for the purpose of ensuring best corporate practices internationally.

A list of other policies on some important matters is prescribed in Table 4.1 for the corporates to frame and implement for the sake of best practices and improved corporate governance.

It may be noted that the policies mentioned under mandatory policies and essential policies are framed on the basis of the Companies Act, 2013 and Rules, 2014 as well as new Listing Requirements of SEBI. The list of policies shown under Table 4.1 is an indicative list only and not an exhaustive list. A company may frame policies on other issues/matters also based on its industry specific laws and rules.

TABLE 4.1 List of Other Important Corporate Policies

Serial No.	Policies
1.	Board Evaluation Policy
2.	Protection of Company's Asset Policy
3.	Delegation of Authority Policy
4.	Performance Appraisal Policy
5.	Transfer, Exit and Termination Policy
6.	Training and Development Policy
7.	Code of Corporate Disclosure Practices for Prevention of Insider Trading
8.	Intellectual Property Rights Policy
9.	Health and Safety Policy
10.	Computer and Internet Usage Policy
11.	Information Security Policy
12.	Anti-corruption and Bribery Policy
13.	Media and External Communication Policy
14.	Blogging and Usage of Social Media Policy

4.4 CONCLUSION

Corporate policies are framed and put into practice by the board of directors in companies for good governance. They lay down the guiding principles and procedures on the basis of which the companies do function. The Companies Act, 2013 and the SEBI Listing Requirements have introduced various provisions to require significant changes in the corporate policies. Besides, various other provisions have discussed about certain important matters and advised the corporate boards to frame policy documents. The new laws have identified a total of 30 corporate policies and classified as: (a) mandatory/compulsory corporate policies, (b) essential corporate policies, and (c) policies for best practices. They have been adequately discussed in this chapter.

The importance of policy documents is immense. They translate the corporate vision, mission and goals in writing and set parameters for governing the course of conduct of business. The policies, when implemented, do introduce the best practices that are followed by the corporates all over the world. Moreover, the written policy documents reduce the chance of misinterpretation, and at the same time, bring in uniformity throughout the organization.

CASE STUDY

SEBI Probe Sends ICRA CEO on Forced Leave

THE CASE

Credit rating agency ICRA has sent its Managing Director and CEO Naresh Takkar on forced leave, pending an enquiry into 'concerns' raised by the Securities and Exchange Board of India (SEBI) which forwarded an anonymous complaint on the ratings of Infrastructure Leasing & Financial Services (ILF&S).

ICRA has appointed its Chief Financial Officer Vipul Agarwal as the interim chief operating officer who will report to the board as informed by ICRA to the bourses. ICRA mentioned that this action has been taken following an anonymous representation to SEBI that was forwarded to ICRA by SEBI expressing the 'concerns'. The action has been taken with immediate effect as stated by the Chairman, ICRA.

PROFILE OF NARESH TAKKAR

Mr. Naresh Takkar joined ICRA as an analyst in 1991 and rose through the ranks in the rating agency. He was previously with Tata Consultancy Services for 3 years in its system consulting division. He is a chartered accountant from ICAI and holds a Bachelor's degree in commerce from the University of Delhi. He was the joint MD and Chief Rating Officer of ICRA prior to becoming CEO. He was recently appointed by the Reserve Bank of India (RBI) as a member of its committee on the development of housing finance securitisation market.

DEVELOPMENT

Though ICRA is silent on the reasons behind its CEO being asked to go on leave, the development comes at a time while the rating agencies are under a cloud following the crisis at IL&FS which at one point was highly rated but defaulted in late August, 2018.

In May, a media report stated that the ICRA top brass was being probed by the market regulator that was acting on a whistleblower complaint which said that the officials had influenced the "AAA" rating for IL&FS.

The IL&FS debacle spooked the credit markets triggering a liquidity crisis as IL&FS unexpectedly defaulted on repayments in September 2018, setting off a liquidity crisis for non-banking finance companies (NBFCs) and throwing the country's financial markets into turmoil. It is alleged that IL&FS and its various group entities owe about ₹ 90000 crore.

The allegations range from failing to detect asset-liability mismatches and low capital cover. IL&FS and its group companies borrowed short term money to fund long term projects, causing a credit squeeze with mutual funds and banks not extending liquidity support to the NBFCs.

FALLOUT

SEBI has already initiated a judicial enquiry into accusations that ICRA top management allegedly influenced the rating, following the whistleblower complaint mentioned above. SEBI is also reportedly examining the role of a large number of entities, including independent directors, auditors, top management personnel, and rating agencies formerly associated with the infrastructure financier, for suspected violation of disclosure and corporate governance norms. Many of them are likely to face stringent penal action.

In its first chargesheet the Serious Fraud Investigation Office (SFIO) had identified a nine-member coterie behind the huge financial fraud at IL&FS Financial Services (IFIN). Similar probes were underway for other IL&FS entities including the parent firm.

On June 10, the Ministry of Corporate Affairs (MCA) had moved the National Company Law Tribunal (NCLT), seeking a 5 year ban on Deloitte Haskins & Sells and BSR Associates who were the auditors of IL&FS Financial Services. The Tribunal is scheduled to hear the matter on July 15. In June 2019 KPMG India affiliate BSR had resigned as an auditor of IL&FS Financial Services.

Questions for Discussion

1. To What should have been the roles of IL&FS as a non-banking financial company?
2. What are the main causes of debacle in IL&FS case?
3. What was the complaint made by the whistleblower to the SEBI against IL&FS?
4. What was role of ICRA and other agencies which contributed to the debacle in IL&FS case?
5. What remedial actions have been taken by ICRA board, SEBI and SFIO till now?

Test Your Knowledge

1. What is meant by Corporate Policy? What is the importance of policy documents in companies?
2. What are the mandatory corporate policies specified by the Indian Companies Act, 2013 and the new SEBI (LODR) Regulations, 2015? Explain in brief.
3. What are the numerous important and essential issues necessitating framing up of board policies to ensure better governance in companies?
4. Is it necessary to frame a whistle blower policy in corporate houses? If so, why?
5. "Besides the mandatory policies and essential corporate policies which are directly driven by the regulatory framework, there are various other important issues or matters that require for having policy documents in place for the purpose of ensuring best corporate practices internationally"—Is it necessary to frame such policies by the corporate houses? If so, list out the policies required for ensuring best corporate practices.
6. Write short notes on:
   (a) Risk management policy
   (b) Code for independent director
   (c) Policy on related party transactions
   (d) Investment policy
   (e) Recruitment and selection policy
   (f) Board evaluation policy

CHAPTER 5

Independent Directors

Learning Objectives	Key Words
After reading this chapter, the readers will be able to understand: • Key issues on Independent Directors • Genesis of appointment of Independent Directors • Definition of Independence and Criteria for designating a board member as an Independent Director • Need for induction of Independent Directors • Credentials, abilities and appointment of Independent Director • Proportion of Independent Directors in the corporate board and board committees • Eligibility of Independent Directors to hold shares/securities • Roles and Responsibilities of Independent Directors and Lead Independent Director • Independent Directors in Family—run/Closely-held Companies • The effectiveness of the board with Independent Directors	• Independent Director • Holding Company • Lead Independent Director • Fiduciary Duty • Non-Executive Director • Nominee Director • Executive Board • Supervisory Board • Closely-held Companies

5.1 INTRODUCTION

A significant trend that has characterized the boards over the last 20 years has been the rise in the independent/outside directors, particularly after the happenings of corporate scandals, viz. Enron, WorldCom, AOL, Time-Warner, Xerox, Global Crossing, etc. in the USA that had shaken the corporate world. There were no checks and balances on functioning of the boards of these companies. Either there were no non-executive independent/outside directors in the boards of these companies or they did not accomplish their duties as they were the clones of the chairmen and other directors. In fact, these directors were never independent in their conduct and functioning in the true sense, which resulted huge loss to these organizations and the ultimate sufferers were the stakeholders, especially shareholders whose investments in these companies were swindled forever.

In order to be 'independent', a director must be independent and he will have no material or pecuniary relationship with the company or the board in which he sits, either directly or indirectly. This excludes not only full-time employees of the company but also family members of employees and the company's lawyer, banker, consultant, suppliers, customers, debtors or creditors, or interlocking directors. In the USA, while the independent directors are called outside directors, in the UK, they are broadly termed as non-executive directors (NEDs). In this chapter, we discuss details about independent directors in the corporate boards.

5.2 KEY ISSUES ON INDEPENDENT DIRECTORS

Of late, there are certain key issues raised from different corners in regard to the effectiveness of the functioning of independent directors in the board management of companies. In this respect, some *pertinent questions* are often asked about independent directors. They are as follows:

(i) What is the genesis of appointment of independent directors in the corporate board management?

(ii) Is there meaningful definition of 'independence' and independent directors or in other words, what are the criteria for designating a board member as an independent director?

(iii) Should there be an appointment of lead independent director in the corporate board?

(iv) What is the need for appointing independent directors in the board?

(v) What credential and abilities does an independent director need?

(vi) What should be the proportion of independent directors and executive directors in the board and board committees?

(vii) How should the independent directors be appointed?

(viii) What are the roles and responsibilities of independent directors in improving corporate governance practices in the companies?

(ix) Is it prudent for the independent directors to hold shares/securities in the companies in which they are appointed as independent directors? Is an independent director entitled to receive the benefit of ESOS?

(x) Are independent directors impotent or ineffective in reality in enforcing adequate corporate governance? What changes are required further to utilize these directors for ensuring greater transparency in the board's performance?

5.3 GENESIS OF APPOINTMENT OF INDEPENDENT DIRECTORS

Evolution or genesis of the appointment of independent directors started from two basic or fundamental *theories* of corporate governance. They are:

(a) Stewardship theory; and

(b) Agency theory.

The *stewardship theory* is based on the belief that stewardship would be exercised by the directors to whom the shareholders have delegated responsibility and authority, while requiring appropriate accountability.

However, Berle and Means in 1932 did challenge the conventional assumptions of stewardship theory. They introduced another theory of corporate governance named as *agency theory*, whereby they pointed out that since the ownership in large public companies had been separated from management, the interests of owners (shareholders) and management (directors) were divergent.

The view taken by the agency theory on directors is that they (agents) cannot be trusted to act in the public welfare, in general, and in the interest of shareholders, in particular. In fact, they need to be constantly monitored and controlled to ensure compliance. Obviously, such checks and balance mechanisms require incurrence of agency costs.

These agency costs being incurred in practice in the public companies are reflected in the board structures by way of induction of outside independent directors, board committees comprising independent directors to be concerned with 'audit' (audit committee), top management 'remuneration' (remuneration/compensation committee), 'nomination' of new directors (nomination committee), and the 'separation' of roles of chairman and CEO.

In reality, a number of high-profile corporate crimes and scams in the US and other countries in the 1970s and 1980s prompted a fresh look at the roles of directors. Academics, investors, and other stakeholders began to put more emphasis on the importance of independent directors, as these directors are not primarily employed by the company. Outsiders are not dependent on the chief executive for promotion, or for legal or consultancy business. Thus, they are relatively free from conflicts of interest, and are capable of protecting the owners' interests better. This, philosophy prompted the corporate houses to increase the number of outside/independent directors in their boards, and more importantly, the ratio of outsiders to insiders in their boards. The corporate critics and commentators also agreed that if outside directors command a powerful majority in the boardroom, they will be able to check better any tendency of those in the top management to abuse their positions of power.

The notion of raising the ratio of independent directors to the executive directors on corporate boards proved extremely popular all over the world. Over the last four decades, the boardrooms of many developed and developing countries like India have witnessed a remarkable growth in the power of independent directors. More efforts and regulatory reforms have been directed not only to make sure that boards have independent directors but also to provide them a structure which makes it possible for them to monitor more effectively.

5.4 DEFINITION OF 'INDEPENDENCE' AND CRITERIA FOR DESIGNATING A BOARD MEMBER AS AN INDEPENDENT DIRECTOR

From the study of various literature on this subject, it is observed that the definition and analysis of independence and independent directors have been given by the various committees, both international as well as national, and the regulatory authorities in different ways. Some of their interpretations on 'independence' and independent directors deserve mention hereunder.

According to the *Combined Code, London Stock Exchange* 1998, the *criteria* for determining 'independence' of a director include:

(a) his employment by the company or group within the last 5 (five) years;
(b) a material business relationship with him within the last 3 (three) years;
(c) any significant shareholding by him in the company; and
(d) his service on the board exceeding 9 (nine) years.

One of the many principles of corporate governance framed by the *OECD* (*1999*) recommends that true independence of the board should be ensured by having a majority of outside directors who do not have any financial or pecuniary involvement with the company and are not in any way related to the promoters or senior executives including the full-time directors of the company.

The Blue Ribbon Committee (*1999*), while reporting on the effectiveness of corporate audit committee prescribed that the board members in the audit committee shall be considered 'independent' if they have no relationship to the corporation that may interfere with the exercise of their independence from management and the corporation. *Examples* of such relationships include:

(a) a director being employed by the corporation or any of its affiliates for the current year or any of the past 5 (five) years;
(b) a director accepting any compensation from the corporation or any of its affiliates other than compensation for board service or benefits under a tax-qualified retirement plan;
(c) a director being a member of the immediate family of an individual who is, or has been in any of the past 5 (five) years, employed by the corporation or any of its affiliates as an executive officer;
(d) a director being a partner in, or a controlling shareholder or an executive officer of, any for-profit business organization to which the corporation made, or from which the corporation received, payments that are or have been significant to the corporation or business organization in any of the past 5 (five) years;
(e) a director being employed as an executive of another company where any of the corporation's executives serves on that company's compensation committee.

The New York Stock Exchange offers a definition of an independent director as the director who is independent of management and free from any relationship which could interfere with the exercise of independent judgement as a committee member.

For the purpose of effective corporate governance, the *Toronto Stock Exchange Committee* (*1994*) stipulated that the board of directors of every corporation should be constituted with a majority of individuals who qualify as 'unrelated (independent) directors'. An 'unrelated director' is a director who is independent of management and is free from any interest and any business or other relationship which could materially interfere with the director's ability to act for the best interests of the corporation, other than interests and relationships arising from shareholding.

The Sarbanes Oxley Act, 2002 of the USA defined an independent director as the director not receiving, other than for service on the board, any consulting, advisory, or other compensatory fee from the company, and as not being an affiliated person or any subsidiary thereof.

In India, *Kumar Mangalam Birla Committee* (*2000*) defined 'independent directors' as the directors who, apart from receiving directors' remuneration do not have any other material pecuniary relationship or transaction with the company, its promoters, management or subsidiaries, which in the judgement of the board may affect their independence of judgement.

The RBI Report of the Advisory Group on Corporate Governance (*2001*) recommended that the board members shall be considered independent if they have no relationship to the company that may interfere with the exercise of their independence from management and the company. They should be identified in the annual report. The directors nominated by the government on the boards of public sector undertakings/ enterprises and public sector banks and all nominees of the regulators should not be considered as independent.

One of the main recommendations of *Naresh Chandra Committee* (*2002*) stipulates that an independent director of a company is a non-executive director who:

(a) apart from receiving director's remuneration, does not have any material pecuniary relationships or transactions with the company, its promoters, its senior management or its holding company, its subsidiaries, and associated companies;

(b) is not related to promoters or management at the board level, or one level below the board (spouse and dependent, parents, children, or siblings);

(c) has not been an executive of the company in the last 3 (three) years;

(d) is not a partner or an executive of the statutory audit firm, the internal audit firm that are associated with the company, and has not been a partner or an executive of any such firm for the last 3 (three) years. This will apply also to legal firm(s), and consulting firm(s) that have a material association with the entity;

(e) is not a significant supplier, vendor or customer of the company;

(f) is not a substantial shareholder of the company, i.e. owning 2% or more of the block of voting shares; and

(g) has not been a director, independent or otherwise, of the company for more than 3 (three) terms of 3 (three) years each [not exceeding 9 (nine) years in any case].

An employee, executive director or nominee of any bank, financial institution, corporations, or trustees of any debenture and bond holders, who is normally called a 'nominee director' will be excluded from the pool of directors in the determination of the number of independent directors. Such a director will not feature either in the numerator or the denominator.

The term 'independent director' has been defined by *N.R. Narayana Murthy Committee* (*2003*), as a non-executive director of the company who:

(a) apart from receiving director's remuneration, does not have any material pecuniary relationships or transactions with the company, its promoters, its senior management or its holding company, its subsidiaries and associated companies;

(b) is not related to promoters or management at the board level or at one level below the board;

(c) has not been an executive of the company in the immediately preceding 3 (three) financial years;

(d) is not a partner or an executive of the statutory audit firm or the internal audit firm that is associated with the company, and has not been a partner or an executive of any such firm for the last 3 (three) years. This will also apply to legal firm(s), and consulting firm(s) that have a material association with the entity;

(e) is not a supplier, service provider or customer of the company. This should include lessor–lessee type relationships also; and

(f) is not a substantial shareholder of the company, i.e., owning 2% or more of the block of voting shares.

J.J. Irani Committee (*2005*) recommended that the expression 'independent director' should mean a non-executive director of the company who:

(a) apart from receiving director's remuneration, does not have, and none of his relatives or firms/companies controlled by him have, any material pecuniary relationships or transactions with the company, its promoters, its directors, its senior management or its holding company, its subsidiary, and associate companies which may affect independence of the director;

(b) is not, and none of his relatives is, related to promoters or persons occupying management positions at the board level or at any one level below the board;

(c) is not affiliated to any non-profit organization that receives significant funding from the company, its promoters, its directors, its senior management or its holding company or subsidiary company;

(d) has not been, and none of his relatives has been, employee of the company in the immediately preceding year;

(e) is not, and none of his relatives is, a partner or part of senior management during the preceding 1 (one) year, of any (i) statutory audit firm or the internal audit firm that is associated with the company, its holding and subsidiary companies, (ii) legal firm(s), and consulting firm(s) that have a material association with the company, its holding and subsidiary companies;

(f) is not, and none of his relatives is, a material supplier, service provider or customer or a lessor or lessee of the company; and

(g) is not, and none of his relatives is, not a substantial shareholder of the company, i.e. owning 2% or more of voting power.

The term 'material pecuniary relationship' should be clearly defined for the purpose of determining whether the director is independent or not. It needs to be defined in terms of percentage. 10% or more of recipient's consolidated gross revenue/receipts for the preceding year should form a material condition affecting 'independence'. Transactions with an entity in which the director or his relatives hold more than 2% shareholding should also be considered.

Nominee directors appointed by a financial institution, bank, or government appointees representing government shareholding should not be deemed to be independent directors as such nominees represent specific interests and cannot, therefore, be termed as 'independent'.

SEBI, in its mandatory requirements (Annexure I of Clause 49 of Listing Agreement) in 2004 defined the expression 'independent director' to mean a non-executive director of the company who:

(a) apart from receiving director's remuneration, does not have, any material pecuniary relationships or transactions with the company, its promoters, its directors, its senior management or its holding company, its subsidiaries and associates which may affect independence of the director;

(b) is not related to promoters or persons occupying management positions at the board level or at any one level below the board;

(c) has not been an executive of the company in the immediately preceding 3 (three) financial years;

(d) is not a partner or an executive or was not partner or an executive during the preceding 3 (three) years, of any of the following:

   (i) the statutory audit firm or the internal audit firm that is associated with the company, and

   (ii) the legal firm(s) and consulting firm(s) that have a material association with the company.

(e) is not a material supplier, service provider or customer or a lessor or lessee of the company, which may affect independence of the director; and

(f) is not a substantial shareholder of the company, i.e., owning 2% or more of the block of voting shares.

SEBI also mentioned in the Clause 49 in 2004 that nominee directors appointed by an institution which has invested in or lent to the company shall be deemed to be independent directors.

However, the entire Clause 49 of the Listing Agreement has been changed and further overhauled by SEBI in alignment with the new Companies Act, 2013 and Rules, 2014. The new Clause 49 which has been made effective from 1st October 2014 no longer recognizes nominee directors as independent directors in the board of corporate houses. Thereafter, the new Clause 49 was also replaced by the SEBI (Listing Obligations and Disclosure Requirements) Regulations, 2015. Further details about the Listing Requirements are available in Chapter 10.

It may not be out of place to mention here that until 2013, the Companies Act, 1956 and its several amendments in 1999, 2000, 2001, etc. did not recognize and classify the company directors as executive, non-executive and independent directors in its provisions. However, it is for the first time in the history of Indian company law that the Central Government introduced new Companies Act, 2013, and Rules, 2014, which recognized the directors as executive, non-executive and independent directors in its provisions and classified them accordingly. The new company law, which has been enforced with effect from 1st April 2014, has defined clearly the criteria for designating a board member as independent director. The new Companies Act has also laid down the Code of Conduct for independent directors in Schedule IV of the Act. Further details of the provisions are available in Chapter 9.

From the host of analyses (mentioned above) defining 'independence' and 'independent directors', it is observed that all the committees and regulatory authorities of the various countries have amply clarified more or less in the same voice as to how the 'independence' is to be judged before appointing a director as 'independent'.

5.5 NEED FOR INDUCTION OF INDEPENDENT DIRECTORS

A burning question often crops up in the mind of people who are concerned with corporate activities as to what is the need for induction of independent directors in the board of directors of companies.

Agency theory of corporate governance has given ample reasons in favour of induction of independent directors in the corporate boards. Some of the cogent *grounds* given for the use of independent directors, both in the survey and in the literature, can be enumerated below:

(i) To give access to relevant external information;
(ii) To provide an independent appraisal and check on management;
(iii) To ensure constant monitoring of board's performance;
(iv) To strengthen the board;
(v) To give new perspectives on the company's direction;
(vi) To provide status to the board; and
(vii) To provide, and be seen to provide, a counterweight to managerial power.

5.6 CREDENTIALS AND ABILITIES OF INDEPENDENT DIRECTORS

Some companies, even today, do not attach much importance to verify credentials and judge abilities of a person before inducting him as independent director in the boards. The only qualification of such person as independent director possibly could be the proximity with the chairman/CEO of the companies. It is needless to say that such appointees are neither beneficial for the stakeholders nor for the improvement in the standard of corporate governance. Such appointees are little respected in the society. Fortunately, the number of such companies is much less in any country.

On the contrary, the professional organizations have felt the need for appointment of people of standing and calibre, with integrity, possessing relevant exercise and experience in their boards as recommended by various committees. There is no denial of the fact that such professional persons should be inducted as independent directors for better implementation of the corporate governance standard, apart from enhancement of the goodwill of companies and also for the sustained growth of the organizations in the present-day critical business conditions.

5.7 APPOINTMENT OF INDEPENDENT DIRECTOR

It is a fact that often appointments of non-executive independent directors are made more from within the circle of the chairman to offer him support, especially if times turned difficult. However, this practice is changing and financial institutions and more active shareholders have started to exert their views vigorously rather than just rubber-stamping a new appointment in the next AGM. As per the mandatory provisions of the company law, the nomination committee is the vehicle by which new non-executive independent directors are brought for selection. Generally, they discuss and agree the brief, choose the search firms, agree the short list and interview final candidates. Considering the requirement of skill sets on the board, eminent people having an independent standing in their respective profession, and who can effectively contribute to the company's business and policy decisions are considered for appointment as independent directors on the board. The committee, inter alia, considers qualification, positive attributes, area of expertise and number of directorships and membership held in various committees of other companies by such persons. The board considers the committee's recommendation, and takes appropriate decision.

However, good number of corporate houses have reported that they are experiencing difficulties in obtaining the non-executive independent directors they really want. Whereas, in the United States, the view is frequently put that scarcity of outside directors is due to their reluctance to take office for fear of litigation. In the UK, the reason is often seen as lack of talent. In India, it is observed that barring a few reputed and professionally-managed companies, such appointments are quite often made from within the circle of the chairman or the promoters of the company. This needs change for the sake of effective corporate governance. Appointments of independent directors may also be considered from the panel kept by the Institute of Directors or by the professional institutes such as ICAI, ICWAI, ICSI, etc. in addition to the search firms. The new Companies Act, 2013 has provided that independent directors are required to be appointed from the data bank maintained by any body, institution, association or agency recognized by the Central Government (Section 150).

5.8 PROPORTION OF INDEPENDENT DIRECTORS IN THE CORPORATE BOARD AND BOARD COMMITTEES

There is no denial of the fact that induction of independent directors in the corporate boards is imperative for the sake of more effectiveness, transparency and more professionalism in the board functioning of companies. But, a natural question arises as to what should be the proportion of independent directors in the board of directors and board committees.

Again, we observe divergent views from the study of various literatures on the subject. Even the company laws of many countries have enacted divergent provisions regarding proportion of independent directors in the boards. Both *Cadbury Committee* and *Hampel Committee* suggested that the board should include a balance of executive directors and non-executive directors, including independent directors, such that no individual or small group of individuals can dominate the board's decision-making. To be effective, non-executive directors need to make up at least one-third of the membership of the board.

The *Combined Code, London Stock Exchange* recommended that the board should include non-executive directors of sufficient calibre and number for their views to carry significant weight in the board's decisions. The non-executive directors should comprise not less than one-third of the board. The majority of non-executive directors should be independent of management and free from any business or other relationship, which could materially interfere with the exercise of their independent judgement.

The *Greenbury Committee* opined for setting up of remuneration committee (board committee), which should consist exclusively of non-executive directors with no personal financial interest, no potential conflicts of interest, and day-to-day involvement in business affairs.

Hampel Committee advocated that each company should establish an audit committee of at least three non-executive directors, with at least two of them independent.

Combined Code, LSE recommended that a majority of board members of nomination committee should be non-executive directors. The board of directors should set up remuneration committee comprising independent non-executive directors exclusively. The board should establish an audit committee consisting of at least three directors, all non-executives, and a majority of them should be independent non-executive directors.

OECD Principles of Corporate Governance, on the other hand, recommended that the majority of the board members must be independent who can contribute sufficiently to the decision-making of the board. Board should establish an audit committee, a remuneration committee, and a nomination committee with a minimum number to be composed entirely of non-executive members.

Blue Ribbon Committee recommended that the audit committee should be composed solely of independent directors.

As we have mentioned before that in line with the requirement of the company laws of the countries, most of the boards in the UK and India are the *majority executive boards* in which non-executive directors, including independent directors, are less in number. The *majority outside board* where non-executive directors form the majority on the board, particularly the independent majority, exists in the USA and Australia. However, the ultimate separation of executive management from non-executive direction is found in the *two-tier supervisory board.* Most boards in the continental European countries, particularly Germany, do have such type of boards. In Germany, the 'supervisory board' (aufsichsrat) has no common membership with the 'executive board' (vorstrand). The members of the German supervisory board represent labour and capital in equal numbers, with the employees appointing the labour members and the shareholders their representatives. Contrary to the western emphasis on the importance of the contribution of independent outside directors, the Japanese board is made up almost entirely on inside *all executive directors.*

In India also, divergent views from various national committees are noticed. For instance, *CII Code* recommended that any listed company with a turnover of ₹1000 million and above should have professionally competent and acclaimed non-executive directors, who should constitute (a) at least 30% of the board, if the chairman of the company is a non-executive director, or (b) at least 50% of the board if the chairman and managing director is the same person.

K.M. Birla Committee recommended that the board of a company should have an optimum combination of executive and non-executive directors with not less than

50% of the board comprising the non-executive directors. In case a company has a non-executive chairman, at least one-third of the board should comprise independent directors, and in case a company has an executive chairman, at least half of the board should be independent. A qualified and independent audit committee should be set up by the board of the company. The committee should have minimum 3 members, all being non-executive directors, with majority being independent, and with at least 1 director having financial and accounting knowledge. The chairman of the committee should be an independent director. The board should set up a remuneration committee which should comprise at least 3 directors, all of who should be non-executive directors, the chairman of the committee being an independent director.

The RBI Report of the Advisory Group recommended that if the CEO is also the chairman of the board, more than 50% of the board members should be independent. The audit committee should be composed solely of independent directors, having a minimum of 3 directors. Boards of companies, banks, and PSUs should set up nomination committees consisting of at least 3 independent board members, and should set up remuneration committees exclusively of independent board members.

Naresh Chandra Committee appointed by the Central Government in 2002 recommended that no less than 50% of the board of directors of any listed company as well as unlisted public limited companies, with a paid-up share capital and free reserves of ₹ 100 million and above or turnover of ₹ 500 million and above, should consist of independent directors. Audit committee of all listed companies, as well as the unlisted public limited companies with a paid up share capital and free reserves of ₹ 100 million and above, or turnover of ₹500 million and above, should consist exclusively of independent directors.

N.R. Narayana Murthy Committee appointed by SEBI in 2003 recommended that all audit committee members shall be non-executive directors.

J.J. Irani Committee appointed by the Central Government in 2005 opined that there should be a minimum of one-third of the total strength of the board as independent directors. Majority of the directors of the audit committee should be independent directors and the chairman of the committee should be independent.

From the above discussion, it is quite clear that there are divergent views on this subject. However, the new Companies Act, 2013 enforced by the Government of India with effect from 1st April 2014 has stipulated that every listed public company shall have at least one-third of the total number of directors as independent directors and the Central Government may prescribe the minimum number of independent directors in case of any class or classes of public companies (Section 149). The audit committee of the board shall consist of a minimum of 3 directors, with independent directors forming a majority (Section 177). The board of directors of every listed company and such other class or classes of companies, as may be prescribed, shall constitute the nomination and remuneration committee consisting of 3 or more non-executive directors out of which not less than one-half shall be independent directors (Section 178). The details of the provisions are available in Chapter 9.

The new SEBI Listing Requirements, 2015 (Regulation 17) has also similarly prescribed the proportion of independent directors in the board of directors and the board committees. The board of directors of the company shall have an optimum combination of executive and non-executive directors with at least one woman director and not less than fifty percent of the board of directors comprising non-executive directors. Where the chairman of the board is a non-executive director, at least one-third of the board should comprise independent directors, and in case the company does not have a regular non-executive chairman, at least half of the board should comprise independent directors. The audit committee shall have minimum three directors as members. Two-thirds of the members of audit committee shall be independent directors and the chairman of the audit committee shall be an independent director (Regulation 18). A company shall set up a nomination and remuneration committee which shall comprise at least three directors, all of whom shall be non-executive directors and at least half shall be independent. Chairman of the committee shall be an independent director (Regulation 19). The details of the provisions of SEBI Listing Regulations are available in Chapter 10.

5.9 ELIGIBILITY OF INDEPENDENT DIRECTORS TO HOLD SHARES/SECURITIES

A burning question that is subject to lot of discussions among the knowledgeable critics and researchers is that whether an independent director should be entitled to hold equity shares and securities of the company in which he is appointed or proposed to be appointed as independent director. There are different views from different quarters in this respect. Various committees set up by different countries, including India, for issue of guidelines on corporate governance have opined in favour of holding of shares and securities by the independent directors in the companies in which they are appointed as directors. Some of the committees in India, viz. Naresh Chandra Committee, N.R. Narayana Murthy Committee, J.J. Irani Committee have even prescribed the maximum limit of holding less than 2% of the block of voting shares by an independent director. The same has also been approved by the regulatory authority, i.e. SEBI in its new Listing Requirements.

On the other hand, many critics have given opposite views in this respect. They are of the opinion that an independent director is a director who is independent of management and free from any relationship pecuniary or otherwise, which could interfere with the exercise of independent judgement as a board member. Therefore, these directors should not hold any shares/securities of the companies because their relationship as shareholders with the companies may likely to interfere with the exercise of independent judgement as committee members of the boards of such companies. In this connection, the definition given by K.M. Birla Committee is very clear, which states that independent directors are the directors who, apart from receiving directors' remuneration, do not have any other material pecuniary relationship or transaction with the company, its promoters, management or subsidiaries, which in the judgement of the board may affect their independence of judgement. The RBI Report of the Advisory Group on Corporate Governance (2001) also recommended that the board members shall be considered independent if they have no relationship to the company that may interfere with the exercise of their independence from management and the company.

From the above divergent viewpoints, the author is of the opinion that for the sake of independent, unbiased, objective and transparent decision-making in the board proceedings, it is prudent for the independent directors not to hold any share or securities of the companies in which they are appointed or proposed to be appointed as independent directors; otherwise, there is always an apprehension of having conflicts of interest in their functioning. In other words, the persons holding equity shares/ securities in any company or companies should not be considered for appointment as independent directors of such company or companies. They also should not be eligible for benefit under ESOS scheme implemented by the companies.

5.10 ROLES AND RESPONSIBILITIES OF INDEPENDENT DIRECTORS

The roles of non-executive/outside directors are to act as fully participating members of the board for performing the following *duties*:

(a) To direct the company as well as to bring wider experience, technical expertise, independent judgement and new ideas to its discussion;

(b) To monitor and challenge the performance of executive directors and management; and

(c) To ensure that there are adequate control systems in place to protect the company's interests and also the interests of the shareholders, and stakeholders, as they enjoy the investors' confidence.

Independent directors play a key role in the decision-making process of the board, as they approve the overall strategy of the company and oversee the performance of management. They are committed to acting in what they believe is in the best interest of the company and its stakeholders.

The independent directors bring to the company a wide range of experience, knowledge, and judgement as they draw on their varied proficiencies in economics, finance, infrastructure, management, accountancy, law, public policy, engineering and corporate strategy. This wide knowledge of both their field of expertise and boardroom practices helps foster varied, unbiased, independent and experienced perspectives. The company benefits immensely from their inputs in achieving its strategic direction.

Non-executive directors have fiduciary duties, as the law does not distinguish between executive and non-executive directors, which means the non-executive directors have similar and equal responsibilities as that of executive directors in the eye of law. In discharging all these responsibilities, the non-executive directors/outside directors, being equal members of the boards have the power to (i) demand information from the management, and (ii) exercise their votes based on their independent judgement.

The Cadbury report highlights a monitoring responsibility for independent directors stating that non-executive directors are in the best position to monitor performance of the board and the CEO. There is a possible danger in that the executive board members might come to see the monitoring role as purely a job of their independent colleagues. Further, this may lead to weakening of the notion that a board is a team of all of whose members share responsibility. The great threat here is the possible outbreak of battles between executive and independent directors. Therefore, the central issue is whether independent directors are supposed to be monitors only or should draw their skills and backgrounds towards progress of the company. Assuming that independent directors will increasingly be chosen for the breadth of experience and skills, which they can bring to a board, then there is a question about appropriateness of limiting their contribution to that of a monitoring role. To deny such directors, the opportunity to exploit their backgrounds by contributing to setting the policy framework would be rather self-defeating.

While responsible outside directors cannot remain passive, their monitoring need not impair constructive collegiality on the board. Finding a way to make a contribution through informed, systematic monitoring of long-term performance, while avoiding friction, is one of the greatest challenges of the outside directors in their board service.

5.11 LEAD INDEPENDENT DIRECTOR

Another question arises: Should there be an appointment of lead independent director in the corporate board? If so, what should be his role in the board's functioning? Having discussed the criteria for designating a director as an independent director of a company, let us now discuss about the necessity of the appointment of a leading independent director.

The international benchmark or standard of corporate governance prescribes as a good governance practice that irrespective of whether the posts of chairman and CEO are held by different persons or by same individual, there should be a strong and independent non-executive element on the board as lead independent director (other than the chairman), to whom concerns can be conveyed.

Roles and responsibilities of lead independent director

The *roles* played by the lead independent director in a company are as follows:

(a) To preside over all meetings of independent directors;
(b) To ensure that there is an adequate and timely flow of information to independent directors;
(c) To liaison between the chairman and the managing director, the management, and the independent directors;
(d) To preside over meetings of the board and shareholders when the chairman and managing director is not present, or where he is an interested party;
(e) To take appropriate steps to present independent directors' views to the chairman and managing director;
(f) To perform such other duties as may be delegated to the lead independent director by the board/independent directors.

It will be the responsibility of lead independent director to (a) act as a spokesperson for independent directors as a group, (b) work closely with the chairman/CEO, and (c) take a lead role in the board's evaluation process, apart from other important broad functions. A lead independent director should be identified in the annual report.

In order to meet the international standard, majority of the companies in the world have initiated appointment of lead independent directors in their boards. However, corporate India's position is dismal in this regard. Only 8% of the listed companies examined have appointed lead independent directors in their boards.

5.12 INDEPENDENT DIRECTORS IN FAMILY-RUN/CLOSELY-HELD COMPANIES

In a family-run business, it is observed that the goals and values of individual family members seem often to clash with their goals and objectives as directors and managers. Of course, there are some family boards which are very effective. These boards often include directors who are outsiders—independent individuals whose only relation with the company or family is that they serve as directors.

The roles, strengths, and influence of family board members are generally not well-established or perceived outside family circles, even to outsiders who work within the firm as directors. Except in a crisis situation, the process of changing family attitudes, values, and goals takes a long time. A trusted, competent outside/independent director can provide the focus that holds the board and the company together during this time.

Roles of outside/independent director in family-run company

The outside/independent director on a family board is required to play a number of important *roles* as mentioned:

(i) Arbitrator: He must be capable of handling disagreements within the family, hostilities, and other emotional stresses or conflicts.

(ii) Resource to the board: He has to supplement internal resources and provide freedom from group and insider thinking when key decision-makers are advocates of a particular view or beneficiaries of a particular action.

(iii) Gap-filler: His role is to fill in the gap when owners of the company lack time or expertise to cope with the difficulties of managing the company in a dynamic situation.

(iv) Catalyst and agent of change: He is required to perform catalytic action needed for significant shift in the goal or objective of the company such as, making a divestment or an acquisition, going public, changing top managerial personnel, etc.

(v) Corporate networking agent: He has to work as the company's networking agent for the benefit of the family firm such as network of potential sources of capital, new business strategy, new technology, information on economic trends, connection in industry, international contracts, connection with the government, etc.

(vi) Devil's advocate: His role as devil's advocate is to pinpoint the defects in presentation when the board needs a champion of the worst cause or case.

(vii) Father confessor: His role as father confessor is complete when the owners, directors, and managers talk to him freely and confidentially and share concerns or troubles, etc.

Therefore, outside directors are required to sort out and help to resolve key issues where accountability, role ambiguity, and old and obsolete strategy result in unsatisfactory corporate performance. They can provide the resources that a closely held company needs in order to survive and improve its performance even after the founder's unexpected death when leadership from within the family has not been established. The independent directors play an important role in separating personal goals from the objectives of the company for family members on the board and for the family members employed in the company.

Qualities of an independent director in family-run company

An outside/independent director must preserve the courage, confidence, and the ability required to act independently, with a view to fulfilling various duties, both legal and moral, of a fiduciary. He must be willing to risk the rapport established with owners and colleagues by way of taking an independent position. He must be prepared even to relinquish directorship rather than be recognized a captive. He must refrain from getting involved either in family problems or in day-to-day company affairs. He must keep that most valuable of traits, his independent perspective, for the larger overall needs of governance.

Benefits of including independent director in the family board

There are plenty of *benefits* of inclusion of independent director in a family board, as mentioned below:

(a) An outside/independent director can support the necessary reorganization and help to moderate its impact on family members.
(b) He can counsel against nepotism on the issue of succession.
(c) He can help to sort out the governance processes for the benefit of family directors.
(d) He can help to identify and resolve conflicts arising from the difference of objectives of owners and the objectives of the company, by way of offering alternatives to the family board.
(e) He can help board members to accommodate change and avoid other emotional crises as his objectivity can often save the family company from some of its emotionally charged relationships. He can negotiate differences of opinion between generations or between groups that may be represented on the board.
(f) Non-family directors are often in a better position than family member directors to assess the impact of estate planning on non-family employees, strategic positioning, and the long-term future of the company.
(g) When ownership is being transferred, particularly to younger family members, the independent directors are capable of providing continuity on the board.
(h) Outside/independent directors can influence the board on major corporate decisions, viz. corporate strategy, growth objectives, strategy on diversification and divestment, etc.
(g) Non-family directors can play a unique role in controlling nepotism and group thinking in management development, in succession, in the selection of candidates for directors, etc.

5.13 HOW EFFECTIVE ARE THE BOARDS WITH INDEPENDENT DIRECTORS? HOW EFFECTIVENESS CAN BE IMPROVED?

As mentioned earlier that over the last four decades, the boardrooms of many developed and developing countries like India have witnessed a remarkable growth in the power of independent directors. More efforts and regulatory reforms have been directed not only to make sure that boards have adequate number of independent directors but also to provide them a structure which makes it possible for them to monitor more effectively. One recent study indicates that outside/independent directors constituted around 65% of the directors of a sample of Fortune 500 companies, whereas inside executive directors constituted only 35%. The main reason for this change has been the growing concern that inside directors tend to be self-serving. But, in practice, all these efforts and reform measures expected to improve the quality of board functioning have appeared to be not as successful as expected.

In the year 1971, Myles Mace, a Harvard Business School professor, conducted a landmark study on corporate boards. He concluded that the independent directors were nothing but "ornaments on a corporate Christmas tree". Despite increase in the number of independent directors, the boards of the corporate houses have seldom succeeded in overseeing management's performance effectively. In practice, it is the CEO/chairman who wields the power in the board proceedings, and the directors mostly serve at his pleasure. However, except in extreme situations, the very human impulse of many independent directors is to feel loyalty to the company's CEO, the leader in whose hands the future of the organization is seen as resting.

Vance (1983) contended that outside directors are even more obligated to the CEO for their position than are inside directors, and thus, are likely to be less forceful at monitoring and challenging senior management. In another study, Gautschi and Jones (1987) concluded that firms with higher proportions of outside/independent directors on their boards tended to have more criminal violations than those with lower proportions. The evidence to date does not seem to support the belief that the stockholders are better served by boards dominated by outsiders. The empirical evidence suggests that outside/independent directors may not necessarily be the solution to the perceived problem of the separation of management and ownership.

This is not to say that directors do not do anything or that they cannot check managerial abuse and misuse. Drieghe (1986) concluded that boards with a higher proportion of outside directors, who had executive experience as well as contractual relationships with the firm, were the most effective at protecting shareholders' interests. But, at the same time, it is true that boards are mostly reactive and not proactive in many companies even now. The evidence suggests that simply adding outside/independent directors to a board will not in and of itself ensure that the board will become more effective.

However, things have improved remarkably over the decades, but outside/independent directors still have a long way to go before they exercise their power to look after stakeholders' interests. They have to function as active monitors of corporate management, not just in crisis, but continually. They should have an active role in the formulation of long-term strategic, financial and organizational goals of the company and should approve plans to achieve those goals. They should engage themselves too in the periodical review of short- and long-term performance as per plan and be prepared to press for correction when in their judgement there is a necessity.

Effective long-term monitoring requires a sympathetic and productive relationship between the outside board members and the CEO, and acknowledgement by the CEO of the legitimacy of the monitoring role and its requisites. Besides, a host of innovative mechanisms may be explored to develop the board's functioning and its transparency.

For instance, a periodic meeting of the independent directors without the presence of CEO might be helpful. Direct access to corporate information and personnel might be possible. Periodic structured meetings between outside/independent directors and large, long-term shareholders might prove productive.

While responsible independent directors cannot be passive, their monitoring need not impair constructive collegiality on the board. They have to find a way to make a contribution through informed, sympathetic monitoring of long-term performance, while minimizing friction.

A director's role should be seen as imbued with some elements of civic responsibility as well. The men and women who accept this responsibility and who perform it conscientiously and well, are performing a service to the whole community and the nation. They deserve our respect. Whereas, the men and women who as directors are passive, who view their role as mere advisors, who are pliable and pleasant, but who do not insist upon a real monitor's role, do small service to anyone and deserve little respect.

5.14 CONCLUSION

The definition and analysis of independence and independent directors have been given by the various committees, both international as well as national, and the regulatory authorities in different ways. However, one of the many principles of corporate governance is that true independence of the board should be ensured by having a majority of outside directors who do not have any financial or pecuniary involvement with the company and are not in any way related to the promoters or senior executives including the full-time directors of the company.

This chapter has dealt with various aspects of independent directors such as criteria for designating a board member as an independent director, genesis of the appointment of independent directors in corporates, roles and responsibilities of independent directors, appointment of independent directors and lead independent directors, need for induction of non-executive outside/independent directors in the boards of corporate houses, their credentials and abilities, eligibility of independent directors to hold share/securities in the companies in which they are appointed or proposed to be appointed as directors, etc.

The chapter ends with the discussion on proportion of independent directors in the corporate boards and board committees, the effectiveness of the boards' functioning with independent directors and independent directors in family-run/closely-held companies.

CASE STUDY–I

Independent Director in General Electric (GE)

INTRODUCTION

General Electric (GE), the world's second most admired company, ranked 5th in Fortune 500 list of companies in the year 2012. It operated a diverse range of businesses covering aircraft engines, power generation, financial services, medical imaging, television programming, and plastics. GE's sales had risen from USD 60 billion in 1993 to USD 210 billion in 2012. GE had established various principles with regard to corporate governance and put in place various systems and processes to implement them.

GE grew from strength to strength under Welch's leadership. It became one of the most admired companies and its stock, one of the most highly valued in the world. Welch laid a great emphasis on services and launched major quality initiatives. He also initiated efforts to make GE a web-centric enterprise. GE Capital became one of the major growth engines for GE.

BOARD OF DIRECTORS

GE's directors were elected each year by the shareholders at the annual general meeting. The board proposed a slate of nominees to the shareholders for directors' election. Between annual shareholders meetings, the board could elect directors to serve until the next annual meeting. The board and the management believed that the long term interests of shareholders could be served by addressing the concerns of all stakeholders including employees, recruits, customers, suppliers, GE communities, government officials, and the public at large.

Out of 17 board directors, 11 of them were independent directors under New York Stock Exchange (NYSE) regulations. There were a minimum of 10 independent directors at all times, and it was the board's goal to have at least two-thirds of board comprising independent directors. GE used various guidelines to determine director's independence. A director did not qualify as independent if, within the preceding 5 years:

I. The director was employed by GE
II. An immediate family member of the director was employed by GE as an officer
III. The director was employed by or affiliated with GE's independent auditor
IV. An immediate family member of the director was employed by GE's independent auditor as a partner or manager
V. A GE executive officer was on the board of directors of a company which employed the GE director, or which employed an immediate family member of the director as an officer

GE attempted to attract directors with an inquisitive and objective perspective, practical wisdom, and mature judgment. It endeavoured to have a board representing diverse experience at policy-making levels in business, government, education and technology, and in areas that were relevant to the company's global activities.

The board neither believed that arbitrary term limits on directors' service were appropriate, nor believed that directors had to be re-nominated annually until they reached mandatory retirement age. The board's self-evaluation process was an important determinant for its tenure. Directors were not generally nominated for election to the board after the age of 73 years. But the full board could nominate candidates under special circumstances.

BOARD RESPONSIBILITIES

The board was responsible for supervising the management and performing specific functions as follows:

- Selecting, evaluating, and compensating the CEO and overseeing CEO succession planning
- Providing counsel and oversight on the selection, evaluation, development, and compensation of senior management
- Reviewing, approving, and monitoring fundamental financial and business strategies and major corporate actions
- Assessing major risks faced by the company and reviewing options for their mitigation
- Ensuring that processes were in place for maintaining the integrity of the company, the financial statements, compliance with law and ethics, relationships with customers and suppliers, and other stakeholders

GE directors and executives were expected to conform to the highest standards of personnel, professional and ethical codes of conduct at all times and to acknowledge adherence to GE's codes. The board did not permit waiver of any ethics policy for any director or executive officer. If an actual or potential conflict of interest arose, the director had to promptly inform the CEO and the presiding director. If a significant conflict of interest existed and was not solved, the director was expected to resign. The board resolved any conflict of interest involving the CEO, the vice chairman or the senior vice president. The CEO resolved any conflict of interest involving any other officer of the company.

The general counsel and the chief financial officer were responsible for providing orientation for new directors, and periodically provided materials or briefing sessions for all directors to assist them in discharging their duties. Within six months of election, each new director to the board spent a day at the corporate headquarters for personal briefing by senior management on the company's strategic plans, its financial statements, and its key policies and practices.

The board of directors had 8 scheduled meetings a year where it reviewed and discussed reports by management on the performance of the company, plans and prospects, as well as issues of immediate concern. Directors were expected to attend all scheduled board and committee meetings.

Questions for Discussion

1. How an independent director was elected in GE and what were the criteria for such selection?
2. What were the responsibilities of the board of GE?
3. How a potential or actual conflict of interest was resolved at the directors' level?

CASE STUDY–II

Infosys Independent Director Settles Charges

INTRODUCTION

Ms. Kiran Mazumdar Shaw, the lead independent director of Infosys, has settled with SEBI a case of alleged delay in making disclosures about the change in her shareholding in the IT services firm.

THE CASE AGAINST SHAW

Ms Shaw was alleged to have violated the provisions of the Prohibition of Insider Trading (PIT) Regulations.

In February, 2019 Infosys had said that Ms. Mazumdar Shaw inadvertently sold 1600 shares of the company through her portfolio management services, without obtaining prior clearance.

THE COMPANY'S REVIEW

The Audit Committee of Infosys examined the case against Ms. Shaw. After a review by the Audit Committee of the company's board of directors which determined and came to the conclusion that there was a violation of the Infosys' insider trading policy and the PIT Regulations.

SEBI INVESTIGATION

The market regulator SEBI had conducted an examination and observed that Ms. Shaw delayed in making the necessary disclosures with respect to the change in her shareholding in the company. A penalty of ₹ 9.5 lakh was imposed on her.

However, before proceeding further and initiating proceedings, SEBI sent a notice of settlement to Ms. Shaw with an intimation that the proceedings may be settled and disposed of upon the filing of an application settlement mechanism along with the remittance of settlement amount of ₹ 3.01 lakh.

SETTLEMENT

Accordingly, Ms. Kiran Mazumdar Shaw filed the settlement application without admitting or denying the default and remitted ₹ 301758 in September, 2019 as settlement charges. The market regulator passed an order saying that "This order disposes of the proceedings that may be initiated for the defaults".

Questions for Discussion

1. Who is Ms. Kiran Mazumdar Shaw?
2. What was the charge against Ms. Kiran Mazumdar Shaw?
3. What are the provisions of the Prohibition of Insider Trading (PIT) Regulations relating to this case?
4. What were the findings of Infosys' Audit Committee and the SEBI in this case?
5. What were the verdict of the market regulator and how the settlement of charges was accomplished?

Test Your Knowledge

1. What do you mean by Independent Director? How should the Independent Directors be appointed?

2. Discuss the pertinent questions that are often asked about Independent Director.
3. Explain the genesis of appointment of Independent Directors in the corporate board management.
4. Explain in brief, the various criteria suggested by the national committees for designating a board member as independent director.
5. Is there any need for induction of Independent Directors in the corporate boards? If yes, discuss critically with cogent reasons.
6. Should there be an appointment of Lead Independent Director in the corporate board? If so, what should be his role in the board functioning?
7. What are the divergent views expressed by various committees in India on proportion of independent directors in the corporate board and board committees in their recommendations on corporate governance?
8. What are the roles and responsibilities of Independent Directors in improving corporate governance practices in the companies?
9. Is it prudent for the Independent Directors to hold shares/securities in the companies in which they are appointed as Independent Directors? Should they be entitled to receive the benefit of ESOS?
10. Do you think the Independent Directors are impotent or ineffective in reality in enforcing adequate corporate governance? What changes, according to you, are required further to utilise them in order to ensure greater transparency in the board's performance?
11. Is there any necessity of appointing independent directors in family-run/closely held companies? If yes, discuss in detail, the roles and responsibilities discharged by an independent director in a family-run company.
12. What are the benefits of including independent director in a family-run corporate board?

CHAPTER 6 Gender Diversity in Corporate Boards

Learning Objectives	Key Words
After reading this chapter, the readers will be able to understand: • Key issues concerned with Gender Diversity and inclusion of Women Directors in the corporate board • Need for Gender Diversity and its adoption by other countries • Desirability of regulatory imposition of Quota System • Effectiveness and efficiency of board's functioning due to Gender Diversity and the stakeholders' benefits • Global initiatives on implementation of Gender Diversity • GAP analysis of Men and Women in corporate boards of different countries • Status of Gender Diversity in India and the present scenario • Regulatory authorities' initiative towards Gender Diversity • Provisions of the Companies Act, 2013 and SEBI (Listing Obligation and Disclosure Requirements) Regulations, 2015 on Gender Diversity • Present scenario and Repository for sustenance of Gender Diversity	• Gender Diversity • Women Directors • Quota System, Return on Equity (ROE) • Return on Capital (ROC) • Gap Analysis • Letter and Spirit

6.1 INTRODUCTION

Gender diversity is the way to create diversity without necessarily increase in the board size. This diversity has been created in the boards of corporate houses all over the world at least a decade ago in order to improve the structure of corporate governance and bring in gender equality and balance in the board's activities. In the words of Philip Hampton, Chairman, Royal Bank of Scotland, "Improving gender balance in the boardroom not only increases the performance of the board and strengthens the business but is also good for the UK economy, as it enhances our competitiveness, ability to attract talent and reputation for good governance in a global market". In India, gender diversity has been recognized by the regulatory bodies in 2013. Accordingly, the new Companies Act, 2013 and the new SEBI Guidelines, 2014 have enacted in favour of inclusion of women directors in the corporate boards by 1st April 2015.

In this chapter we shall discuss at length gender diversity and inclusion of women directors in the boards of companies in different countries, including India.

6.2 LITERATURE REVIEW

There are plenty of literatures available in favour of participation and inclusion of women in corporate boards, a few of which deserve mention here.

Carter et al. (2007) opined that the existence of gender diversity in boards may issue positive signals to markets—labour, products, and capital markets—by providing a greater degree of legitimacy to corporations and improving their reputations. Welbourne et al. (2007) mentioned that diversity enhances creativity and innovation inside the corporation and would lead to more effective problem-solving, since a more diverse board provides a wider variety of perspectives and consequently, a higher number of alternatives to evaluate. Adams and Ferreira (2009) reported that women directors have a significant impact on board inputs and firm outcomes. They have better attendance records and are more likely to join monitoring committees than men directors. Dalton and Dalton (2010) opined that steady increases in the overall participation of women in corporate boards show their presence on key board committees, particularly in the post Sarbanes-Oxley period. Kurup et al. (2011) reported that women are less represented in Indian corporate boards as compared to other countries. India is the lowest with 5.4% of the directorships being held by women, whereas Canada (15%), the USA (14.5%), the UK (12.2%), Hong Kong (8.9%), and Australia (8.3%) have higher percentages. Branson (2012) opined that a diverse board would help avoid "group think", and the presence of women would aid the proliferation perspectives and viewpoints on corporate boards, leading to better assessment of risks and less rubber-stamping of CEOs' decisions; this would be improving the monitoring and oversight capacity of the board.

6.3 ISSUES CONCERNED WITH GENDER DIVERSITY AND INCLUSION OF WOMEN DIRECTORS IN THE BOARD

There are certain questions raised/apprehensions expressed by some critics in regard to gender diversity and inclusion of women directors in the board of directors of companies.

(i) Is there any need for gender diversity through quota system by enactment of law for inclusion of women directors in the corporate boards? Has the gender diversity been practised and followed by other countries?

(ii) Do the effectiveness and efficiency of the board's functioning increase due to participation of women directors in the board's proceedings?

(iii) What advantages are achieved by the stakeholders from gender diversity in the boards of companies?

(iv) Can such a quota system for ensuring gender diversity in boardroom synchronize with the performance aspect of a company?

(v) Is regulatory imposition of quota system (i.e., inclusion of women director in the board) a desirable option? Is it not a challenge against the principle of autonomy based on ownership?

(vi) What is the experience in other countries that have adopted quota system by way of inclusion of women directors in their corporate boards?

(vii) What are the other global initiatives on implementation of gender diversity?

(viii) What are the rules made by the Companies Act, 2013 and requirements made by the SEBI Guidelines in favour of the gender diversity?

We shall make an endeavour to find answers to these questions/apprehensions in the paragraphs that follow.

6.4 NEED FOR GENDER DIVERSITY AND ITS ADOPTION BY OTHER COUNTRIES

Gender diversity is often seen by some critics as the apparent intention of the interference on the company's affairs. But, when we look at the inherent cardinal intention behind imposition of law on this issue, we find that the ultimate purpose of the adoption of gender diversity is to boost corporate governance so that the decision-making becomes robust in the dynamic and diverse global environment.

Gender diversity has been adopted by many countries. The path finder is Norway in this regard. In 2003, Norway became the first country in the world to impose gender quota in its corporate houses. It required 500 companies, including 175 companies listed on the Oslo Stock Exchange, to raise the proportion of women on their boards to 40%. Initially, the law was meant for voluntary participation and was supposed to be withdrawn had the companies voluntarily filed the gender quota with the scheduled date, i.e., 1st July 2005. Since the deadline was ignored and not adhered to by most of the companies, the Norway Government introduced official legislation that same year. The penal provision was also severe in that the companies would be subjected to penalties for non-compliance as on 1st January 2008 with fines, thereafter with deregistration by the stock exchange, and finally, mandatory dissolution by 2008. The result was that all the companies did comply the requirement by April 2008 in order to avoid their punishment. The number of female directorships was increased by 260% (from 165 to 592 seats) in that period. In 2011, as per Governance Metrics International (GMI) Rating, about 93% companies in Norway had appointed at least one female director. In fact, Norway has the greatest number of female directors, thereby filling 35.6% of the total board seats.

Taking Norway example, many countries, viz. Belgium, Iceland, Italy, Finland, France, Spain and Malaysia have started imposing gender quotas for their corporate boards. The European Commission has been seriously considering imposition of gender quotas across all European nations. On 6th March 2015, Germany has introduced an enactment, whereby it requires some of the Europe's large companies to provide 30% of supervisory seats to women starting from next year.

6.5 DESIRABILITY OF REGULATORY IMPOSITION OF QUOTA SYSTEM

The Norway experience clearly makes us understood that when the requirement for adoption of gender diversity in corporate boards was voluntary and left to the companies to get implemented, the companies did not care to participate in the venture for gender equality and diversity. But, when it was enforced on them as legal requirement to take steps to implement gender diversity and maintain gender balance, the result was quick and remarkable towards gender diversity. Therefore, it is evident that there is a need to impose upon the corporates to take steps in order to maintain gender diversity in boards at least to begin with. Such imposition ultimately enhances sensitivity to build up a culture, which (i) respects diversity, (ii) helps in improving governance and (iii) adds value to the stakeholders. In other words, the route of imposition of legislation for ensuring gender diversity in the boards can be considered as a tool to improve upon corporate governance. Therefore, imposition of law in such case should not be seen as a challenge against the principle of autonomy based on ownership.

6.6 EFFECTIVENESS AND EFFICIENCY OF BOARD'S FUNCTIONING DUE TO GENDER DIVERSITY AND THE STAKEHOLDERS' BENEFITS

According to Jo Iwasaki, Head of Corporate Governance, The Institute of Chartered Accountants, England and Wales "*We believe that diversity is just the starting point to make a board and company effective. It needs to be done efficiently. The goal is to have a meaningful boardroom discussion and rigorous process and diversity should help achieving it—not to meet a number-based target*". Various researchers have studied the performance of the companies vis-à-vis the representation of women in the boards. Though the results of many such research works have remained inconclusive, some of these studies have indicated a positive correlation.

It has been observed by **Catalyst** in its recent report titled: *The Bottom Line: Corporate Performance and Women's Representation on Boards* that Fortune 500 companies having the highest representation of women directors in the boards have achieved significantly higher financial performance than those with the lowest representation of women directors in their boards. The report also mentions on average, companies with 3 or more women board directors performed remarkably stronger than average performance as compared to the companies with lowest or no representation, in three critical financial parameters such as (i) Return on Equity (ROE), (ii) Return on Sales, and (iii) Return on Capital (ROC) invested.

(i) Return on Equity (ROE): On average, companies having highest percentage of women board directors have outperformed the companies with lowest representation by 53%.

(ii) Return on Sales: On average, companies with the highest percentage of women board directors have outperformed the companies with lowest representation by 42%.

(iii) Return on Capital (ROC) invested: On average, companies having highest percentage of women board directors have outperformed the companies with lowest representation by 66%.

McKinsey published a report titled: "*Women Matter-Gender diversity, a corporate performance driver*" in 2007. It compared 89 European listed companies with the best diversity score against their industry average. The financial performance of these companies was measured based on ROE, operating profits earning before interest and tax (EBIT), and stock price growth. As per the results, the more gender diverse companies achieved higher ROE, EBIT, and stock price growth by 11%, 91%, and 36%, respectively, as compared to the least diverse companies.

Diversity Leads in its report published in 2014 also states that companies having higher percentage of women on top management teams and boards perform better in many fronts such as higher sales revenue, greater number of customers, greater market share, higher relative profits, stronger links to clients and customers, retaining best talents, etc.

All the above studies do indicate that women in the corporate boards enhance performance of companies, which ultimately benefits the stakeholders, especially the shareholders in terms of higher profits and dividends and higher allocation of funds for the upliftment of other stakeholders and the society at large.

6.7 OTHER GLOBAL INITIATIVES ON IMPLEMENTATION OF GENDER DIVERSITY

As we are aware, voluntary compliance and disclosure is a good approach adopted by many countries' boards. The corporate governance codes are self-regulatory measures used to promote gender-balanced company boards. If gender diversity in boards gets due recognition while building up the governance structure, it is more likely to influence and bring a cultural change that is sustainable in the long run. It is observed that gender diversity in the corporate governance codes has some influence on the composition of boards in listed companies in Australia and the United Kingdom.

The Australian Securities Exchange (ASX) Corporate Governance Council has implemented a policy that requires all publicly listed companies in Australia to set gender diversity targets. These companies are required to report on their targets and provide explanations if they are not in place. It has been reported that as on April 2012, 14% of directors in the ASX 200 were women as compared to 13.4% in the year 2011.

In the United Kingdom, Davies Report in 2011 called for voluntary targets of 25% women on the Financial Times Stock Exchange (FTSE) 100 company boards by the year 2015. The report mentions that representation of women on FTSE 100 company boards now stands at 23.5%, with 18% women's representation on FTSE 250 company boards.

Since 2009 in the USA, the Securities and Exchange Commission (SEC) has required disclosures from companies designed to assist the investors who are interested in the diversity of company boards. Item 407(c) of Regulation S-K requires the companies to disclose their policy towards implementation of gender diversity while considering nominees for directors. The rule requires disclosure of (i) whether diversity is considered in identifying nominees and, if so how; and (ii) if a company has a policy for considering diversity, then a description of how the policy is implemented and how the company assesses the effectiveness of this policy.

In May 2012, Denmark announced legislative amendments to strike a balance between the need for real progress in increasing the proportion of women in boards and flexibility for companies. The amendments made are mentioned as follows:

(i) The 100 largest companies are required to set a target for the proportion of the under-represented gender in the board that needs to be realistic and ambitious.
(ii) These companies must have a policy that must be presented in the company's annual report for the purpose of increasing the proportion of the under-represented gender at the management level of the companies.
(iii) The companies must report on the status of fulfilling the target set out in the annual report and explain if so, why the companies have failed to achieve the target set.
(iv) Fines can be imposed for non-disclosure of information by companies.

6.8 GAP ANALYSIS OF MEN AND WOMEN IN CORPORATE BOARDS OF DIFFERENT COUNTRIES

In order to examine the gap of men and women's participation in corporate boards of various countries of the world, let us look at some statistics provided in Table 6.1.

TABLE 6.1 Representation of Men and Women in Corporate Boards—Country-wise with Rank and Year of Enactment

Country	Women (%)	Men (%)	Rank	Year of enactment of women quota boards	Type of quota
Norway	35.5	64.5	1	2003	Legislative
Finland	29.9	70.1	2	2004	Legislative
France	29.7	70.3	3	2010	Legislative
Sweden	28.8	71.2	4	2004	Voluntary
Belgium	23.4	76.6	5	2011	Legislative
United Kingdom	22.8	77.2	6	2010	Voluntary
Denmark	21.9	78.1	7	2013	Legislative
Netherland	21	79	8	2012	Legislative
Canada	20.8	79.2	9		
United States	19.2	80.8	10	2010	Voluntary
Australia	19.2	80.8	11	2011	Voluntary
Germany	18.5	81.5	12	2014	Legislative
Spain	18.2	81.8	13	2007	Legislative
Switzerland	17	83	14		
Austria	13	87	15	2011	Legislative
Ireland	10.3	89.7	16	2004	Legislative
Hong Kong	10.2	89.8	17	2011	Voluntary
India	9.5	90.5	18	2013	Legislative
Portugal	7.9	92.1	19	2012	Legislative
Japan	3.1	96.9	20		

Source: Catalyst Census: Women Board Directors (2014), Corporate Women Directors International (2013 and 2014).

It may be observed from Table 6.1 that top five nations with highest percentage of women in corporate boards are European countries. Norway has secured the top position with 35.5% women participation, followed by Finland (29.9%), and then by France (29.7%), whereas Japan has the lowest 3.1% women's participation in board, followed by Portugal (7.9%) and then by India (9.5%) at 18th position. The position will be more clear and vivid if we look at Figure 6.1.

Figure 6.1 depicts the global analysis of gap between men and women representation in corporate boards, wherein Japan is having maximum gap of 93.8%, followed by

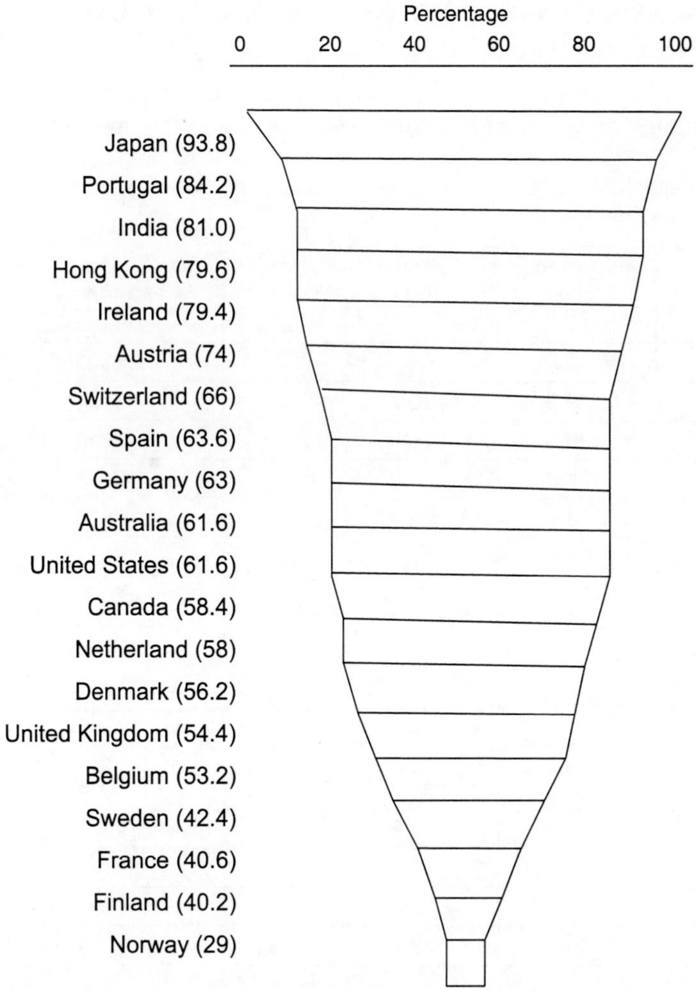

Figure 6.1 Global analysis of gap between men and women representation in corporate boards.

Portugal (84.2%) and then by India (81%). The main reasons for such a huge gender gap in India in women representation in boards of companies are that apart from social barriers in which some women find it difficult to obtain the education and training required to advance into management positions, corporate cultures and environment are also responsible for alienating women. Lack of mentoring, management training and opportunities for career advancement, biased rating and testing systems, lack of consistent monitoring and prevention programmes, lack of support from higher management to address and eliminate gender issues are some of the main issues narrowing the percentage of women in senior positions, and thereby widening gender gap in India.

6.9 STATUS OF GENDER DIVERSITY IN INDIA

India ranks 108 out of 145 countries in the World Economic Forum's Global Gender Gap Index. Iceland, Norway, Finland, Sweden and Ireland top the Index. Even India's neighbours—Bangladesh, China and Sri Lanka—are ranked higher than India. Therefore, gender diversity in the corporate boards in India can be regarded as an ideal example of women empowerment. A lot of discussions are held in various fora for women empowerment in this country, but the reality is that nothing much has progressed in this direction. Naturally, it is an accepted fact that no progress has been made in regard to gender diversity in the boards of Indian companies. There are various factors responsible for the poor status of gender diversity in India as mentioned below:

First, there was hardly any initiative on the part of regulatory authorities to pressurize the corporate houses for inclusion of women directors in their boards until the introduction of the new Companies Act, 2013 and the revised SEBI Guidelines, 2014 (later on replaced by the SEBI (Listing obligation and Disclosure Requirements) Regulations, 2015.

Second, most of the Indian companies did not care for gender diversity and strike a gender balance in their boards' functioning. Many companies have not even opened their account on placing a woman director in their boards. No disclosures have ever been made by these companies nor asked for in this regard.

Third, there has been a total non-committal stance taken by the India Inc. in order to circumvent the spirit of the regulation made by the Companies Act, 2013 and the SEBI Guidelines, 2014 while complying with its words.

A detailed study undertaken by this author on 38 companies listed in BSE Sensex and NSE Nifty reveals that in the year 2013–2014, only 27 board directors are women representing 6% of the total board strength of these companies. These women directors have achieved the board positions, some of them as CEO/Chairpersons, mainly on their own calibre, hard work, qualifications and wide experience. 15 companies out of 38 do not have a woman director in their boards. Therefore, they have failed to comply with the minimum statutory requirement of appointing at least one woman director in the board.

6.10 REGULATORY AUTHORITIES' INITIATIVE TOWARDS GENDER DIVERSITY

Having reviewed corporate governance norms in India, SEBI, the capital market regulator, brought out a consultative paper in the year 2013. It realized that corporate governance must be dynamic, evolving and must change with the changing context and time. Therefore, a company should strive to bring in diversity of thought, experience, knowledge, understanding, perspective, gender and age in the board. It also acknowledged that only a handful of women directors in the board of Indian listed companies expressed the necessity for bringing gender diversity in the board.

Further, the Standing Committee on Finance (2011–12) in its 57th report on the Companies Bill, 2011 also acknowledged the need for aligning gender diversity and corporate governance and expected that provisions of the bill would make the companies more alive to give proper recognition and due importance to the female gender in the realm of corporate governance. This would also reflect the government policy to encourage women's participation in decision-making at every level in the society. However, it is no denying the fact that the regulatory initiative in India has been a landmark step in the direction of gender equality by the legislature.

6.11 PROVISIONS OF THE COMPANIES ACT, 2013 AND SEBI (LISTING OBLIGATION AND DISCLOSURE REQUIREMENTS) REGULATIONS, 2015 ON GENDER DIVERSITY

Section 149 (1) of the Companies Act, 2013 and Rule 3 of the Companies (Appointment and Qualification of Directors) Rules, 2014 provide that (i) every listed company, and (ii) every other public company having (a) paid up share capital of ₹ 100 crore or more, or (b) turnover of ₹ 300 crore or more shall appoint at least one woman director. Provided that a company, which has been incorporated under the Act and is covered under provisions of second proviso to subsection (1) of Section 149 shall comply with such provisions within a period of six months from the date of incorporation. Provided further that any intermittent vacancy of a woman director shall be filled up by the board at the earliest, but not later than immediate next board meeting or three months from the date of such vacancy, whichever is later.

Similarly, Clause 49 II A of the SEBI Listing Agreement replaced by SEBI (Listing Obligations and Disclosure Requirements) Regulations, 2015 (Listing Regulations) also requires that the board of the company shall have an optimum combination of executive and non-executive directors with at least one woman director and not less than 50% of the board of directors comprising non-executive directors.

SEBI has also announced that listed companies failing to appoint at least one woman director in their boards by 31st March would be penalized a minimum of ₹ 50,000 fine. Those companies complying between 1st July and 30th September this year will need to pay ₹ 50,000 and an additional ₹ 1000 per day fine till compliance.

6.12 PRESENT SCENARIO

Although the above regulation is a concrete step taken by the regulatory authorities in order to align India Inc. to demonstrate sensitivity towards diversity and also to improve upon their governance structure, it appears that Indian corporate, in its entirety, has not displayed till now its commitment towards embracing gender diversity to improve its corporate governance. The same view has also been expressed by the Hon'ble Minister of State for Finance during Question Hour Session on 24th April 2015 in Lok Sabha, when he informed the House that as many as 2015 (38%) companies listed on the BSE and 263 (16%) on the NSE did not comply the SEBI directive to appoint at least one woman director in their boards. This also included 32 defaulting PSEs.

While framing the guidelines on inclusion of women directors in the boards, SEBI adopted a prudent approach to ease the process of implementation. It extended the deadline to 31st March 2015 from the initial deadline of 1st October 2014, as it received representations from different market participants, including companies and industry associations mentioning certain practical difficulties in ensuring compliance, seeking clarifications on interpretation of certain provisions.

With SEBI deadline as on 1st April 2015, many listed companies are scrambling to meet the deadline and there has been a spur of activity in appointment of women directors. Since the corporate houses found it difficult to meet deadline to appoint women to their boards, many of them found an easy solution to meet the *letter* of the law, but certainly not the intention or *spirit* of the law by way of giving appointment to promoters' wives and relatives as women directors.

In such situation, when the entire India Inc. is avoiding compliance to regulation in *letter and spirit*, quota system is likely to remain restricted to merely increase minimum number of female seats in the boardroom as a token gesture only. Whatever may be the scenario, imposition of quota system will ensure presence of woman in every board proceedings and serve as a starting point to establish and enhance gender diversity.

Moreover, the legislative mandate of having one woman director in every corporate board is a token introduction in India, whereas the prevailing trend is around 20% or even more in developed countries. The justification of such token introduction can be interpreted in that the legislature has sought to introduce the issue in the first instance and thereafter may, in future, go for higher proportion in favour of gender equality as being followed in many countries. No matter what critics point out against gender diversity, the fact remains that in the long run, Indian legislation is bound to bring a sea change in the boardroom gender bias leading to a better representation of gender in the corporate decision-making process.

Of late, the present situation has improved considerably with effect from 1st April 2015. The survey conducted by the author from annual reports 2015–2016 of different large-cap listed companies revealed that out of 32 such companies, only 2 companies—ONGC and Tata Power—have not appointed any woman director in their boards till date, thereby violating the provisions of the Companies Act and SEBI Regulations. Out of 345 directors in the boards of these companies, only 42 are women directors representing 12% of the total board strength of these companies. The details are available in Table 11.7 (Chapter 11) and Appendix 9.

6.13 REPOSITORY FOR SUSTENANCE OF GENDER DIVERSITY

In order to develop, locate, groom talents, the companies are required to upgrade the HR process, with a view to identifying the excellent potential women for future board positions. Besides, a repository of women directors needs to be in place in order to provide the companies a source of drawing capable, qualified and experienced women for their boards. Some of the *suggestions* towards repository of women directors can be cited as follows:

(i) A repository of women directors similar to the repository of independent directors formed by the bodies, professional institutes and associations in the form of data bank as required by Section 150 of the Companies Act, 2013 can be created by the same bodies, professional institutes and associations for sourcing of talented women in directors' position.

(ii) Database on women from other domain/areas needs to be organized in similar repository framework for sourcing women directors. It may be placed under the aegis of various Chambers of Commerce or any such representative body to ensure sustained quality and reliability in the database.

(iii) Global initiatives that have been undertaken in other countries, viz. Finland, the USA and Malaysia can also be adopted in India. For example, in the year 2012, Finland Chamber of Commerce launched a top level monitoring programme consisting of mentoring, seminars, and networking for women executives.

In the USA, an organization named Women Corporate Directors (WCDs) has been set up in New York as a global membership organization of women directors of public and large privately held companies. The mission of this organization is to become a powerful and trusted community of women corporate directors with a focus on development, diversity of thought and experience, education, new board placement opportunities and an effective dialogue on best practices in corporate governance.

The women directors' sourcing initiative undertaken in Malaysia also supports the listed companies in the search and selection process for qualified women directors for their boards.

All such initiatives and programmes can be implemented in India also by different bodies, industry associations, Chambers of Commerce, professional institutes, and the Ministries of the Government. Such endeavours will definitely contribute to a great extent in the creation of repository and development of human potential of women to future board positions.

6.14 CONCLUSION

Gender diversity is a way of creating diversity without necessarily increasing the board's size. It is in practice in many countries across the globe in order to uplift the standard of corporate governance. Regulatory intervention undertaken by the regulatory authorities is the need of the hour in this country, as the entire India Inc. is yet to display its maturity to improve upon its governance structure. It is expected that the intervention by way of new legal provisions and new guidelines will primarily act as catalyst for changing the culture, realigning mindset and neutralizing the existing bias. The measures taken by the Government of India to promote gender diversity in corporate board is really a positive and revolutionary measure, but nowhere in this Act, the status and qualification of a woman director has been mentioned. However, for ensuring sustainability and enhancing the value proposition, such regulatory framework needs to be dovetailed with generating a skilled pool from where such vacancies will get filled.

CASE STUDY
Gender Diversity and Woman Directors

INTRODUCTION

Gender diversity is the way to create diversity without necessarily increase in the board size. This diversity has been created in the boards of corporate houses all over the world at least a decade ago in order to improve the corporate governance structure and bring in gender equality and balance in the board activities.

GENDER DIVERSITY AND ITS ADOPTION BY OTHER COUNTRIES

Gender diversity has been adopted by many countries. The path finder is Norway in this regard. In 2003 Norway became the first country in the world to impose gender quota in its corporate houses. It required 500 companies, including 175 companies listed on the Oslo Stock Exchange, to raise the proportion of women on their boards to 40%. Initially, the law was meant for voluntary participation and was supposed to be withdrawn had the companies voluntarily filed the gender quota with the scheduled date, i.e. 1st July 2005. Since the deadline was ignored and not adhered to by most of the companies, the Norway Government introduced official legislation that same year. The penal provision was also severe in that the companies would be subjected to penalties for non-compliance as on 1st January 2008 with fines, thereafter with deregistration by the stock exchange and finally mandatory dissolution by 2008. The result was that all the companies did comply with the requirement by April 2008 in order to avoid their punishment. The number of female directorships was increased by 260% (from 165 to 592 seats) in that period. In 2011, as per Governance Metrics International (GMI) Rating, about 93% companies in Norway had appointed at least one female director. In fact Norway has the greatest number of female directors, thereby filling 35.6% of the total board seats.

Many other countries viz. Belgium, Iceland, Italy, Finland, France, Spain and Malaysia have also started imposing gender quotas for their corporate boards. The European Commission has been seriously considering imposition of gender quotas across all European nations. On 6th March 2015, Germany has introduced an enactment whereby it requires some of the Europe's large companies to provide 30% of supervisory seats to women starting from next year.

The Australian Securities Exchange (ASX) Corporate Governance Council has implemented a policy that requires all publicly listed companies in Australia to set gender diversity targets. These companies are required to report on their targets and provide explanations if they are not in place. It has been reported that as on April 2012, 14% of directors in the ASX 200 were women as compared to 13.4% in the year 2011.

In the United Kingdom, Davies Report in 2011 called for voluntary targets of 25% women on the Financial Times Stock Exchange (FTSE) 100 company boards by the year 2015. The report mentions that representation of women on FTSE 100 company boards now stands at 23.5%, with 18% women's representation on FTSE 250 company boards.

Since 2009 in the USA, the Securities and Exchange Commission (SEC) has required disclosures from companies. Item 407(c) of Regulation S-K requires the companies to disclose their policy towards implementation of gender diversity while considering nominees for directors. The rule requires disclosure of (i) whether diversity is considered in identifying nominees and, if so how; and (ii) if a company has a policy for considering diversity, then a description of how the policy is implemented and how the company assesses the effectiveness of this policy.

In May 2012 Denmark announced legislative amendments to strike a balance between the need for real progress in increasing the proportion of women on boards and flexibility for companies.

EFFECTIVENESS AND EFFECIENCY OF BOARD FUNCTIONING DUE TO GENDER DIVERSITY

Efficiency and effectiveness of board functioning due to gender diversity has been published by some renowned management consultancy organisations. It has been observed by **Catalyst** in its recent report titled:

The Bottom Line: Corporate Performance and Women's Representation on Boards that Fortune 500 companies having the highest representation of women directors in the boards have achieved significantly higher financial performance than those with the lowest representation of women directors in their boards. The report also mentions on average, companies with 3 or more women board directors performed remarkably stronger than average performance as compared to the companies with lowest or no representation, in three critical financial parameters such as (i) Return on Equity (ROE), (ii) Return on Sales, and (iii) Return on Capital (ROC) invested.

- *Return on Equity (ROE)*: On average, companies having highest percentage of women board directors have outperformed the companies with lowest representation by 53%.
- *Return on Sales*: On average, companies with the highest percentage of women board directors have outperformed the companies with lowest representation by 42%.
- *Return on Capital (ROC) invested*: On average, companies having highest percentage of women board directors have outperformed the companies with lowest representation by 66%.

McKinsey published a report titled: *"Women Matter-Gender diversity, a corporate performance driver"* in 2007. It compared 89 European listed companies with the best diversity score against their industry average. The financial performance of these companies was measured based on ROE, Operating profits/Earnings before Interest and Tax (EBIT), and Stock price growth. The results found was that the more gender diverse companies achieved higher ROE, EBIT, and Stock price growth by 11%, 91%, and 36% respectively as compared to the least diverse companies.

Diversity Leads in its report published in 2014 also states that companies having higher percentage of women on top management teams and boards perform better in many fronts such as higher sales revenue, greater number of customers, greater market share, higher relative profits, stronger links to clients and customers, retaining best talents etc.

All the above studies do indicate that women in the corporate boards enhance performance of companies which ultimately benefits the stakeholders, especially the shareholders in terms of higher profits and dividends and higher allocation of funds for the upliftment of other stakeholders and the society at large.

GAP ANALYSIS OF MEN AND WOMEN ON CORPORATE BOARDS OF DIFFERENT COUNTRIES

It has been observed that top five nations with highest percentage of women on corporate boards are European countries. Norway has secured the top position with 35.5% women participation, followed by Finland (29.9%), and then by France (29.7%), whereas Japan has the lowest 3.1% women participation on board, followed by Portugal (7.9%) and then by India (9.5%) at 18th position.

The global analysis of gap between men and women representation on corporate boards indicates that whereas Japan has maximum gap of 93.8%, followed by Portugal (84.2%) and then by India (81%). The main reasons for such a huge gender gap in India in women representation on boards of companies are that apart from social barriers in which some women find it difficult to obtain the education and training required to advance into management positions, corporate cultures and environment are also responsible for alienating women. Lack of mentoring, management training and opportunities for career advancement, biased rating and testing systems, lack of consistent monitoring and prevention programmes, lack of support from higher management to address and eliminate gender issues are some of the main issues narrowing the percentage of women in senior positions and thereby widening gender gap in India.

STATUS OF GENDER DIVERSITY IN INDIA

India ranks 108 out of 145 countries in the World Economic Forum's Global gender Gap Index. Iceland, Norway, Finland, Sweden and Ireland top the Index. Even India's neighbours–Bangladesh, China and Sri Lanka–are ranked higher than India. Therefore, gender diversity in the corporate boards in India can be regarded as an ideal example of women empowerment. It is an accepted fact that no progress has been made in regard to gender diversity in the boards of Indian companies. There are various factors responsible for the poor status of gender diversity in India as mentioned below:

- First, there was hardly any initiative on the part of regulatory authorities to pressurise the corporate houses for inclusion of women directors in their boards.
- Second, most of the Indian companies did not care for gender diversity and strike a gender balance in their boards functioning. No disclosures have ever been made by these companies nor asked for in this regard.
- Third, there has been a total non-committal stance taken by the India Inc. in order to circumvent the spirit of the regulation made by the Companies Act, 2013 and the SEBI Guidelines, 2014 while complying with its words.

PROVISIONS OF THE COMPANIES ACT, 2013 AND SEBI (LISTING OBLIGATION AND DISCLOSURE REQUIREMENTS) REGULATIONS, 2015 ON GENDER DIVERSITY

Section 149 (1) of the Companies Act, 2013 and Rule 3 of the Companies (Appointment and Qualification of Directors) Rules 2014 provide that (i) every listed company, and (ii) every other public company having (a) paid up share capital of ₹ 100 crore or more, or (b) turnover of ₹ 300 crore or more shall appoint at least one woman director. Provided that a company, which has been incorporated under the Act and is covered under provisions of second proviso to subsection (1) of Section 149 shall comply with such provisions within a period of six months from the date of incorporation. Provided further that any intermittent vacancy of a woman director shall be filled up by the board at the earliest but not later than immediate next board meeting or three months from the date of such vacancy whichever is later.

Similarly, Clause 49 II A of the SEBI Listing Agreement replaced by SEBI (Listing Obligations and Disclosure Requirements) Regulations 2015 (Listing Regulations) also requires that the board of the company shall have an optimum combination of executive and non-executive directors with at least one women director and not less than 50% of the board of directors comprising non-executive directors.

PRESENT SCENARIO

Although the above regulation is a concrete step taken by the regulatory authorities in order to align India Inc. to demonstrate sensitivity towards diversity and also improve upon their governance structure, however, the corporate India it appears, in its entirety has not displayed till now its commitment towards embracing gender diversity to improve their corporate governance.

With SEBI deadline as on 1st April 2015, many listed companies are scrambling to meet the deadline and there has been a spur of activity in appointment of women directors. Since the corporate houses found it difficult to meet deadline to appoint women to their boards, many of them found an easy solution to meet the letter of the law but certainly not the intention or spirit of the law by way of giving appointment to promoters' wives and relatives as women directors.

Whatever may be the scenario, imposition of quota system will ensure presence of woman in every board proceedings and serve as a starting point to establish and enhance gender diversity. Moreover, the legislative mandate of having one woman director in every corporate board is a token introduction in India, whereas the prevailing trend is around 20% or even more in developed countries. No matter what critics point out against gender diversity the fact remains that in the long run Indian legislation is bound to bring a sea change in the boardroom gender bias leading to a better representation of gender in the corporate decision making process.

Of late, the present situation has improved considerably with effect from 1st April 2015. The survey conducted from annual reports 2015–2016 of different large-cap listed companies revealed that out of 32 such companies, only 2 companies ONGC and TATA Power have not appointed any woman director in their boards till date, thereby violating the provisions of the Companies Act and SEBI Regulations. Out of 345 directors in the boards of these companies, only 42 are women directors representing 12% of the total board strength of these companies.

All global initiatives and programmes can be implemented in India also by different bodies, industry associations, Chambers of Commerce, professional institutes, and the Ministries of the Government. Such endeavours will definitely contribute to a great extent in the creation of repository and development of human potential of women to future board positions.

Questions for Discussion

1. What is gender diversity? What are the initiatives taken by various countries for inclusion of women directors in the board of companies?
2. What is the status of gender diversity in India?
3. What actions have been taken by the Indian Regulatory Authorities for ensuring gender diversity in Indian corporate boards?

Test Your Knowledge

1. What is meant by Gender Diversity? What are the key issues concerning Gender Diversity and inclusion of Women Directors in the corporate board?
2. What is the need for gender diversity in the corporate boards? How different countries have adopted gender diversity in their corporate boards?
3. Why Regulatory Authorities' imposition of Quota System is required? What are the initiatives taken by the regulatory authorities for implementation of gender diversity in the corporate boards?
4. "Effectiveness and efficiency of board's functioning can be increased due to participation of Women Directors in the board proceedings"—Discuss.
5. What advantages are achieved by the stakeholders from gender diversity in the boards of companies?
6. Explain the global initiatives on implementation of Gender Diversity.
7. Discuss the present status of gender diversity in Indian corporate houses.
8. What are the provisions of the Companies Act, 2013 and SEBI Guidelines in favour of the gender diversity?
9. "In the long run Indian legislation is bound to bring a sea change in the board room gender bias leading to a better representation of gender in the corporate decision making process". Discuss.
10. What would be your suggestions for a repository of women directors to provide companies a source of drawing capable, qualified, and experienced women for their boards?
11. "The route of imposition of legislation for ensuring gender diversity in the boards can be considered as a tool to improve upon corporate governance".—Do you agree with this statement? If so, discuss how such imposition enhances the standards of corporate governance in the boards of companies.
12. Write short notes on:
    (a) Gender Diversity in corporate boards
    (b) Gap Analysis of Men and Women in the board of directors of companies
    (c) Status of Gender Diversity in India
    (d) Repository for sustenance of Gender Diversity

CHAPTER 7 Corporate Governance Code The World Over: Various Committees' Reports, A Comparative Study

Learning Objectives	Key Words
After reading this chapter, the readers will be able to understand: ☛ The need for corporate governance code consequent to the several incidents of corporate failures in different countries ☛ The various International Committees' Reports and their recommendations in pursuit of bringing in effective corporate governance practices in the corporate world ☛ The salient features of the reports/recommendations of (i) Cadbury Committee, (ii) Greenbury Committee, (iii) Hampel Committee, (iv) LSE Combined Code, (v) OECD Principles for Corporate Governance, (vi) Blue Ribbon Committee etc. ☛ A comparative study and analysis of the various Committees' Reports/ Codes of best practices ☛ Corporate governance system in vogue in various industrialised countries of the world	☛ Code of Best Practice ☛ External Auditors ☛ Combined Code ☛ Accounting Standards

7.1 INTRODUCTION

In Chapter 3, we have discussed in depth, various conceptual issues on corporate governance. We deliberate in this chapter upon various committees' reports and attempt to make a comparative study of their recommendations on principles and practice of governance in order to assess the trend of corporate governance code world over.

Consequent to the several incidents of corporate failures, many countries in the world had felt the need for corporate governance code. Accordingly, the codes or principles have been drawn upon various aspects of corporate governance, like establishing directors' and CEO's accountability, defining the roles and responsibilities of the board of directors (boards) and stakeholders and setting out the guidelines for more effective and improved performance. By implementing the corporate governance code, the boards are now challenged to bring changes in the operating systems and improve face of relationship between supervisory and executive bodies.

In pursuit of bringing in effective corporate governance practices in the corporate world, the following committees' reports on corporate governance deserve special mention:

- Report of the Cadbury Committee on 'The Financial Aspects of Corporate Governance: The Code of Best Practice';
- Directors' Remuneration, Report of a Study Group chaired by Sir Richard Greenbury;
- Recommendations of The Treadway Commission on Audit Committee;
- Report and Recommendations of The Blue Ribbon Committee on Improving the Effectiveness of Corporate Audit Committees;
- The Hampel Committee on Corporate Governance;
- The Combined Code, Principles of Good Governance and Code of Best Practice, London Stock Exchange;
- The Turnbull Committee Report on 'Internal Control, Guidance for Directors on the Combined Code', The Institute of Chartered Accountants in England and Wales;
- The Organization for Economic Co-operation and Development (OECD) Principles on Corporate Governance;
- The King Committee Recommendations on Corporate Governance in South Africa;
- The Vie'not Report on Corporate Governance in France;
- Report of the Working Party, Centre for European Policy Studies (CEPS) on Guidelines of Good Practice and Governance Standards in the European Union (EU);
- Recommendations of Secretariat Committee on Corporate Governance in Netherlands, for Sound Governance, Supervision and Effective Accountability;
- Report of the Toronto Stock Exchange Committee—Guidelines for Improved Corporate Governance in Canada.

Besides, certain Institutional Shareholders' Committees/Associations, as also the renowned corporates, etc. have issued guidelines on good corporate governance standards and practices to be followed by their investee organizations as also by themselves respectively, and they also deserve to be mentioned hereunder:

- Recommendations of Institutional Shareholders' Committee, London on: (a) The Role and Duties of Directors—A Statement of Best Practice, and (b) The Responsibilities of Institutional Shareholders in the UK—Principles of Good Practice;
- Teachers Insurance and Authority Association—College Retirement Equities Fund (TIAA-CREF)'s guidelines on 'Important Elements of Good Corporate Governance' (USA);
- Pension Investment Association of Canada (PIAC)'s guidelines on the 'General Principles in Corporate Governance Standards';
- General Motors, Washington, 'Guidelines on Significant Corporate Goverance Issues' (1995);

- Atlantic Richfield Company (ARCO), Los Angeles' Corporate Governance Principles (1995);
- 'Statement of General Business Principles'—Royal Dutch/Shell Group;
- 'Statement of Corporate Governance'—British Telecom (BT).

The contents of this chapter are divided into three sections:

- Constitution of some of the most renowned committees and salient features of their recommendations on corporate governance principles, guidelines and best practices;
- A comparative study and an analysis of these recommendations; and
- Corporate governance system in various industrially developed countries of the world.

7.2 CONSTITUTION OF SOME RENOWNED COMMITTEES AND SALIENT FEATURES OF THEIR REPORTS/RECOMMENDATIONS ON CORPORATE GOVERNANCE

Out of many Committees' reports/recommendations on the issue, we select reports and recommendations of the following renowned international Committees for our deliberation:

- Cadbury Committee (1992)
- Greenbury Committee (1995)
- Hampel Committee (1998)
- LSE Combined Code (1998)
- OECD Principles for Corporate Governance (1999)
- Blue Ribbon Committee (1999)

It may be mentioned that the reports of the other committees have not been considered here because their recommendations are found to be almost in line with recommendations of the above-mentioned Committees.

7.2.1 The Cadbury Committee Report (1992)

Consequent upon a number of scams and failures in the corporate sector in the late 1980s and the early 1990s the Cadbury Committee was set up in May 1991 by the Financial Reporting Council, the London Stock Exchange, and the accountancy profession to address the financial aspects of corporate governance. The Committee issued a draft report for public comment on 27th May 1992. Its final report was published on 1st December 1992. The contents of the report are segregated into three parts:

(a) reviewing the structure and responsibilities of boards of directors and recommending a Code of Best Practice;

(b) considering the roles of auditors and addressing a number of recommendations to the accountancy profession; and

(c) dealing with the rights and responsibilities of shareholders.

Further, the Code of Best Practice is divided into four sections:

First, concerning the role of the board of directors, duties of a board and its composition; second, dealing with the role of the outside non-executive directors; third, concerning the executive directors and their remuneration; and fourth, addressing questions of financial reporting and financial controls.

The major recommendations of the report defining a code of best practice for companies are summarised below:

(a) All listed companies should comply with the code in order to strengthen accountability of the board to the shareholders and that the stock exchanges should require the annual report of all listed companies to include a statement about the extent of compliance. In case of non-compliance, the board should provide reasons for its non-compliance.

(b) The Committee favoured separation of the offices of chairman and chief executive to prevent excessive concentration of power in boardrooms. Where the offices are combined, there should be a strong group of non-executive directors with an appointed leader to counter balance the power of chief executive.

(c) It promoted the power and influence of non-executive directors who should be independent and of high calibre so that their views would carry weight in board discussions. They should be in the best position to monitor the performance of the company and of the executive directors without any potential conflicts of interest.

(d) It recommended majority/whole membership of non-executive directors in the nomination committee, audit committee and remuneration committee to play major roles in improving the standards of corporate governance.

(e) It also recommended that directors' total emoluments and those of the chairman and highest paid directors should be disclosed in the company's annual report, including break-up between salary and performance related pay.

(f) It emphasized the responsibility of the board to present a balanced and understandable assessment of their company's position in reporting of financial statements for the sake of 'true and fair' financial reporting.

(g) It called for a professional and objective relationship between the boards and the auditors. It also recommended for a regular rotation of audit partners to prevent unhealthy relationship between auditors and the management. It also recommended for disclosure of payments to the auditors for non-audit services to the company.

(h) It also encouraged the institutional investors to make greater use of their voting rights and take active interest in the board functioning.

7.2.2 The Greenbury Committee Report (1995)

In January 1995, the Confederation of British Industry (CBI) organized a Committee to study executive pay issues and provided the recommendations for governance reform. On July 17, 1995, Sir Richard Greenbury, chairman of the Committee, released a report concerning director compensation at publicly traded British companies entitled 'Directors' Remuneration—Report of a Study Group chaired by Sir Richard Greenbury'.

The contents of the Code of Best Practice and its recommendations are segregated into four parts:

(a) The Remuneration Committee;
(b) Disclosure and Approval Provisions;
(c) Remuneration Policy; and
(d) Service Contract and Compensation.

The code contains the following recommendations:

(i) The board of directors should set up remuneration committee of the non-executive directors to determine the company's policy on executive remuneration and specific remuneration packages for each of the executive directors, including pension rights and any compensation payments.

(ii) The chairman of the remuneration committee should be accountable directly to the shareholders.

(iii) The remuneration committee should consist exclusively of non-executive directors with no personal financial interest (except being shareholders), no potential conflicts of interest (arising out of cross-directorships), and no day-to-day involvement in business affairs.

(iv) The board should determine the remuneration of the non-executive directors, including members of the remuneration committee.

(v) The chairman of the committee should attend the company's annual general meeting to answer shareholders' questions on directors' remuneration.

(vi) The remuneration committee reports should be included as a separate section in the annual report and should fully disclose all elements of pay for all company directors, including base pay, incentive, bonus plans and benefits. The report should also explain why the company is not in compliance with the code of best practice, if any.

(vii) The remuneration policy should attract, retain and motivate directors of the required quality in the long-term interests of the company.

(viii) Executive pay packages should link rewards to performance and should 'align the interests of directors and shareholders in promoting the company's progress'. Management pay levels should be sensitive to employee wage levels.

(ix) The shareholders should be able to vote on all new long-term incentive plans, including share option schemes and on existing pay packages that have 'attracted controversy'.

(x) Stock options should be granted in phases based on 'challenging performance criteria'. They 'should never be issued at a discount', and should not be exercisable for three years from the date of grant. The directors should be encouraged to own meaningful levels of stock. Stock options in the newly privatized companies should not be granted for at least six months after the initial offering.

(xi) Contract terms for directors should be disclosed. Terms in excess of one year maximum up to two years are discouraged. If service contracts of over one year's notice are needed to recruit key directors, the notice period should be reduced to one year after an initial period.

(xii) While compensating directors for departure on early termination of their contracts, account should be taken of the reasons for departure. A tough stance on compensation for poor performance should be taken. Consideration should be given to paying compensation in installments to avail an opportunity to reduce or stop them when the concerned director finds a new employment.

7.2.3 The Hampel Committee on Corporate Governance (1998)

The Hampel Committee started work in November 1995 with a view to assessing progress of implementation of Cadbury and Greenbury recommendations.

The sponsors of the Hampel Committee were the London Stock Exchange (LSE), the Confederation of British Industry (CBI), the Institute of Directors (IOD), the Consultative Committee of Accountancy Bodies (CCAB), the National Association of Pension Funds (NAPF), and the Association of British Insurers (ABI).

The Committee submitted its final report in June 1998.

The final report of the Committee containing recommendations is divided into seven chapters:

(a) Corporate governance
(b) Principles of corporate governance
(c) The role of directors
(d) Directors' remuneration
(e) The role of shareholders
(f) Accountability and audit
(g) Summary of conclusions and recommendations.

Some of the most important recommendations of the Hampel Committee are summarized below:

(i) Companies should include in their annual reports a narrative account of how they apply the broad principles of corporate governance, and the companies should also explain the circumstances justifying departure from best practice.

(ii) Every listed company should be headed by an effective board, which should lead and control the company.

(iii) There are two key tasks at the top of every public company—the running of the board and the executive responsibility for running of the company's business. Separation of the roles of chairman and chief executive is preferred. However, a decision to combine these roles in one individual should be publicly explained.

(iv) The board should include a balance of executive directors and non-executive directors (including independent non-executives) such that no individual or small group of individuals can dominate the board's decision-making. To be effective, non-executive directors need to make up at least one-third of the membership of the board.

(v) There should be a formal and transparent procedure for the appointment of new directors to the board. Companies should set up nomination committees to make recommendations to the boards on all new board appointments. The remuneration committee should be made up of independent non-executive directors.

(vi) All directors should be required to submit themselves for re-election at regular intervals, at least every three years.

(vii) The majority of non-executive directors should be independent, and boards should disclose in the annual report which of the non-executive directors are considered to be independent.

(viii) Boards should consider introducing procedures for assessing their own collective performance and that of individual directors.

(ix) Whether or not the roles of chairman and chief executive officer are combined, a senior non-executive director should be identified in the annual report, to whom concerns can be conveyed.

(x) Levels of remuneration should be sufficient to attract and retain the directors, needed to run the company successfully. The component parts of remuneration should be structured so as to link rewards to corporate and individual performance.

(xi) Companies should establish a formal and transparent procedure for developing policy on executive remuneration and for fixing the remuneration package of individual executive directors. The company's annual report should contain a statement of remuneration policy and details of the remuneration of each director.

(xii) When evaluating companies' governance arrangements, particularly those relating to board structure and composition, institutional investors and their advisers should give due weight to all relevant factors drawn to their attention.

(xiii) The board should present a balanced and understandable assessment of the company's position and prospects.

(xiv) The board should maintain a sound system of internal control to safeguard shareholders' investment and the company's assets. The directors should report on the company's system for internal control.

(xv) The external auditors should independently report to shareholders in accordance with statutory and professional requirements and independently assure the board on the discharge of its responsibilities (financial reporting, internal control) in accordance with professional guidance.

(xvi) Each company should establish an audit committee of at least three non-executive directors, at least two of them independent. The audit committee should keep under review the overall financial relationship between the company and its auditors, to ensure a balance between the maintenance of objectivity and value for money.

(xvii) The bodies concerned should consider reducing from 10%, the limit on the proportion of total income, which an audit firm may earn from one audit client.

(xviii) The requirement on directors to include a 'going concern' statement in the annual report should be retained.

7.2.4 The Combined Code, Principles of Good Governance and Code of Best Practice, London Stock Exchange (1998)

Consequent to the submission of Cadbury Report and Greenbury Recommendations, there was a substantial pressure from the investing public, institutions and the legislators on the London Stock Exchange (LSE) to implement the voluntary codes into compulsory provisions through listing requirements for the companies in the UK. A Committee was set up by the LSE thereafter, whose terms of remit were to: (i) examine the reports and recommendations of Cadbury and Greenbury, and (ii) suggest to LSE a set of principles of good governance and codes of best practice for the UK companies finally for implementation.

The Combined Code included a number of changes made by the LSE, with the Committee's agreement. Accordingly, the LSE introduced a requirement on listed companies to make a disclosure statement in two parts. In the first part of the statement, the company would be required to report on how it has applied the principles in the Combined Code. In the second part of the statement, the company would be required either to confirm that it has complied with the code provisions or where it has not, it has to provide explanation for non-compliance. The Committee's report envisaged that the companies should be ready to explain their governance policies, including any circumstances justifying departure from the best practice.

There are two sections of the Combined Code. Section 1 contains the corporate governance principles and code provisions applicable to all listed companies incorporated in the UK. Section 2 contains principles and code provisions applicable to institutional shareholders with regard to their voting, dialogue with companies, and evaluation of a company's governance arrangements. Section 1 of the Combined Code is divided into four parts:

(a) Directors: (i) The board, (ii) Chairman and CEO, (iii) Board balance, (iv) Supply of information, (v) Appointments of the board, and (vi) Re-election;

(b) Directors' remuneration: (i) The level and make up of remuneration, (ii) Procedure, and (iii) Disclosure;

(c) Relations with shareholders: (i) Dialogue with institutional shareholders, and (ii) Constructive use of the AGM;

(d) Accountability and audit: (i) Financial reporting, (ii) Internal control, and (iii) Audit committee and auditors.

Section 2 deals with the institutional investors: (i) Shareholders voting, (ii) Dialogue with companies, and (iii) Evaluation of governance disclosures. Besides, two schedules (A and B) concerning provisions on the design of performance related remuneration and provisions on the items to be included in the remuneration report have been annexed to the Committee's report.

Some essential items of the Combined Code of best practice enunciated by the committee are mentioned hereunder:

(i) The board should meet regularly. It should have a formal schedule of matters specifically reserved to it for decision. The board should take independent professional advice if necessary, at the company's expense. All directors should bring an independent judgement to bear on issues of strategy, performance, resources, including key appointments, and standards of conduct. Every director should receive appropriate training on the first occasion when he or she is appointed to the board of a listed company, and subsequently as necessary.

(ii) A decision to combine the posts of chairman and CEO in one person should be publicly justified. Whether the posts are held by different people or by the same person, there should be a strong and independent non-executive element on the board, with a recognized senior member other than the chairman, to whom concerns can be conveyed. They should be identified in the annual report.

(iii) The board should include non-executive directors of sufficient calibre and number for their views to carry significant weight in the board's decisions. The non-executive directors should comprise not less than one-third of the board. The majority of non-executive directors should be independent of management and free from any business or other relationship, which could materially interfere with the exercise of their independent judgement. They should be identified in the annual report.

(iv) Unless the board is small, a nomination committee should be established to make recommendations to the board on all new board appointments. A majority of the members of this committee should be non-executive directors, and the chairman should be either the chairman of the board or a non-executive director. They should be identified in the annual report.

(v) The non-executive directors should be appointed for specified terms. The removal of a director and re-appointment should not be automatic. All directors should be subject to election by shareholders at the first opportunity after their appointment, and to re-election thereafter at intervals of no more than three years. The names of the directors submitted for election or re-election should be accompanied by sufficient biographical details to enable shareholders to take an informed decision.

(vi) Board of directors should set up remuneration committee comprising exclusively of independent non-executive directors to make recommendations to the board on the company's framework of executive remuneration and its cost, and to determine on specific remuneration packages for each of the executive directors. The members of the committee should be listed each year in the board's remuneration report to the shareholders. The board itself or the shareholders should fix up the remuneration of the non-executive directors including members of the remuneration committee. The committee should consult the chairman and/or CEO about their proposals relating to the remuneration of other executive directors. The chairman of the board should ensure that the company maintains contact with its principal shareholders on remuneration affair.

(vii) The remuneration committee should provide the packages needed to attract, retain and motivate directors of the quality but should avoid paying more than necessary. The committee should be aware, what comparable companies are paying and should take account of relative performance but they should use such comparisons with caution. They should be sensitive to the wider scene, including pay and employment conditions elsewhere in the group while determining annual salary increases. The performance-related elements of remuneration should form a significant proportion of the total remuneration package of executive directors so as to give these directors keen incentives to perform at the highest levels. Executive share options should not be offered at a discount.

(viii) There is a strong case for setting notice or contract period at one year or less. The remuneration committees should consider what compensation commitments (including pension contributions) their directors' contracts of service would entail in the case of early termination. The broad aim should be to avoid rewarding poor performance while dealing fairly with cases where departure is not due to poor performance and to take a tough stand on reducing compensation to reflect departing directors' obligation to mitigate the loss.

(ix) The board should report to the shareholders each year on remuneration. The report should set out the company's policy on executive directors' remuneration. The shareholders should be invited specifically to approve all new long-term incentive schemes.

(x) Companies should count all the proxy votes and should indicate the level of proxies lodged on each resolution and the balance for and against the resolution. Companies should propose a separate resolution at the AGM on each substantially separate Issue and should propose a resolution at the AGM relating to the report and accounts. The chairman should ensure presence of the chairmen of audit, remuneration and nomination committees to answer questions at the AGM. Notice of the AGM and all related papers should be sent to the shareholders at least 20 working days before the meeting.

(xi) The directors should be responsible for preparing the accounts and there should be auditor's statement about their reporting responsibilities. They should present a balanced and understandable assessment reports and they also should report that the business is a going concern.

(xii) The directors should annually conduct a review of the effectiveness of the group's system of internal control and should report to the shareholders. The review should cover all controls including financial, operational and compliance controls and risk management.

(xiii) The board should establish an audit committee consisting of at least three directors, all non-executives with clear terms of reference of its authority and duties. A majority of the members should be independent non-executive directors. The duties of the committee should include keeping under review the scope and results of the audit, its cost effectiveness and the independence and objectivity of the auditors.

7.2.5 The Organization for Economic Co-operation and Development (OECD) Principles on Corporate Governance (1999)

Corporate governance mechanisms differ among countries. The governance mechanism of each country is shaped by its political, economic and social history as also by its legal framework. Despite the differences in shareholder philosophies across countries, good governance mechanisms need to be encouraged among all corporate and non-corporate entities.

While the multilateral organizations like World Bank and Asian Development Bank have evinced a keen interest in the subject of corporate governance, an effective and intellectual lead has been given by the Organization for Economic Co-operation and Development (OECD) in evolving a set of cogent principles of corporate governance which are internationally recognized to serve as good benchmarks. Being an inter-governmental organization of the industrially developed nations of the world, OECD has come out with a set of clearly defined principles, which are useful to all countries irrespective of their stages of development, legal systems, institutional framework, and traditions.

The main objective of the OECD in drafting these principles is to assist both its member governments as also non-member governments to bring about suitable improvements in their legal, institutional and regulatory framework for facilitating good corporate governance regimes. The OECD principles not only incorporate codes to protect interests of the shareholders but also give due importance to safeguarding interests of the stakeholders like employees, creditors, suppliers, customers, environment etc. as OECD believes that effective co-operation of all the stakeholders is essential for creating wealth for the shareholders and building financially sound corporates.

The OECD principles of corporate governance were released in late 1999, and these have been accepted as an international benchmark. These standards were evolved in recognition of growing awareness of the importance of good corporate governance and the demands from the OECD country ministries in 1998 to develop a set of standards and guidelines. The OECD principles represent the first major international effort in evolving core elements of good corporate governance regimes.

The OECD corporate governance principles have covered five major areas:

(a) Rights of shareholders—dealing with (i) market for takeovers, and (ii) role of institutional investors;

(b) Equitable treatment of shareholders—dealing with (i) voting by custodians, (ii) hassles in voting, (iii) insider trading, and (iv) disclosure by directors;

(c) Role of stakeholders;

(d) Disclosures and transparency—dealing with (i) financial health, (ii) company objectives, (iii) major share ownership and voting rights, (iv) risk factors, and (v) quality of financial reporting;

(e) Responsibilities of the board.

The principles of corporate governance framed by OECD and its recommendations are summarized below:

(i) The majority of the board members must be independent who can contribute sufficiently to the decision-making of the board.

(ii) The board should ensure a formal and transparent board nomination process. Service on too many boards can interfere with performance. The members of the board should ensure that they enjoy legitimacy and confidence in the eyes of the shareholders.

(iii) A sufficient number of board members should not be employed by the company and should not be closely related to the company or its management through significant economic, family or either ties. However, this does not prevent shareholders from being the members.

(iv) The board members should be required to disclose any material interests in transactions or matters affecting the corporation.

(v) The board should fulfill certain few functions, viz. (a) reviewing and guiding corporate strategy, risk policy, annual budget and business plans, setting performance objectives, monitoring corporate performance and overseeing major capital expenditures and acquisitions; (b) selecting, compensating and monitoring key executives; (c) reviewing key executive and board remuneration; (d) monitoring and managing potential conflicts of interest of management, board members and shareholders; (e) ensuring the integrity of corporation's accounting and financial reporting systems; (f) monitoring the effectiveness of the governance practices; and (g) overseeing the process of disclosure and communications.

(vi) Companies are generally expected to disclose sufficient information on the remuneration of board members and key executives (either individually or in the aggregate) for investors to properly assess the costs and benefits of remuneration plans and the contribution of incentive schemes, such as stock option schemes, to performance.

(vii) Board should consider establishing an audit committee, a remuneration committee and a nomination committee with a minimum number to be composed entirely of non-executive members.

(viii) The corporate governance framework should protect the shareholders' rights. Shareholders should have the opportunity to participate effectively and vote in general meetings and they should have access to information about rules, including voting procedures that govern general shareholders' meetings. They should receive sufficient and timely information about the date, location and agenda of general meetings. They should have the opportunity to ask questions to the board and place items on agenda. They should be able to vote in person or in absentia, with equal weight for the two. Shareholders, including institutional investors, should consider the costs and benefits of exercising their voting rights.

(ix) Processes and procedures for general shareholders' meetings should allow for equal treatment of all shareholders.

(x) An independent auditor should conduct an annual audit in order to provide an external and objective assurance on the way in which financial statements have been prepared and presented.

(xi) The corporate governance framework should recognize the rights of stakeholders as established by law and encourage active co-operation between corporations and stakeholders in creating wealth, jobs, and the sustainability of financially sound enterprises. The framework should also permit performance-enhancing mechanisms for stakeholder communication.

(xii) Information should be prepared, audited and disclosed in accordance with high standards of accounting, financial, and non-financial disclosures, and audit. The principles should support the development of high quality internationally recognized standards, which should improve the compatibility of information between countries.

(xiii) A key responsibility of the board is to ensure that appropriate systems of control are in place, in particular, systems for monitoring risk, financial control, and compliance with the law.

(xiv) The corporate governance framework should ensure that timely and accurate disclosure is made on all material matters including the financial situation, performance, ownership and governance of the company.

(xv) Disclosure should include material information on the financial and operating results of the company, and material foreseeable risk factors. Capital structures and arrangements that enable certain shareholders to obtain a degree of control disproportionate to their equity ownership should be disclosed. Managers must disclose any material interests in transactions or matters affecting the corporation. Companies should be encouraged to report on how they apply relevant corporate governance principles in practice.

7.2.6 The Blue Ribbon Committee Report on Effectiveness of Corporate Audit Committees (1999)

The Blue Ribbon Committee, co-chaired by John Whitehead and Ira Millstein was set up on October 6,1998, by the Securities and Exchange Commission (SEC), the New York Stock Exchange (NYSE), and the National Association of Securities Dealers (NASD) in response to the concerns expressed by Arthur Levitt, Chairman the Security and Exchange Commission (SEC) about the financial reporting process.

The Committee submitted their final report in early 1999.

The Committee's ten recommendations are explained under seven segments:

- Independence of the audit committee;
- Financial literacy of the audit committee members;
- Audit committee structure and process;
- Audit committee relationships with management including the internal auditor and with the outside auditors;
- Practical improvements to audit committee oversight and enhancing the outside auditors' communication with the audit committee;
- Instituting audit committee disclosure;
- Mandating auditor interim financial review.

Besides, Blue Ribbon Committee also outlined five 'Guiding Principles' for best practices on the following issues:

(a) The audit committee's key role in monitoring the other component parts of the audit process;

(b) Independent communication and information flow between the audit committee and the internal auditor;

(c) Independent communication and information flow between the audit committee and the outside auditors;

(d) Candid discussions with management, the internal auditor, and outside auditors regarding issues implicating judgment and impacting quality;

(e) Diligent and knowledgeable audit committee membership.

The recommendations of the Blue Ribbon Panel are summarized below:

(i) The audit committee should be comprised solely of independent directors.

(ii) It should be comprised of a minimum of three directors, each of who is financially literate or becomes financially literate within a reasonable period of time after the appointment. Further, at least one member of the audit committee should have accounting or related financial management expertise.

(iii) The audit committee of each listed company should: (a) adopt a formal written charter approved by the full board of directors specifying the committee's audit responsibilities, including its structure, processes and membership requirements, and (b) review and reassess the adequacy of the audit committee charter on an annual basis.

(iv) It shall disclose in the company's proxy statement for its annual meeting of shareholders whether the audit committee has adopted a formal written charter, and if so, whether the audit committee satisfied its responsibilities during the prior year in compliance with its charter.

(v) The audit committee charter shall specify that the outside auditor is ultimately accountable to the board of directors and the audit committee. The audit committee, as representative of shareholders shall have the ultimate authority and responsibility to propose appointment and replacement of the outside auditor.

(vi) The charter shall specify that the audit committee is responsible for ensuring its receipt of a formal written statement from the outside auditor delineating all relationships between the auditor and the company.

(vii) Generally Accepted Auditing Standards (GAAS) require that a company's outside auditor discusses with the audit committee, the auditor's judgements about the quality, not just the acceptability, of the company's accounting principles as applied in its financial reporting.

(viii) The audit committee chairman shall publish a report in the corporate governance report certifying that (a) management has reviewed the audited financial statements with the audit committee, (b) the outside auditors have discussed with the audit committee the outside auditors' judgements of the quality of accounting principles, (c) the members of the audit committee have discussed among themselves without management or the outside auditor's presence, the information disclosed to the audit committee and (d) the audit committee believes that the company's financial statements are fairly presented in conformity with Generally Accepted Accounting Principles (GAAP) in all material respects.

Comments on the recommendations of various Committees

The **Cadbury Report** is primarily concerned with the boardroom and accounting aspects of governance rather than the operation of the capital market and the role of takeovers in disciplining managements. The report places particular emphasis on the need for fair and accurate reporting of a company's progress to its shareholders, which is the responsibility of the board, and is subject to attestation by its auditors. It is no denial of the fact that although in some respects the recommendations of the Cadbury Committee seem unduly timid, debatable and the proposed voluntary code of conduct lacks effective sanctions and the proposed changes in legislation are minor, nevertheless, the committee has made useful proposals for improving the system of corporate governance in Britain. Companies quoted on the London Stock Exchange (LSE) are now required to report annually to shareholders on their conformity with the code. The institutional investors are increasingly taking note of areas of non-compliance. The code, in fact, is now seen as a 'floor' rather than as a 'ceiling' and the better companies now seek to set best practice in key areas. The work of the Cadbury Committee has laid a foundation on which others have built. This process has proceeded in three directions: first, the further development of codes of practice, second, the exploration of wider governance issues, and third, the drive for better governance practice from enlightened company directors.

The companies listed on the London Stock Exchange have been asked to report performance against the code's recommendations but, like Cadbury Code, the **Greenbury Codes** compliance is not mandatory. The Greenbury Report has unleashed a range of concerns and emotions, which is greater than the impact of Cadbury. It is still too early to judge the long-term effect of these recommendations, but they have begun to force greater openness into the issue of remuneration and have brought greater accountability in time. In fact, the Greenbury Report has forced the debate on 'rewards' into the public arena and that 'doubtful practices' are now subject to the challenge from the shareholders.

The **Hampel Committee** tried to address the positive aspect of self-regulation. It felt the need for board of directors to enhance the prosperity of the business over time and to take into account the relevant interests of stakeholders in the company's business. There is some dilution of the Cadbury emphasis on separating the roles of chairman and chief executive, the independence of non-executive directors, and recognition of the dubiousness of paying them partially in company shares. The Committee prescribed that 'box ticking' as required by Cadbury and Greenbury should be dropped in favour of a 'narrative account' of how the Hampel principles are applied. However, it is a matter of doubt whether Hampel has advanced the work of Cadbury and Greenbury or merely made it easier to avoid specific accountability. Although like Cadbury, Hampel Committee saw a need to use governance to build ' business prosperity' but did not address the question of how it would be done or how the different stakeholders in the company would be taken into account.

The **Combined Code** of best practice and governance principles prescribed by the committee are mostly a consolidation of the works of the Cadbury, Greenbury Committees as well as the works of their own. They have retained the substance of the two earlier codes except in those few cases where the committee has taken a different view from the predecessors. For example, the committee has taken a different view from the Greenbury Committee in regard to the status of the remuneration committee, and the compensation payable to an executive director on loss of office. Thereafter, the UK Government and the London Stock Exchange (LSE) made a sweeping revision in the Combined Code with effect from 1st November 2003. The UK Government had also proposed company law reforms in this regard.

The **OECD** has made the governance principles non-binding on the member countries in view of diversity among the countries. It is argued that the OECD principles may not be highly suitable for some of the Asian countries, as these have been drafted keeping in view the situation of the OECD countries. This argument seems to be invalid in view of the explicit recognition of the factors by OECD before formulating its governance principles. The OECD principles did not rely on the template of any particular country. They have been framed by picking up the best elements of good corporate governance as noted in different countries having varied historical and cultural backgrounds, different legal systems, institutional frameworks and traditions. So adoption of the OECD principles would be in the best interests of all countries which are serious in trying to integrate themselves in the emerging competitive global economy as most of the member countries have given effect to their commitments under the World Trade Organization (WTO) agreements. The process of convergence in corporate governance has gathered momentum due to growing international integration of financial markets. As the inflow of direct and portfolio foreign investment have increased, there has been substantial demand to address the concerns and requirements of foreign investors in regard to corporate governance standards and practices. Companies, which are highly transparent and attach considerable importance to good corporate governance standards as enunciated in the OECD principles, should invariably command a high premium in the capital markets.

The OECD established the study into the role of corporate governance in enhancing economic competitiveness. Its most convincing finding is that globalizing markets will increase pressure on companies to be outstanding in order to attract and retain the financial and intellectual capital needed to compete in the long term. Transparent and motivating corporate governance practices are seen as a major factor in attracting the support needed to prosper in conditions of increasing uncertainty. The report recommends that each company should experiment and adopt to find its own best practice, subject to agreed minimum standards and to universal rules for accounting.

The OECD study, has in fact, integrated best practice from all major economies. It advocates shareholder value as being the accepted objective of business. It also recognizes the need to be responsive to the demands and expectations of other stakeholders. A convergence between the US philosophy of maximizing shareholder value over the long run and the societal focus of German and Japanese companies is expected to occur as globalization forces the companies to compete without any protection. The report also expects the governments to have a distinct and important responsibility in providing a regulatory framework and thereby allowing investors and corporations to adapt corporate governance practices in rapidly changing circumstances. It recommends further work to encourage the member nations to establish an enabling regulatory framework to support the improvement of corporate governance. Such work might produce a public policy document, a code of best practice and a set of reporting standards.

The **Blue Ribbon Committee** was set up at that point of time when many US companies resorted to improper and unlawful practices in financial reporting to their shareholders, viz. misuse of acquisition accounting, inappropriate overstatement of future earnings, premature revenue recognition, improper deferral of expenses, misuse of the concept of materiality etc. Therefore, the sponsors of the committee felt an urgent need to strengthen the role of the audit committees with pragmatic and progressive recommendations which would ensure the functioning of more effective and efficient audit committees and more transparent and reliable financial reporting process. The committee's recommendations are built on the two essential factors. First, an audit committee with actual practices and overall performance that reflect the professionalism embodied by the full board of which it is a part, and second, a legal regulatory and self-regulatory framework that emphasizes disclosure and transparency and accountability. The committee views the recommendations as an integrated set of objectives, which must be adopted in entirety, in order to accomplish the intended results. To this end, the Blue Ribbon Committee in the USA has contributed remarkably in establishing the best concept of audit committees.

7.3 A COMPARATIVE STUDY AND ANALYSIS OF THE VARIOUS COMMITTEES' REPORTS/CODES OF BEST PRACTICES

In this section, we attempt a comparative study of the above-mentioned committees' reports and analyze their recommendations/codes of best practices to find out the depth and coverage of their recommendations for corporate governance.

The comparative study and analysis of these recommendations can be grouped under three broad heads:

(a) ***Areas of governance where various Committees expressed same or similar views, e.g.,***

- Selection of the directors
- Age limit of the directors
- Duties, responsibility and accountability to the shareholders
- Orientation and training of directors
- Access to information and consultation
- Board meetings and matters to be reserved for board decision
- General meetings

(b) ***Areas of governance where various Committees extended their views further to the Cadbury Recommendations/codes, e.g.,***

- Composition and size of the board of directors
- Tenure of directors
- Board's performance evaluation
- Chairman and CEO
- Remuneration of directors, service contract and compensation
- Audit committee

- Remuneration committee
- Nomination committee
- Auditors
- Stakeholders
- Accounting standards
- Financial reporting
- Disclosure and transparency

(c) ***Areas of governance where various Committees hold totally different views, e.g.,***

- Independent directors
- Disclosure of directors' remuneration
- Shareholders' rights and shareholders' voting
- Shareholders' involvement in determining directors remuneration
- Evaluation of governance disclosure
- Internal control and internal audit

Some of the governance issues where various Committees have expressed same or **similar views** may be iterated here.

Most of the Committees did recommend a formal and transparent procedure for **selection of directors** with requisite skill, knowledge and personal attributes best suited to the role expected of them.

The Committees were of the opinion that there should be no fixed rules for the length of service or **age limit** of the directors but the boards should be vigilant against the risk of their becoming less efficient with advancing age.

So far as the **duties, responsibility** and **accountability** to **the shareholders** are concerned, the Committees recommended that the boards should present a balanced and understandable assessment of the company's position and prospects. The directors should act in good faith in the interests of the companies and to exercise care and skill in all their review and monitoring functions.

The Committees were also in favour of regular **orientation and training** of all directors on appointment and even thereafter and they should have free **access to information and consultation** or independent professional advice at the company's expense.

In regard to the **board meetings and matters to be reserved for board decision**, the Committees recommended that board should meet regularly and the board should have formal schedule of matters specifically reserved to it for decision.

Regarding the **general meetings** of shareholders the Committees prescribed that the board should use the AGM to communicate with private investors and encourage their participation. The companies should count all proxy votes and announce the result on each resolution after it has dealt with on a show of hands.

Let us now highlight some of the areas of governance where various Committees have **extended views** further to the Cadbury Code.

As far as the **'composition and size'** of the board is concerned, Cadbury Code mentions minimum requirement of three non-executive directors, of whom one may be the chairman of the company, provided he is not CEO and two non-executive directors should be independent. Both Hampel Committee and Combined Code (LSE) agree to this but prescribe minimum membership to be 1/3rd of the board. As per the revised Combined Code w.e.f. 1st November 2003, the minimum membership of non-executive directors in the board has been 50%.

In regard to **'tenure'** of executive director's service both Hampel Committee, and Combined Code (LSE) agree with the Cadbury Code (i.e. 3 years), though Hampel and Combined Code suggest for reduction of contract period to one year or less. As per revised Combined Code w.e.f. 1st November 2003, tenure of non-executive directors in excess of six years should not be viewed as 'extraordinary'.

Regarding **'board's performance evaluation'** no other Committee except Combined Code (LSE) have dealt with this specifically. The Combined Code recommends that boards should undertake a formal and rigorous annual evaluation of their own performance and that of the main board committees as well as the individual directors. The annual report should explain how such evaluations have been conducted. Non-executive directors led by the senior independent director should be responsible for performance evaluation of the chairman, taking into account the views of directors.

As regards **'chairman and CEO'** issue, the Cadbury Code clearly advocates (although not firmly) in favour of segregation of the post of chairman and CEO at the helm of affairs in order to ensure balance of power and authority. The code also requires immediate installation of a senior strong independent director on the board where the chairman and CEO is the same person. Both Hampel Committee and Combined Code (LSE), while agreeing to the Cadbury Code, also prescribe that the company should justify and explain in the annual report, its decision to combine the role of chairman and CEO in one person in case the company decides so. Moreover, irrespective of whatever decision taken, the company must install a senior independent director on the board to whom the concerns can be conveyed. The chairman, CEO and the senior independent director should be identified in the annual report.

While agreeing with the Cadbury Code in regard to **'remuneration of directors'** recommended by a remuneration committee, the Greenbury Committee prescribes in detail, the responsibilities of the remuneration committee for directors' remuneration including performance related payment, annual bonus, stock options, pension schemes, service contract, compensation in case of early retirement due to reasons other than poor performance, payment of compensation in installments, tax procedure on stock option etc. Hampel Committee agrees to the recommendation of Greenbury but gives a 'caution' in the use of 'inter- company comparisons and remuneration surveys in setting levels of directors' remuneration (as suggested by Greenbury) in view of the risk involved, resulting in a upward ratchet of remuneration levels with no corresponding improvement in performance.

As far as the constitution of **'audit committee'** is concerned, the Cadbury Code requires the board to set up an audit committee of at least three non-executive directors (not necessarily independent) as a sub-committee of the main board. They should have a written terms of reference, should meet at least twice a year and should discuss with the external auditors at least once a year without the presence of executive board members. The external auditor, head of internal audit and director (finance) should attend audit committee meetings. The chairman of the committee should answer audit questions at the AGM. While agreeing with the Cadbury Code, the Hampel Committee has gone a step forward. It requires at least two out of three non-executive directors to be independent and also requires only the board chairman to decide on who should answer audit questions in AGM, although chairman, audit committee may be present there. Again the Combined Code (LSE) has revised its code w.e.f. 1st November 2003, whereby it requires an audit committee to be exclusively comprised of independent non-executive directors—at least two in case of small companies and three in other case. On the other, Blue Ribbon Committee prescribes that an audit committee should be comprised solely of independent directors—at least three members, each one of whom must be financially literate and at least one of them to have accounting or financial management expertise. They should meet at least four times a year.

Regarding constitution of the **'remuneration committee'** and the **'nomination committee'** whereas the Cadbury Committee recommends wholly or mainly non-executive directors to be in these committees whose membership should be disclosed in the annual report, Greenbury prescribes that non-executive board members in these committees should be independent and the chairmen of the respective committees should answer all questions regarding directors' remuneration and nomination in the AGM. Hampel, while agreeing with Cadbury Code and Greenbury recommendations, prescribes that only the board chairman should decide on who should answer these questions in AGM. Again the Combined Code (LSE) has revised its code w.e.f. 1st November 2003, whereby it requires a remuneration committee and nomination committee to be exclusively comprised of independent non-executive directors—at least two in case of small companies in each such committee and three in other cases and the chairman of the board should be the chairman of the nomination committee. The OECD principles on corporate governance prescribes that all members of the nomination committee should be the non-executive directors.

Among many recommendations of the Cadbury Committee on the **'auditors',** one of which is that the fees paid to the auditors for non-audit work should be fully disclosed in the annual report. No ceiling on the fees for non-audit work from a single client has been prescribed by Cadbury. While agreeing with the Cadbury, Hampel goes a step forward in suggesting that the bodies concerned should consider reducing from 10%, the limit on the proportion of total income, which an audit firm may earn from one audit client.

No other Committees except OECD have recommended specifically on the **'stakeholders'**. The OECD recommends that the corporate governance framework should recognize the rights of stakeholders and encourage active co-operation between companies and stakeholders in creating wealth, jobs etc.

While Cadbury Code recommends for the development and use of **'accounting standards'** which would enable auditors in exercising their professional judgement, the OECD advocates further for a high quality internationally recognized standards to improve the compatibility of information between the countries.

As regards the issue of **'financial reporting'** the Cadbury Code recommends that the directors should explain in a statement their responsibility for preparing the accounts next to the auditor's statement about their reporting responsibilities. The directors should also report that the business is a going concern. Hampel, while fully agreeing with Cadbury Code, goes a step forward in suggesting that the companies should also include in the Directors' Responsibility Statement, a narrative account of how they have applied the corporate governance principles.

In so far as the issue of **'disclosure and transparency'** is concerned, the Cadbury Code is specific which states that all listed companies in the UK should include a statement about the compliance of the code, with full explanations in case of any areas of non-compliance. In this respect, the Combined Code vide its revised code w.e.f. 1st November 2003 requires the board to give adequate disclosure of the board's role in providing entrepreneurial leadership. The OECD, on the other hand, requires the board to disclose in the annual report, the capital structures and arrangement, which have enabled certain shareholders to obtain a degree of control disproportionate to their equity ownership.

Besides, certain areas of governance where various Committees have expressed totally **different views** from one another have been noticed. Some examples may be cited here.

First, the Cadbury, Greenbury and Hampel—all these Committees did approach corporate governance from the different perspectives. Both the Cadbury and Greenbury reports were responses to things which were perceived to have gone wrong—corporate failures in the first case, unjustified compensation packages in the listed companies in the second. Understandably, both were concerned on the negative aspects of corporate governance and therefore, both concentrated largely on the prevention of abuse. On the other, Hampel was concerned with the positive contribution which good corporate governance can make.

Second, the experience of the UK companies on Cadbury and Greenbury Codes has been rather different. They believe that the codes have been treated as sets of prescriptive rules. The shareholders would be interested only on whether the letter of the rule has been complied with—yes or no. A 'yes' would receive a tick; thereby a 'box ticking' approach has been encouraged. Hampel has strongly objected to this approach and rightly so, because 'box ticking' takes no account of the diversity of circumstances and experience among the companies, and within the same company over time. It can be seized on as an easier option than the diligent pursuit of corporate governance objectives. It would then be easy for lazy or unscrupulous directors or shareholders to arrange matters so that the letter of every governance rule is complied with but not the substance. So, 'box ticking' as suggested by Cadbury, seems to be unfair and nor likely to be efficient in preventing abuse. Nevertheless, the true safeguard for good corporate governance lies in the application of informed and independent judgement by experienced and qualified individuals—executive and non-executive directors, shareholders and auditors. That is why Hampel has prescribed for a listing requirement whereby the board has to make a statement in the annual report how they have applied the governance principles and complied with the code to justify any significant variances. At the same time shareholders should evaluate them with flexibility with due regard to the company's circumstance.

Third, on the issue of 'independent directors', the Cadbury requires the non-executive directors to be independent of management and be free from any business or other relationship. A good practice for non-executive directors would be not to participate in share option and pension schemes of the company they serve. The Hampel, on the other, does not find any objection to paying remuneration to a non-executive director in company's shares without however, making it an universal practice.

Fourth, in regard to the issue of 'disclosure of directors' remuneration', the Cadbury Code clearly requires the board of directors to disclose in the annual report, full and clear information of total emoluments of directors, chairman, and of the highest paid UK director including pension contribution and stock options, separate figure for salary and performance related payments, and the basis of measurement. But the Greenbury Code requires the remuneration committee to disclose directors' remuneration in the form of a report (to be annexed to the annual report) to the shareholders directly. It also prescribes inclusion of the company's remuneration policy, in addition to the above information. The Hampel does not agree with the Greenbury Code, and holds the view in support of Cadbury that the report on directors remuneration should be in the name of the board only, rather than of the remuneration committee (being a recommendatory body) as this is a matter for the board (as decision-making authority). The Combined Code also holds a different view from the Greenbury relating to the status of the remuneration committee, and the compensation payable to an executive director on loss of office.

Fifth, in regard to the issue of 'shareholders' rights and shareholders' voting', the Cadbury Code prescribes, among other things, that the institutional shareholders should encourage regular, systematic contact at senior executive level in the company to exchange dialogue and information of strategy, performance, board membership and quality of management. However, the Hampel does not recommend any such dialogue between companies and institutional shareholders, rather it advises that institutional shareholders should remain free to abstain from such dialogue with the company possibly the reason is that there is a risk that close contact between individual companies and shareholders may lead to different shareholders receiving unequal information. In particular, price sensitive information maybe given to individual shareholders as inside information, depriving them of the legal right to trade the shares or benefiting them unduly. Therefore, companies should have a policy on investor communication, ideally communicated to those outside the company, with whom it deals, stating how the company handles price sensitive information.

Sixth, The Greenbury Code recommends shareholders' approval of all new long-term incentive plans including share option schemes, existing pay package etc. It also recommends for shareholders' approval for the Remuneration Report. On the contrary, Hampel though advocates shareholders' approval for new long term incentive plans, yet does not favour obliging companies to seek shareholders' approval for the remuneration report.

Last, The Cadbury Code recommends the directors to report on the 'effectiveness' of the company's system of internal control. While agreeing in principle with the Cadbury Recommendation, the Hampel advises that the word 'effectiveness', as recommended by Cadbury, should be dropped. This is because and rightly so that both the directors and auditors may find it practically difficult in confirming the effectiveness of the company's internal control system in the context of public reporting. They may be even exposed to legal liability if an unintentional misstatement or loss of any kind is found to have occurred thereafter. In this context, the Turnbull Committee has exclusively dealt with this issue and given detailed guidelines, which no other code has given so far.

7.4 CORPORATE GOVERNANCE SYSTEM IN VARIOUS INDUSTRIALIZED COUNTRIES OF THE WORLD

In the light of the recommendations of the above-mentioned Committees, many industrially developed countries of the world have implemented most of the recommendations of governance in their corporates. In this section, we select four such countries, viz. the USA, the UK, Germany and Japan to understand the governance systems in vogue in their corporates. The reasons for selection of these countries for the purpose of the current study are threefold.

First, the USA, the UK, Germany and Japan are the most advanced and industrially developed countries of the world where almost all the renowned companies were set up. Therefore, the governance systems in vogue in these companies are clear reflection of the governance systems adopted by these countries.

Second, the corporate governance systems of these four countries are age-old. The regulations of the US Securities and Exchange Commission (SEC) set up in 1934 are the heart of US corporate governance. The audit committees were set up in the US corporates in 1978 as per listing requirements of New York Stock Exchange (NYSE). The British Companies Act, 1948 set the tone of corporate governance in the UK. Since 16th century (1697) the London Stock Exchange (LSE) was active in regulating this system. Many developments thereafter, viz. introduction of Institutional Shareholders' Committee (1991), publishing of practical guide for non-executive directors (PRONED 1987) and guidelines for directors (1990), followed by implementation of the recommendations of various Committees (Cadbury, Greenbury and Hampel) for improved governance by the UK government, and LSE, enriched the governance system in the UK corporates. Germany has had a governance system in vogue in all companies since 18th century. Japan had developed a unique corporate governance system for their corporates in the years following World War II. Right from that time, the 'commercial code' has been governing the formulation, structure and conduct of Japanese companies.

Third, these countries adopted governance systems in their companies, which are different from one another, viz. the USA introduced a 'single-tier majority outside directors' board', the UK introduced a 'single-tier majority inside directors' board' with non-executive chairman, Germany on the other hand, set up a 'two-tier board system', and Japan introduced a 'single-tier majority of all inside directors' board' with employee directors. Other countries have simply followed suit and adopted the same governance systems. For example, India adopted UK model of corporate governance system and France adopted both Anglo-American model and German model of corporate governance for their companies to choose from any of these models.

Accordingly, some of the features of corporate governance in vogue in these countries are explained in Appendix 5.

7.5 CONCLUDING OBSERVATION

It is observed from the deliberations of the corporate governance system prevalent in various industrially developed countries of the world that no two governance systems of two countries are exactly the same and similar to each other. This is because of the fact that different countries have adopted different corporate governance systems based on their practices, culture, ideologies, legal systems, institutional framework, regulatory and macroeconomic circumstances causing an ultimate difference in functioning of the boards—their structures, styles, processes, roles and activities etc. in their companies. Despite the fact that there is a need for further reforms in the corporate governance system in these countries, there is hardly any doubt on the tremendous positive impact created by the recommendations of the various renowned Committees on companies situated all over the world in implementing a reasonably good corporate governance system best suited to them. With the revision in the Company Law and economic legislation and pressure from inside and outside, the companies all over the world have now started adopting the corporate governance principles gradually, and practicing them effectively for their better standing, creating wealth for the shareholders, providing benefits for the stakeholders and bringing upliftment of the society.

CASE STUDY

Auditor finds gaps in McLeod Books

INTRODUCTION

The auditor of India's largest bulk tea producer, McLeod Russel India Ltd. (MRIL) has raised questions about the company's ability to continue as a "going concern" unless lenders agree to a financial restructuring of its short-term borrowing and the promoters manage to sell more assets.

Picking holes in the annual financial statement published by McLeod Russel, promoted by the B.M. Khaitan family, the independent auditor Deloitte Haskins and Sells LLP stated that the current liabilities of the company exceeded current assets by ₹ 1435.66 crore for the financial year ending March 2019. It added that the company had failed to pay up financial and statutory liabilities during the same period.

McLeod Russel declared a profit after tax amounting to ₹ 38.82 crore on a consolidated basis in 2018–19 compared with ₹ 219.16 crore a year ago, backed by the sale of 16 tea gardens in India and shares in two companies in Rwanda. On the contrary, Deloitte said the bottom-line was understated by ₹ 1821.71 crore.

The "adverse opinion" expressed by Deloitte has come a day after Price Waterhouse and Co. LLP (PWC), Chartered Accountants, quit Eveready Industries Ltd., another Khaitan family company, as an independent auditor. It is interesting to note that Deloitte is now under fire from the Government of India for allegedly bungling its fiduciary duty as an independent auditor of disgraced infrastructure lender IL&FS Financial Services Ltd.

If a company fails to remain a going concern, it is indicative of an acute liquidity crisis and questions its ability to remain in the business in the long run. It is often taken as a precursor to bankruptcy.

THE MESS

The company management reported that current borrowing of the company went up to ₹ 1425.79 crore from ₹ 522.86 crore as it had to support the ailing company of the promoter group. Consequently, the annual finance cost went up to ₹ 337.57 crore from ₹ 180.37 crore in 2017–18.

It is widely believed that McLeod and Eveready had to bail out troubled infrastructure company McNally Bharat Engineering Co. Ltd. Incidentally Deloitte is the auditor of McNally where it has raised questions about the company's ability to continue as "going concern".

During the year 2018–19, McLeod Russel had extended advances totalling to ₹ 841.75 crore to certain promoter group companies as capital advances. The promoter group companies to whom such advances were given have substantially lent these onward to another promoter group company. Out of these total capital advances, ₹ 775.75 crore was converted into intercorporate deposits (ICDs) as on March 31, 2019, Deloitte noted.

As on March 31, 2019, ICDs worth ₹ 1744.68 crore given to promoter group companies and other companies, including ₹ 775.75 crore and ₹ 77.03 crore interest accrued on such ICDs (net of provision of ₹ 85.09 crore), respectively, are doubtful recoveries considering the financial condition of the promoter group companies and the other companies to whom these ICDs were given.

Deloitte stated "However, the parent company MRIL has not made any provision for the outstanding amounts recorded as ICDs and interest accrued thereon. Consequently, the non-current portion of loans and interest accrued thereon are overstated and loss for the year is understated by ₹ 1821.71 crore".

McNally, in its financial results for the year 2018–19, had disclosed that it deferred repayment and converted the advance received from certain companies under the same promoter group worth ₹ 985.92 crore into interest-free long term loans/ICDs repayable in five equated annual instalments commencing after 20 years. Moreover, it booked a fair value gain of ₹ 874.82 crore from those transactions in the balance sheet.

The auditor stated that ICDs outstanding at the end of the last fiscal exceeded the limits on lending under Section 186 of the Companies Act, 2013, by ₹ 611.56 crore for which shareholders' approval was not obtained.

MANAGEMENT'S VIEWS

The company stated that promoter group level restructuring is in progress in order to monetise assets to meet the liabilities of those companies, including these ICDs. The management believes that the outstanding dues will be recovered/adjusted and therefore no further provision is necessary at this stage.

The company also argued that the financial performance has been adversely affected due to the downturn in the tea industry and operational issues largely due to the increased cost of production. However, the company could mitigate such increased costs through several cost reduction measures as well as an increase in the selling prices.

The company also mentioned that it had sold the assets of certain tea estates during the year to repay the financial obligations. In addition to the cash flows from the sale of assets and cost reduction measures, the company had to seek short term borrowings to fund various promoter group companies to enable them to meet their financial obligations.

The company also stated that all these have resulted in higher finance costs during the year and an increase in current liabilities. There have been working capital constraints and external factors beyond the control of the company.

Moreover, the liquidity issues faced by the company are now being discussed with the lenders. One of the risk mitigation options being considered by the company is to convert short term loans from lenders into long term loans in order to ease the company's liquidity constraints together with further sale of assets of certain tea estates. The company stated it is hopeful that the proposal of the company for refinancing would be favourably considered.

The company stated that its management is confident to improve its operational efficiency by way of various cost reduction measures. With the lenders' support and other measures the company would be able to generate sufficient cash flows by way of profitable operations, improvement in its net working capital position so that it would be possible to discharge its short term and long term liabilities. Hence, the financial statements of the company have been prepared on a "going concern" basis.

Questions for Discussion

1. What is the auditor's observation on the books of accounts prepared by McLeod for the financial year 2018–19 ?
2. What are the management views and arguments against the qualifications given by the independent auditor Deloitte in their audit report on financial statements of McLeod?
3. Is there any lapse in exercising the proper corporate governance by the board of directors of McLeod Russel?

Test Your Knowledge

1. List out the names of various international committees' reports for implementing effective corporate governance practices in the corporate world?
2. What are the major recommendations of the report of Cadbury Committee in 1992 defining a code of best practice for companies?
3. What are the major recommendations of the report of Greenbury Committee in 1995 containing the code of best practice in respect of 'Directors' remuneration'?
4. Explain in brief, some of the most important recommendations of the Hampel Committee (1998) on corporate governance.
5. Discuss some of the essential items of the Combined Code of best practice enunciated by the Committee appointed by London Stock Exchange in 1998.
6. "The OECD principles of corporate governance have been accepted as an international benchmark and they represent the first major international effort in evolving core elements of good corporate governance regimes"—Discuss some of the principles of corporate governance framed by OECD (1999) in light of the above statement.

7. "Blue Ribbon Committee (1999) outlined five Guiding Principles for best practice in corporates"—What are these principles? Explain some of the most important recommendations of the Committee.
8. Examine critically the recommendations made by the various International Committees highlighting the (a) areas of governance where various Committees expressed same or similar views, (b) areas of governance where various Committees extended their views further to the Cadbury Recommendations/codes, and (c) areas of governance where various Committees hold totally different views.
9. Discuss briefly some of the features of corporate governance system in vogue in various industrialised countries of the world viz. the USA, the UK, Germany and Japan.

CHAPTER 8 Corporate Governance in India: National Committees' Recommendations

Learning Objectives	Key Words
After reading this chapter, the readers will be able to understand: • Corporate governance system in India vis-a-vis the USA, the UK, Germany and Japan • The various National Committees' Reports and their recommendations in pursuit of bringing in effective corporate governance practices in the corporate world • The salient features of the reports/recommendations of (i) CII Code of Desirable Corporate Governance, (ii) Kumar Mangalam Birla Committee, (iii) RBI Report of the Advisory Group on Corporate Governance, (iv) Naresh Chandra Committee, (v) N.R. Narayana Murthy Committee, and (vi) J. J. Irani Committee • The impact of International Committee recommendations and enactments on corporate governance standards in India	• Cash Flow Rights • Control Rights • Directors' Report • Postal Ballot • Stock Options • Credit Rating

8.1 INTRODUCTION

In this chapter, we discuss the corporate governance system in India which has been greatly influenced by the governance systems of the industrially developed countries during this period, especially after the economic reforms since 1991 and onwards. Therefore, our objectives in this chapter are two-fold:

(a) To make a comparative study on corporate governance system adopted in India vis-à-vis that adopted in some industrialized countries with a view to finding out:

  (i) whether and to what extent Indian companies are lagging behind, and

  (ii) whether the existing codes of corporate governance and guidelines are adequate;

(b) To identify the areas wherein further improvement in terms of governance is necessary.

8.2 CORPORATE GOVERNANCE SYSTEM IN INDIA VIS-À-VIS THE USA, THE UK, GERMANY AND JAPAN

8.2.1 Governance Issues

The corporate governance in India can be analyzed under the following major heads.

(a) Ownership system—(i) cash flow rights, and (ii) control rights
(b) Governance rules
(c) Role of governance
(d) Market for corporate control
(e) Governance system

8.2.2 Analysis

(a) So far as **ownership system** (*cash flow rights*) is concerned, majority of the equity shareholdings of Indian corporates (around 40%) rests with the family controlled large business groups (i.e. insider system). The institutional shareholders hold the majority stake in companies in the USA, the UK, and Japan (outsider system). In Germany, the cash flow rights are strongly controlled by commercial banks. Small shareholders in India hold negligible proportion of the total equity holding (about 10%) like that of the UK and Germany. There is significant and major cross shareholdings among the Indian companies of large business groups as that of Germany and Japan. In India, the *'Control Rights'* are mostly exercised by the promoter-directors under the 'family controlled business' regime unlike in other countries, viz. the USA, and the UK where the companies are managed and controlled by the professional managers.

(b) So far as **governance rules** are concerned unlike Germany, where two-tier board system is in vogue, India follows a single-tier majority inside board system like the UK, and Japan whereas the USA follows a single-tier majority outside the board system. In India, the audit committee has been instituted in the listed companies, which is in line with the rules followed by the corporates of other countries, viz., the USA, the UK, and Japan. The legal rule regarding protection of shareholders' rights in Indian companies is strong and stands at the same footing as in the USA, the UK, and Japan. Like the UK, the 'proxy solicitation by mail' for general meetings is not compulsory in the Indian companies whereas in the USA, this is compulsory because the US companies have to ensure at least 50% of the total outside shares to be voted in the AGMs.

(c) So far as the **role of governance** is concerned, India stands in much lower position as compared to the other countries. There is a clear dominance of 'internal capital markets' over 'external capital markets', expropriation of wealth and funds from a company to others to the detriment of interest of small individual shareholders, ineffective monitoring of financial institutions, dismal performance of state owned organizations, lack of transparency in financial reporting leading to corruption etc. in the Indian companies unlike that of other industrialized countries, viz., the USA, the UK, Japan, and Germany which follow much better, higher standard and quality of corporate governance.

(d) In regard to **market for corporate control** unlike the USA and the UK, the capital market and stock exchanges in India are not strong enough or developed due to high level of concentration of control rights and dominance of internal capital market system. Even the takeover market is not developed in India as compared to these countries for check and removal of inefficient management. Role of Indian banks in the corporate governance system is either non-existent or insignificant as compared to the commercial banks in Germany.

(e) India, through its economic reforms, enacted by its political structure in early 1990s followed by certain measures by the regulators, is fast catching up the other industrialized countries for upliftment of the standards of **governance system** in its companies.

In this context, the quality of corporate governance institutions in India relative to some developed countries is presented in Table 8.1.

It is evident from Table 8.1 that India is very much at par with the developed countries with respect to the rights of minority investors and creditors, anti directors' rights and oppressed minority mechanisms. India is at par with the UK with regard to creditor rights and has more protective laws in the books than either the USA, Japan and Germany. However, this favourable ranking of Indian governance system seems to be inconsistent with the general perception that in India the minority investor rights and creditor rights are weak. Besides, the concentration of ownership and control in India has been mainly in response to the existence of weak minority investor rights. However, the fact remains that while important investor protection legislations are in paper, their implementation leaves much to be desired relative to international best practices. What is clearly lacking is in the area of implementation of governance regulations, which is evident from the low score that India has with respect to the rule of law, corruption, risk of expropriation and weak accounting standards.

8.3 CORPORATE GOVERNANCE CODE: NATIONAL COMMITTEES' RECOMMENDATIONS

In Chapter 2 (Subsection 2.2.3) while discussing the reforms processes in India under Anglo-American system, we also discussed about the formation of various committees and submission of their reports on corporate governance during the period 1998–2005. In this subsection, an attempt is made to present various recommendations made by these committees in order to understand the standards of governance desired by them for implementation in Indian corporate houses.

8.3.1 CII Code of Desirable Corporate Governance (1998)

For the first time in the history of corporate governance in India, the Confederation of Indian Industry (CII) framed a voluntary code of corporate governance for the listed companies, which is known as CII Code of desirable corporate governance.

The main recommendations of the Code are summarized below:

(a) Any listed company with a turnover of ₹ 1000 million and above should have professionally competent and acclaimed non-executive directors, who should

TABLE 8.1 A Comparative Assessment of the Quality of Corporate Governance Institutions in India vis-à-vis Major Developed Countries in the 1990s.

Country	Legal origin	Legal variables					Variables representing shareholder protection*							Variables representing creditor rights**				
		Efficiency of the judicial system (1)	*Rule of law (2)*	*Corruption (3)*	*Risk of expropriation (4)*	*Accounting standards (Rating) (5)*	*One-share, one vote*	*Proxy by mail allowed*	*Shares not blocked before meeting*	*Cumulative voting*	*Oppressed minorities mechanism*	*Anti-director rights (6)*	*Mandatory dividend*	*Restrictions for going into reorganization*	*No automatic stay on secured assets*	*Secured creditors first*	*Management does not stay in reorganizations*	*Creditors rights (7)*
US	English origin	10.0	10.0	8.63	9.98	71	1	1	1	1	1	5	0	0	0	1	0	1
UK	English origin	10.0	8.57	9.10	9.71	78	0	1	1	0	1	5	0	1	1	1	1	4
Germany	German origin	9.0	9.23	8.93	9.90	62	0	0	0	0	0	1	0	1	1	1	0	3
Japan	German origin	10.0	8.98	8.52	9.67	65	1	0	1	1	1	4	0	0	0	1	1	2
India	English origin	8.0	4.17	4.58	7.75	57	1	0	1	1	1	5	0	1	1	1	1	4

Source: Sarker, J. and Sarker, S., "Corporate Governance Reforms and Corporate Sector Development in India", in Reed, D. and Mukherjee, S. (Eds.) "Corporate Governance, Economic Reforms, and Development", Oxford University Press, New Delhi, 2004.

Note:

1. Scale from 0 to 10, with lower scores showing lower efficiency levels.
2. Scale from 0 to 10, with lower scores for less tradition of law and order.
3. Scale from 0 to 10, with lower scores for higher levels of corruption.
4. Scale from 0 to 10, with lower scores for higher risks.
5. The score is given on a scale ranging from 0 to 100, with higher scores showing more stringent accounting standards.
6. The index ranges from 0 to 6, with higher values signifying stronger 'Anti-Director Rights'.
7. The index ranges from 0 to 4, with higher values signifying stronger 'Creditor Rights'.

* Except for 'Anti-Director Rights', a value of 1 shows the presence of the relevant feature (i.e. implying that investor protection is in the law.)

** Except for 'Creditor Rights', a value of 1 shows the presence of the relevant feature (i.e. implying that creditor protection is in the law.)

constitute: (i) at least 30% of the board, if the chairman of the company is a non-executive director, or (ii) at least 50% of the board if the chairman and managing director is the same person.

(b) For the non-executive directors to play an important role in corporate decision-making and maximising long-term shareholder value, they need to: (i) become active participants in boards, not passive advisors, (ii) have clearly defined responsibilities within the board, and (iii) know how to read a balance sheet, profit and loss account, cash flow statements and financial ratios, and have some knowledge of various company laws.

(c) No single person should hold directorships in more than 10 listed companies. This ceiling excludes directorship in subsidiaries (where the group has over 50% equity stake) or associate companies (where the group has over 25% but no more than 50% equity stake).

(d) The full board should meet a minimum of six times a year, preferably at an interval of two months, and each meeting should have agenda items that require at least half-a-days discussion.

(e) While reappointing the members of the board, companies should keep attendance record of the concerned directors. If a director has not been present (absent with or without leave) for 50% or more meetings, then this should be explicitly stated in the resolution that is put to vote. As a general rule, one should not reappoint any non-executive director who has not had the time to attend even one-half of the meetings.

(f) Various key information must be reported to, and placed before the board, viz., annual budgets, quarterly results, internal audit reports, show cause, demand and prosecution notices received, fatal accidents and pollution problem, default in payment of principal and interest to the creditors, inter corporate deposits, joint venture, foreign exchange exposures.

(g) Listed companies with either a turnover of over ₹ 1000 million or a paid up capital of ₹ 200 million, whichever is less, should set up audit committees within 2 years. The committee should consist of at least three members, who should have adequate knowledge of finance, accounts, and basic elements of company law. The committees should provide effective supervision of the financial reporting process. The audit committees should periodically interact with statutory auditors and internal auditors to ascertain the quality and veracity of the company's accounts as well as the capability of the auditors themselves.

(h) Consolidation of group accounts should be optional. If a company chooses to voluntarily consolidate, it should not be necessary to annex the accounts of its subsidiary companies in its annual report.

(i) Major Indian stock exchanges should insist on a compliance certificate, signed by the CEO and the CFO which would clearly state that: (a) the management is responsible for the preparation, integrity and fair presentation of the financial statements and other information in the annual report, and the company will continue in business in the course of the following year, (b) the accounting policies and principles conform to the standard practice, and where they do not, full disclosure has been made regarding any material departures, (c) the board has overseen the company's system of internal accounting and administrative control systems either through its audit committee or directly.

(j) In order to secure better effort from non-executive directors, the companies should: (a) pay a commission over and above the sitting fees for the use of the professional inputs. The present commission of 1% of net profit (if the company has a managing director), or 3% (if there is no managing director) is sufficient, (b) consider offering stock options, so as to relate rewards to performance. An appropriate mix of the commission and stock option can align a non-executive director towards keeping an eye on short-term profits as well as long-term shareholder value.

(k) For audit committees to discharge their fiduciary responsibilities with due diligence, management must ensure that members of the committee have full access to financial data of the company, its subsidiary and associated companies, including data on contingent liabilities, debt exposure, current liabilities, loans and investments.

(l) The listed companies should have in place a strong internal audit department, or an external auditor to do internal audits without which any audit committee will be toothless.

(m) Under 'Additional Shareholders' Information' the listed public companies should give data on: (a) high and low monthly averages of share prices in all the stock exchanges where the company is listed for the reporting year, (b) statement on value added, which is the total income minus the cost of all inputs and administrative expenses, (c) greater detail on business segments or divisions up to 10% of turnover, giving share in sales revenue, share in contribution, review of operations, analysis of the market and future prospects.

(n) If any company goes to more than one credit rating agency, it must divulge in the prospectus and issue documents regarding the rating of all the agencies that did such an exercise. These must be given in a tabular format that shows where the company stands relative to higher and lower ranking.

(o) Companies that default in fixed deposits should not be permitted to: (a) accept further deposits and make inter-corporate loans or investments until the default is made good, (b) declare dividends until the default is made good.

(p) It would be desirable for Foreign Investors (FIs) as pure creditors to rewrite their covenants to eliminate having nominee directors except: (a) in the event of serious and systematic debt fault, and (b) in case of the debt company not providing, six-monthly or quarterly operational data to the FI(s) concerned. They should take a policy decision to withdraw nominee directors from the boards of companies where they have little or no debt exposure and where their individual shareholding is 5% or less or total FI holding is under 10%.

8.3.2 Kumar Mangalam Birla Committee (2000)

Another Committee named as K.M. Birla Committee was set up by SEBI in the year 2000. In fact, this Committee's recommendation culminated in the introduction of Clause 49 of the Listing Agreement to be complied with by all listed companies. Practically most of the recommendations were accepted and included by SEBI in its new Clause 49 of the Listing Agreement in 2000.

The main recommendations of the Committee are:

(a) The board of a company should have an optimum combination of executive and non-executive directors with not less than 50% of the board comprising the non-executive directors. In case, a company has a non-executive chairman, at least one-third of board should be comprised of independent directors and in case, a company has an executive chairman, at least half of the board should be independent.

(b) Independent directors are directors who apart from receiving director's remuneration do not have any other material pecuniary relationship or transaction with the company, its promoters, management or subsidiaries, which in the judgement of the board may affect their independence of judgement.

(c) A director should not be a member in more than ten committees or act as chairman of more than five committees across all companies in which he is a director. It should be a mandatory annual requirement for every director to inform the company about the committee positions he occupies in other companies and notify changes as and when they take place.

(d) The disclosures should be made in the section on corporate governance of the annual report: (i) all elements of remuneration package of all the directors, i.e., salary, benefits, bonus, stock options, pension etc., (ii) details of fixed component and performance linked incentives along with the performance criteria, (iii) service contracts, notice period, severance fees, (iv) stock option details, if any, and whether issued at a discount as well as the period over which accrued and exercisable.

(e) In case of appointment of a new director or re-appointment of a director, the shareholders must be provided with the information: (i) a brief resume of the director, (ii) nature of his experience in specific functional areas, and (iii) names of companies in which the person also holds the directorship and the membership of committees of the board.

(f) Board meetings should be held at least 4 times in a year, with a maximum time gap of 4 months between any two meetings. The minimum information (specified by the Committee in Annexure A of the report) should be available to the board such as: annual operating plans and budgets, capital budgets, manpower and overhead budgets, quarterly results, internal audit reports, show cause, demand and prosecution notices received from revenue authorities, fatal accidents and pollution problem, default in payment of principal and interest to the creditors and inter corporate deposits, any issue involving public or product liability claims of a substantial nature including any judgement or order which may have either passed strictures on the conduct of the company, joint venture, transactions that involve substantial payment for goodwill, brand equity or intellectual property, recruitment and remuneration of senior officers just below the board level, labour problems, foreign exchange exposures, minutes of meetings of audit committee and other committees of the board, sale of material nature of investments, subsidiaries, assets, which is not in normal course of business, non-compliance of any regulatory, statutory nature or listing requirements and shareholders service such as non-payment of dividend, delay in share transfer etc.

(g) A qualified and independent audit committee should be set up by the board of the company in order to enhance the credibility of the financial disclosures of a company and promote transparency. The committee should have minimum three members, all being non-executive directors, with majority being independent, and with at least one director having financial and accounting knowledge. The chairman of the committee should be an independent director and he should be present at AGM to answer shareholder queries. Finance director and head of internal audit and when required, a representative of the external auditor should be present as invitees for the meetings of the audit committee. The committee should meet at least thrice a year. One meeting should be held before finalization of annual accounts and one necessarily every six months. The quorum of the meeting should be either two members or one-third of the members of the committee, whichever is higher and there should be a minimum of two independent directors.

(h) The board should set up a remuneration committee to determine on their behalf and on behalf of the shareholders with agreed terms of reference, the company's policy on specific remuneration packages for executive directors including pension rights and any compensation payment. The committee should be comprised of at least 3 directors, all of them should be non-executive directors, the chairman of the committee being an independent director. All the members of the remuneration committee should be present at the meeting. The chairman of the remuneration committee should be present at the AGM to answer the shareholders' queries.

(i) A board committee under the chairmanship of a non-executive director should be formed to specifically look into the redressal of shareholder complaints like transfer of shares, non-receipt of balance sheet, declared dividends etc. The committee should focus the attention of the company on shareholders' grievances and sensitize the management to redressal of their grievances.

(j) The companies should be required to give consolidated accounts in respect of all their subsidiaries in which they hold 51% or more of the share capital.

(k) Disclosures must be made by the management to the board relating to all material, financial and commercial transactions, where they have personal interest that may have a potential conflict with the interest of the company at large. All pecuniary relationships or transactions of the non-executive directors should be disclosed in the annual report.

(l) As part of the Directors' Report or as an addition thereto, a management discussion and analysis report should form part of the annual report to the shareholders. This report should include discussion on the following matters within the limits set by the company's competitive position: (i) industry structure and developments; (ii) opportunities and threats; (iii) segment-wise or product-wise performance; (iv) outlook; (v) risks and concerns; (vi) internal control systems and their adequacy; (vii) discussion on financial performance with respect to operational performance; (viii) material developments in human resources/industrial relations front, including number of people employed.

(m) The half-yearly declaration of financial performance including summary of the significant events in last six months should be sent to each household of shareholders.

(n) The company should arrange to obtain a certificate from the auditors of a company regarding the compliance of mandatory recommendations and annex the certificate with the directors' report, which is sent annually to all the shareholders of the company. The same certificate should also be sent to the stock exchanges along with the annual returns filed by the company.

(o) There should be a separate section on corporate governance in the annual reports of companies, with a detailed compliance report on corporate governance. Non-compliance of any mandatory recommendation with reasons thereof and the extent to which the non-mandatory recommendations have been adopted should be specifically highlighted.

(p) Powers of the audit committee should include power: (i) to investigate any activity within its terms of reference, (ii) to seek information from any employee, (iii) to obtain outside legal or other professional advice, (iv) to secure attendance of outsiders with relevant expertise, if necessary.

(q) The role of the audit committee should include: (1) oversight of the company's financial reporting process and the disclosure of its financial information to ensure that the financial statement is correct, sufficient and credible; (2) recommending the appointment and removal of external auditor, fixation of audit fee, and also approval for payment for any other services; (3) reviewing with management the annual financial statements before submission to the board, focusing primarily on any changes in accounting policies and practices, major accounting entries based on the exercise of management judgement, qualifications in draft audit report, significant adjustments arising out of audit, the going concern assumption, compliance with accounting standards, compliance with stock exchange and legal requirements, any related party transactions; (4) reviewing with the management, external and internal auditors, the adequacy of internal control systems; (5) reviewing the adequacy of internal audit function, the structure of internal audit department, staffing and seniority of the official heading the department, reporting structure, coverage and frequency of internal audit; (6) discussion with internal auditors of any significant findings and follow up thereon; (7) reviewing the findings of any internal investigations by the internal auditors into matters where there is suspected fraud or irregularity or a failure of internal control system of a material nature and reporting the matter to the board; (8) discussion with external auditors before the audit commences as also post-audit discussion; (9) reviewing the company's financial and risk management policies; (10) looking into the reasons for substantial defaults in payment to the depositors, debenture holders, shareholders and creditors.

(r) To expedite the process of share transfers, the board should delegate the power of share transfer to an officer, or a committee or to the registrar and share transfer agents. The delegated authority should attend to share transfer formalities at least once in a fortnight.

(s) All the shareholders of a company should be given the right to vote on certain critical matters through a postal ballot system. Some of the critical matters requiring shareholders' decision are: (1) matters relating to alteration in the memorandum of association such as changes in name, objects, address of registered office etc.; (2) sale of whole or substantially the whole of the undertaking; (3) sale of investments in the companies, where the shareholding or the voting rights of the company exceeds 25%; (4) making a further issue of shares through preferential allotment or private placement basis; (5) corporate restructuring; (6) entering a new business area not germane to the existing business; (7) variation in rights attached to class of securities.

(t) Financial reporting in respect of each product segment should be available to shareholders and the market to obtain a complete financial picture of the company.

Annexure 4 of the recommendations suggested a list of the following items to be included in the report on corporate governance in the annual report of companies:

(a) A brief statement on company's philosophy on code of governance.

(b) *Board of Directors:* (i) composition and category of directors, for example promoter, executive, non-executive, independent non-executive, nominee director, which institution represented as lender or as equity investor, (ii) attendance of each director at the board meetings and the last AGM, (iii) number of board meetings held, dates on which held.

(c) *Audit Committee:* (i) brief description of terms of reference, (ii) composition, name of members and chairperson, (iii) meetings and attendance during the year.

(d) *Remuneration Committee:* (i) brief description of terms of reference, (ii) composition, name of members and chairperson, (iii) attendance during the year, (iv) remuneration policy, (v) details of remuneration to all the directors.

(e) *Shareholders Committee:* (i) name of non-executive director heading the committee, (ii) name and designation of the compliance officer, (iii) number of shareholders' complaints received so far, (iv) number not solved to the satisfaction of shareholders, (v) number of pending share transfers.

(f) *General Body Meetings:* (i) location and timing where last 3 AGMs held, (ii) whether special resolutions: (a) were put through postal ballot last year, details of voting pattern, (b) person who conducted the postal ballot exercise, (c) are proposed to be conducted through postal ballot, (d) procedure for postal ballot.

(g) *Disclosures:* (i) disclosures on materially significant related party transactions, i.e. transactions of the company of material nature, with its promoters, the directors or the management, their subsidiaries or relatives etc. that may have potential conflict with the interests of company at large, (ii) details of non-compliance by the company, penalties, strictures imposed on the company by stock exchange or SEBI or any statutory authority, on any matter related to capital markets, during the last 3 years.

(h) *Means of Communication:* (i) The half-yearly report sent to each household shareholders, (ii) quarterly results: (a) which newspapers normally published in, (b) any website, where displayed, (c) whether it also displays official news releases, and (d) the presentations made to institutional investors or to the analysts, (iii) whether MD& A is a part of annual report or not.

(i) *General Shareholder Information:* (i) AGM: date, time and venue, (ii) financial calendar, (iii) date of book closure, (iv) dividend payment date, (v) listing on stock exchanges, (vi) stock code, (vii) market price data: high, low during each month in last financial year, (viii) performance in comparison to broad-based indices such as BSE Sensex, CRISIL Index etc. (ix) registrar and transfer agents, (x) share transfer system, (xi) distribution on shareholding, (xii) dematerialization of shares and liquidity, (xiii) outstanding GDRs/ADRs/Warrants or any convertible instruments, conversion date and likely impact on equity, (xiv) plant locations, (xv) address for correspondence.

8.3.3 Reserve Bank of India (RBI) Report of the Advisory Group on Corporate Governance (2001)

An Advisory Group on corporate governance under chairmanship of Dr. R.H. Patil, then managing director, National Stock Exchange was constituted by a standing committee of RBI in 2000 for evolving sound standards based on recognized best practices and for adopting transparency while adhering to the codes. They submitted their report in March 2001.

The Group adopted the OECD principles of corporate governance as the main benchmark for comparing the extent of compliance by the Indian corporate entities. The Group has relied on (a) the Combined Code of LSE, (b) the Cadbury Report, (c) Greenbury Report and (d) the Blue Ribbon Committee Report on improving the effectiveness of corporate governance.

The report contained several *recommendations* on corporate governance to be applicable to all companies, especially the public sector banks (PSBs) and public sector enterprises (PSEs), as follows:

1. The responsibility of the company as also the bank-board should be clearly defined to include the key functions: (i) reviewing and guiding corporate strategy, risk policy, annual budget and business plans, setting performance objectives, monitoring corporate performance and overseeing major capital expenditures and acquisitions; (ii) selecting, compensating and monitoring key executives; (iii) reviewing key executive and board remuneration; (iv) monitoring and managing potential conflicts of interest of management, board members and shareholders; (v) ensuring the integrity of company's accounting and financial reporting systems; (vi) monitoring the effectiveness of the governance practices; and (vii) overseeing the process of disclosure and communication.

   Banks need to follow the best practices in functioning of the boards. They need to develop mechanisms to ensure percolation of corporate strategic objectives and sound values throughout the organization. The board should ensure implementation of policies that prohibit activities and relationships that diminish the quality of corporate governance such as conflicts of interest, self-dealing and preferential treatment to related parties. Bank boards should oversee the management approaches towards different kinds of risks, viz. credit, market, liquidity and operational.

2. The boards of companies, including PSEs, should be accountable to the owners of the companies. However, they should respect the contractual obligations to the stakeholders such as employees, creditors, suppliers, customers, environmental impact of the operations of the companies.

3. In order to fulfil their responsibilities, board members should have access to accurate, relevant and timely information. They should be free to acquire, at the expense of the company, independent professional advice regarding the company affairs.

   The board meeting should be conducted properly with clearly laid down agenda for discussion, that should be circulated well in advance and supported by substantive information. The minutes of the board meeting should be circulated well in advance of the next board meeting.

4. Independent and executive directors of the companies should be appointed to the board, based on the recommendations of a nomination committee comprising the independent directors of the board. The committee should adopt clear and transparent criteria for selection of independent directors. The criteria for choosing non-executive directors should be disclosed in the annual report.

   It is essential to look into the composition of board of directors of nationalized banks and induct professionals. The board with nominated members cannot be regarded as being truly independent.

   An independent high powered selection board of eminent persons on the lines of the UPSC to select full time directors for the PSUs should be set up. Its decisions should be final and not subject to approval of the concerned administrative ministry. The selection board should also prepare a panel of experts for nomination as independent or professional directors.

5. All listed companies should have minimum of 8 board members so as to have professionals/experts from different disciplines. Companies including PSEs with net worth of ₹ 150 million or more should have at least 10 directors of which at least 5 should be independent directors.

   All banks should have minimum of 10 board members.

6. The board should have core group of excellent, professionally qualified non-executive directors performing dual role: (a) appreciating the issues put forward by management, and (b) honestly discharging their fiduciary responsibilities towards the company's shareholders and creditors. It is important to have high proportion of non-executive independent directors.

   There is a need to review and take a stand on reasonable bank board level representation for private shareholders in case of mixed ownership between government and the private sector.

7. The board members shall be considered independent if they have no relationship to the company that may interfere with the exercise of their independence from management and the company. They should be identified in the annual report.

   The directors nominated by the government on the boards of PSUs and PSBs and all nominees of the regulators should not be considered as independent.
8. Only the experts having financial, technical or legal knowledge or specialization in the area of operations of the company, should be appointed to the board. The training on board practices should be imparted to the elected members at the cost of the company.
9. In case of all companies, the maximum limit for a director serving on multiple boards should be 10. The same director should also not be a member of too many committees (preferably not more than 5/6 committees).
10. If the CEO is also the chairman of the board, more than 50% of the board members should be independent. It is preferable to separate the role of CEO from the chairman of the board. The chairman should be independent, objective, ethical and experienced enough to manage the diversities among shareholders, stakeholders and management.

    Immediate steps should be taken to de-link the posts of chairman and CEO of the PSEs from the officials of the administrative ministries.
11. All types of companies need to ensure that the audit committee of the board functions effectively and independently. The majority of the members of the committee should be non-official professionals. The audit committees should be comprised solely of independent directors, having a minimum of three directors, each of whom is financially literate or becomes financially literate within a reasonable period. At least one member of the committee should have accounting or related financial management expertise. The committee should (i) adopt a formal written charter that is approved by the full board of directors and that specifies the scope of the committee's responsibilities, including structure, processes, and membership requirements, (ii) review and reassess the adequacy of the charter on an annual basis. The committee should be responsible for ensuring its receipt from the outside auditors in the form of a written statement delineating all relationships between the auditors and the company.

    All reporting companies should include a report from the audit committee in the company's annual report disclosing whether or not (i) management has reviewed the audited financial statements with the audit committee, (ii) the outside auditors have discussed with the audit committee the auditors' judgement about the quality of the company's accounting principles, (iii) the members of the committee have discussed among themselves the information disclosed to the committee, (iv) the committee believes that the company's financial statements are fairly presented in conformity with GAAP in all material respects.
12. Boards of companies, banks, and PSUs should set up nomination committees consisting of at least three independent board members. The committee should have the responsibility of proposing new nominees for the board and assessing directors on an ongoing basis. Such a review should be conducted on an annual basis.

13. Boards of companies, banks, and PSUs should set up remuneration committees. The committee should be made-up exclusively of non-executive independent directors who make recommendations on the company's framework of remuneration for the full-time directors and senior employees of the company. The committee should operate independently and be granted full authority to seek counsel from both inside and outside sources.
14. A board committee under the chairmanship of a non-executive director should be formed to specifically look into the redress of shareholder complaints relating to transfer of shares, non-receipt of balance sheet etc. The board should delegate the power of share transfer to an officer or a committee or to the registrars and share transfer agents.
15. The boards of large companies and banks should meet at least six times a year. Through suitable legal provisions in the Companies Act, attending of board meetings through video-conferencing facilities should be recognized as valid attendance.
16. The term limits for independent directors may preferably be up to 10 years at a stretch.
17. All companies should ideally follow the maximum age limit of 65 years for whole-time directors and 75 years for part-time directors.
18. The liability of non-executive directors should be limited. They should not be held responsible for the matters that are not disclosed to the board by the executive directors. The main responsibility and liability thereof in respect of all statutory compliance should solely rest with the CEO/MD.
19. To protect commercial interests the lending institutions may stipulate a clause in the loan agreement to appoint nominee directors on the boards of companies. As institutions have much better access to information and better monitoring capabilities, they should take interest in corporate governance. Institutions should use their voting rights to get eminent and competent professionals elected as independent directors on the boards of companies, especially where they have sizeable shareholdings.
20. The necessary biographical details of directors should be provided in the annual report. All such details should be given to the shareholders when a new director is being elected by them at the general meeting of shareholders.
21. The remuneration of executive directors should be decided by the board's remuneration committee. Besides the usual sitting fees, the non-executive directors should be suitably remunerated for the time devoted by them for the affairs of the company. There should be no upper limit for sitting fees. To secure deeper involvement of non-executive directors, companies should pay a commission over and above the sitting fees for use of the professional inputs. Companies may also consider offering stock options. An appropriate mix of commissions, and stock options would align a non-executive director towards keeping an eye on short-term profits as well as long-term shareholder value.
22. The remuneration committee should follow a clearly laid down and transparent procedure for determining remuneration to the board. The committee should take care to position the company among others in the industry so as not to

overpay the directors. Executive share options should not be priced at a discount except when authorized by the listing rules.

23. The remuneration packages of all directors should be disclosed in the annual report. Membership in the remuneration committee must be annually reported to the shareholders. The annual report should include statements to shareholders regarding remuneration policy and the state of accounts. The report of the committee should identify directors individually and specify their compensation packages. Directors' total remuneration package, including share options and pension arrangements, should be subject to audit.
24. The shareholders should have the final say in approving remuneration of the full-time as well as the non-executive directors. The remuneration packages of senior executives should be approved by the board and full details thereof should be disclosed to the shareholders.
25. A system of electronic voting should be introduced to enable the shareholders to vote at the AGMs. Institutional investors should favour a dialogue with companies to determine mutual objectives. They should encourage regular and systematic contact at senior executive level to exchange views and information on strategy, performance, board membership and quality of management. They should provide checks and balances to prevent unhealthy concentration of decision-making power. The institutional shareholders can also play a role in the appointment of independent non-executive directors of necessary caliber, competence, and experience.
26. The AGMs should be held at the town/city, where the CEO of the company is located/headquartered. The company should also hold one or two general meetings of shareholders a year by rotation at different places where a large number of shareholders resides so that common shareholders have the opportunities to interact with the board and management of the company.
27. Companies should make special efforts in explaining company's governance policies, business ethics, and the environment and other public policy commitments. All large companies should arrange to get evaluated the quality of all their disclosures to the shareholders and the stakeholders. This evaluation job should be entrusted to an independent agency, which can audit the quality of disclosures. This evaluation report should be sent to all the shareholders.
28. The boards of all companies should ensure the integrity and consistency of their reports and meet the financial reporting standards in letter as well as in spirit. They should also report certain key financial ratios, which reflect the health of the company.
29. Disclosure standards of banks in India need further improvement to reflect the affairs of the banks in a true and fair manner. Banks should, on their own, disclose all material information relating to the true state of their affairs, their vision statements, future business strategies. To bring more transparency, banks should disclose more information on risk management strategies and practices, transaction with affiliated and connected parties, classification of assets, off-balance items etc. It is essential to present a fair view of the activities and the

accounts of the subsidiaries of public sector banks. This would bring transparency and disclosure in the accounts of these banks at par with the private sector banks and other companies. All banks particularly the bigger ones should have their own websites, where they should put all information for the benefit of the public, shareholders and depositors. The shareholding pattern, in particular the shares of institutional investors, Foreign Institutional Investors (FIIs), and mutual funds and other major shareholders must be disclosed by the public and private sector banks.

30. Banks and companies should prepare and present consolidated financial statements including those of all their subsidiaries. There should be disclosure about related entities, the nature of relationship, type of transactions etc., where the parent is having 26% or more shareholding. They should present desegregated segmental information for each significant product or service segment and for each significant geographical market. The companies should present the aggregate amount and period of defaults on repayment obligation on loans, bonds, debentures and public deposits.
31. An annual review of the effectiveness of the company's internal controls over financial, operational, and compliance matters should be conducted and reported to shareholders.

    In banks there should be much stronger internal control systems, including effective internal and external audit mechanisms, risk management functions independent of business lines, and other checks and balances.
32. Boards should take measures to enhance the independence and stature of auditors. The findings of auditors should be utilized in a timely and effective manner. The head of the audit firm should report to the board or the audit committee in an independent manner.
33. In principle, the bank's board should have obligation, but not accountability to stakeholders. However, a sound corporate governance should consider their interests and ensure that individual banks are conducting their business in such a way as not to harm the interests of depositors.
34. Some items, viz. outlook, risk and concerns, internal control systems and their adequacy should be covered in the annual report of companies.

    Banks should be encouraged to make disclosures on senior management structures, i.e. responsibilities, reporting lines, qualifications and experience, and broad incentive structures, i.e. remuneration policies, executive compensation, bonuses, stock options.
35. The extent of compliance with governance requirements should be disclosed in the 'directors' report' of all companies.

8.3.4 Naresh Chandra Committee (2002)

Consequent to the several corporate debacles in the USA in 2001, followed by the stringent enactments of Sarbanes Oxley Act, Government of India appointed Naresh Chandra Committee in 2002 to examine and recommend drastic amendments to the law pertaining to auditor-client relationships and the role of independent directors.

The main recommendations of the Committee are given below:

(a) The minimum board size of all listed companies as well as unlisted public limited companies with paid up share capital and free reserves of ₹ 100 million and above, or turnover of ₹ 500 million and above, should be 7, of which at least 4 should be independent directors. However this will not apply to (i) unlisted public companies having not more than 50 shareholders and without debt of any kind from the public, banks, or FIs, as long as they do not change their character, (ii) unlisted subsidiaries of listed companies.

(b) No less than 50% of the board of directors of any listed company as well as unlisted public limited companies with a paid-up share capital and free reserves of ₹ 100 million and above or turnover of ₹ 500 million and above, should consist of independent directors.

(c) In line with the international best practices, the committee recommended a list of disqualification for audit assignment which included:

1. prohibition of any direct financial interest in the audit client by the audit firm, its partners or members of the engagement team as well as their direct relatives. This prohibition would also apply if any 'relative' of the partners of the audit firm or member of the engagement team has an interest of more than 2% of the share of profit or equity capital of the audit client.
2. prohibition of receiving any loans and/or guarantees from or on behalf of the audit client by the audit firm, its partners or any member of the engagement team and their direct relatives.
3. prohibition of any business relationship with the audit client by the audit firm, its partners or any member of the engagement team and their direct relatives.
4. prohibition of personal relationships, which would exclude any partner of the audit firm or member of the engagement team being a 'relative' of any of key officers of the client company, i.e. any whole time director, CEO, CFO, CS, senior manager belonging to the top two managerial levels of the company, and the officer who is in default.
5. prohibition of service or cooling-off period under which any partner or member of the engagement team of an audit firm who wants to join an audit client, or any key officer of the client company wanting to join the audit firm, would only be allowed to do so after 2 years from the time they were involved in the preparation of accounts and audit of that client.
6. prohibition of undue dependence on an audit client, so that no audit firm is unduly dependent on an audit client, the fees received from any one client and its subsidiaries and affiliates, altogether, should not exceed 25% of the total revenues of the audit firm. However, to help newer and smaller audit firm, this requirement will not be applicable to audit firms for the first 5 years from the date of commencement of their activities, and for those whose total revenues are less than ₹ 1.5 million per year. [Note: A 'direct relative' is defined as the individual concerned, his or her spouse, dependent parents, children or dependent siblings.]

(d) Certain services should not be provided by an audit firm to any audit client, viz. (1) accounting and book keeping services, related to the accounting records or financial statements of the audit client; (2) internal audit services; (3) financial information systems design and implementation, including services related to IT systems for preparing financial or management accounts and information flows of a company; (4) actuarial services; (5) broker, dealer, investment advisor, or investment banking services; (6) outsourced financial services; (7) management functions, including the provision of temporary staff to the audit clients; (8) any form of staff recruitment, and particularly hiring of senior management staff for the audit client; (9) valuation services and fairness opinion.

In case the firm undertakes any service other than audit, or the prohibited services listed above, it should be done only with the approval of the audit committee.

(e) The audit partners and at least 50% of the engagement team responsible for the audit of either a listed company, or companies whose paid up capital and free reserves exceeds ₹ 100 million or companies whose turnover exceeds ₹ 500 million, should be rotated every 5 years. Persons who are compulsorily rotated could, if need be, allowed to return after a break of 3 years.

(f) Before agreeing to be appointed, the audit firm must submit a certificate of independence to the audit committee or to the board of directors of the client company certifying that the firm and its consulting and specialized services affiliates, subsidiaries, and associated companies:

1. are independent and have arm's length relationship with the client company;
2. have not engaged in any non-audit services; and
3. are not disqualified from audit assignments by virtue of breaching any of the limits, restrictions and prohibitions.

(g) There should be a certification by the CEO (either executive chairman or the managing director) and the CFO (whole time finance director or otherwise), which should state that, to the best of their knowledge and belief:

1. they have reviewed the balance sheet and profit & loss account and all its schedules and notes on accounts, as well as the cash flow statements and the directors' report;
2. these statements do not contain any material untrue statement or omit any material fact nor do they contain statements that might be misleading;
3. these statements represent a true and fair picture of the financial and operational state of the company, and are in compliance with the existing accounting standards and/or applicable laws/regulations;
4. they are responsible for establishing and maintaining internal controls to ensure that all material information is periodically made known to them; and have evaluated the effectiveness of internal control systems of the company;
5. they have disclosed to the auditors as well as the audit committee deficiencies in the design or operation of internal controls, if any, and what they have done or propose to do to rectify these deficiencies;

6. they have disclosed to the auditors as well as the audit committee instances of significant fraud, if any, that involves management or employees having a significant role in the company's internal control systems;
7. they have indicated to the auditors, the audit committee and in the notes on accounts, whether or not there were significant changes in internal control and/or of accounting policies during the year under review;
8. in the event of any materially significant misstatements or omission, the signing officers will return to the company that part of any bonus or incentive or equity based compensation which was inflated on account of such errors, as decided by the audit committee.

(h) An independent director of a company is a non-executive director who:

1. apart from receiving director's remuneration, does not have any material pecuniary relationships or transactions with the company, its promoters, its senior management or its holding company, its subsidiaries and associated companies;
2. is not related to promoters or management at the board level, or one level below the board (spouse and dependent, parents, children or siblings);
3. has not been an executive of the company in the last 3 years;
4. is not a partner or an executive of the statutory audit firm and the internal audit firm that are associated with the company, and has not been a partner or an executive of any such firm for the last 3 years. This will apply also to legal firm(s) and consulting firm(s) that have a material association with the entity;
5. is not a significant supplier, vendor or customer of the company;
6. is not a substantial shareholder of the company, i.e. owning 2% or more of the block of voting shares;
7. has not been a director, independent or otherwise, of the company for more than 3 terms of 3 years each (not exceeding 9 years in any case).

(i) An employee, executive director or nominee of any bank, financial institution corporations or trustees of any debenture and bond holders, who is normally called a 'nominee director' will be excluded from the pool of directors in the determination of the number of independent directors. In other words, such a director will not feature either in the numerator or the denominator.

(j) The statutory limit on sitting fees should be reviewed. Loss making companies should be permitted by the DCA (now MCA) to pay special fees to any independent director, subject to reasonable caps, in order to attract the best restructuring and strategic talent to the boards of such companies. The present provision relating to stock options, and to the 1% commission on net profits, is adequate and does not, at present, need any revision. However, the vesting schedule of stock options should be staggered over at least 3 years.

(k) If a director is not physically present but wants to participate in the proceedings of the board and its committees, then a minuted and signed proceedings of a tele-conference or video conference should constitute the proof of his or her participation. Accordingly, this should be treated as presence in the meeting(s). The minutes of all such meetings should be signed and confirmed by the director(s) who has/have attended the meeting through video conferencing.

(l) The minutes of board meetings and audit committee meetings of all listed companies as well as unlisted public limited companies with a paid-up share capital and free reserves of ₹ 100 million and above or turnover of ₹ 500 million, must disclose the timing and duration of each such meeting, in addition to the date and members in attendance.

(m) All independent directors should be required to attend at least one training course before assuming responsibilities as an independent director, or within one year of becoming an independent director.

(n) Where an audit firm has subsidiary, associate or affiliated entities, yardstick of not more than 25% of revenues coming from a single audit client should be widened to accommodate the consolidated entity. Thus, not more than 25% of the revenues of the consolidated entity should come from a single corporate client with whom there is also an audit engagement.

The other prohibitions should also apply in full to all the affiliated consulting and specialized service entities of any audit firm that are either subsidiaries of the audit firm, or have common ownership of over 50% with the audit firm.

(o) A special resolution of shareholders needs to be passed, in case an auditor, while being eligible to reappointment, is sought to be replaced. An explanatory statement accompanying such a special resolution must disclose the management's reasons for such a replacement, on which the outgoing auditor shall have the right to comment. The audit committee will have to verify that this explanatory statement is 'true and fair'.

(p) Audit committee of all the listed companies, as well as the unlisted public limited companies with a paid up share capital and free reserves of ₹ 100 million and above, or turnover of ₹ 500 million and above, should consist exclusively of independent directors.

In addition to disclosing the names of the members of the audit committee and the dates and frequency of meetings, the chairman of the audit committee must annually certify whether and to what extent each of the functions listed in the audit committee charter were discharged in the course of the year. This will serve as the committee's 'action taken report' to the shareholders. This report would also include the audit committee's views on the adequacy of internal control system, perceptions of risks and, in the event of any qualifications, why the committee accepted and recommended the financial statements with qualifications. This statement should also certify whether the audit committee met with the statutory and internal auditors of the company without the presence of management, and whether such meetings revealed materially significant issues or risks.

To discharge the fiduciary responsibility, the audit committee shall (a) discuss the annual work programme with the auditor, (b) review the independence of the audit firm, (c) recommend to the board, with reasons, either the appointment/

reappointment or removal of the external auditor, along with the annual audit remuneration.

(q) Management should provide a clear description of each material liability and its risks, which should be followed by the auditor's clearly worded comments on the management's view. This should be highlighted in the significant accounting policies and notes on accounts as well as in the auditor's report, where necessary. Qualifications to accounts, if any, must form a distinct, and adequately highlighted section of the auditor's report to the shareholders. It should also be mandatory for the audit firm to separately send a copy of the qualified report to the ROC, the SEBI and the principal stock exchange, with a copy of the letter being sent to the management of the company.

(r) Consolidated financial statements should be made mandatory for companies having subsidiaries.

(s) Companies should be required to establish, and publish an 'internal code' of ethics.

It is interesting to note that majority of the recommendations of this committee are the culmination of the provisions of Sarbanes Oxley Act of the USA.

8.3.5 N.R. Narayana Murthy Committee (2003)

SEBI constituted this Committee under the chairmanship of N.R. Narayana Murthy, chairman and mentor of Infosys, and mandated the Committee to review the performance of corporate governance in India and make appropriate recommendations. The Committee submitted its report in February 2003.

The main items of Committee recommendations are as follows:

(a) Persons should be eligible for the office of non-executive director so long as the term of office did not exceed nine years (in three terms of three years each, running continuously).

(b) The age limit for directors to retire should be decided by companies themselves. Corporate boards should have an adequate mechanism of self-renewal, as part of corporate governance best practices. It would be a good practice for directors to retire after a particular age. Companies may fix the retirement age at either 65 or 70 years.

(c) All audit committee members shall be non-executive directors. They should be financially literate and at least 1 member should have accounting or related financial management expertise. [*Explanation 1*: The term 'financial literate' means the ability to read and understand basic financial statements, i.e. balance sheet, profit & loss account, and statement of cash flows. *Explanation 2*: A member will be considered to have accounting or related financial management expertise if he or she possesses experience in finance or accounting, or requisite professional certification in accounting, or any other comparable experience or background which results in the individual's financial sophistication, including being or having been a chief executive officer, chief financial officer or other senior officer with financial oversight responsibilities.]

(d) Audit committee of listed companies shall review mandatorily the information, viz., (a) financial statements and draft audit reports, (b) management discussion and analysis of financial condition and operating results, (c) risk management reports, (d) statutory auditors' letter to management regarding internal control weaknesses, and (e) related party transactions.

(e) The audit committee of the parent company shall also review the financial statements, in particular, the investments made by the subsidiary company.

(f) A statement of all transactions with related parties including their bases should be placed before the independent audit committee for formal approval/ratification. If any transaction is not on an arm's length basis, management should provide an explanation to the audit committee, justifying the same.

(g) Procedures should be in place to inform the board members about the risk assessment and minimization procedures. These procedures should be periodically reviewed to ensure that executive management controls risk through the means of a properly defined framework.

(h) Companies raising money through an Initial Public Offering (IPO) shall disclose to the audit committee, the uses/application of funds by major category (capital expenditure, sales and marketing, working capital etc.), on a quarterly basis. On an annual basis, the company shall prepare a statement of funds utilized for purposes other than those stated in the offer document/prospectus. This statement shall be certified by the independent auditors of the company. The audit committee should make appropriate recommendations to the board to take up steps in this matter.

(i) It should be obligatory for the board of a company to lay down the code of conduct for all board members and senior management of a company. They shall affirm compliance with the code on an annual basis. The annual report of the company shall contain a declaration to this effect signed off by the CEO and COO.

(j) A director, to become independent, shall satisfy the various conditions laid down by the committee. The term 'independent director' is defined as a non-executive director of the company who:

1. apart from receiving director remuneration, does not have any material pecuniary relationships or transactions with the company, its promoters, its senior management or its holding company, its subsidiaries and associated companies;
2. is not related to promoters or management at the board level or at one level below the board;
3. has not been an executive of the company in the immediately preceding 3 financial years;
4. is not a partner or an executive of the statutory audit firm or the internal audit firm that is associated with the company, and has not been a partner or an executive of any such firm for the last 3 years. This will also apply to legal firm(s) and consulting firm(s) that have a material association with the entity;

5. is not a supplier, service provider or customer of the company. This should include lessor-lessee type relationships also; and
6. is not a substantial shareholder of the company, i.e. owning 2% or more of the block of voting shares.

(k) Personnel who observe an unethical or improper practice (not necessarily a violation of law) should be able to approach the audit committee without necessarily informing their supervisors. Companies shall take measures to ensure that this right of access is communicated to all employees through means of internal circulars etc. Companies shall annually affirm that they have not denied any personal access to the audit committee of the company (in respect of matters involving alleged misconduct) and that they have provided protection to whistle blowers from unfair termination and other unfair or prejudicial employment practices. Such affirmation shall form a part of the board report on corporate governance that is required to be prepared and submitted together with the annual report.

(l) For all listed companies there should be a certification by the CEO and CFO confirming, the financial statements as true and fair in compliance with the existing accounting standards, effectiveness of internal control system, disclosure of significant fraud and significant changes in internal control and/or of accounting policies to the auditors and the audit committee.

(m) The provisions relating to the composition of the board of directors of the holding company should be made applicable to the composition of the board of directors of subsidiary companies. At least 1 independent director on the board of directors of the parent company shall be a director on the board of directors of the subsidiary company. The minutes of the board meetings of the subsidiary company shall be placed for review at the board meeting of the parent company.

(n) The appointment, removal and terms of remuneration of the chief internal auditor must be subject to review by the audit committee.

(o) Management should place a report before the entire board of directors every quarter documenting the business risks faced by the company, measures to address and minimize such risks, and any limitations to the risk taking capacity of the company. This document should be formally approved by the board.

(p) In case a company has followed a treatment different from that prescribed in an accounting standard, management should justify why they believe such alternative treatment is more representative of the underlying business transaction. Management should also clearly explain the alternative accounting treatment in the footnotes to the financial statements.

(q) Non-executive directors should be required to disclose their stock holding (both own or held by/for other persons on a beneficial basis) in the listed company in which they are proposed to be appointed as directors, prior to their appointment. These details should accompany their notice of appointment.

(r) Companies should be encouraged to train their board members in the business model of the company as well as the risk profile of the business parameters of the company, their responsibilities as directors, and the best ways to discharge them.

(s) Corporate governance ratings are desirable. However, it should be left to the management of companies to decide whether they want to be rated or not, on corporate governance.

(t) There shall be no nominee directors. Where an institution wishes to appoint a director on the board, such appointment should be made by the shareholders. An institutional director, so appointed, shall have the same responsibilities and shall be subject to the same liabilities, as any other director. Nominee of the government on public sector companies shall be similarly elected and shall be subject to the same responsibilities and liabilities as other directors.

(u) All compensation paid to non-executive directors should be fixed by the board of directors and approved by the shareholders in general meeting. Limits should be set for the maximum number of stock options that can be granted to non-executive directors in any financial year and in aggregate. The stock options granted to the non-executive directors shall vest after a period of at least 1 year from the date such non-executive directors have retired from the board of the company. The considerations as regards remuneration paid to an independent director shall be the same as those applied to a non-executive director.

(v) Companies should publish their compensation philosophy and statement of entitled compensation in respect of non-executive directors in their annual report. Alternatively, this may be put up on the company's website and reference drawn thereto in the annual report. Companies should disclose on an annual basis, details of shares held by non-executive directors, including on an 'if converted' basis.

(w) Legal provisions must specifically exempt the non-executive and independent directors from criminal and civil liabilities under certain circumstances. Such exemptions need to be specifically spelt out for the relevant laws by the relevant departments of the government and independent regulators, as the case may be.

(x) Independent directors should periodically review legal compliance reports prepared by the company as well as steps taken by the company to cure any taint. In the event of any proceedings against an independent director in connection with the affairs of the company, defence should not be permitted on the ground that the independent director was unaware of this responsibility.

(y) The performance evaluation of non-executive directors should be done by a peer group comprising the entire board of directors, excluding the director being evaluated. Peer group evaluation should be the mechanism to determine whether to extend/continue the terms of appointment of non-executive directors.

(z) Management should provide a clear description of each material contingent liability and its risks, which should be accompanied by the auditor's clearly worded comments on the management's view. This action should be highlighted in significant accounting policies and notes on accounts, as well as, in the auditor's report, where necessary.

It is worth noting here that majority of the recommendations of this committee have been accepted by SEBI and thereby incorporated in the revised Clause 49 of the Listing Agreement in 2003 and 2004.

8.3.6 J.J. Irani Committee (2005)

The J.J. Irani Committee was constituted by the Government of India in December, 2004 to evaluate the comments and suggestions received on 'concept paper' and provide recommendations to the Government in making a simplified modern law. The Committee submitted its report to the Government in May 2005.

The main features of its recommendations pertaining to corporate governance are as follows:

(a) The (new) company law should provide for minimum number of directors necessary for various classes of companies. There need not be any limit to the maximum numbers of directors in a company. This should be decided by the companies or by its Articles of Association. Every company should have at least one director resident in India to ensure availability in case of any issue regarding accountability of the board.

(b) Both the managing director as also the whole time directors should not be appointed for more than 5 years at a time. The committee is in favour of retaining the existing option of the Companies Act (Section 265) regarding adoption of proportionate representation in the board.

(c) No age limit may be prescribed in the law. There should be adequate disclosure of age of the directors in the company's document. In case of a public company, appointment of directors beyond a prescribed age (say) seventy years should be subject to a special resolution passed by the shareholders.

(d) A minimum of one-third of the total strength of the board as independent directors should be adequate, irrespective of whether the chairman is executive or non-executive, independent or not. A director to be independent should satisfy certain conditions laid down by the committee. The expression 'independent director' should mean a non-executive director of the company who:

1. apart from receiving director's remuneration, does not have, and none of his relatives or firms/companies controlled by him have, any material pecuniary relationships or transactions with the company, its promoters, its directors, its senior management or its holding company, its subsidiaries, and associate companies which may affect independence of the director;
2. is not, and none of his relatives is, related to promoters or persons occupying management positions at the board level, or at any one level below the board;
3. is not affiliated to any non-profit organization that receives significant funding from the company, its promoters, its directors, its senior management or its holding or subsidiary company;
4. has not been, and none of his relatives has been, employee of the company in the immediately preceding year;
5. is not, and none of his relatives is, a partner or part of senior management during the preceding one year, of any (i) statutory audit firm or the internal audit firm that is associated with the company, its holding and subsidiary companies, (ii) legal firm(s), and consulting firm(s) that have a material association with the company, its holding and subsidiary companies;

6. is not, and none of his relatives is, a material supplier, service provider or customer or a lessor or lessee of the company;
7. is not, and none of his relatives is, a substantial shareholder of the company, i.e. owning 2% or more of voting power.

(e) The total number of directorships any one individual may hold should be limited to a maximum of 15. The number of alternate directorships a person holds should fall within the overall limit of directorships. An individual should not be appointed as an alternate director for more than one director in the same company. An alternate director may be allowed to be appointed for an independent director. Such alternate director should also be an independent director.

(f) Companies should adopt remuneration policies that attract and maintain talented and motivated directors and employees for enhanced performance. However, this should be transparent and based on principles that ensure fairness, reasonableness and accountability. There should be a clear relationship between responsibility and performance vis-à-vis remuneration. The policy underlying directors' remuneration should be articulated, disclosed and understood by investors/stakeholders.

(g) There need not be any limit prescribed to sitting fees payable to non-executive directors including independent directors. The company with the approval of shareholders may decide on remuneration in the form of sitting fees and/or profit related commissions payable to such directors for attending board and committee meetings, and should disclose it in its directors' remuneration report forming part of the annual report of the company. The information may contain all elements of remuneration package of directors, including severance package and other details like company's policy on directors' remuneration for the following year, performance graph etc.

(h) The requirement of the Companies Act, 1956 to hold a board meeting every 3 months and at least 4 meetings in a year should continue. The gap between two board meetings should not exceed 4 months. Meetings of the board by electronic means (teleconferencing and video conferencing included) should be allowed and directors who participate through electronic means should be counted for attendance and form part of quorum. Minutes should be approved/accepted by such directors by use of digital signature certification. If any director has some reservation about the contents of the minutes, he may raise the issue in succeeding meeting and the dissent, if any, may be recorded in the minutes of that meeting.

Notice of every board meeting should be given well in advance (say a period of 7 days) to ensure participation by maximum number of directors. Meetings at short notices should be held only to transact emergency business. In such meetings the mandatory presence of at least 1 independent director should be required in order to ensure that only well-considered decisions are taken. If even 1 independent director is not present in the emergency meeting, then decisions taken in such meeting should be subject to ratification by at least 1 independent director. Failure to attend board meetings for a continuous period of 1 year should be a sufficient ground for vacation of office by the concerned director regardless of leave of absence being given by the board.

(i) Majority of the directors of the audit committee should be independent directors if the company is required to appoint independent directors. The chairman of the committee should be independent. At least one member of the audit committee should have knowledge of financial management or audit or accounts. The recommendation of the committee, if overruled by the board, should be disclosed in the Directors' Report along with the reasons for overruling.

(j) There should be an obligation on the board of a public listed company to constitute a remuneration committee, comprising non-executive directors including at least 1 independent director. The chairman of the committee should be an independent director. The committee will determine the company's policy as well as specific remuneration packages for its managing/executive directors/ senior management. The chairman or in his absence at least 1 member of the remuneration committee should be present in the general meeting to answer the shareholders' queries.

(k) The rights of minority shareholders should be protected during general meetings of the company. There should be extensive use of postal ballot including electronic media to enable shareholders to participate in meetings. Every company should be permitted to transact any item of business through postal ballot, except the items of ordinary business, viz., consideration of annual accounts, reports of directors and auditors, declaration of dividends, appointment of directors, and appointment and fixation of remuneration of the auditors.

(l) Appointment of auditors should be made by the shareholders taking into account the recommendation of the board after obtaining the recommendation of the audit committee. Reimbursement of expenses to auditors should be disclosed separately in the financial statements along with the auditors' fees. All non-audit services may be pre-approved by the audit committee.

(m) Public listed companies should be required to have a regime of internal financial controls for their own observance. Internal controls should be certified by the CEO and CFO of the company and mentioned in the Directors Report.

(n) Detail of transactions of the company with its holding or subsidiary or associate companies in the ordinary course of business and transacted on an arm's length basis should be placed periodically before the board through the audit committee. The transactions not in a normal course of business and/or not on an arm's length basis should be placed before the board with management justification for the same. A summary of such transaction should form part of the annual report of the company.

(o) Every director should disclose to the company on his directorships and shareholdings in the company and in other companies. He should also disclose to the company, the contracts or arrangements with the company in which he has any interest or concern directly or indirectly. In case of failure to make disclosure, the concerned director should be held liable to penalties and he should be deemed to have vacated his office.

(p) In order to lay down more responsibilities on companies seeking public subscription, the companies should be required to preserve the composition of the board of directors for 2 years or till the procured funds are utilized as per the objectives stated in the prospectus, whichever is earlier. In case the director resigns from such a company, his liability should continue till the above period.

(q) The appointment of independent directors should be made by the companies from among persons with integrity, possessing relevant expertise and experience and who satisfy the above criteria for independence. The term 'material pecuniary relationship' should be clearly defined for the purpose of determining whether the director is independent or not. It needs to be defined in terms of percentage. 10% or more of recipient's consolidated gross revenue/receipts for the preceding year should form a material condition affecting independence. Transactions with an entity in which the director or his relatives hold more than 2% shareholding should also be considered.

(r) An independent director should make a self-declaration at the time of appointment and at the time of change in his status that he satisfies the legal conditions for being an independent director. Board should disclose in the 'directors' report' that independent directors have given self-declaration and that also in the judgement of the board they are independent. The board should also disclose the basis for determination.

(s) A non-executive/independent director should be held liable only in respect of any contravention of any provisions of the Act, which had taken place with his knowledge (attributable through board process) and where he has not acted diligently, or with his consent or connivance. If the independent director does not initiate any action upon knowledge of any wrong, such director should be held liable. Any follow-up action/dissent of such independent directors, upon knowledge of any wrong, should be recorded in the minutes of the board meeting.

(t) Independent directors/non-executive directors should have the right to (i) call upon the board for due diligence or obtain records for seeking professional opinion by the board, (ii) inspect records of the company, (iii) review legal compliance reports prepared by the company, (iv) in case of disagreement, record their dissent in the minutes.

(u) There should be specific executive development training programmes aimed at developing the awareness levels of board level appointees. Such persons should also be provided an insight into corporate law compliance requirements.

(v) Nominee directors appointed by a financial institution, bank, or government appointees representing government shareholding should not be deemed to be independent directors as such nominees represent specific interests and cannot, therefore, be termed as 'independent'.

(w) The issue of remuneration and its decision need not be taken by the government on behalf of the company but should be left to its shareholders whose approval should necessarily be taken. Such approval should take into account the recommendations of remuneration committee, through the board. No quantified limits on remuneration need be prescribed as emphasis should be on disclosures rather than providing limits/ceilings. Remuneration received by the directors of the holding company from its subsidiary companies should be disclosed in the annual report of the holding company.

(x) There should be a requirement of disclosure of directors' background, education, training and qualifications, as well as relationships with managers and shareholders.

(y) All matters relating to appointment of auditors, examination of the auditors' report along with financial statements prior to consideration and approval by the board, related party transactions, valuations and other matters involving conflicts of interest should be referred to the board only through the audit committee.

(z) Companies having a combined shareholder/deposit holder/debenture holder base of 1000 or more should be required to constitute a 'stakeholders' relationship committee' to monitor the redressal of their grievances. The committee should be chaired by a non-executive director.

(aa) The financial information and disclosures to be provided to shareholders should not be in excessively technical format but should be simple to understand. The information could also be made available through other means like print, electronic media, company website etc.

(bb) An audit firm should be prohibited from rendering the following non-audit services to its audit client and its subsidiaries:

   (i) accounting and book-keeping services relating to accounting records;
   (ii) internal audit;
   (iii) design and implementation of financial information systems including services related to IT systems for preparing financial or management accounts and information flows of a company;
   (iv) actuarial services;
   (v) investment advisory or investment banking services;
   (vi) rendering of outsourced financial services;
   (vii) management function including provision of temporary staff to audit clients.

(cc) Auditors are required to carry out their work with highest standards of excellence and independence within the discipline of the legal provisions and the accounting standards. Non-compliance with such standards should invite stringent penalties to be prescribed in the rules.

(dd) A regime of stringent disclosure norms should be provided for in case of companies accessing funds through public offers. There should be adequate and deterrent penalties in law against wrong disclosures. At par with international practices in regard to the related party transactions in which directors or their relatives are interested, a 'shareholder approval and disclosure-based regime' should be practised rather than 'government approval-based regime'.

(ee) In addition to the existing requirements [under Section 217(2AA) of the Companies (Amendment) Act, 2000] the 'directors responsibility statement' should include that the related party transactions have been entered into at arm's length, and if not, the relationships of the directors in such transactions along with the amounts involved have been disclosed as a part of the 'directors' report' along with management justification thereof.

(ff) There should be no requirement for a subsidiary company to necessarily co-opt an independent director of the holding company as an independent director on its board.

(gg) Consolidation of financial statements of subsidiaries with those of holding companies should be mandatory. Presentation of consolidated financial statements by the holding company should be in addition to the mandatory presentation of individual financial statements of that holding company.

(hh) There should be an interactive dialogue between professional bodies and corporate sector to enable evolution of corporate governance codes. The 'codes of conduct for directors' should be developed and disseminated by private sector and professional organizations. Such codes should detail the minimum procedures and care that make up due diligence and care. The presence of such codes would serve to educate both directors and investing public.

(ii) There is a need for regulators to monitor the end use of funds collected from the public. This should be the responsibility of the shareholders of the company who should charge company management with the responsibility coupled with adequate authority to ensure prudent and proper use of funds collected from the public.

(jj) Credit rating would be a good evaluation mechanism and its wide use would be generally beneficial. However, there is no need to mandate credit rating by law except for companies accepting public deposits. The companies accepting the public deposits should be required to:

 (i) appoint independent directors;
 (ii) appoint audit/remuneration/stakeholders relationship committees;
 (iii) undertake deposit insurance;
 (iv) undertake credit rating;
 (v) create adequate cash reserves being set aside for repayment of deposits;
 (vi) be subjected to close monitoring in respect of implementation of any scheme for payment of deposits that may be sanctioned by CLB/Tribunal/court;
 (vii) be subjected to a stringent disclosure regime; and
 (viii) be subjected to stringent penalties for irresponsible/fraudulent behaviour by the companies.

(kk) In addition to CEO, CFO, and CS, equally important would be the role of qualified professionals such as the accountant, auditor, lawyer, providing corporate advice. Such individuals should also be held liable for wrong-doing if it can be established that they had not specifically advised against actions or behaviour violative of the law.

(ll) The committee recognizes the 'whistle-blower concept' by enabling protection to individuals who expose offences by companies, particularly those involving fraud. Such protection should extend to normal terms and conditions of service and from harassment.

It is important to mention here that despite various recommendations made by the above Committees on corporate governance, the Committees kept silence on two major issues on corporate governance. They are:

(i) Chairman and CEO duality (particularly in regard to separation of these two posts), and

(ii) Appointment of nomination committee.

8.4 IMPACT OF INTERNATIONAL COMMITTEE RECOMMENDATIONS AND ENACTMENTS ON CORPORATE GOVERNANCE STANDARDS IN INDIA

If we look at the code of best practices and the corporate governance principles world over, and compare them with the governance standards presently followed in Indian corporates, it will not be difficult to trace that our governance standards prescribed by the regulatory authorities based on the recommendations of various national Committees have, in fact, been culminated from the recommendations of various world renowned Committees and enactments on this issue. The impact of international Committees' recommendations on the recommendations of the national committees and their effect in enactments of SEBI regulations and Companies Act, is given in Appendix 6.

It is quite evident from Appendix 6 that the contribution of international Committees and enactments towards implementation and upgradation of our corporate governance system through the national Committees that have given similar recommendations, are significant. It is not difficult to realize that the current governance standards are much improved and superior to the previous standards that existed in 2000. This is because of the fact that significant amendments/revisions have been made in the Companies Act, 2013 and Company Rules, 2014 and as also in the SEBI (Listing Obligation and Disclosure Requirements) Regulations, 2015, the details of which have been provided in the next two chapters. More and more requirements have been included in the regulations and enactments in order to ensure full disclosures and transparency in the functioning of corporate management and introducing more accountability of the board of directors to the stakeholders. It is expected that this will go a long way in bringing more integrity and fairness, transparency and disclosures, and accountability and responsibility in the functioning of corporates towards attaining a new height of achievement of corporate governance standards.

8.5 SUMMARY AND CONCLUSION

Corporate India has a long history of its corporate governance system, which started from 1850, under the British Rule. Since then the corporate governance system and practice in India have been greatly influenced by the British system of governance. India follows the Anglo-American system of corporate governance with a unitary majority executive board structure. In fact, corporate governance system in India started changing with the liberalization of Indian economy in 1991. Consequently, the changes in corporate governance in many developed economies of the world had their share of influence also on India's corporate governance system. An analysis of India's corporate governance system vis-à-vis some industrially developed countries discussed in this chapter, clearly reveals that India's corporate governance system and practices are far below the international standards and practices.

In late 1990s and early 2000, Government of India, through its own Ministry, Ministry of Corporate Affairs (MCA) and SEBI, appointed several expert committees to suggest measures for improvement in the standards of corporate governance. In an endeavour to improve the standards of corporate governance system, the Indian Companies Act, 1956, have been rewritten and a new Companies Act, 2013, and Company Rules, 2014 have been introduced and enforced. Similarly, in line with new provisions of the company law, the SEBI also introduced new listing requirements, 2015, applicable to all listed companies for the same purpose. The details of these provisions towards corporate governance reforms in India will be discussed in the next two chapters.

CASE STUDY

Lapses of Corporate Governance in the Nationalised Banks

INTRODUCTION

The Corporate Governance is a system of structuring, operating, and controlling a company/body corporate with a view to achieving long-term strategic goals to satisfying its shareholders, creditors, employees, customers and suppliers. It includes the policies and procedures adopted by an organisation to achieve its objectives in relation to its all stakeholders. A framework of effective accountability to the stakeholders is the essence of corporate governance.

The principles or cornerstones of corporate governance in an organisation revolve around the basic interrelated segments such as, (i) Integrity and Fairness, (ii) Transparency and Disclosures, and (iii) Accountability and Responsibility. In order to ensure compliance of these principles by the corporate houses in India the Government of India and SEBI, post Harshad Mehta, Ketan Parekh and Ramesh Gailie scams appointed national committees viz. CII Code of Desirable Corporate Governance (1998), K.M. Birla Committee, RBI Report of the Advisory Group on Corporate Governance (2001), Naresh Chandra Committee (2002), N.R. Narayana Murthy Committee (2003), and J.J. Irani Committee (2005). These committees submitted their reports that included various guidelines to be followed by the companies/banks in order to uplift the standards of corporate governance. Moreover, a new Companies Act, 2013 and SEBI (LODR) Regulations, 2015 were introduced by the regulatory authorities based on the recommendations of these committees.

Unfortunately, in our country, most of the corporate houses do practice these principles/guidelines only in black and white, more so our commercial banks in general, nationalised banks in particular. Right from the year 1992 and onwards till date, mis-governance in the Banking Sector is continuing, resulting in thousands of crores of rupees fraud in banks' lending transactions, thereby weakening our financial system. Recent cases of frauds perpetrated by the absconding fraud stars like Vijay Mallya, Jatin Mehta, Nirav Modi, Mehul Choksi etc. only points out to us that nothing has improved in the matter of corporate governance in our banking system post Harshad Mehta, Ketan Parekh, and Ramesh Gailie cases. It is estimated that around ₹ 30,000 crore public money has been swindled by these fugitive offenders involving State Bank of India, Punjab National Bank, Canara Bank, Indian Bank, Oriental Bank of Commerce, United Bank of India, Allahabad Bank etc. and a few Private Sector Banks.

LAPSES OF CORPORATE GOVERNANCE IN BANKS

On a closure look at the present functioning of these banks many loopholes are observed, some of which deserve immediate attention, as follows:

- Inadequate Internal Financial Control System in banks' functioning
- Ineffective performance of the banks' Boards
- Ineffective and inefficient follow up and monitoring system adopted by the Risk Management Committee, and Audit Committee of the Board of Directors
- Lack of proper Risk Management Policy of the Banks and the process of mitigation
- Lack of Monitoring System in banks' functioning, particularly the lending transactions
- Inadequate coverage or no coverage of insurance on the moneys lent to the big clients/borrowers
- Loopholes in drafting Loan Agreements causing inadequate pledge or charge on the borrowers' assets
- Tremendous political pressure on bank officials advocating for bank loans for their vested interests
- Failure of Internal Auditors in detecting frauds and irregularities
- Lack of proper functioning of the banks' Vigilance Cell in discharging vigilance activities
- Huge vacancies in the position of Independent Directors in the Public Sector Banks' Boards & Board Committees and the Ministry's lackadaisical attitude in regard to filling the posts of Independent Directors
- Failure in proper discharging of audit activities by the Banks' Statutory Auditors
- Lack of Transparency & Disclosure in Banks' reporting, and
- Lack of Accountability & Responsibility of Banks' officers at various levels
- Lack of demanding accountability by RBI on the Banks

It has also been observed that in total 30 bank officials were prosecuted for corruption from the period January 2015 to December 2017, of whom 5 officials belonged to Punjab National Bank (PNB), 5 to United Bank of India (UBI), 4 to State Bank of India (SBI), and 16 to 10 other Banks. During the same period, a total of 5000 PSB staff were punished for fraud (not referred to CVC), of whom 184 staff belonged to PNB, 141 to UBI, 1538 to SBI, and 3137 to other Banks.

The affected banks, RBI and the Central Government have suddenly wakened up and started fire fighting activities to control damage any further. In the process several properties and bank accounts of the fraud perpetrators have been seized, confiscated and frozen. But the quantum of recovery as on date is negligible as compared to the total monies siphoned off from the banking system. However, the Central Government has taken certain actions after the damage is done. The Government has moved on setting up a new agency viz. National Financial Reporting Authority (NFRA) provided for in the Companies Act to take away "Review and Disciplinary" functions of the Institute of Chartered Accountants of India (ICAI). In addition, the Government has also asked the PSBs to fix operational gaps within 15 days and they must check all bad loan accounts over ₹ 50 crore for possible fraud and wilful default and refer such cases to CBI and other investigating agencies. The Govt. has also brought a Bill in the Parliament for enactment against such fugitive offenders.

As a matter of abundant caution, the Central Vigilance Commission (CVC) advisory has been issued soon after the PNB fraud unfolded, to transfer officers having completed 3 years of service in a bank branch and clerical staff having completed 5 years as on December 31, 2017. Accordingly, some 7000 PSB employees from across Gujarat have been transferred. But all these actions of the Government so far are not going to stop the menace permanently. In order to curb or minimise the bank fraud of this huge magnitude, host of permanent and objective remedial measures are required to be taken immediately.

REMEDIAL MEASURES

There has to be integrity and fairness in the mind of bank officials and they have to feel that they are the public servants and the society largely depends on them for safe preservation of public deposits and wise investments. They must be accountable and responsible to the public at large for their business dealings. Therefore, good corporate governance prescribes a Code of Corporate Conduct as well as a Code of Ethics which should be prepared and distributed to the employees to follow strictly. The books of accounts and the reporting system of Banks should be such as to ensure highest standard of Disclosure and Transparency of the banking transactions.

Under Section 134 of the Companies Act, 2013 a Directors' Responsibility Statement (DRS) is required to be furnished in the Annual Report of the banks, duly certified by no other than the Chairman/CMD of the Bank. It is observed that the Chairpersons/CMDs of all Banks have certified adequacy and effective operations of Internal Financial Control System in DRS published in the Annual Reports. It is for sure that had there been adequate and effective Internal Financial Control System in operation in true sense, the Banks would not have suffered in this manner. Therefore, the Chairpersons/CMDs of all Banks should be more careful in certifying DRS in order to avoid inviting trouble for themselves in future in terms of civil and criminal proceedings against them for false declaration in the Annual Report.

All Banks mentioned in their Annual Reports, 2016–17 that they have put in strong credit appraisal and risk management frameworks in place for identification, measurement, monitoring and control of the risks in credit exposures regularly. Here the question is, if there was strong credit appraisal and risk management frameworks in place and the Credit Concentration Risk adequately managed, then how so much of public money were swindled by these fugitive offenders over the time? And what type of follow up and monitoring system was adopted by the Risk Management Committee, and Audit Committee of the Board of Directors? It is no denying the fact that there is a clear lack of proper Risk Management Policy of the Banks and its process of mitigation. There is a lack of Monitoring System as well, in banks' functioning, particularly the lending transactions, which needs to be relooked.

In the midst of these incidents a question naturally arises: Was there adequate coverage of insurance on the moneys lent to the big clients repeatedly? Were there loopholes in drafting Loan Agreements causing inadequate pledge or charge on the borrowers' assets? Proper answers to these questions can be provided only by the senior officials and Board members of the affected Banks. In any case, there should be immediate adequate coverage of insurance on the large credits to the borrowers if not taken earlier. The Loan Agreements must be foolproof enough not to give any undue leeway to the borrowers in regard to the pledge or charge on their assets.

There is no doubt that prima facie officials of both Internal Audit Department and Vigilance Department of the affected Banks have failed to discharge their duties properly and effectively. Otherwise, the fraud of this huge magnitude would have been detected. Audit Committee of the board has also failed in monitoring the functions of the Internal Audit Department. There is a need for redefining the roles of Internal Audit officers and the responsibility fixed on them on such lapses.

Role of the Statutory Auditors of the affected Banks in these episodes are dismal no doubt. It is no denying the fact that they did not discharge their duties honestly and diligently. Time is ripe that not only the concerned auditors but the audit firms also should be punished severely. Exemplary punishment (both civil and criminal) should be given to the audit firms debarring them from audit jobs of the listed companies for a period 3 to 5 years depending on the magnitude of the lapses.

Last but not the least, both RBI and the Central Government cannot avoid their responsibility for the recent banks' frauds. Pressure on bank officials advocating for bank loans for the vested interests of the political parties must stop so that the bank officials can work freely and fearlessly. Accountability and Responsibility must be demanded by these Agencies from the senior officials of the Banks regularly in order to avoid recurrence of this type of debacle in future. At the same time the Government should seriously think of providing complete autonomy in the functioning and decision making activities of the public sector banks particularly in regard to appointment of Directors in the Banks' boards and remuneration of senior officials and Board Members. The posts of Independent Directors in the Banks' Boards must be filled immediately from the lists/registers kept by the professional Institutes of our country in order to ensure appointment of genuine capable, experienced and qualified persons in the Board of Directors of the Banks. After all, an effective and vibrant Board of Directors, with ethical principles, can confirm improvement in the standard of Corporate Governance at the International level by way of their valuable contribution to the Boards and the society at large.

Questions for Discussion

1. What were the lapses of corporate governance in the nationalised banks in the recent past?
2. What remedial measures do you suggest in order to stop these lapses and ensure improvement in the standards of corporate governance in banks?

Test Your Knowledge

1. Explain Corporate Governance system in India vis-à-vis the USA, the UK, Germany and Japan on various governance issues.
2. List out the names of various national committees' reports for implementing effective corporate governance practices in India?
3. For the first time in the history of corporate governance in India, which Industry Association framed a voluntary code of corporate governance for the listed companies? Discuss some of its recommendations.
4. Which Committee's recommendations culminated in the introduction of Clause 49 of the Listing Agreement to be complied with by all listed companies? Discuss some of its recommendations which were accepted and included by SEBI in its new Clause 49 of the Listing Agreement in 2000.
5. Explain in brief, some of the important recommendations made in Reserve Bank of India (RBI) report on corporate governance in public sector banks.
6. What are the disqualifications for audit assignment suggested by Naresh Chandra Committee in the year 2002?
7. Discuss the main features of N.R. Narayana Murthy Committee's recommendations on corporate governance in the year 2003.
8. What are the main points highlighted by J.J. Irani Committee in the year 2005 on corporate governance reforms while recommending to the Govt. of India in making simplified modern company law?
9. Discuss the impact of International Committee recommendations and enactments on corporate governance standards in India.

CHAPTER 9

Indian Companies Act, 2013 and Rules, 2014 Concerning Corporate Governance

Learning Objectives

After reading this chapter, the readers will be able to understand:

- The important enactments of Indian Companies Act, 2013 and Rules, 2014 concerning the corporate board of directors and corporate governance viz.
  - Directors' Responsibility Statement [Section 134(5)]
  - Corporate Social Responsibility [Section 135]
  - Company to have Board of Directors [Section 2(10) and Section 149]
  - Manner of Selection of Independent Directors and Maintenance of Data Bank of Independent Directors [Section 150]
  - Appointment of Director Elected by Small Shareholders [Section 151]
  - Number of Directorships [Section 165]
  - Duties of Directors [Section 166]
  - Audit Committee [Section 177]
  - Nomination and Remuneration Committee and Stakeholders' Relationship Committee [Section 178]
  - Disclosure of Interest by Director [Section 184]
  - Related Party Transactions [Section 188]
- The Code for Independent Directors
- A Critical Analysis of New Company Law and a few Suggestions for improvement

Key Words

- Executive Directors
- Related Party Transactions
- Forward Dealings
- Accounting Policies
- True and Fair View
- Internal Controls
- Disclosure of Interest
- Insider Trading

9.1 INTRODUCTION

India took up its economic reforms programme in 1990s. Again, a need was felt for a comprehensive review of the Companies Act, 1956, which had become the bulkiest and archaic with 781 sections and 15 schedules by this time. Three unsuccessful attempts were made in 1993, 1997 and then in 2003 to rewrite the company law. As many as 24 amendments to this Act were made since 1956.

Thereafter, in the year 2013, the GOI introduced a new and revised Companies Act, 2013 and Rules, 2014. The Act is now sleek and thoroughly overhauled and revised with 29 chapters, 470 sections, 7 schedules and 95 definitions. The new Act has been enforced with effect from 1st April 2014. Many provisions of the erstwhile Act have been omitted, many existing provisions revised, merged, extended and re-written, and many provisions have been newly introduced as per the requirement of current conditions and reality. It is the first time in the history of company law that the corporate directors have been recognized and classified as executive directors, non-executive directors and independent directors in the new Companies Act, 2013. The roles, powers, and responsibilities of these directors have been specified in much more clear detail in this Act.

Consequent to the introduction of the Companies Act, 2013 and Rules 2014, several doses of amendments to the Act and Rules were made in the year 2015, 2016, 2017, 2018, and 2019. All these amendments have been incorporated in the sections relevant to the corporate governance in this chapter.

9.2 IMPORTANT ENACTMENTS OF INDIAN COMPANIES ACT, 2013 AND RULES, 2014 (AS AMENDED UPTO 2019) CONCERNING THE CORPORATE BOARD OF DIRECTORS

Some of the important sections of the Companies Act, 2013, and Rules, 2014 concerning the board of directors of companies are discussed below:

1. Directors' responsibility statement [Section 134(5)]
2. Corporate social responsibility [Section 135]
3. Company to have board of directors [Section 2(10) and Section 149]
4. Manner of selection of independent directors and maintenance of databank of independent directors [Section 150]
5. Appointment of director elected by small shareholders [Section 151]
6. Number of directorships [Section 165]
7. Duties of directors [Section 166]
8. Audit Committee [Section 177]
9. Nomination and remuneration committee and stakeholders' relationship committee [Section 178]
10. Disclosure of interest by director [Section 184]
11. Related party transactions [Section 188]

Let us discuss some of the *provisions* of the above sections in brief at this stage.

9.2.1 Directors' Responsibility Statement [Section 134(5)] [Corresponding to Section 217(2AA) of the Companies (Amendment) Act, 2000] [Enforced with effect from 13/12/2000]

Under this section, the board's report shall include a 'directors' responsibility statement' indicating therein:

(a) that in the preparation of annual accounts, the applicable accounting standards had been followed along with proper explanation relating to material departures;

(b) that the directors had selected such accounting policies and applied them consistently and made judgements and estimates that are reasonable and prudent so as to give a true and fair view of the state of affairs of the company at the end of the financial year and of the profit or loss of the company for that period;

(c) that the directors had taken proper and sufficient care for the maintenance of adequate accounting records in accordance with the provisions of the Act for safeguarding the assets of the company and for preventing and detecting fraud and other irregularities;

(d) that the directors had prepared the annual accounts on a going concern basis;

(e) that the directors, in the case of a listed company, had laid down internal financial controls to be followed by the company and that such internal financial controls are adequate and were operating effectively; and

(f) that the directors had devised proper systems to ensure compliance with the provisions of all applicable laws and that such systems were adequate and operating effectively.

Explanation: For the purpose of clause (e), the term "internal financial controls" means the policies and procedures adopted by the company for ensuring the orderly and efficient conduct of its business, including adherence to company's policies, the safeguarding of its assets, the prevention and detection of frauds and errors, the accuracy and completeness of the accounting records, and the timely preparation of reliable financial information.

9.2.2 Corporate Social Responsibility [Section 135]

1. Every company having net worth of ₹ 500 crore or more or turnover of ₹ 1000 crore or more or a net profit of ₹ 5 crore or more during the immediately preceding financial year shall constitute a corporate social responsibility committee of the board consisting of 3 or more directors, out of which at least 1 director shall be an independent director.

   Provided that where a company is not required to appoint an independent director under sub-section (4) of Section 149, it shall have in its Corporate Social Responsibility Committee two or more directors.
2. The board's report under Section 134(3) shall disclose the composition of the corporate social responsibility committee.
3. The corporate social responsibility committee shall
   (a) formulate and recommend to the board, a corporate social responsibility policy which shall indicate the activities to be undertaken by the company in areas or subject, specified in Schedule VII;
   (b) recommend the amount of expenditure to be incurred on the activities referred to in clause (a); and
   (c) monitor the corporate social responsibility policy of the company from time to time.
4. The board of every company referred to in sub-section (1) shall:
   (a) after taking into account the recommendations made by the corporate

social responsibility committee, approve the corporate social responsibility policy for the company and disclose contents of such policy in its report, and also place it on the company's website, if any, in such manner as may be prescribed; and

(b) ensure that the activities, as are included in corporate social responsibility policy of the company, are undertaken by the company.

5. The board of every company referred to in sub-section (1) shall ensure that the company spends, in every financial year, at least 2% of the average net profits of the company made during the three immediately preceding financial years, or where the company has not completed the period of 3 financial years since its incorporation, during such immediately preceding financial years,' in pursuance of its corporate social responsibility policy:

   Provided that the company shall give preference to the local area and areas around it where it operates, for spending the amount earmarked for corporate social responsibility activities.

   Provided further that if the company fails to spend such amount, the board shall, in its report, made under clause (o) of sub-section (3) of Section 134, specify the reasons for not spending the amount and unless the unspent amount relates to any ongoing project referred to in sub-section (6), transfer such unspent amount to a Fund specified in Schedule VII, within a period of 6 months of the expiry of the financial year.

6. Any amount remaining unspent under sub-section (5), pursuant to any ongoing project, fulfilling such conditions as may be prescribed, undertaken by a company in pursuance of its corporate social responsibility policy, shall be transferred by the company within a period of 30 days from the end of the financial year to a special account to be opened by the company in that behalf for that financial year in any scheduled bank to be called the Unspent Corporate Social Responsibility Account, and such amount shall be spent by the company in pursuance of its obligation towards the corporate social responsibility policy within a period of 3 financial years from the date of such transfer, failing which, the company shall transfer the same to a Fund specified in Schedule VII, within a period of 30 days from the date of completion of the third financial year.

7. If a company contravenes the provisions of sub-section (5) or sub-section (6), the company shall be punishable with fine which shall not be less than ₹ 50,000 but which may extend to ₹ 25 lakh and every officer of such company who is in default shall be punishable with imprisonment for a term which may extend to 3 years or with fine which shall not be less than ₹ 50,000 but which may extend to ₹ 5 lakh or with both.

8. The Central Government may give such general or special directions to a company or class of companies as it considers necessary to ensure compliance of provisions of this section and such company or class of companies shall comply with such directions.

Explanation: For the purpose of this section "net profit" shall not include such sums as may be prescribed, and shall be calculated in accordance with the provisions of Section 198.

Companies (Corporate Social Responsibility Policy) Rules, 2014

In exercise of the powers conferred under Section 135 and sub-sections (1) and (2) of Section 469 of the Companies Act, 2013, the Central Government hereby makes the following rules, namely:

1. Short title and commencement

(i) These rules may be called the Companies (Corporate Social Responsibility Policy) Rules, 2014.

(ii) They shall come into force on the 1st day of April, 2014.

2. Definition

In these rules, unless the context otherwise requires:

(a) "Act" means the Companies Act, 2013;

(b) "Annexure" means Annexure appended to these rules;

(c) "Corporate Social Responsibility (CSR)" means and includes but is not limited to:

  (i) Projects or programmes relating to activities, areas or subjects specified in Schedule VII to the Act; or

  (ii) Projects or programmes relating to activities undertaken by the board of directors of a company (board) in pursuance of recommendations of the CSR committee of the board as per declared CSR policy of the company subject to the condition that such policy will include activities, areas or subjects specified in Schedule VII of the Act.

(d) "CSR committee" means the corporate social responsibility committee of the board referred to in Section 135 of the Act.

(e) "CSR policy" relates to the activities to be undertaken by the company in areas or subjects specified in Schedule VII to the Act and the expenditure thereon, excluding activities undertaken in pursuance of normal course of business of a company;

(f) "Net profit" means the net profit of a company as per its financial statement prepared in accordance with the applicable provisions of the Act, but shall not include the following, viz.

  (i) any profit arising from any overseas branch or branches of the company, whether operated as a separated company or otherwise; and

  (ii) any dividend received from other companies in India, which are covered under and complying with the provisions of Section 135 of the Act:

Provided that net profit in respect of a financial year for which the relevant financial statements were prepared in accordance with the provisions of the Companies Act, 1956 (1 of 1956) shall not be required to be re-calculated in accordance with the provisions of the Act;

Provided further that in case of a foreign company covered under these rules, net profit means the net profit of such company as per profit and loss account prepared in terms of clause (a) of sub-section (1) of Section 381 read with Section 198 of the Act.

3. Corporate social responsibility

(1) Every company including its holding or subsidiary, and a foreign company having its branch office or project office in India, which fulfills the criteria specified in Section 135(1) of the Act shall comply with the provisions of Section 135 of the Act and these rules:

Provided that net worth, turnover or net profit of a foreign company shall be computed in accordance with balance sheet and profit and loss account of such company prepared in accordance with the provisions of clause (a) of sub-section (1) of Section 381 and Section 198 of the Act.

(2) Every company which ceases to be a company covered under Section 135(1) of the Act for three consecutive financial years shall not be required to:

(a) constitute a CSR Committee; and

(b) comply with the provisions contained in sub-section (2) to (5) of the said section, till such time it meets the criteria specified in Section 135(1).

4. CSR activities

(1) The CSR activities shall be undertaken by the company, as per its stated CSR policy, as projects or programmes or activities (either new or on-going), excluding activities undertaken in pursuance of its normal course of business.

(2) The board of a company may decide to undertake its CSR activities approved by the CSR committee, through

(a) a company established under Section 8 of the Act or a registered trust or a registered society, established by the company, either singly or along with any other company, or

(b) a company established under Section 8 of the Act or a registered trust or a registered society, established by the Central Government or State Government or any entity established under an Act of Parliament or a State legislature:

Provided that if, the board of a company decides to undertake its CSR activities through a company established under Section 8 of the Act or a registered trust or a registered society, other those specified in this sub-rule, such company or trust or society shall have an established track record of 3 years in undertaking similar programmes or projects, and the company has specified the projects or programmes to be undertaken, the modalities of utilisation of funds of such projects and programmes and the monitoring and reporting mechanism.

(3) A company may also collaborate with other companies for undertaking such projects and programmes or CSR activities in such a manner that the CSR committees of respective companies are in a position to report separately on such projects and programmes in accordance with these rules.

(4) Subject to provisions Section 135(5) of the Act, the CSR projects or programmes or activities undertaken in India only shall amount to CSR expenditure.

(5) The CSR projects or programmes or activities that benefit only the employees of the company and their families shall not be considered as CSR activities in accordance with Section 135 of the Act.

(6) Companies may build CSR capacities of their own personnel as well as those of their implementing agencies through institutions with established track records of at least three financial years, but such expenditure including expenditure on administrative overheads shall not exceed 5% of the total CSR expenditure of the company in one financial year.

(7) Contribution of any amount directly or indirectly to any political party under Section 182 of the Act, shall not be considered as CSR activity.

5. CSR committees

(1) The companies mentioned in rule 3 shall constitute CSR committee as under:

(i) a company covered under Section 135(1) which is not required to appoint an independent director pursuant to Section 149 (4) of the Act, shall have its CSR committee without such director;

(ii) a private company having only 2 directors in its board shall constitute its CSR committee with 2 such directors;

(iii) with respect to a foreign company covered under these rules, the CSR committee shall comprise at least 2 persons of which 1 person shall be as specified under clause (d) of sub-section (1) of Section 380 of the Act and another person shall be nominated by the foreign company.

(2) The CSR committee shall institute a transparent monitoring mechanism for implementation of the CSR projects or programmes or activities undertaken by the company.

6. CSR policy

(1) The CSR policy of the company shall, *inter alia*, include the following, viz.:

(a) a list of CSR projects or programmes which a company plans to undertake areas or subjects specified in the Schedule VII of the Act, specifying modalities of execution of such projects or programmes and implementation schedules for the same; and

(b) monitoring process of such projects or programmes:

Provided that the CSR activities do not include the activities undertaken in pursuance of normal course of business of a company;

Provided further that the board of directors shall ensure that activities included by a company in its CSR policy are related to the areas or subjects specified in Schedule VII of the Act.

(2) The CSR policy of the company shall specify that the surplus arising out of the CSR projects or programmes or activities shall not form part of the business profit of a company.

7. CSR expenditure

CSR expenditure shall include all expenditure, including contribution to corpus, or on projects or programmes relating to CSR activities approved by the board on the recommendation of its CSR committee, but does not include any expenditure on an item not in conformity or not in line with the activities which fall within the areas or subjects, specified in Schedule VII of the Act.

8. CSR reporting

(1) The board's report of a company covered under these rules pertaining to a financial year commencing on or after the 1st day of April 2014 shall include an annual report on CSR containing particulars specified in Annexure.

(2) In case of a foreign company, the balance sheet filed under sub-clause (b) of sub-section (1) of Section 381 shall contain an Annexure regarding report on CSR.

9. Display of CSR activities on its website

The board of directors of the company shall, after taking into account the recommendations of CSR committee, approve the CSR policy for the company and disclose contents of such policy in its report and the same shall be displayed on the company's website, if any, as per the particulars specified in the Annexure.

Annexure

Format for the annual report on CSR activities to be included in the board's report

1. A brief outline of the company's CSR policy, including overview of projects or programmes proposed to be undertaken and a reference to the weblink to the CSR policy and projects or programmes;
2. The composition of the CSR committee;
3. Average net profit of the company for the last 3 financial years;
4. Prescribed CSR expenditure (2% of the amount as in item 3 above);
5. Details of CSR spent during the financial year:
   (a) Total amount to be spent for the financial year
   (b) Amount unspent, if any

Manner in which the amount spent during the financial year is detailed below:

1	2	3	4	5	6	7	8
S.No.	CSR project or activity identified	Sector in which the project is covered	Projects or Programs: 1. Local area or other programme 2. Specify the state and district where products or programmes were undertaken	Amount outlay (budget): Project or programme-wise	Amount spent on the projects or programmes (sub-heads): 1. Direct expenditure on projects or programmes 2. Overheads	Cumulative expenditure upto the reporting period	Amount spent Direct or through: implementing agency (Give details of implementing agency)
1.							
2.							
Total							

Give details of implementing agency

6. In case the company has failed to spend the 2% of the average net profit of the last 3 financial years or any part thereof, the company shall provide the reasons for not spending the amount in its board report.
7. A responsibility statement of the CSR committee that the implementation and monitoring of CSR policy is in compliance with CSR objectives and policy of the company.

Sd/- (Chief executive officer or managing director or director)	Sd/- (Chairman CSR committee)	Sd/- (Person specified under Section 380 (1) (d) of the Act) [wherever applicable]

Schedule VII

[Enforced with effect from 1st April 2014]

Activities which may be included by companies in their corporate social responsibility policies

Activities relating to:

(i) Eradicating hunger, poverty and malnutrition, promoting health care including preventive health care and sanitation including contribution to the Swachh Bharat Kosh set-up by the Central Government for the promotion of sanitation and making available safe drinking water;

(ii) Promoting education, including special education and employment enhancing vocation skills especially among children, women, elderly, and the differently abled and livelihood enhancement projects;

(iii) Promoting gender equality, empowering women, setting up homes and hostels for women and orphans; setting up old age homes, day care centres and such other facilities for senior citizens and measures for reducing inequalities faced by socially and economically backward groups;

(iv) Ensuring environmental sustainability, ecological balance, protection of flora and fauna, animal welfare, agro forestry, conservation of natural resources and maintaining quality of soil, air, and water, including contribution to the Clean Ganga Fund set-up by the Central Government for rejuvenation of river Ganga;

(v) Protection of natural heritage, art and culture including restoration of buildings and sites of historical importance and works of art; setting up public libraries; promotion and development of traditional arts and handicrafts;

(vi) Measures for the benefit of armed forces veterans, war widows and their dependents;

(vii) Training to promote rural sports, nationally recognized sports, paralympic sports and Olympic sports;

(viii) Contribution to the Prime Minister's National Relief Fund or any other fund set up by the Central Government for socio-economic development and relief and welfare of the Scheduled Castes, the Scheduled Tribes, other backward classes, minorities and women;

(ix) Contributions or funds provided to technology incubators located within academic institutions which are approved by the Central Government;

(x) Rural development projects.

(xi) Slum area development;

Explanation: For the purpose of this item, the term 'slum area' shall mean any area declared as such by the Central Government or any State Government or any other competent authority under any law for the time being in force.

(xii) Disaster management, including relief, rehabilitation and reconstruction activities.

9.2.3 Company to have Board of Directors [Section 2(10) and Section 149] [Corresponding to Sections 252 and 253 of the Companies Act, 1956]

According to Section 2(10) of the Companies Act, 2013 "Board of Directors" or "Board", in relation to a company, means the collective body of the directors of the company.

Section 149 provides that:

1. Every company shall have a board of directors consisting of individuals as directors and shall have:
   (i) a minimum number of three directors in the case of a public company, two directors in the case of a private company, and one director in the case of a one-person company; and
   (ii) a maximum of fifteen directors;

Provided that a company may appoint more than fifteen directors after passing a special resolution;

Provided further that such class or classes of companies as may be prescribed [under Rule 3 of the Companies (Appointment and Qualification of Directors) Rules 2014], shall have atleast one woman director.

[Rule 3 of the Companies (Appointment and Qualification of Directors) Rules 2014 states that the following class of companies shall appoint at least one woman director:

(i) every listed company;

(ii) every other public company having:

(a) paid-up share capital of ₹ 100 crore or more; or

(b) turnover of ₹ 300 crore or more;

Provided that a company, which has been incorporated under the Act and is covered under provisions of second proviso to sub-section (1) of Section 149 shall comply with such provisions within a period of six months from the date of incorporation:

Provided further that any intermittent vacancy of a woman director shall be filled up by the board at the earliest, but not later than immediate next board meeting or three months from the date of such vacancy, whichever is later.].

2. Every company existing on or before the date of commencement of this Act shall within one year from such commencement comply with the requirements of the provisions of sub-section (1).
3. Every company shall have at least one director who stays in India for a total period of not less than 182 days during the financial year.

   Provided that in case of a newly incorporated company the requirement under this sub-section shall apply proportionately at the end of the financial year in which it is incorporated.
4. Every listed public company shall have at least one-third of the total number of directors as independent directors and the Central Government may prescribe [under Rule 4 of the Companies (Appointment and Qualification of Directors) Rules 2014] the minimum number of independent directors in case of any class or classes of public companies.

   Explanation: For the purposes of this sub-section, any fraction contained in such one-third number shall be rounded off as one.

   [Rule 4 of the Companies (Appointment and Qualification of Directors) Rules 2014 states that the following class or classes of companies shall have at least two directors as independent directors:

   (i) the public companies having paid-up share capital of ₹ 10 crore or more; or

   (ii) the public companies having turnover of ₹ 100 crore or more; or

   (iii) the public companies which have, in aggregate, outstanding loans, debentures and deposits, exceeding ₹ 50 crore:

   Provided that in case a company covered under this rule is required to appoint a higher number of independent directors due to composition of its audit committee, such higher number of independent directors shall be applicable to it;

   Provided further that any intermittent vacancy of an independent director shall be filled up by the board at the earliest, but not later than immediate next board meeting or three months from the date of such vacancy, whichever is later;

   Provided also that where a company ceases to fulfill any of three conditions laid down in sub-rule (1) for three consecutive years, it shall not be required to comply with these provisions until such time as it meets any of such conditions;

   Provided that a company belonging to any class of companies for which a higher number of independent directors has been specified in the law for the time being in force, shall comply with the requirements specified in such law].
5. Every company existing on or before the date of commencement of this Act shall, within one year from such commencement or from the date of notification of the rules in this regard as may be applicable, comply with the requirements of the provisions of sub-section (4).
6. An independent director in relation to a company, means a director other than a managing director or a whole time director or a nominee director:

   (a) who, in the opinion of the board, is a person of integrity and possesses relevant expertise and experience;

   (b) (i) who is or was not a promoter of the company or its holding, subsidiary or associate company;

(ii) who is not related to promoters or directors in the company, its holding, subsidiary or associate company;

(c) who has or had no pecuniary relationship, other than remuneration as such director or having transaction not exceeding 10% of his total income or such amount as may be prescribed, with the company, its holding, subsidiary or associate company, or their promoters or directors, during the two immediately preceding financial years or during the current financial year;

(d) none of whose relatives:

(i) is holding any security of or interest in the company, its holding, subsidiary or associate company during the two immediately preceding financial years or during the current financial year.

Provided that the relative may hold security of or interest in the company of face value not exceeding ₹ 50 lakh or 2% of the paid-up capital of the company, its holding, subsidiary or associate company or such higher sum as may be prescribed;

(ii) is indebted to the company, its holding, subsidiary or associate company or their promoters, or directors, in excess of such amount as may be prescribed during the two immediately preceding financial years or during the current financial year;

(iii) has given a guarantee or provided any security in connection with the indebtedness of any third person to the company, its holding, subsidiary or associate company or their promoters, or directors of such holding company, for such amount as may be prescribed during the two immediately preceding financial years or during the current financial year; or

(iv) has any other pecuniary transaction or relationship with the company, or its subsidiary, or holding, or associate company amounting to 2% or more of its gross turnover or total income singly or in combination with the transactions referred to in sub-clause (i), (ii) or (iii);

(e) who, neither himself nor any of its relatives:

(i) holds or has held the position of a key managerial personnel or is or has been employee of the company or its holding, subsidiary or associate company in any of the three financial years immediately preceding the financial year in which he is proposed to be appointed;

Provided that in case of a relative who is an employee, the restriction under this clause shall not apply for his employment during preceding 3 financial years.

(ii) is or has been an employee or proprietor or a partner, in any of the three financial years immediately preceding the financial year in which he is proposed to be appointed, of:

(A) a firm of auditors or company secretaries in practice or cost auditors of the company or its holding, subsidiary or associate company; or

(B) any legal or a consulting firm that has or had any transaction with the company, its holding, subsidiary or associate company amounting to ten percent or more of the gross turnover of such firm;

(iii) holds together with his relatives two percent or more of the total voting power of the company; or

(iv) is a chief executive or director, by whatever name called, of any non-profit organization that receives twenty-five percent or more of its receipts from the company, any of its promoters, directors or its holding, subsidiary or associate company or that holds two percent or more of the total voting power of the company; or

(f) who possesses such other qualifications as may be prescribed.

[Rule 5 of the Companies (Appointment and Qualification of Directors) Rules 2014 states that an independent director shall possess appropriate skills, experience and knowledge in one or more fields of finance, law, management, sales, marketing, administration, research, corporate governance, technical operation, or other disciplines related to the company's business].

7. Every independent director shall at the first meeting of the board in which he participates as a director and thereafter at the first meeting of the board in every financial year or whenever there is any change in the circumstances which may affect his status as an independent director, give a declaration that he meets the criteria of independence as provided in sub-section (6).

'*Explanation:* For the purposes of this section, "nominee director" means a director nominated by any financial institution in pursuance of the provisions of any law for the time being in force, or of any agreement, or appointed by any government, or any other person to represent its interests.'

8. The company and independent directors shall abide by the provisions specified in Schedule IV. (Schedule IV to the Companies Act, 2013 has been provided in Para 7.3).

9. Notwithstanding anything contained in any other provisions of this Act, but subject to the provisions of Sections 197 and 198, an independent director shall not be entitled to any stock option and may receive remuneration by way of fee provided under sub-section (5) of Section 197, reimbursement of expenses for participation in the board and other meetings and profit-related commission as may be approved by the members.

[Section 197(5) states that a director may receive remuneration by way of fee for attending meetings of the board or committee thereof or for any other purpose whatsoever as may be decided by the board:

Provided that the amount of such fees shall not exceed the amount as may be prescribed (under Rule 4 of the Companies (Appointment and Remuneration of Managerial Personnel) Rules, 2014).

Provided further that different fees for different classes of companies and fees in respect of independent director may be such as may be prescribed].

[Rule 4 of the Companies (Appointment and Remuneration of Managerial Personnel) Rules, 2014 states that a company may pay a sitting fee to a director for attending meetings of the board or committees thereof, such sum as may be decided by the board of directors thereof which shall not exceed one lakh rupees per meeting of the board or committee thereof:

Provided that for independent directors and women directors, the sitting fee shall not be less than the sitting fee payable to other directors].

10. Subject to the provisions of Section 152, an independent director shall hold office for a term upto five consecutive years on the board of a company, but shall be eligible for re-appointment on passing of a special resolution by the company and disclosure of such appointment in the board's report.
11. Notwithstanding anything contained in sub-section (10), no independent director shall hold office for more than two consecutive terms, but such independent director shall be eligible for appointment after the expiration of three years of ceasing to become an independent director:

    Provided that an independent director shall not, during the said period of three years, be appointed or be associated with the company in any other capacity, either directly or indirectly.

    Explanation: For the purpose of sub-sections (10) and (11), any tenure of an independent director on the date of commencement of this Act shall not be counted as a term under those sub-sections.
12. Notwithstanding anything contained in this Act,
    (i) an independent director;
    (ii) a non-executive director not being promoter or key managerial personnel,

    shall be held liable, only in respect of such acts of omission or commission by a company which had occurred with his knowledge, attributable through board processes, and with his consent or connivance or where he had not acted diligently.
13. The provisions of sub-sections (6) and (7) of Section 152 in respect of retirement of directors by rotation shall not be applicable to appointment of independent directors.

9.2.4 Manner of Selection of Independent Directors and Maintenance of Data Bank of Independent Directors [Section 150]

1. Subject to the provisions contained in Section 149(6), an independent director may be selected from a data bank containing names, addresses and qualifications of persons who are eligible and willing to act as independent directors, maintained by any body, institute or association, as may be notified by the Central Government, having expertise in creation and maintenance of such data bank and put on their website for the use by the company making the appointment of such directors:

    Provided that responsibility of exercising due diligence before selecting a person from the data bank as an independent director shall lie with the company making such appointment.
2. The appointment of independent director shall be approved by the company in general meeting as provided in Section 152(2) and the explanatory statement annexed to the notice of the general meeting called to consider the said appointment shall indicate the justification for choosing the appointee for appointment as independent director.

3. The data bank shall create and maintain data of persons willing to act as independent director in accordance with such rules as may be prescribed [under Rule 6 of the Companies (Appointment and Qualification of Directors) Rules 2014].

   [Rule 6 of the Companies (Appointment and Qualification of Directors) Rules 2014 states that

   (i) Any body, institute or association (hereinafter to be referred to as "the agency"), which has been authorized in this behalf by the Central Government shall create and maintain a data bank of persons willing and eligible to be appointed as independent director and such data bank shall be placed on the website of the Ministry of Corporate Affairs or on any other website as may be approved or notified by the Central Government.

   (ii) The data bank shall contain the following details in respect of each person included in the data bank to be eligible and willing to be appointed as independent director:

      (a) Director Identification Number (DIN);
      (b) the name and surname in full;
      (c) the father's name;
      (d) the date of birth;
      (e) gender;
      (f) the nationality;
      (g) the occupation;
      (h) full address with PIN Code (present and permanent);
      (i) phone number;
      (j) e-mail id;
      (k) the educational and professional qualifications;
      (l) experience and expertise, if any;
      (m) any legal proceedings initiated or pending against such person;
      (n) the list of limited liability partnerships in which he is or was a designated partner along with:
         (i) the name of the limited liability partnerships;
         (ii) the nature of industry; and
         (iii) the duration with dates;
      (o) the list of companies in which he is or was director along with:
         (i) the name of the company;
         (ii) the nature of industry;
         (iii) the nature of directorship—executive or non-executive or managing director or independent director or nominee director; and
         (iv) duration with dates.

   (iii) A disclaimer shall be conspicuously displayed on the website hosting the data bank that a company must carry out its own due diligence before appointment of any person as an independent director and the 'agency' maintaining the data bank or the Central Government shall not be held responsible for the accuracy of information or lack of suitability of the person whose particulars form part of the data bank.

(iv) Any person who desires to get his name included in the data bank of independent directors shall make an application to the 'agency'.

(v) The agency may charge a reasonable fee from the applicant for inclusion of his name in the data bank of independent directors.

(vi) Any person who has applied for inclusion of his name in the data bank of independent directors or any person whose name appears in the data bank, shall intimate to the agency about any changes in his particulars within 15 days of such change.

(vii) The data bank posted on the website shall:

(a) be accessible at the specified website;

(b) be substantially identical to the physical version of the data bank;

(c) be searchable on the parameters specified in sub-rule 2;

(d) be presented in a format or formats convenient for both printing and viewing online; and

(e) contain a link to obtain the software required to view or print the particulars free of charge.].

4. The Central Government may prescribe the manner and procedure of selection of independent directors who fulfill the qualifications and requirements specified under Section 149.

9.2.5 Appointment of Director Elected by Small Shareholders [Section 151] [Corresponding to Section 252 of the Companies Act, 1956]

A listed company may have one director elected by such small shareholders in such manner and with such terms and conditions as may be prescribed [under Rule 7 of the Companies (Appointment and Qualification of Directors) Rules, 2014].

Explanation: For the purpose of this section, "small shareholders" means a shareholder holding shares of nominal value of not more than ₹ 20,000 or such other sum as may be prescribed.

[Rule 7 of the Companies (Appointment and Qualification of Directors) Rules, 2014 states that:

1. A listed company may, upon notice of not less than 1000 small shareholders or one-tenth of the total number of such shareholders, whichever is lower, have a small shareholders' director elected by the small shareholders.
2. The small shareholders intending to propose a person as a candidate for the post of small shareholders' director shall leave a notice of their intention with the company at least 14 days before the meeting under their signatures specifying the name, address, shares held and folio number of the person whose name is being proposed for the post of director and of the small shareholders who are proposing such person for the office of director.
3. The notice shall be accompanied by a statement signed by the person whose name is being proposed for the post of small shareholders' director stating:

(a) his director identification number;

(b) that he is not disqualified to become a director under the Act; and
(c) his consent to act as a director of the company.

4. Such director shall be considered as an independent director subject to his being eligible under Section 149(6) and his giving a declaration of his independence in accordance with Section 149(7) of the Act.
5. The appointment of small shareholders' director shall be subject to the provisions of Section 152 except that:
   (a) such director shall not be liable to retire by rotation;
   (b) such director's tenure as small shareholders' director shall not exceed a period of 3 consecutive years; and
   (c) on the expiry of the tenure, such director shall not be eligible for re-appointment.
6. A person shall not be appointed as small shareholders' director of a company, if the person is not eligible for appointment in terms of Section 164.
7. A person appointed as small shareholders' director shall vacate the office if:
   (a) the director incurs any of the disqualifications specified in Section 164;
   (b) the office of the director becomes vacant in pursuance of Section 167;
   (c) the director ceases to meet the criteria of independence as provided in Section 149(6).
8. No person shall hold the position of small shareholders' director in more than 2 companies at the same time:

   Provided that the second company in which he has been appointed shall not be in a business which is competing or is in conflict with the business of the first company.
9. A small shareholders' director shall not, for a period of 3 years from the date on which he ceases to hold office as a small shareholders' director in a company, be appointed in or be associated with such company in any other capacity, either directly or indirectly].

9.2.6 Number of Directorships [Section 165] [Corresponding to Sections 275, 276, 278 and 279 of the Companies Act, 1956]

1. No person, after the commencement of this Act, shall hold office as a director, including any alternate directorship, in more than 20 companies at the same time:

   Provided that the maximum number of public companies in which a person can be appointed as a director shall not exceed 10.

   Explanation: For reckoning the limit of public companies in which a person can be appointed as a director, directorship in private companies that are either holding or subsidiary company of a public company shall be included.
2. Subject to the provisions of sub-section(1), the members of a company may, by special resolution, specify any lesser number of companies in which a director of the company may act as directors.

3. Any person holding office as director in companies more than limits as specified in sub-section (1), immediately before the commencement of this Act shall, within a period of 1 year from such commencement:
   (a) choose not more than the specified limit of those companies, as companies in which he wishes to continue to hold the office of director;
   (b) resign his office as director in the other remaining companies; and
   (c) intimate the choice made by him under clause (a), to each of the companies in which he was holding the office of director before such commencement and to the registrar having jurisdiction in respect of each such company.
4. Any resignation made in pursuance of clause (b) of sub-section (3) shall become effective immediately on the dispatch thereof to the company concerned.
5. No such person shall act as director in more than the specified number of companies:
   (a) after dispatching the resignation of his office as director or non-executive director thereof, in pursuance of clause (b) of sub-section (3); or
   (b) after the expiry of 1 year from the commencement of this Act, whichever is earlier.
6. If a person accepts an appointment as a director in contravention of sub-section (1), he shall be liable to a penalty of ₹ 5000 for each day after the first during which such contravention continues.

9.2.7 Duties of Directors [Section 166] [Corresponding to Sections 312 and 388 of the Companies Act, 1956]

1. Subject to the provisions of this Act, a director of a company shall act in accordance with the articles of the company.
2. A director of a company shall act in good faith in order to promote the objects of the company for the benefit of its members as a whole, and in the best interests of the company, its employees, the shareholders, the community and for the protection of environment.
3. A director of a company shall exercise duties with due and reasonable care, skill and diligence and shall exercise independent judgement.
4. A director of a company shall not involve in a situation in which he may have a direct or indirect interest that conflicts, or possibly may conflict, with the interest of the company.
5. A director of a company shall not achieve or attempt to achieve any undue gain or advantage either to himself or to his relatives, partners, associates and if such director is found guilty of making any undue gain, he shall be liable to pay an amount equal to that gain to the company.
6. A director of a company shall not assign his office and any assignment so made shall be void.
7. If a director of the company contravenes the provisions of this section, such director shall be punishable with fine which shall not be less than ₹ 1 lakh but, which may extend to ₹ 5 lakh.

9.2.8 Audit Committee [Section 177] [Corresponding to Section 292A of the Companies (Amendment) Act, 2000]

1. The board of directors of every listed company and such other class or classes of companies, as may be prescribed [under Rule 6 of the Companies (Meetings of Board and its Powers) Rules, 2014], shall constitute an audit committee.

   [Rule 6 of the Companies (Meetings of Board and its Powers) Rules, 2014 states that the board of directors of every listed company and the following classes of companies shall constitute an audit committee and a nomination and remuneration committee of the board:

   (i) all public companies with a paid-up capital of ₹ 10 crore or more;
   (ii) all public companies having turnover of ₹ 100 crore or more;
   (iii) all public companies, having in aggregate, outstanding loans or borrowings or debentures or deposits exceeding ₹ 50 crore or more].

2. The audit committee shall consist of a minimum of 3 directors with independent directors forming a majority:

   Provided that majority of members of audit committee, including its chairperson, shall be persons with ability to read and understand, the financial statement.

3. Every audit committee of a company existing immediately before the commencement of this Act shall, within 1 year of such commencement, be reconstituted in accordance with sub-section (2).

4. Every audit committee shall act in accordance with the terms of reference specified in writing by the board which shall *inter alia*, include:

   (i) the recommendation for appointment, remuneration and terms of appointment of auditors of the company;
   (ii) review and monitor the auditor's independence and performance and effectiveness of audit process;
   (iii) examination of the financial statement and the auditors' report thereon;
   (iv) approval or any subsequent modification of transactions of the company with related parties;

   Provided that the audit committee may make omnibus approval for related party transactions proposed to be entered into by the company subject to such conditions as may be prescribed [under Rule 6A of the Companies (Meetings of Board and its Powers) Rules, 2014.

   [Rule 6A of the Companies (Meetings of Board and its Powers) Rules, 2014 states that all related party transactions shall require approval of the audit committee and the audit committee may make omnibus approval for related party transactions proposed to be entered into by the company subject to the following conditions, namely:

   (1) The audit committee shall, after obtaining approval of the board of directors, specify the criteria for making the omnibus approval which shall include the following, namely:

      (a) maximum value of the transaction, in aggregate, which can be allowed under the omnibus route in a year;
      (b) the maximum value per transaction which can be allowed;

(c) extent and manner of disclosures to be made to the audit committee at the time of seeking omnibus approval;

(d) review, at such intervals as the audit committee may deem fit, related party transaction entered into by the company pursuant to each of the omnibus approval made;

(e) transactions which cannot be subject to the omnibus approval by the audit committee.

(2) The audit committee shall consider the following factors while specifying the criteria for making omnibus approval, namely:

(a) repetitiveness of the transactions (in past or in future);

(b) justification for the need of omnibus approval.

(3) The audit committee shall satisfy itself on the need for omnibus approval for transactions of repetitive nature and that such approval is in the interest of the company.

(4) The omnibus approval shall contain or indicate the following:

(a) name of the related parties;

(b) nature and duration of the transaction;

(c) maximum amount of transaction that can be entered into;

(d) the indicative base price or current contracted price and the formula for variation in the price, if any; and

(e) any other information relevant or important for the audit committee to take a decision on the proposed transaction:

Provided that where the need for related party transaction cannot be foreseen and aforesaid details are not available, audit committee may make omnibus approval for such transactions subject to their value not exceeding ₹ 1 crore per transaction.

(5) Omnibus approval shall be valid for a period not exceeding one financial year and shall require fresh approval after the expiry of such financial year.

(6) Omnibus approval shall not be made for transactions in respect of selling or disposing of the undertaking of the company.

(7) Any other conditions as the audit committee may deem fit.

Provided further that in case of transaction, other than transactions referred to in Section 188, and where audit committee does not approve the transaction, it shall make its recommendations to the board:

Provided also that in case of any transaction involving any amount not exceeding ₹ 1 crore is entered into by a director or officer of the company without obtaining the approval of the audit committee and it is not ratified by the audit committee within 3 months from the date of the transaction, such transaction shall be voidable at the option of the audit committee and if the transaction is with the related party to any director or is authorised by any other director, the director concerned shall indemnify the company against any loss incurred by it:

Provided also that the provisions of this clause shall not apply to a transaction, other than a transaction referred to in Section 188, between a holding company and its wholly owned subsidiary company.'

(v) scrutiny of intercorporate loans and investments;

(vi) valuation of undertakings or assets of the company, wherever it is necessary;

(vii) evaluation of internal financial controls and risk management systems;

(viii) monitoring the end-use of funds raised through public offers and related matters.

5. The audit committee may call for the comments of the auditors about internal control systems, the scope of audit, including the observations of the auditors and review of financial statement before their submission to the board and may also discuss any related issues with the internal and statutory auditors and the management of the company.
6. The audit committee shall have authority to investigate into any matter in relation to the items specified in sub-section (4) or referred to it by the board and for this purpose, shall have power to obtain professional advice from external sources and have full access to information contained in the records of the company.
7. The auditors of a company and the key managerial personnel shall have a right to be heard in the meetings of the audit committee when it considers the auditors' report, but shall not have the right to vote.
8. The board's report under Section 134(3) shall disclose the composition of an audit committee and where the board had not accepted any recommendation of the audit committee, the same shall be disclosed in such report along with the reasons there for.
9. Every listed company or such class or classes of companies, as may be prescribed, shall establish a vigil mechanism for directors and employees to report genuine concerns in such manner as may be prescribed [under Rule 7 of the Companies (Meetings of Board and its Powers) Rules, 2014].

[Rule 7 of the Companies (Meetings of Board and its Powers) Rules, 2014 states that

(i) Every listed company and the companies belonging to the following class or classes shall establish a vigil mechanism for their directors and employees to report their genuine concerns or grievances:

(a) the companies which accept deposits from the public;

(b) the companies which have borrowed money from banks and public financial institutions in excess of ₹ 50 crore.

(ii) The companies which are required to constitute an audit committee shall oversee the vigil mechanism through the committee and if any of the members of the committee have a conflict of interest in a given case, they should recue themselves and the others on the committee would deal with the matter on hand.

(iii) In case of other companies, the board of directors shall nominate a director to play the role of audit committee for the purpose of vigil mechanism to whom other directors and employees may report their concerns.

(iv) The vigil mechanism shall provide for adequate safeguards against victimization of employees and directors who avail of the vigil mechanism and also provide for direct access to the chairperson of the audit committee or the director nominated to play the role of audit committee, as the case may be, in exceptional cases.

(v) In case of repeated frivolous complaints being filed by a director or an employee, the audit committee or the director nominated to play the role of audit committee may take suitable action against the concerned director or employee including reprimand].

10. The vigil mechanism under sub-section (9) shall provide for adequate safeguards against victimization of persons who use such mechanism and make provision for direct access to the chairperson of the audit committee in appropriate or exceptional cases:

Provided that the details of the establishment of such mechanism shall be disclosed by the company on its website, if any, and in the board's report.

9.2.9 Nomination and Remuneration Committee and Stakeholders' Relationship Committee [Section 178]

1. The board of directors of every listed company and such other class or classes of companies, as may be prescribed [under Rule 6 of the Companies (Meetings of Board and its Powers) Rules, 2014], shall constitute the nomination and remuneration committee consisting of 3 or more non-executive directors out of which not less than one-half shall be independent directors:

   Provided that the chairperson of the company (whether executive or non-executive) may be appointed as a member of the nomination and remuneration committee, but shall not chair such committee.
2. The nomination and remuneration committee shall identify persons who are qualified to become directors and who may be appointed in senior management in accordance with the criteria laid down, recommend to the board their appointment and removal and shall specify the manner for effective evaluation of performance of board, its committees and individual directors to be carried out either by the board, by the nomination and remuneration committee or by an independent external agency and review its implementation and compliance.
3. The nomination and remuneration committee shall formulate the criteria for determining qualifications, positive attributes and independence of a director and recommend to the board a policy, relating to the remuneration for the directors, key managerial personnel and other employees.
4. The nomination and remuneration committee shall, while formulating the policy under sub-section (3), ensure that:

   (a) the level and composition of remuneration is reasonable and sufficient to attract, retain and motivate directors of the quality required to run the company successfully;

   (b) relationship of remuneration to performance is clear and meets appropriate performance benchmarks; and

(c) remuneration to directors, key managerial personnel and senior management involves a balance between fixed and incentive pay reflecting short- and long-term performance objectives appropriate to the working of the company and its goals:

Provided that such policy shall be placed on the website of the company, if any, and the salient features of the policy and changes therein, if any, along with the web address of the policy, if any, shall be disclosed in the board's report.

5. The board of directors of a company which consists of more than 1000 shareholders, debenture holders, deposit holders and any other security holders at any time during a financial year shall constitute a stakeholders' relationship committee consisting of a chairperson who shall be a non-executive director and such other members as may be decided by the board.
6. The stakeholders' relationship committee shall consider and resolve the grievances of security holders of the company.
7. The chairperson of each of the committees constituted under this section or, in his absence, any other member of the committee authorized by him in this behalf shall attend the general meetings of the company.
8. In case of any contravention of the provisions of Section 177 and this section, the company shall be punishable with fine which shall not be less than ₹ 1 lakh, but which may extend to ₹ 5 lakh and every officer of the company who is in default shall be punishable with imprisonment for a term which may extend to 1 year or with fine which shall not be less than ₹ 25000, but which may extend to ₹ 1 lakh, or with both:

   Provided that inability to resolve or consider any grievance by the stakeholders' relationship committee in good faith shall not constitute a contravention of this section.

Explanation: The expression "senior management" means personnel of the company who are members of its core management team excluding board of directors comprising all members of management one level below the executive directors, including the functional heads.

9.2.10 Disclosure of Interest by Director [Section 184] [Corresponding to Sections 299 and 305 of the Companies Act, 1956]

1. Every director shall at the first meeting of the board in which he participates as a director and thereafter at the first meeting of the board in every financial year or whenever there is any change in the disclosures already made, then at the first board meeting held after such change, disclose his concern or interest in any company or companies or bodies corporate, firms, or other association of individuals which shall include the shareholding, in such manner as may be prescribed [under Rule 9 of the Companies (Meetings of Board and its Powers) Rules, 2014].

   [Rule 9 of the Companies (Meetings of Board and its Powers) Rules, 2014 states that:

(i) Every director shall disclose his concern or interest in any company or companies or bodies corporate (including shareholding interest), firms, or other association of individuals, by giving a notice in writing in Form MBP 1.

(ii) It shall be the duty of the director giving notice of interest to cause it to be disclosed at the meeting held immediately after the date of the notice.

(iii) All notices shall be kept at the registered office and such notices shall be preserved for a period of 8 years from the end of the financial year to which it relates and shall be kept in the custody of the company secretary of the company or any other person authorized by the board for the purpose].

2. Every director of a company who is in any way, whether directly or indirectly, concerned or interested in a contract or arrangement or proposed contract or arrangement entered into or to be entered into:

   (a) with a body corporate in which such director or such director in association with any other director, holds more than 2% shareholding of that body corporate, or is a promoter, manager, chief executive officer of that body corporate; or

   (b) with a firm or other entity in which, such director is a partner, owner or member, as the case may be,

   shall disclose the nature of his concern or interest at the meeting of the board in which the contract or arrangement is discussed and shall not participate in such meeting:

   Provided that where any director who is not so concerned or interested at the time of entering into such contract or arrangement, he shall, if he becomes concerned or interested after the contract or arrangement is entered into, disclose his concern or interest forthwith when he becomes concerned or interested or at the first meeting of the board held after he becomes so concerned or interested.

3. A contract or arrangement entered into by the company without disclosure under sub-section (2) or with participation by a director who is concerned or interested in any way, directly or indirectly, in the contract or arrangement, shall be voidable at the option of the company.

4. If a director of the company contravenes the provisions of sub-section (1) or sub-section (2), such director shall be punishable with imprisonment for a term which may extend to 1 year or with fine which may extend to ₹ 1 lakh, or with both.

5. Nothing in this section:

   (a) shall be taken to prejudice the operation of any rule of law restricting a director of a company from having any concern or interest in any contract or arrangement with the company;

   (b) shall apply to any contract or arrangement entered into or to be entered into between two companies or between one or more companies and one or more bodies corporate where any of the directors of the one company or two or more of them together holds or hold not more than 2% of the paid-up share capital in the other company or the body corporate.

9.2.11 Related Party Transactions [Section 188] [Corresponding to Sections 294, 294A, 297 and 314 of the Companies Act, 1956]

1. Except with the consent of the board of directors given by a resolution at a meeting of the board and subject to such conditions as may be prescribed [under Rule 15 of the Companies (Meetings of Board and its Powers) Rules, 2014], no company shall enter into any contract or arrangement with a related party with respect to:

   (a) sale, purchase or supply of any goods or materials;

   (b) selling or otherwise disposing of, or buying, property of any kind;

   (c) leasing of property of any kind;

   (d) availing or rendering of any services;

   (e) appointment of any agent for purchase or sale of goods, materials, services or property;

   (f) such related party's appointment to any office or place of profit in the company, its subsidiary company or associate company; and

   (g) underwriting the subscription of any securities or derivatives thereof, of the company:

   Provided that no contract or arrangement, in the case of a company having a paid-up share capital of not less than such amount, or transactions exceeding such sums as may be prescribed [under Rule 15 of the Companies (Meetings of Board and its Powers) Rules, 2014], shall be entered into except with the prior approval of the company by a resolution;

   Provided further that no member of the company shall vote on such special resolution, to approve any contract or arrangement which may be entered into by the company, if such member is a related party;

   Provided also that nothing in this sub-section shall apply to any transactions entered into by the company in its ordinary course of business other than transactions which are not on arm's length basis.

   Provided also that the requirement of passing the resolution under first proviso shall not be applicable for transactions entered into between a holding company and its wholly owned subsidiary whose accounts are consolidated with such holding company and placed before the shareholders at the general meeting for approval.

   Explanation: In this sub-section:

   (a) the expression "office or place of profit" means any office or place:

      (i) where such office or place is held by a director, if the director holding it receives from the company anything by way of remuneration over and the remuneration to which he is entitled as director, by way of salary, fee, commission, perquisites, any rent-free accommodation, or otherwise;

      (ii) where such office or place is held by an individual other than a director or by any firm, private company or other body corporate, if the individual, firm, private company or body corporate holding it receives from the company anything by way of remuneration, salary, fee, commission, perquisites, any rent-free accommodation, or otherwise;

(b) the expression "arm's length transaction" means a transaction between two related parties that is conducted as if they were unrelated, so that there is no conflict of interest.

[Rule 15 of the Companies (Meetings of Board and its Powers) Rules, 2014 states that a company shall enter into any contract or arrangement with a related party subject to the following conditions, viz.

(1) The agenda of the board meeting at which the resolution is proposed to be moved shall disclose:
   (a) the name of the related party and nature of relationship;
   (b) the nature, duration of the contract and particulars of the contract or arrangement;
   (c) the material terms of the contract or arrangement including the value, if any;
   (d) any advance paid or received for the contract or arrangement, if any;
   (e) the manner of determining the pricing and other commercial terms, both included as part of contract and not considered as part of the contract;
   (f) whether all factors relevant to the contract have been considered, if not, the details of factors not considered with the rationale for not considering those factors; and
   (g) any other information relevant or important for the board to take a decision on the proposed transaction.

(2) Where any director is interested in any contract or arrangement with a related party, such director shall not be present at the meeting during discussion on the subject matter of the resolution relating to such contract or arrangement.

(3) For the purposes of first proviso to sub-section (1) of Section 188, except with the prior approval of the company by a resolution, a company shall not enter into a transaction or transactions, where the transaction or transactions to be entered into:
   (a) as contracts or arrangements with respect to clauses (a) to (e) of sub-section (1) of Section 188, with criteria as mentioned below:
      (i) sale, purchase or supply of any goods or materials, directly or through appointment of agent, amounting to 10% or more of the turnover of the company or ₹ 100 crore, whichever is lower, as mentioned in clause (a) and clause (e) respectively of sub-section (1) of Section 188;
      (ii) selling or otherwise disposing of or buying property of any kind, directly or through appointment of agent, amounting to 10% or more of net worth of the company or ₹ 100 crore, whichever is lower, as mentioned in clause (b) and clause (e) respectively of sub-section (1) of Section 188;
      (iii) leasing of property of any kind amounting to 10% or more of net worth of the company or 10% or more of the turnover of

the company or ₹ 100 crore, whichever is lower, as mentioned in clause (c) of sub-section (1) of Section 188;

(iv) availing or rendering of any services, directly or through appointment of agent, amounting to 10% or more of the turnover of the company or ₹ 50 crore, whichever is lower, as mentioned in clause (d) and clause (e) respectively of sub-section (1) of Section 188;

Explanation: It is hereby clarified that the limits specified in sub-section (i) to (iv) shall apply for transaction or transactions to be entered into either individually or taken together with the previous transactions during a financial year.

(b) is for appointment to any office or place of profit in the company, its subsidiary company or associate company at a monthly remuneration exceeding ₹ 2.50 lakh as mentioned in clause (f) of sub-section (1) of Section 188; or

(c) is for remuneration for underwriting the subscription of any securities or derivatives thereof, of the company exceeding 1% of the net worth as mentioned in clause (g) of sub-section (1) of Section 188.

Explanation:

(1) The turnover or net worth referred to in the above sub-rules shall be computed on the basis of the audited financial statement of the preceding financial year.

(2) In case of a wholly-owned subsidiary, the resolution passed by the holding company shall be sufficient for the purpose of entering into transactions between the wholly-owned subsidiary and the holding company.

(3) The explanatory statement to be annexed to the notice of a general meeting convened pursuant to Section 101 shall contain the following particulars, namely:

(a) name of the related party;

(b) name of the director or key managerial personnel who is related, if any;

(c) nature of relationship;

(d) nature, material terms, monetary value and particulars of the contract or arrangement;

(e) any other information relevant or important for the members to take a decision on the proposed resolution.

2. Every contract or arrangement entered into under sub-section (1) shall be referred to in the board's report to the shareholders along with the justification for entering into such contract or arrangement.

3. Where any contract or arrangement is entered into by a director or any other employee, without obtaining the consent of the board or approval by a resolution in the general meeting under sub-section (1) and if it is not ratified by the board

or, as the case may be, by the shareholders at a meeting within 3 months from the date on which such contract or arrangement was entered into, such contract or arrangement shall be voidable at the option of the board and if the contract or arrangement is with a related party to any director, or is authorized by another director, the directors concerned shall indemnify the company against any loss incurred by it.

4. Without prejudice to anything contained in sub-section (3), it shall be open to the company to proceed against a director or any other employee who had entered into such contract or arrangement in contravention of the provisions of this section for recovery of any loss sustained by it as a result of such contract or arrangement.
5. Any director or any other employee of a company, who had entered into or authorized the contract or arrangement in violation of the provisions of this section, shall:
   (i) in case of listed company, be punishable with imprisonment for a term which may extend to 1 year or with fine which shall not be less than ₹ 25,000, but which may extend to ₹ 5 lakh, or with both; and
   (ii) in case of any other company, be punishable with fine which shall not be less than ₹ 25,000 but which may extend to ₹ 5 lakh.

9.3 CODE FOR INDEPENDENT DIRECTORS

The new Companies Act has also provided the following *guidelines/code of conduct* to be followed by independent directors.

Code for Independent Directors

[Schedule IV to the Companies Act, 2013]

The Code is guide to professional conduct for independent directors. Adherence to these standards by independent directors and fulfillment of their responsibilities in a professional and faithful manner will promote confidence of the investment community, particularly minority shareholders, regulators and companies in the institution of independent directors.

I. Guidelines of professional conduct

An independent director shall:

1. uphold ethical standards of integrity and probity;
2. act objectively and constructively while exercising his duties;
3. exercise his responsibilities in a bona fide manner in the interest of the company;
4. devote sufficient time and attention to his professional obligations for informed and balanced decision-making;
5. not allow any extraneous considerations that will vitiate his exercise of objective independent judgement in the paramount interest of the company as a whole, while concurring in or dissenting from the collective judgement of the board in its decision-making;

6. not abuse his position to the detriment of the company or its shareholders or for the purpose of gaining direct or indirect personal advantage or advantage for any associated person;
7. refrain from any action that would lead to loss of his independence;
8. where circumstances arise which make an independent director lose his independence, the independent director must immediately inform the board accordingly;
9. assist the company in implementing the best corporate governance practices.

II. Role and functions

The independent directors shall:

1. help in bringing an independent judgement to bear on the board's deliberations, especially on issues of strategy, performance, risk management, resources, key appointments and standards of conduct;
2. bring an objective view in the evaluation of performance of board and management;
3. scrutinize the performance of management in meeting agreed goals and objectives and monitor the reporting of performance;
4. satisfy themselves on the integrity of financial information and that financial controls and the systems of risk management are robust and defensible;
5. safeguard the interests of all stakeholders, particularly the minority shareholders;
6. balance the conflicting interest of the stakeholders;
7. determine appropriate levels of remuneration of executive directors, key managerial personnel and senior management and have a prime role in appointing and, where necessary, recommend removal of executive directors, key managerial personnel and senior management;
8. moderate and arbitrate in the interest of the company as a whole, in situations of conflict between management and shareholders' interest.

III. Duties

The independent directors shall:

1. undertake appropriate induction and regularly update and refresh their skills, knowledge and familiarity with the company;
2. seek appropriate clarification or amplification of information and, where necessary, take and follow appropriate professional advice and opinion of the outside experts at the expense of the company;
3. strive to attend all meetings of the board of directors and of the board committees of which he is a member;
4. participate constructively and actively in the committees of the board in which they are chairpersons or members;
5. strive to attend the general meetings of the company;
6. where they have concerns about the running of the company or a proposed action, ensure that these are addressed by the board and, to the extent that

they are not resolved, insist that their concerns are recorded in the minutes of the board meeting;

7. keep themselves well informed about the company and the external environment in which it operates;
8. not to unfairly obstruct the functioning of an otherwise proper board or committee of the board;
9. pay sufficient attention and ensure that adequate deliberations are held before approving related party transactions and assure themselves that the same are in the interest of the company;
10. ascertain and ensure that the company has an adequate and functional vigil mechanism and to ensure that the interests of a person who uses such mechanism are not prejudicially affected on account of such use;
11. report concerns about unethical behaviour, actual or suspected fraud or violation of the company's code of conduct or ethics policy;
12. act within their authority, assist in protecting the legitimate interests of the company, shareholders and its employees;
13. not disclose confidential information, including commercial secrets, technologies, advertising and sales promotion plans, unpublished price-sensitive information, unless such disclosure is expressly approved by the board or required by law.

IV. Manner of appointment

1. Appointment process of independent directors shall be independent of the company management, while selecting independent directors the board shall ensure that there is appropriate balance of skills, experience and knowledge in the board so as to enable the board to discharge its functions and duties effectively.
2. The appointment of independent director(s) of the company shall be approved at the meeting of the shareholders.
3. The explanatory statement attached to the notice of the meeting for approving the appointment of independent director shall include a statement that in the opinion of the board, the independent director proposed to be appointed fulfills the conditions specified in the Act and the rules made thereunder and that the proposed director is independent of the management.
4. The appointment of independent directors shall be finalized through a letter of appointment, which shall set out:
   (a) the term of appointment;
   (b) the expectation of the board from the appointed director, the board level committee(s) in which the director is expected to serve and its tasks;
   (c) the fiduciary duties that come with such an appointment along with accompanying liabilities;
   (d) provision for directors and officers (D and O) insurance, if any;
   (e) the code of business ethics that the company expects its directors and employees to follow;

(f) the list of actions that a director should not do while functioning as such in the company; and

(g) the remuneration, mentioning periodic fees, reimbursement of expenses for participation in the board's and other meetings and profit-related commission, if any.

5. The terms and conditions of appointment of independent directors shall be open for inspection at the registered office of the company by any member during normal business hours.
6. The terms and conditions of appointment of independent directors shall also be posted on the company's website.

V. Re-appointment

The re-appointment of independent director shall be on the basis of report of performance evaluation.

VI. Resignation or removal

1. The resignation or removal of an independent director shall be in the same manner as is provided in Sections 168 and 169 of the Act.
2. An independent director who resigns or is removed from the board of the company shall be replaced by a new independent director within a period of 3 months from the date of such resignation or removal, as the case may be.
3. Where the company fulfills the requirement of independent directors in its board even without filling the vacancy created by such resignation or removal, as the case may be, the requirement of replacement by a new independent director shall not apply.

VII. Separate meetings

1. The independent directors of the company shall hold at least one meeting in a financial year, without the attendance of non-independent directors and members of management;
2. All the independent directors of the company shall strive to be present at such meeting;
3. The meeting shall:
   (a) review the performance of non-independent directors and the board as a whole;
   (b) review the performance of the chairperson of the company, taking into account the views of executive directors and non-executive directors;
   (c) assess the quality, quantity and timeliness of flow of information between the company management and the board that is necessary for the board to effectively and reasonably perform their duties.

VIII. Evaluation mechanism

1. The performance evaluation of independent directors shall be done by the entire board of directors, excluding the director being evaluated.

2. On the basis of the report of performance evaluation, it shall be determined whether to extend or continue the term of appointment of the independent director.

Note: The provisions of sub-paragraphs (2) and (7) of Paragraph II, Paragraph IV, Paragraph V, clauses (a) and (b) of sub-paragraph (3) of Paragraph VII and Paragraph VIII shall not apply in the case of a Government company as defined under clause (45) of Section 2 of the Companies Act, 2013 (18 of 2013), if the requirements in respect of matters specified in these paragraphs are specified by the concerned Ministries or Departments of the Central Government or as the case may be, the State Governments, and such requirements are complied with by the Government companies.

9.4 A CRITICAL ANALYSIS OF NEW COMPANY LAW AND A FEW SUGGESTIONS FOR IMPROVEMENT

We have discussed at length in the previous section the provisions contained in different sections of the Companies Act, 2013 relating to the corporate directors. At this stage, it will be prudent to highlight some of the important analyses.

1. It is the first time in the history of company law that the corporate directors have been recognized and classified as executive directors, non-executive directors, and independent directors.
2. It is the first time that the company law has defined clearly the criteria for designating a board member as independent director.
3. It is for the first time that the company law mandated the provision for introduction of corporate social responsibility committee in the corporate houses, along with CSR policy rules and a separate schedule specifying the activities to be included by companies in their CSR policies.
4. It is the first time that the company law has provided guidelines/code of conduct to be followed by independent directors.
5. Out of 39 sections concerning directors of companies, 4 sections were newly added and enforced with effect from 1st April 2014. They are Section 135 (Corporate Social Responsibility), Section 150 (Manner of selection of independent directors and maintenance of data bank of independent directors), Section 168 (Resignation of director), and Section 178 (Nomination and Remuneration Committee and Shareholders Relationship Committee).
6. There are 6 sections out of 39, which have been enforced with effect from 12th September 2013. They are Section 180 (Restrictions on powers of board), Section 185 (Loan to directors, etc.), Section 192 (Restrictions on non-cash transactions involving directors), Section 194 (Prohibition of forward dealings in securities of company by director or key managerial personnel), Section 195 (Prohibition on insider trading of securities), and Section 202 (Compensation for loss of office of managing, or whole time director or manager). The provisions of the rest 33 sections have been enforced with effect from 1st April 2014. Subsequently Section 194 and Section 195 have been omitted by the Companies (Amendment) Act, 2017, w.e.f. 9th February, 2018.

7. As many as 62 sections (Sections 197A, 198, 201, 202, 215, 216, 217, 252, 253, 254, 255, 256, 260, 262, 264, 266A, 266B, 266C, 266D, 266E, 266F, 266G, 267, 274, 275, 276, 278, 279, 283, 284, 286, 287, 288, 289, 291, 292, 292A, 293, 294, 294A, 295, 296, 297, 299, 301, 303, 305, 307, 309, 310, 312, 313, 314, 317, 318, 319, 320, 321(4), 384, 385, 387, 388) have been condensed into 32 sections of the new Companies Act, 2013.
8. The provisions of 13 sections have been re-written and completely overhauled. These sections are Section 153 (Application for allotment of Director Identification Number), Section 154 (Allotment of Director Identification Number), Section 155 (Prohibition to obtain more than one Director Identification Number), Section 156 (Director to intimate Director Identification Number), Section 157 (Company to inform Director Identification Number to Registrar), Section 158 (Obligation to indicate Director Identification Number), Section 159 (Punishment for contravention), Section 166 (Duties of directors), Section 177 (Audit Committee), Section 184 (Disclosure of interest by director), Section 188 (Related party transactions), Section 189 (Register of contracts or arrangements in which directors are interested), and Section 191 (Payment to director for loss of office, etc. in connection with transfer of undertaking, property or shares.
9. New provisions have been included and thereby 15 sections have been extended. These sections are Section 134(5) (Directors' responsibility statement), Section 149 (Company to have board of directors), Section 151 (Appointment of director elected by small shareholders), Section 152 (Appointment of directors), Section 161 (Appointment of additional director, alternate director and nominee director), Section 164 (Disqualifications for appointment of director), Section 165 (Number of directorships), Section 173 (Meetings of board), Section 174 (Quorum for meetings of board), Section 175 (Passing of resolution by circulation), Section 179 (Powers of board), Section 180 (Restrictions on powers of board), Section 185 (Loan to directors), Section 196 (Appointment of managing director, whole time director or manager), and Section 197 (Overall maximum managerial remuneration and managerial remuneration in case of absence or inadequacy of profits).

All these initiatives have been taken by the Ministry of Corporate Affairs, GOI, not only to make the new company law sleek but also to make it more effective, up-to-date and unambiguous. There is no doubt that adherence to these provisions by corporate directors and fulfillment of their responsibilities in a professional and faithful manner will go a long way to promote confidence of the investment community, particularly minority shareholders, regulators and companies and ensure international standard of corporate governance.

However, on further analysis of the new regulations and enactments, we have observed certain *gaps in the current enactments* relating to corporate governance, some of which are highlighted below:

Minimum number of directors [Section 149]

Under this section, a public company shall have at least three directors, which appear to be insufficient for managing a company. The minimum number should be increased substantially in order to position them in various board committees required for corporate governance.

Small shareholders' director [Section 151]

This section provides for election of one director by small shareholders. Implementation of this provision shall pose a problem. The questions will come up: How the small shareholders will elect their nominee—is it by show of hands or will there be a separate poll for this purpose? Will it serve any useful purpose when only a small number of small shareholders attend general meetings? What will be the role of such elected director? Is there any real necessity for appointment of such a director in the board when there are independent directors to take care of the interests of all shareholders including the small shareholders?

All these questions need to be addressed properly and the section should be modified accordingly.

Directors' Responsibility Statement (DRS) [Section 134(5)]

Directors' Responsibility Statement (DRS), enacted by the new Act, is not complete. It should include an additional statement to the effect that every director has made relevant disclosure of his interest or concern. Moreover, DRS should also include another clause that the related party transactions have been entered into at arm's length, and if not, the relationships of the directors in such transactions along with the amount involved have been disclosed as a part of the directors' report along with justification.

Maximum number of directorships in companies [Section 165]

Section 165 of the Companies Act, 2013 prescribes the maximum number of directorships to 10 in public companies. But, in the present era of stiff business competition—domestic and international, when the company directors are to concentrate heavily on the day-to-day management for its survival and growth, it is time that the maximum number of directorships should be reduced to 5 in public companies, of which as member in not more than 2 committees and as chairman in not more than 1 committee. This will ensure justice towards improved corporate governance on all these companies.

Audit committee [Section 177]

This section leaves a huge gap in its enactment as it has not mentioned anything about (i) periodicity of the meeting, (ii) quorum for meeting, (iii) specific powers of the committee and (iv) secretary to the committee. It is no denying the fact that the intention of the law in regard to formation of the audit committee is not to induct any promoter—director or the executive director in the committee. But, the current provision lays the foundation for such induction, which is likely to vitiate the very purpose of audit committee formation.

It is, therefore, proposed that these gaps should be plugged expeditiously by way of further amendment. Besides, the Government should consider constitution of audit committee only with independent directors to serve its purpose and thereby change the current provision accordingly.

Protection to whistle blowers

The company law should recognize the 'whistle blower' concept by introducing a separate section to provide for protection to individuals who expose offences by companies, particularly those involving fraud. Such protection should be extended to normal terms and conditions of service and from harassment. The section should also explain in detail as to how individual protection can be provided, what the responsibilities of the companies are and what the remedies available in the company law are for the whistle blowers if adequate protections are not provided.

9.5 CONCLUSION

As we have mentioned earlier that India took up its economic reforms programme in 1990s. A need was felt for a comprehensive review of the Companies Act, 1956 which had become the bulkiest and archaic by the course of time. Thereafter, in the year 2013, the GOI introduced a new and revised Companies Act, 2013 and the Rules, 2014. The Act is now sleek and thoroughly overhauled and revised with 29 chapters, 470 sections and 7 schedules. The new Act has been enforced with effect from 1st April 2014. Many provisions of the erstwhile Act have been omitted, many existing provisions revised, merged, extended and re-written, and many provisions have been newly introduced as per the requirement of current conditions and reality. It is for the first time that the corporate directors have been recognized and classified as executive directors, non-executive directors and independent directors in the new Companies Act, 2013. Subsequently, some of these provisions of the new Act have been amended by the Companies (Amendment) Act, 2019. Adherence to these provisions by corporate directors and fulfillment of their responsibilities in a professional and faithful manner will go a long way to promote confidence of the investment community, particularly minority shareholders, regulators and companies and ensure international standard of corporate governance. However, on further analysis of the new regulations and enactments, we have observed certain gaps in the current enactments relating to corporate governance, some of which have been highlighted and suggestions provided.

CASE STUDY

Board of Directors of Citigroup

INTRODUCTION

In the year 2012, Citigroup, headquartered in New York, was the 7th largest company in the world according to the Fortune Global 500. The group generated net revenues of USD 172 billion and net income of USD 36 billion. Citigroup formed by the merger of Travellers Group and Citicorp in 1998 had emerged as the largest financial services company in the world offering services to its clients thro: four global business groups across 100 countries.

Citigroup was organised into various business segments. Global Consumer Group (GCG) offered services such as, banking, lending and investment services, credit cards and debit cards, such as, Master card and VISA, truck financing, construction, material handling, health care, office equipment finance and consumer finance etc.

Global Corporate and Investment bank (GCIB) provided various services to corporate, institutional and retail investors such as, underwriting, syndicated loans, foreign exchange and futures, strategic and financial advisory services etc.

Global Investment Management (GIM) took care of personalised wealth management services for affluent clients, asset management, retirement and insurance. Citigroup International (CI) looked after providing personal financial services all over the world.

BOARD OF DIRECTORS

The board's primary responsibility was to ensure effective governance that would protect the interests of its stakeholders. It was also responsible for the formation of committees for various functions and overseeing the management of the organisation and compliance with various standards, laws, rules and regulations.

Board Structure

The board consisted of 17 directors of whom 14 were independent directors, 2 were executive directors, and 1 was an honorary director. The honorary director participated in board meetings but could not vote. Members of the board or senior management were required to hold at least 75% of the shares of Citigroup common stock. Citigroup did not adopt term limits for directors.

Directors–Appointment and Tenure

Candidates for nomination to the board were selected by the nomination and corporate governance committee, and were recommended to the board for approval. The stockholders, at each annual meeting, elected directors to serve for a one year term. Directors who served on the board till the next annual meeting of the company following their 72nd birthday were not elected, unless this requirement was waived off by the board or the nomination and corporate governance committee for a valid reason.

Directors–Orientation and Continuing Education

Citigroup provided an orientation programme for new directors. The programme included visits to the company's major facilities. All members of the board could also participate in continuing education programmes provided by the company and third parties.

Board Meetings

Citigroup's directors were expected to attend all board meetings and meetings of committees on which they served. The directors were provided with necessary and appropriate information before the meeting. The chairman established a standard agenda for the year, which contained issues to be discussed at each meeting. Board members were allowed to suggest items for inclusion. The Citigroup board met 16 times in the year 2012.

The independent directors met 7 times in executive sessions, in the absence of the CEO. The chairman of the nomination and corporate governance committee presided over all such meetings. Individual board members, from time to time, met or otherwise communicated with various other constituent units involved with Citigroup, only after consultation with senior management.

Directors had full and free access to senior management and other employees of the company. The board welcomed regular attendance by the senior management of the company at each board meeting. The CEO could also request additional company personnel to attend board meetings with prior approval of the board.

Directors–Compensation

Based on the recommendations of the nomination and corporate governance committee and annual review of the compensation structure, the board decided the directors' compensation. Apart from the salary, the executive directors did not receive any compensation for their service as directors. Independent directors could not enter into any paid consulting arrangements with the company. Independent directors and the honorary director received an annual retainer of USD 125000, payable either 100% in common stock, or up to 50% in cash to cover taxes and the remainder in common stock. Directors could receive all or a part of this compensation in the form of an option, to purchase shares of the company's stock.

CEO Performance and Succession Planning

The personnel and compensation committee conducted an annual review of the CEO's performance, followed by a review by the board to assess whether the CEO was providing the best leadership for the company in the short and long run. The committee also presented a report to the board on succession planning to facilitate nomination and evaluation of potential successors to the CEO. The CEO made available his recommendations and evaluations of potential successors, and a review of any development plans recommended for such individuals.

Questions for Discussion

1. What was the board structure of Citigroup?
2. How the directors of Citigroup were appointed and compensated?
3. How the CEO's performance was evaluated and succession planning conducted?

Test Your Knowledge

1. List out the important enactments of Indian Companies Act, 2013 and Rules, 2014 concerning the corporate board of directors and corporate governance.
2. What are the provisions of the Companies Act, 2013 in regard to 'Directors' Responsibility Statement'?
3. Discuss the provisions of the company law in regard to Corporate Social Responsibility.
4. Enumerate the 'Duties of Directors' as provided in the Companies Act, 2013.
5. Discuss the manner of selection of independent directors and maintenance of databank of independent directors as required by the Companies Act, 2013.

6. Discuss the provisions of the Companies Act, 2013 in regard to formation, roles and responsibilities of the Audit Committee.
7. What are the provisions of the Companies Act, 2013 regarding disclosure of interest by director?
8. What do you mean by the legal term 'Related Party'? What are the provisions of the Companies Act, 2013 regarding 'Related Party Transactions'?
9. What are the provisions of the Companies Act, 2013 regarding prohibition of forward dealings in securities of company by director or key managerial personnel?
10. What do you mean by the legal term 'Insider Trading'? What are the prohibitions under the Companies Act, 2013 on 'Insider Trading of Securities'?
11. Discuss the Code for Independent Directors as provided by the new Companies Act, 2013.
12. Highlight some of the important analyses of new Company Law and offer your suggestions for improvement.
13. Write short notes on:
    (a) Appointment of Director Elected by Small Shareholders
    (b) Number of Directorships
    (c) Nomination and Remuneration Committee and Stakeholders' Relationship Committee

CHAPTER 10

Role of Securities and Exchange Board of India (SEBI) Concerning Corporate Governance

Learning Objectives	Key Words
After reading this chapter, the readers will be able to understand: • The functions and powers of SEBI, SEBI Regulations, Guidelines and Schemes • Revised (New) Clause 49 of the SEBI Listing Agreement • SEBI (Listing Obligations and Disclosure Requirements) Regulations, 2015 [as amended on and upto 29th July 2019] pertaining to Corporate Governance • The Gaps in the SEBI Listing Regulations, 2015 and a few Suggestions for Modification • Comparison between the SEBI Listing Regulations, 2015 and the Companies Act, 2013 (amended upto 2019)	• Listing Agreement • Risk Management • Board Responsibilities • Whistle Blowers • Means of Communication

10.1 INTRODUCTION

SEBI formulated various rules and regulations for the purpose of regulating the operations of the players of the capital market, which were aimed at promotion of more responsible corporate governance. In this chapter, we discuss about revised Clause 49 of the Listing Agreement introduced by SEBI with effect from 1st October 2014 for compliance by all listed companies in regard to governance by all directors (executive, non-executive, and independent). Subsequently, this clause has been replaced by the new SEBI (Listing Obligation and Disclosure Requirements) 2015, which has been effective from December 2015. Subsequently, there were several amendments in between the years 2015 and 2019 in regard to SEBI Listing Regulations.

10.2 THE SECURITIES AND EXCHANGE BOARD OF INDIA (SEBI)

With the abolition of the office of the Controller of Capital Issues (CCI), the Securities and Exchange Board of India (SEBI) was constituted. It was established originally in 1988, but was only given statutory power with the enactment of the SEBI Act in January 1992. The SEBI did not obtain complete autonomy and authority to pursue its twin goals of *investor protection* and *market development*. The authority in key areas remained with the Department of Company Affairs (DCA). Gradually, its powers were expanded, but not to the extent enjoyed by the Securities and Exchange Commission (SEC of the USA). The statutory and regulatory powers to SEBI have been given by the Government, with the mission to move from control regime to prudential regulation. SEBI was empowered to regulate the working of the stock exchanges, monitoring the members of the stock exchanges and all the players of the capital market, including the boards of all listed companies. The bankers and registrars to the issue, merchant bankers, underwriters, portfolio managers, credit rating agencies, Foreign Institutional Investors (FIIs), Venture Capital Funds (VCFs), Mutual Funds (MFs) and Asset Management Companies (AMCs) also came within the purview of SEBI operations.

SEBI, thereafter, formulated various rules and regulations for the purpose of regulating the operations of the players of the capital market, which were aimed at promotion of more responsible governance in companies.

10.2.1 Functions and Powers of SEBI

According to Section 11(1) of the SEBI Act, SEBI has the responsibility to protect the interests of investors in securities and to promote the development of and to regulate the securities markets by way of taking appropriate *measures*, as mentioned under:

1. Regulating the business in stock exchanges and any other securities markets;
2. Registering and regulating the working of stock-brokers, sub-brokers, share transfer agents, bankers to an issue, trustees of trust deeds, registrars to an issue, merchant bankers, underwriters, portfolio managers, investment advisors, and such other intermediaries associated with the securities markets in any manner;
3. Registering and regulating the functioning of collective investment schemes, including mutual funds;
4. Promoting and regulating self-regulatory organizations;
5. Prohibiting fraudulent and unfair trade practices in the securities market;
6. Promoting investor education and trading of securities in securities market;
7. Prohibiting insider trading in securities;
8. Regulating substantial acquisition of shares and takeover of companies;
9. Calling for information from, undertaking inspection, conducting enquiries and audits of the stock exchanges, intermediaries, and self-regulatory organizations in the securities market;
10. Performing such functions and exercising such powers under the provisions of the Securities Contracts (Regulation) Act, 1956, as may be delegated to it by the Central Government;
11. Levying fees and other charges for carrying out the purposes of Section 11 of the Act;
12. Conducting research for the above purpose;
13. Performing such other functions as may be prescribed by the government.

SEBI exercises *powers* under Sections 11 and 11B of the SEBI Act, 1992, and other regulations. With its powers, SEBI can perform the following *functions*:

1. Ask for information from any intermediary or market participant;
2. Inspect books of depository participants (DPs), issuers or beneficiary owners;
3. Suspend or cancel certificate of registration granted to a DP or issuer;
4. Request the RBI to inspect books of a banker to an issue, and suspend or cancel certificate of registration granted to the banker to an issue;
5. Suspend or cancel certificate of registration granted to the custodian of securities;
6. Suspend or cancel certificate of registration issued to the FIIs;
7. Investigate and inspect books of accounts and records of insiders;
8. Investigate an acquirer, a seller, or a merchant banker for violation of takeover rules;
9. Suspend or cancel certificate of registration granted to a merchant banker;
10. Investigate the affairs of mutual funds, their trustees and AMCs;
11. Suspend or cancel certificate of registration issued to the portfolio managers;
12. Investigate any person dealing in securities on complaint of contravention of trading regulations;
13. Suspend or cancel certificate of registration issued to the registrars and share transfer agents;
14. Suspend or cancel certificate of registration issued to the brokers who fail to furnish information of transactions in securities or who furnish false information.

10.2.2 SEBI Regulations, Guidelines and Schemes

SEBI has introduced several *regulations, guidelines and schemes* since its operations, the details of which are mentioned in Appendix 4.

In principle, all these regulations should help to promote more responsible corporate governance by:

(a) providing investors with greater information to make informed choices;
(b) curbing insider trading and manipulations on one hand and ensuring transparency and fair play, integrity and confidence of the investors on the other hand;
(c) providing investors with more effective means of redress in cases of abuse;
(d) providing equality of treatment and opportunities to minority shareholders, protection of the interest of minority shareholders, free and full disclosure of all material facts by the acquirers;
(e) preventing the actions that do not respect the interest of the shareholders, viz. manipulation of stock exchanges, including price rigging and artificially increasing/decreasing share prices; and
(f) ensuring greater transparency in the market for corporate control and facilitating the process for replacement of underperforming management through takeovers.

10.3 REVISED (NEW) CLAUSE 49 OF THE SEBI LISTING AGREEMENT

A code of corporate governance was introduced by the recommendations of the K.M. Birla Committee set up by SEBI in the year 2000. This culminated in the introduction of Clause 49 of the standard Listing Agreement to be complied with by all listed companies in stipulated phases. Birla Committee recommended:

(1) board of directors to set up qualified and independent audit committee to enhance credibility of financial disclosures and to promote transparency;
(2) corporates to provide consolidated statements in respect of all its subsidiaries having a shareholding of 51% or more of the share capital;
(3) shareholders to exhibit a greater degree of interest and involvement in the appointment of directors and auditors, etc.

In the year 2002, SEBI, while analyzing the status of compliance with Clause 49 by the listed companies, a need was felt to look beyond mere systems and procedures in order to make the corporate governance more effective in protecting the interest of investors. SEBI, therefore, constituted a committee under the chairmanship of N.R. Narayana Murthy, Chairman and Mentor of Infosys, and mandated the committee to review the performance of corporate governance in India and make appropriate recommendations. The committee submitted its report in February 2003.

Following the recommendations of Narayana Murthy Committee on corporate governance, SEBI, in exercise of powers conferred by Section 11(1) of the SEBI Act 1992, read with Section 10 of the SC(R) Act, 1956, revised Clause 49 again vide its Circular (SEMI/MRD/SE/2003/26/08) dated 26th August 2003. But, this circular was deferred for implementation, and finally, withdrawn by SEBI due to its controversial and debatable provisions. It was replaced by a new SEBI Circular (SEBI/CFD/DIL/CG/1/2004/12/10) dated 29th October 2004, after complete overhaul of Clause 49 (revised Clause 49), superseding all previous circulars issued by SEBI in this regard.

Thereafter, the Companies Act, 2013 was enacted on 30th August 2013 which provided for a major overhaul in the governance norms for all companies. The rules pertaining to corporate governance were notified on 27th March 2014. The requirements under the Companies Act, 2013 and the rules notified thereunder would be applicable for every company or a class of companies (both listed and unlisted) as may be provided therein. SEBI, therefore, decided to review the provisions of the Listing Agreement in this regard, with the objective to align with the provisions of the Companies Act, 2013, adopt best practices on corporate governance and to make the governance framework more effective. Accordingly, SEBI issued a new Circular (no. CIR/CFD/POLICY CELL/2014) on 17th April 2014, superseding all other earlier circulars issued by SEBI on Clause 35B (provision of e-voting facility to the shareholders) and Clause 49 of the Equity Listing Agreement.

10.4 SEBI (LISTING OBLIGATIONS AND DISCLOSURE REQUIREMENTS) REGULATIONS, 2015

The revised Clause 49 has also been replaced by the new SEBI (Listing Obligations and Disclosure Requirements) Regulations, 2015 (in short Listing Regulations), which has been effective from December, 2015. Thereafter, several amendments to SEBI Listing Regulations took place in between the years 2015 and 2019.

For the benefit of the readers, we reproduce below the full text of the relevant extracts of the Listing Regulations, 2015 as amended on and upto 29th July, 2019, pertaining to corporate governance.

10.4.1 Regulation 3: Applicability of the Regulations

Unless otherwise provided, these regulations shall apply to the listed entity who has listed any of the following designated securities on recognised stock exchange(s):

(a) specified securities listed on main board or SME Exchange or institutional trading platform;
(b) non-convertible debt securities, non-convertible redeemable preference shares, perpetual debt instrument, perpetual non-cumulative preference shares;
(c) Indian depository receipts;
(d) securitised debt instruments;
(da) security receipts;
(e) units issued by mutual funds;
(f) any other securities as may be specified by the Board.

10.4.2 Principles Governing Disclosures and Obligations

Regulation 4(1)

The listed entity which has listed securities shall make disclosures and abide by its obligations under these regulations, in accordance with the following principles:

(a) Information shall be prepared and disclosed in accordance with applicable standards of accounting and financial disclosure.
(b) The listed entity shall implement the prescribed accounting standards in letter and spirit in the preparation of financial statements taking into consideration the interest of all stakeholders and shall also ensure that the annual audit is conducted by an independent, competent and qualified auditor.
(c) The listed entity shall refrain from misrepresentation and ensure that the information provided to recognised stock exchange(s) and investors is not misleading.
(d) The listed entity shall provide adequate and timely information to recognised stock exchange(s) and investors.
(e) The listed entity shall ensure that disseminations made under provisions of these regulations and circulars made thereunder, are adequate, accurate, explicit, timely and presented in a simple language.
(f) Channels for disseminating information shall provide for equal, timely and cost efficient access to relevant information by investors.
(g) The listed entity shall abide by all the provisions of the applicable laws including the securities laws and also such other guidelines as may be issued from time to time by the Board and the recognised stock exchange(s) in this regard and as may be applicable.
(h) The listed entity shall make the specified disclosures and follow its obligations in letter and spirit taking into consideration the interest of all stakeholders.

(i) Filings, reports, statements, documents and information which are event based or are filed periodically shall contain relevant information.

(j) Periodic filings, reports, statements, documents and information reports shall contain information that shall enable investors to track the performance of a listed entity over regular intervals of time and shall provide sufficient information to enable investors to assess the current status of a listed entity.

Regulation 4(2)

The listed entity which has listed its specified securities shall comply with the corporate governance provisions as specified in chapter IV which shall be implemented in a manner so as to achieve the objectives of the principles as mentioned below.

(a) **The rights of shareholders:** The listed entity shall seek to protect and facilitate the exercise of the following rights of shareholders:

(i) right to participate in, and to be sufficiently informed of, decisions concerning fundamental corporate changes.

(ii) opportunity to participate effectively and vote in general shareholder meetings.

(iii) being informed of the rules, including voting procedures that govern general shareholder meetings.

(iv) opportunity to ask questions to the board of directors, to place items on the agenda of general meetings, and to propose resolutions, subject to reasonable limitations.

(v) Effective shareholder participation in key corporate governance decisions, such as the nomination and election of members of board of directors.

(vi) exercise of ownership rights by all shareholders, including institutional investors.

(vii) adequate mechanism to address the grievances of the shareholders.

(viii) protection of minority shareholders from abusive actions by, or in the interest of, controlling shareholders acting either directly or indirectly, and effective means of redress.

(b) **Timely information:** The listed entity shall provide adequate and timely information to shareholders, including but not limited to the following:

(i) sufficient and timely information concerning the date, location and agenda of general meetings, as well as full and timely information regarding the issues to be discussed at the meeting.

(ii) Capital structures and arrangements that enable certain shareholders to obtain a degree of control disproportionate to their equity ownership.

(iii) rights attached to all series and classes of shares, which shall be disclosed to investors before they acquire shares.

(c) **Equitable treatment:** The listed entity shall ensure equitable treatment of all shareholders, including minority and foreign shareholders, in the following manner:

(i) All shareholders of the same series of a class shall be treated equally.

(ii) Effective shareholder participation in key corporate governance decisions, such as the nomination and election of members of board of directors, shall be facilitated.

(iii) Exercise of voting rights by foreign shareholders shall be facilitated.

(iv) The listed entity shall devise a framework to avoid insider trading and abusive self-dealing.

(v) Processes and procedures for general shareholder meetings shall allow for equitable treatment of all shareholders.

(vi) Procedures of listed entity shall not make it unduly difficult or expensive to cast votes.

(d) **Role of stakeholders in corporate governance:** The listed entity shall recognise the rights of its stakeholders and encourage co-operation between listed entity and the stakeholders, in the following manner:

(i) The listed entity shall respect the rights of stakeholders that are established by law or through mutual agreements.

(ii) Stakeholders shall have the opportunity to obtain effective redress for violation of their rights.

(iii) Stakeholders shall have access to relevant, sufficient and reliable information on a timely and regular basis to enable them to participate in corporate governance process.

(iv) The listed entity shall devise an effective whistle blower mechanism enabling stakeholders, including individual employees and their representative bodies, to freely communicate their concerns about illegal or unethical practices.

(e) **Disclosure and transparency:** The listed entity shall ensure timely and accurate disclosure on all material matters including the financial situation, performance, ownership, and governance of the listed entity, in the following manner:

(i) Information shall be prepared and disclosed in accordance with the prescribed standards of accounting, financial and non-financial disclosure.

(ii) Channels for disseminating information shall provide for equal, timely and cost efficient access to relevant information by users.

(iii) Minutes of the meeting shall be maintained explicitly recording dissenting opinions, if any.

(f) **Responsibilities of the board of directors:** The board of directors of the listed entity shall have the following responsibilities:

(i) Disclosure of information:

1. Members of board of directors and key managerial personnel shall disclose to the board of directors whether they, directly, indirectly, or on behalf of third parties, have a material interest in any transaction or matter directly affecting the listed entity.
2. The board of directors and senior management shall conduct themselves so as to meet the expectations of operational transparency to stakeholders

while at the same time maintaining confidentiality of information in order to foster a culture of good decision-making.

(ii) Key functions of the board of directors:

1. Reviewing and guiding corporate strategy, major plans of action, risk policy, annual budgets and business plans, setting performance objectives, monitoring implementation and corporate performance, and overseeing major capital expenditures, acquisitions and divestments.
2. Monitoring the effectiveness of the listed entity's governance practices and making changes as needed.
3. Selecting, compensating, monitoring and, when necessary, replacing key managerial personnel and overseeing succession planning.
4. Aligning key managerial personnel and remuneration of board of directors with the longer term interests of the listed entity and its shareholders.
5. Ensuring a transparent nomination process to the board of directors with the diversity of thought, experience, knowledge, perspective and gender in the board of directors.
6. Monitoring and managing potential conflicts of interest of management, members of the board of directors and shareholders, including misuse of corporate assets and abuse in related party transactions.
7. Ensuring the integrity of the listed entity's accounting and financial reporting systems, including the independent audit, and that appropriate systems of control are in place, in particular, systems for risk management, financial and operational control, and compliance with the law and relevant standards.
8. Overseeing the process of disclosure and communications.
9. Monitoring and reviewing board of director's evaluation framework.

(iii) Other responsibilities:

1. The board of directors shall provide strategic guidance to the listed entity, ensure effective monitoring of the management and shall be accountable to the listed entity and the shareholders.
2. The board of directors shall set a corporate culture and the values by which executives throughout a group shall behave.
3. Members of the board of directors shall act on a fully informed basis, in good faith, with due diligence and care, and in the best interest of the listed entity and the shareholders.
4. The board of directors shall encourage continuing directors training to ensure that the members of board of directors are kept up to date.
5. Where decisions of the board of directors may affect different shareholder groups differently, the board of directors shall treat all shareholders fairly.
6. The board of directors shall maintain high ethical standards and shall take into account the interests of stakeholders.
7. The board of directors shall exercise objective independent judgement on corporate affairs.

8. The board of directors shall consider assigning a sufficient number of non-executive members of the board of directors capable of exercising independent judgement to tasks where there is a potential for conflict of interest.
9. The board of directors shall ensure that, while rightly encouraging positive thinking, these do not result in over-optimism that either leads to significant risks not being recognised or exposes the listed entity to excessive risk.
10. The board of directors shall have ability to 'step back' to assist executive management by challenging the assumptions underlying: strategy, strategic initiatives (such as acquisitions), risk appetite, exposures and the key areas of the listed entity's focus.
11. When committees of the board of directors are established, their mandate, composition and working procedures shall be well defined and disclosed by the board of directors.
12. Members of the board of directors shall be able to commit themselves effectively to their responsibilities.
13. In order to fulfil their responsibilities, members of the board of directors shall have access to accurate, relevant and timely information.
14. The board of directors and senior management shall facilitate the independent directors to perform their role effectively as a member of the board of directors and also a member of a committee of board of directors.

10.4.3 Common Obligations of Listed Entities

Regulation 13: Grievance Redressal Mechanism

1. The listed entity shall ensure that adequate steps are taken for expeditious redressal of investor complaints.
2. The listed entity shall ensure that it is registered on the SCORES platform or such other electronic platform or system of the Board as shall be mandated from time to time, in order to handle investor complaints electronically in the manner specified by the Board.
3. The listed entity shall file with the recognised stock exchange(s) on a quarterly basis, within twenty one days from the end of each quarter, a statement giving the number of investor complaints pending at the beginning of the quarter, those received during the quarter, disposed of during the quarter and those remaining unresolved at the end of the quarter.
4. The statement as specified in sub-regulation (3) shall be placed, on quarterly basis, before the board of directors of the listed entity.

10.4.4 Obligations of Listed Entity Which Has Listed Its Specified Securities

Regulation 15: Applicability

(1) The provisions of this chapter shall apply to a listed entity which has listed its specified securities on any recognised stock exchange(s) either on the main board or on SME Exchange or on institutional trading platform:

(2) The compliance with the corporate governance provisions as specified in regulations 17,

17A, 18, 19, 20, 21, 22, 23, 24, 24A, 25, 26, 27 and clauses (b) to (i) of sub-regulation 2 of regulation 46 and para C, D and E of Schedule V shall not apply, in respect of:

(a) the listed entity having paid up equity share capital not exceeding rupees ten crore and net worth not exceeding rupees twenty five crore, as on the last day of the previous financial year:

Provided that where the provisions of the regulations specified in this regulation becomes applicable to a listed entity at a later date, such listed entity shall comply with the requirements those regulations within six months from the date on which the provisions became applicable to the listed entity.

(b) the listed entity which has listed its specified securities on the SME Exchange: Provided that for other listed entities which are not companies, but body corporate or are subject to regulations under other statues, the provisions of corporate governance provisions as specified in regulation 17, 17A, 18, 19, 20, 21, 22, 23, 24, 24A, 25, 26, 27 and clauses (b) to (i) of sub-regulation (2) of regulation 46 and para C, D and E of Schedule V shall apply to the extent that it does not violate their respective statutes and guidelines or directives issued by the relevant authorities.

(2A) The provisions as specified in regulation 17 shall not be applicable during the insolvency resolution process period in respect of a listed entity which is undergoing corporate insolvency resolution process under the Insolvency Code:

Provided that the role and responsibilities of the board of directors as specified under regulation 17 shall be fulfilled by the interim resolution professional or resolution professional in accordance with sections 17 and 23 of the Insolvency Code.

(2B) The provisions as specified in regulations 18, 19, 20 and 21 shall not be applicable during the insolvency resolution process period in respect of a listed entity which is undergoing corporate insolvency resolution process under the Insolvency Code:

Provided that the roles and responsibilities of the committees specified in the respective regulations shall be fulfilled by the interim resolution professional or resolution professional.

(3) Notwithstanding sub-regulation (2) above, the provisions of Companies Act, 2013 shall continue to apply, wherever applicable.

Regulation 16: Definitions

1. For the purpose of this chapter, unless the context otherwise requires:

(a) "control" shall have the same meaning as assigned to it under the Securities and Exchange Board of India (Substantial Acquisition of Shares and Takeovers) Regulations, 2011;

(b) "independent director" means a non-executive director, other than a nominee director of the listed entity:

(i) who, in the opinion of the board of directors, is a person of integrity and possesses relevant expertise and experience;

(ii) who is or was not a promoter of the listed entity or its holding, subsidiary or associate company or member of the promoter group of the listed entity;

(iii) who is not related to promoters or directors in the listed entity, its holding, subsidiary or associate company;

(iv) who, apart from receiving director's remuneration, has or had no material pecuniary relationship with the listed entity, its holding, subsidiary or associate company, or their promoters, or directors, during the two immediately preceding financial years or during the current financial year;

(v) none of whose relatives has or had pecuniary relationship or transaction with the listed entity, its holding, subsidiary or associate company, or their promoters, or directors, amounting to two per cent. or more of its gross turnover or total income or fifty lakh rupees or such higher amount as may be prescribed from time to time, whichever is lower, during the two immediately preceding financial years or during the current financial year;

(vi) who, neither himself, nor whose relative(s):

(A) holds or has held the position of a key managerial personnel or is or has been an employee of the listed entity or its holding, subsidiary or associate company in any of the three financial years immediately preceding the financial year in which he is proposed to be appointed;

(B) is or has been an employee or proprietor or a partner, in any of the three financial years immediately preceding the financial year in which he is proposed to be appointed, of:

(1) a firm of auditors or company secretaries in practice or cost auditors of the listed entity or its holding, subsidiary or associate company; or

(2) any legal or a consulting firm that has or had any transaction with the listed entity, its holding, subsidiary or associate company amounting to ten per cent or more of the gross turnover of such firm;

(C) holds together with his relatives two per cent or more of the total voting power of the listed entity; or

(D) is a chief executive or director, by whatever name called, of any non-profit organisation that receives twenty-five per cent or more of its receipts or corpus from the listed entity, any of its promoters, directors or its holding, subsidiary or associate company or that holds two per cent or more of the total voting power of the listed entity;

(E) is a material supplier, service provider or customer or a lessor or lessee of the listed entity;

(vii) who is not less than 21 years of age.

(viii) who is not a non-independent director of another company on the board of which any non-independent director of the listed entity is an independent director:

(c) "material subsidiary" shall mean a subsidiary, whose income or net worth exceeds [19][ten] percent of the consolidated income or net worth respectively, of the listed entity and its subsidiaries in the immediately preceding accounting year.

Explanation: The listed entity shall formulate a policy for determining 'material' subsidiary.

(d) "senior management" shall mean officers/personnel of the listed entity who are members of its core management team excluding board of directors and normally this shall comprise all members of management one level below the "chief executive officer/managing director/whole time director/manager (including chief executive officer/manager, in case they are not part of the board) and shall specifically include company secretary and chief financial officer.

Regulation 17: Board of Directors

(1) The composition of board of directors of the listed entity shall be as follows:

(a) board of directors shall have an optimum combination of executive and non-executive directors with at least one woman director and not less than fifty per cent. of the board of directors shall comprise of non-executive directors;

Provided that the Board of directors of the top 500 listed entities shall have at least one independent woman director by April 1, 2019 and the Board of directors of the top 1000 listed entities shall have at least one independent woman director by April 1, 2020;

Explanation: The top 500 and 1000 entities shall be determined on the basis of market capitalisation, as at the end of the immediate previous financial year.

(b) where the chairperson of the board of directors is a non-executive director, at least one-third of the board of directors shall comprise of independent directors and where the listed entity does not have a regular non-executive chairperson, at least half of the board of directors shall comprise of independent directors:

Provided that where the regular non-executive chairperson is a promoter of the listed entity or is related to any promoter or person occupying management positions at the level of board of director or at one level below the board of directors, at least half of the board of directors of the listed entity shall consist of independent directors.

Explanation: For the purpose of this clause, the expression "related to any promoter" shall have the following meaning:

(i) if the promoter is a listed entity, its directors other than the independent directors, its employees or its nominees shall be deemed to be related to it;

(ii) if the promoter is an unlisted entity, its directors, its employees or its nominees shall be deemed to be related to it.

(c) The board of directors of the top 1000 listed entities (with effect from April 1, 2019) and the top 2000 listed entities (with effect from April 1, 2020) shall comprise of not less than six directors.

Explanation: The top 1000 and 2000 entities shall be determined on the basis of market capitalisation as at the end of the immediate previous financial year.

(d) where the listed company has outstanding SR equity shares, at least half of the board of directors shall comprise of independent directors.

(1A) No listed entity shall appoint a person or continue the directorship of any person as a non-executive director who has attained the age of seventy five years unless a special resolution is passed to that effect, in which case the explanatory statement annexed to the notice for such motion shall indicate the justification for appointing such a person.

(1B) With effect from April 1, 2020, the top 500 listed entities shall ensure that the Chairperson of the board of such listed entity shall—

(a) be a non-executive director;

(b) not be related to the Managing Director or the Chief Executive Officer as per the definition of the term "relative" defined under the Companies Act, 2013:

Provided that this sub-regulation shall not be applicable to the listed entities which do not have any identifiable promoters as per the shareholding pattern filed with stock exchanges.

Explanation: The top 500 entities shall be determined on the basis of market capitalisation, as at the end of the immediate previous financial year.

(2) The board of directors shall meet at least four times a year, with a maximum time gap of one hundred and twenty days between any two meetings.

(2A) The quorum for every meeting of the board of directors of the top 1000 listed entities with effect from April 1, 2019 and of the top 2000 listed entities with effect from April 1, 2020 shall be one-third of its total strength or three directors, whichever is higher, including at least one independent director.

Explanation I: For removal of doubts, it is clarified that the participation of the directors by video conferencing or by other audio-visual means shall also be counted for the purposes of such quorum.

Explanation II: The top 1000 and 2000 entities shall be determined on the basis of market capitalisation, as at the end of the immediate previous financial year.

(3) The board of directors shall periodically review compliance reports pertaining to all laws applicable to the listed entity, prepared by the listed entity as well as steps taken by the listed entity to rectify instances of non-compliances.

(4) The board of directors of the listed entity shall satisfy itself that plans are in place for orderly succession for appointment to the board of directors and senior management.

(5) (a) The board of directors shall lay down a code of conduct for all members of board of directors and senior management of the listed entity.

(b) The code of conduct shall suitably incorporate the duties of independent directors as laid down in the Companies Act, 2013.

(6) (a) The board of directors shall recommend all fees or compensation, if any, paid to non-executive directors, including independent directors and shall require approval of shareholders in general meeting.

(b) The requirement of obtaining approval of shareholders in general meeting shall not apply to payment of sitting fees to non-executive directors, if made within the limits prescribed under the Companies Act, 2013 for payment of sitting fees without approval of the Central Government.

(c) The approval of shareholders mentioned in clause (a), shall specify the limits for the maximum number of stock options that may be granted to non-executive directors, in any financial year and in aggregate.

(ca) The approval of shareholders by special resolution shall be obtained every year, in which the annual remuneration payable to a single non-executive director exceeds fifty per cent of the total annual remuneration payable to all non-executive directors, giving details of the remuneration thereof.

(d) Independent directors shall not be entitled to any stock option.

(e) The fees or compensation payable to executive directors who are promoters or members of the promoter group, shall be subject to the approval of the shareholders by special resolution in general meeting, if:

(i) the annual remuneration payable to such executive director exceeds rupees 5 crore or 2.5 per cent of the net profits of the listed entity, whichever is higher; or

(ii) where there is more than one such director, the aggregate annual remuneration to such directors exceeds 5 per cent of the net profits of the listed entity:

Provided that the approval of the shareholders under this provision shall be valid only till the expiry of the term of such director.

Explanation: For the purposes of this clause, net profits shall be calculated as per section 198 of the Companies Act, 2013.

(7) The minimum information to be placed before the board of directors is specified in Part A of Schedule II.

(8) The chief executive officer and the chief financial officer shall provide the compliance certificate to the board of directors as specified in Part B of Schedule II.

(9) (a) The listed entity shall lay down procedures to inform members of board of directors about risk assessment and minimization procedures.

(b) The board of directors shall be responsible for framing, implementing and monitoring the risk management plan for the listed entity.

(10) The evaluation of independent directors shall be done by the entire board of directors which shall include:

(a) performance of the directors; and

(b) fulfillment of the independence criteria as specified in these regulations and their independence from the management:

Provided that in the above evaluation, the directors who are subject to evaluation shall not participate.

(11) The statement to be annexed to the notice as referred to in sub-section (1) of section 102 of the Companies Act, 2013 for each item of special business to be transacted at a general meeting shall also set forth clearly the recommendation of the board to the shareholders on each of the specific items.

Regulation 17 A: Maximum Number of Directorships

The directors of listed entities shall comply with the following conditions with respect to the maximum number of directorships, including any alternate directorships that can be held by them at any point of time:

(1) A person shall not be a director in more than eight listed entities with effect from April 1, 2019 and in not more than seven listed entities with effect from April 1, 2020:

Provided that a person shall not serve as an independent director in more than seven listed entities.

(2) Notwithstanding the above, any person who is serving as a whole time director/ managing director in any listed entity shall serve as an independent director in not more than three listed entities.

For the purpose of this sub-regulation, the count for the number of listed entities on which a person is a director/independent director shall be only those whose equity shares are listed on a stock exchange.

Regulation 18: Audit Committee

1. Every listed entity shall constitute a qualified and independent audit committee in accordance with the terms of reference, subject to the following:

(a) The audit committee shall have minimum three directors as members.

(b) Two-thirds of the members of audit committee shall be independent directors and in case of a listed entity having outstanding SR equity shares, the audit committee shall only comprise of independent directors.

(c) All members of audit committee shall be financially literate and at least one member shall have accounting or related financial management expertise.

Explanation 1: For the purpose of this regulation, "financially literate" shall mean the ability to read and understand basic financial statements i.e. balance sheet, profit and loss account, and statement of cash flows.

Explanation 2: For the purpose of this regulation, a member shall be considered to have accounting or related financial management expertise if he or she possesses experience in finance or accounting, or requisite professional certification in accounting, or any other comparable experience or background which results in the individual's financial sophistication, including being or having been a chief executive officer, chief financial officer or other senior officer with financial oversight responsibilities.

(d) The chairperson of the audit committee shall be an independent director and he shall be present at Annual general meeting to answer shareholder queries.

(e) The Company Secretary shall act as the secretary to the audit committee.

(f) The audit committee at its discretion shall invite the finance director or head of the finance function, head of internal audit and a representative of the statutory auditor and any other such executives to be present at the meetings of the committee: Provided that occasionally the audit committee may meet without the presence of any executives of the listed entity.

2. The listed entity shall conduct the meetings of the audit committee in the following manner:

   (a) The audit committee shall meet at least four times in a year and not more than one hundred and twenty days shall elapse between two meetings.

   (b) The quorum for audit committee meeting shall either be two members or one third of the members of the audit committee, whichever is greater, with at least two independent directors.

   (c) The audit committee shall have powers to investigate any activity within its terms of reference, seek information from any employee, obtain outside legal or other professional advice and secure attendance of outsiders with relevant expertise, if it considers necessary.

3. The role of the audit committee and the information to be reviewed by the audit committee shall be as specified in Part C of Schedule II.

Regulation 19: Nomination and Remuneration Committee

1. The board of directors shall constitute the nomination and remuneration committee as follows:

   (a) the committee shall comprise of at least three directors;

   (b) all directors of the committee shall be non-executive directors; and

   (c) at least fifty percent of the directors shall be independent directors and in case of a listed entity having outstanding SR equity shares, two thirds of the nomination and remuneration committee shall comprise of independent directors.

2. The Chairperson of the nomination and remuneration committee shall be an independent director:

   Provided that the chairperson of the listed entity, whether executive or non-executive, may be appointed as a member of the Nomination and Remuneration Committee and shall not chair such Committee.

2A. The quorum for a meeting of the nomination and remuneration committee shall be either two members or one third of the members of the committee, whichever is greater, including at least one independent director in attendance.

3. The Chairperson of the nomination and remuneration committee may be present at the annual general meeting, to answer the shareholders' queries; however, it shall be up to the chairperson to decide who shall answer the queries.

3A. The nomination and remuneration committee shall meet at least once in a year.

4. The role of the nomination and remuneration committee shall be as specified as in Part D of the Schedule II.

Regulation 20: Stakeholders Relationship Committee

1. The listed entity shall constitute a Stakeholders Relationship Committee to specifically look into various aspects of interest of shareholders, debenture holders and other security holders.

2. The chairperson of this committee shall be a non-executive director.

2A. At least three directors, with at least one being an independent director, shall be members of the Committee and in case of a listed entity having outstanding SR equity shares, at least two thirds of the Stakeholders Relationship Committee shall comprise of independent directors.

3. The Chairperson of the Stakeholders Relationship Committee shall be present at the annual general meetings to answer queries of the security holders.

3A. The stakeholders relationship committee shall meet at least once in a year.

4. The role of the Stakeholders Relationship Committee shall be as specified as in Part D of the Schedule II.

Regulation 21: Risk Management Committee

1. The board of directors shall constitute a Risk Management Committee.

2. The majority of members of Risk Management Committee shall consist of members of the board of directors and in case of a listed entity having outstanding SR equity shares, at least two thirds of the Risk Management Committee shall comprise of independent directors.

3. The Chairperson of the Risk management committee shall be a member of the board of directors and senior executives of the listed entity may be members of the committee.

3A. The risk management committee shall meet at least once in a year.

4. The board of directors shall define the role and responsibility of the Risk Management Committee and may delegate monitoring and reviewing of the risk management plan to the committee and such other functions as it may deem fit such function shall specifically cover cyber security.

5. The provisions of this regulation shall be applicable to top 500 listed entities, determined on the basis of market capitalisation, as at the end of the immediate previous financial year.

Regulation 22: Vigil Mechanism

1. The listed entity shall formulate a vigil mechanism for directors and employees to report genuine concerns.

2. The vigil mechanism shall provide for adequate safeguards against victimization of director(s) or employee(s) or any other person who avail the mechanism and also provide for direct access to the chairperson of the audit committee in appropriate or exceptional cases.

Regulation 23: Related Party Transactions

1. The listed entity shall formulate a policy on materiality of related party transactions and on dealing with related party transactions including clear threshold limits duly approved by the board of directors and such policy shall be reviewed by the board of directors at least once every three years and updated accordingly:

   Explanation: A transaction with a related party shall be considered material if the transaction(s) to be entered into individually or taken together with previous transactions during a financial year, exceeds ten percent of the annual consolidated turnover of the listed entity as per the last audited financial statements of the listed entity.

1A. Notwithstanding the above, [with effect from July 01, 2019 a transaction involving payments made to a related party with respect to brand usage or royalty shall be considered material if the transaction(s) to be entered into individually or taken together with previous transactions during a financial year, exceed five percent of the annual consolidated turnover of the listed entity as per the last audited financial statements of the listed entity.

2. All related party transactions shall require prior approval of the audit committee.
3. Audit committee may grant omnibus approval for related party transactions proposed to be entered into by the listed entity subject to the following conditions, namely:
   (a) the audit committee shall lay down the criteria for granting the omnibus approval in line with the policy on related party transactions of the listed entity and such approval shall be applicable in respect of transactions which are repetitive in nature;
   (b) the audit committee shall satisfy itself regarding the need for such omnibus approval and that such approval is in the interest of the listed entity;
   (c) the omnibus approval shall specify:
      (i) the name(s) of the related party, nature of transaction, period of transaction, maximum amount of transactions that shall be entered into,
      (ii) the indicative base price/current contracted price and the formula for variation in the price if any; and
      (iii) such other conditions as the audit committee may deem fit:

      Provided that where the need for related party transaction cannot be foreseen and aforesaid details are not available, audit committee may grant omnibus approval for such transactions subject to their value not exceeding rupees one crore per transaction.
   (d) the audit committee shall review, at least on a quarterly basis, the details of related party transactions entered into by the listed entity pursuant to each of the omnibus approvals given.
   (e) Such omnibus approvals shall be valid for a period not exceeding one year and shall require fresh approvals after the expiry of one year:

4. All material related party transactions shall require approval of the shareholders through resolution and no related party shall vote to approve such resolutions whether the entity is a related party to the particular transaction or not:

   Provided that the requirements specified under this sub-regulation shall not apply in respect of a resolution plan approved under section 31 of the Insolvency Code, subject to the event being disclosed to the recognized stock exchanges within one day of the resolution plan being approved;
5. The provisions of sub-regulations (2), (3) and (4) shall not be applicable in the following cases:
   (a) transactions entered into between two government companies;
   (b) transactions entered into between a holding company and its wholly owned subsidiary whose accounts are consolidated with such holding company and placed before the shareholders at the general meeting for approval.

   Explanation: For the purpose of clause (a), "government company(ies)" means Government company as defined in sub-section (45) of section 2 of the Companies Act, 2013.
6. The provisions of this regulation shall be applicable to all prospective transactions.
7. For the purpose of this regulation, all entities falling under the definition of related parties shall not vote to approve the relevant transaction irrespective of whether the entity is a party to the particular transaction or not.
8. All existing material related party contracts or arrangements entered into prior to the date of notification of these regulations and which may continue beyond such date shall be placed for approval of the shareholders in the first General Meeting subsequent to notification of these regulations.
9. The listed entity shall submit within 30 days from the date of publication of its standalone and consolidated financial results for the half year, disclosures of related party transactions on a consolidated basis, in the format specified in the relevant accounting standards for annual results to the stock exchanges and publish the same on its website.

Regulation 24: Corporate Governance Requirements with respect to Subsidiary of Listed Entity

1. At least one independent director on the board of directors of the listed entity shall be a director on the board of directors of an unlisted material subsidiary, whether incorporated in India or not.

   Explanation: For the purposes of this provision, notwithstanding anything to the contrary contained in regulation 16, the term "material subsidiary" shall mean a subsidiary, whose income or net worth exceeds twenty percent of the consolidated income or net worth respectively, of the listed entity and its subsidiaries in the immediately preceding accounting year.
2. The audit committee of the listed entity shall also review the financial statements, in particular, the investments made by the unlisted subsidiary.
3. The minutes of the meetings of the board of directors of the unlisted subsidiary shall be placed at the meeting of the board of directors of the listed entity.

4. The management of the unlisted subsidiary shall periodically bring to the notice of the board of directors of the listed entity, a statement of all significant transactions and arrangements entered into by the unlisted subsidiary.

   Explanation: For the purpose of this regulation, the term "significant transaction or arrangement" shall mean any individual transaction or arrangement that exceeds or is likely to exceed ten percent of the total revenues or total expenses or total assets or total liabilities, as the case may be, of the unlisted subsidiary for the immediately preceding accounting year.
5. A listed entity shall not dispose of shares in its material subsidiary resulting in reduction of its shareholding (either on its own or together with other subsidiaries) to less than fifty percent or cease the exercise of control over the subsidiary without passing a special resolution in its General Meeting except in cases where such divestment is made under a scheme of arrangement duly approved by a Court/Tribunal, or under a resolution plan duly approved under section 31 of the Insolvency Code and such an event is disclosed to the recognized stock exchanges within one day of the resolution plan being approved.
6. Selling, disposing and leasing of assets amounting to more than twenty percent of the assets of the material subsidiary on an aggregate basis during a financial year shall require prior approval of shareholders by way of special resolution, unless the sale/disposal/lease is made under a scheme of arrangement duly approved by a Court/Tribunal, or under a resolution plan duly approved under section 31 of the Insolvency Code and such an event is disclosed to the recognized stock exchanges within one day of the resolution plan being approved.
7. Where a listed entity has a listed subsidiary, which is itself a holding company, the provisions of this regulation shall apply to the listed subsidiary in so far as its subsidiaries are concerned.

Regulation 24 A: Secretarial Audit

Every listed entity and its material unlisted subsidiaries incorporated in India shall undertake secretarial audit and shall annex with its annual report, a secretarial audit report, given by a company secretary in practice, in such form as may be specified with effect from the year ended March 31, 2019.

Regulation 25: Obligations with respect to Independent Directors

1. No person shall be appointed or continue as an alternate director for an independent director of a listed entity with effect from October 1, 2018.
2. The maximum tenure of independent directors shall be in accordance with the Companies Act, 2013 and rules made thereunder, in this regard, from time to time.
3. The independent directors of the listed entity shall hold at least one meeting in a year, without the presence of non-independent directors and members of the management and all the independent directors shall strive to be present at such meeting.
4. The independent directors in the meeting referred in sub-regulation (3) shall, *inter alia*:

(a) review the performance of non-independent directors and the board of directors as a whole;
(b) review the performance of the chairperson of the listed entity, taking into account the views of executive directors and non-executive directors;
(c) assess the quality, quantity and timeliness of flow of information between the management of the listed entity and the board of directors that is necessary for the board of directors to effectively and reasonably perform their duties.

5. An independent director shall be held liable, only in respect of such acts of omission or commission by the listed entity which had occurred with his knowledge, attributable through processes of board of directors, and with his consent or connivance or where he had not acted diligently with respect to the provisions contained in these regulations.

6. An independent director who resigns or is removed from the board of directors of the listed entity shall be replaced by a new independent director by listed entity at the earliest but not later than the immediate next meeting of the board of directors or three months from the date of such vacancy, whichever is later:

Provided that where the listed entity fulfils the requirement of independent directors in its board of directors without filling the vacancy created by such resignation or removal, the requirement of replacement by a new independent director shall not apply.

7. The listed entity shall familiarise the independent directors through various programmes about the listed entity, including the following:
(a) nature of the industry in which the listed entity operates;
(b) business model of the listed entity;
(c) roles, rights, responsibilities of independent directors; and
(d) any other relevant information.

8. Every independent director shall, at the first meeting of the board in which he participates as a director and thereafter at the first meeting of the board in every financial year or whenever there is any change in the circumstances which may affect his status as an independent director, submit a declaration that he meets the criteria of independence as provided in clause (b) of sub-regulation (1) of regulation 16 and that he is not aware of any circumstance or situation, which exist or may be reasonably anticipated, that could impair or impact his ability to discharge his duties with an objective independent judgment and without any external influence.

9. The board of directors of the listed entity shall take on record the declaration and confirmation submitted by the independent director under sub-regulation (8) after undertaking due assessment of the veracity of the same.

10. With effect from October 1, 2018, the top 500 listed entities by market capitalization calculated as on March 31 of the preceding financial year, shall undertake Directors and Officers insurance ('D and O insurance') for all their independent directors of such quantum and for such risks as may be determined by its board of directors.

Regulation 26: Obligations with respect to Employees including Senior Management, key Managerial Personnel, Directors and Promoters

1. A director shall not be a member in more than ten committees or act as chairperson of more than five committees across all listed entities in which he is a director which shall be determined as follows:
   (a) the limit of the committees on which a director may serve in all public limited companies, whether listed or not, shall be included and all other companies including private limited companies, foreign companies and companies under Section 8 of the Companies Act, 2013 shall be excluded;
   (b) for the purpose of determination of limit, chairpersonship and membership of the audit committee and the Stakeholders' Relationship Committee alone shall be considered.
2. Every director shall inform the listed entity about the committee positions he or she occupies in other listed entities and notify changes as and when they take place.
3. All members of the board of directors and senior management personnel shall affirm compliance with the code of conduct of board of directors and senior management on an annual basis.
4. Non-executive directors shall disclose their shareholding, held either by them or on a beneficial basis for any other persons in the listed entity in which they are proposed to be appointed as directors, in the notice to the general meeting called for appointment of such director.
5. Senior management shall make disclosures to the board of directors relating to all material, financial and commercial transactions, where they have personal interest that may have a potential conflict with the interest of the listed entity at large.

   Explanation: For the purpose of this sub-regulation, conflict of interest relates to dealing in the shares of listed entity, commercial dealings with bodies, which have shareholding of management and their relatives etc.
6. No employee including key managerial personnel or director or promoter of a listed entity shall enter into any agreement for himself or on behalf of any other person, with any shareholder or any other third party with regard to compensation or profit sharing in connection with dealings in the securities of such listed entity, unless prior approval for the same has been obtained from the Board of Directors as well as public shareholders by way of an ordinary resolution:

   Provided that such agreement, if any, whether subsisting or expired, entered during the preceding three years from the date of coming into force of this sub-regulation, shall be disclosed to the stock exchanges for public dissemination:

   Provided further that subsisting agreement, if any, as on the date of coming into force of this sub-regulation shall be placed for approval before the Board of Directors in the forthcoming Board meeting:

   Provided further that if the Board of Directors approve such agreement, the same shall be placed before the public shareholders for approval by way of an ordinary resolution in the forthcoming general meeting:

Provided further that all interested persons involved in the transaction covered under the agreement shall abstain from voting in the general meeting.

Explanation: For the purposes of this sub-regulation, 'interested person' shall mean any person holding voting rights in the listed entity and who is in any manner, whether directly or indirectly, interested in an agreement or proposed agreement, entered into or to be entered into by such a person or by any employee or key managerial personnel or director or promoter of such listed entity with any shareholder or any other third party with respect to compensation or profit sharing in connection with the securities of such listed entity.

Regulation 27: Other Corporate Governance Requirements

1. The listed entity may, at its discretion, comply with requirements as specified in Part E of Schedule II.
2. (a) The listed entity shall submit a quarterly compliance report on corporate governance in the formats specified by the Board from time to time to the recognised stock exchange(s) within fifteen days from close of the quarter.
   (b) Details of all material transactions with related parties shall be disclosed along with the report mentioned in clause (a) of sub-regulation (2).
   (c) The report mentioned in clause (a) of sub-regulation (2) shall be signed either by the compliance officer or the chief executive officer of the listed entity.

Regulation 34: Annual Report

1. The listed entity shall submit to the stock exchange and publish on its website:
   (a) a copy of the annual report sent to the shareholders along with the notice of the annual general meeting not later than the day of commencement of dispatch to its shareholders;
   (b) in the event of any changes to the annual report, the revised copy along with the details of and explanation for the changes shall be sent not later than 48 hours after the annual general meeting.
2. The annual report shall contain the following:
   (a) audited financial statements i.e. balance sheets, profit and loss accounts etc, and Statement on Impact of Audit Qualifications as stipulated in regulation 33(3)(d), if applicable;
   (b) consolidated financial statements audited by its statutory auditors;
   (c) cash flow statement presented only under the indirect method as prescribed in Accounting Standard-3 or Indian Accounting Standard 7, as applicable, specified in Section 133 of the Companies Act, 2013 read with relevant rules framed thereunder or as specified by the Institute of Chartered Accountants of India, whichever is applicable;
   (d) directors report;
   (e) management discussion and analysis report—either as a part of directors report or addition thereto;

(f) for the top five hundred listed entities based on market capitalization (calculated as on March 31 of every financial year), business responsibility report describing the initiatives taken by them from an environmental, social and governance perspective, in the format as specified by the Board from time to time:

Provided that listed entities other than top five hundred listed companies based on market capitalization and listed entities which have listed their specified securities on SME Exchange, may include these business responsibility reports on a voluntary basis in the format as specified.

3. The annual report shall contain any other disclosures specified in Companies Act, 2013 along with other requirements as specified in Schedule V of these regulations.

Regulation 36: Documents and Information to Shareholders

1. The listed entity shall send the annual report in the following manner to the shareholders:
   (a) Soft copies of full annual report to all those shareholder(s) who have registered their email address(es) either with the listed entity or with any depository;
   (b) Hard copy of statement containing the salient features of all the documents, as prescribed in Section 136 of Companies Act, 2013 or rules made thereunder to those shareholder(s) who have not so registered;
   (c) Hard copies of full annual reports to those shareholders, who request for the same.
2. The listed entity shall send annual report referred to in sub-regulation (1), to the holders of securities, not less than twenty-one days before the annual general meeting.
3. In case of the appointment of a new director or re-appointment of a director the shareholders must be provided with the following information:
   (a) a brief resume of the director;
   (b) nature of his expertise in specific functional areas;
   (c) disclosure of relationships between directors inter-se;
   (d) names of listed entities in which the person also holds the directorship and the membership of Committees of the board; and
   (e) shareholding of non-executive directors.
4. The disclosures made by the listed entity with immediate effect from date of notification of these amendments:
   (a) to the stock exchanges shall be in XBRL format in accordance with the guidelines specified by the stock exchanges from time to time; and
   (b) to the stock exchanges and on its website, shall be in a format that allows users to find relevant information easily through a searching tool:

   Provided that the requirement to make disclosures in searchable formats shall not apply in case there is a statutory requirement to make such disclosures in formats which may not be searchable, such as copies of scanned documents.

5. The notice being sent to shareholders for an annual general meeting, where the statutory auditor(s) is/are proposed to be appointed/re-appointed shall include the following disclosures as a part of the explanatory statement to the notice:
   (a) Proposed fees payable to the statutory auditor(s) along with terms of appointment and in case of a new auditor, any material change in the fee payable to such auditor from that paid to the outgoing auditor along with the rationale for such change;
   (b) Basis of recommendation for appointment including the details in relation to and credentials of the statutory auditor(s) proposed to be appointed.

Regulation 43A: Dividend Distribution Policy

1. The top five hundred listed entities based on market capitalization (calculated as on March 31 of every financial year) shall formulate a dividend distribution policy which shall be disclosed in their annual reports and on their websites.
2. The dividend distribution policy shall include the following parameters:
   (a) the circumstances under which the shareholders of the listed entities may or may not expect dividend;
   (b) the financial parameters that shall be considered while declaring dividend;
   (c) internal and external factors that shall be considered for declaration of dividend;
   (d) policy as to how the retained earnings shall be utilized; and
   (e) parameters that shall be adopted with regard to various classes of shares:

   Provided that if the listed entity proposes to declare dividend on the basis of parameters in addition to clauses (a) to (e) or proposes to change such additional parameters or the dividend distribution policy contained in any of the parameters, it shall disclose such changes along with the rationale for the same in its annual report and on its website.
3. The listed entities other than top five hundred listed entities based on market capitalization may disclose their dividend distribution policies on a voluntary basis in their annual reports and on their websites.

Regulation 44: Meeting of Shareholders and Voting

1. The listed entity shall provide the facility of remote e-voting facility to its shareholders, in respect of all shareholders' resolutions.
2. The e-voting facility to be provided to shareholders in terms of sub-regulation (1), shall be provided in compliance with the conditions specified under the Companies (Management and Administration) Rules, 2014, or amendments made thereto.
3. The listed entity shall submit to the stock exchange, within forty eight hours of conclusion of its General Meeting, details regarding the voting results in the format specified by the Board.
4. The listed entity shall send proxy forms to holders of securities in all cases mentioning that a holder may vote either for or against each resolution.
5. The top 100 listed entities by market capitalization, determined as on March

31st of every financial year, shall hold their annual general meetings within a period of five months from the date of closing of the financial year.

6. The top 100 listed entities shall provide one-way live webcast of the proceedings of the annual general meetings.

Explanation: The top 100 entities shall be determined on the basis of market capitalisation, as at the end of the immediate previous financial year.

Regulation 48: Accounting Standards

The listed entity shall comply with all the applicable and notified Accounting Standards from time to time.

Regulation 72: Corporate Governance

1. The listed entity shall comply with the corporate governance provisions as applicable in its home country and other jurisdictions in which its equity shares are listed.
2. The listed entity shall submit to stock exchange a comparative analysis of the corporate governance provisions that are applicable in its home country and in the other jurisdictions in which its equity shares are listed along with the compliance of the same vis-à-vis the corporate governance requirements applicable under regulation 17 to regulation 27, to other listed entities.

SCHEDULE II
CORPORATE GOVERNANCE

PART A—MINIMUM INFORMATION TO BE PLACED BEFORE BOARD OF DIRECTORS

[*See* Regulation 17(7)]

A. Annual operating plans and budgets and any updates.

B. Capital budgets and any updates.

C. Quarterly results for the listed entity and its operating divisions or business segments.

D. Minutes of meetings of audit committee and other committees of the board of directors.

E. The information on recruitment and remuneration of senior officers just below the level of board of directors, including appointment or removal of Chief Financial Officer and the Company Secretary.

F. Show cause, demand, prosecution notices and penalty notices, which are materially important.

G. Fatal or serious accidents, dangerous occurrences, any material effluent or pollution problems.

H. Any material default in financial obligations to and by the listed entity, or substantial non-payment for goods sold by the listed entity.

I. Any issue, which involves possible public or product liability claims of substantial nature, including any judgement or order which, may have passed strictures on the conduct of the listed entity or taken an adverse view regarding another enterprise that may have negative implications on the listed entity.

J. Details of any joint venture or collaboration agreement.

K. Transactions that involve substantial payment towards goodwill, brand equity, or intellectual property.

L. Significant labour problems and their proposed solutions. Any significant development in Human Resources/Industrial Relations front like signing of wage agreement, implementation of Voluntary Retirement Scheme etc.

M. Sale of investments, subsidiaries, assets which are material in nature and not in normal course of business.

N. Quarterly details of foreign exchange exposures and the steps taken by management to limit the risks of adverse exchange rate movement, if material.

O. Non-compliance of any regulatory, statutory or listing requirements and shareholders service such as non-payment of dividend, delay in share transfer etc.

PART B—COMPLIANCE CERTIFICATE

[*See* Regulation 17(8)]

The following compliance certificate shall be furnished by chief executive officer and chief financial officer:

A. They have reviewed financial statements and the cash flow statement for the year and that to the best of their knowledge and belief:
   1. these statements do not contain any materially untrue statement or omit any material fact or contain statements that might be misleading;
   2. these statements together present a true and fair view of the listed entity's affairs and are in compliance with existing accounting standards, applicable laws and regulations.

B. There are, to the best of their knowledge and belief, no transactions entered into by the listed entity during the year which are fraudulent, illegal or violative of the listed entity's code of conduct.

C. They accept responsibility for establishing and maintaining internal controls for financial reporting and that they have evaluated the effectiveness of internal control systems of the listed entity pertaining to financial reporting and they have disclosed to the auditors and the audit committee, deficiencies in the design or operation of such internal controls, if any, of which they are aware and the steps they have taken or propose to take to rectify these deficiencies.

D. They have indicated to the auditors and the Audit committee
   1. significant changes in internal control over financial reporting during the year;
   2. significant changes in accounting policies during the year and that the same have been disclosed in the notes to the financial statements; and
   3. instances of significant fraud of which they have become aware and the involvement therein, if any, of the management or an employee having a significant role in the listed entity's internal control system over financial reporting.

PART C—ROLE OF THE AUDIT COMMITTEE AND REVIEW OF INFORMATION BY AUDIT COMMITTEE

[*See* Regulation 18(3)]

A. The role of the audit committee shall include the following:

1. Oversight of the listed entity's financial reporting process and the disclosure of its financial information to ensure that the financial statement is correct, sufficient and credible;
2. Recommendation for appointment, remuneration and terms of appointment of auditors of the listed entity;
3. Approval of payment to statutory auditors for any other services rendered by the statutory auditors;
4. Reviewing, with the management, the annual financial statements and auditor's report thereon before submission to the board for approval, with particular reference to:
    - (a) Matters required to be included in the director's responsibility statement to be included in the board's report in terms of clause (c) of sub-section (3) of Section 134 of the Companies Act, 2013;
    - (b) Changes, if any, in accounting policies and practices and reasons for the same;
    - (c) Major accounting entries involving estimates based on the exercise of judgment by management;
    - (d) Significant adjustments made in the financial statements arising out of audit findings;
    - (e) Compliance with listing and other legal requirements relating to financial statements;
    - (f) Disclosure of any related party transactions;
    - (g) Modified opinion(s) in the draft audit report;
5. Reviewing, with the management, the quarterly financial statements before submission to the board for approval;
6. Reviewing, with the management, the statement of uses/application of funds raised through an issue (public issue, rights issue, preferential issue, etc.), the statement of funds utilized for purposes other than those stated in the offer document/prospectus/notice and the report submitted by the monitoring agency monitoring the utilisation of proceeds of a public or rights issue, and making appropriate recommendations to the board to take up steps in this matter;
7. Reviewing and monitoring the auditor's independence and performance, and effectiveness of audit process;
8. Approval or any subsequent modification of transactions of the listed entity with related parties;
9. Scrutiny of inter-corporate loans and investments;
10. Valuation of undertakings or assets of the listed entity, wherever it is necessary;

11. Evaluation of internal financial controls and risk management systems;
12. Reviewing, with the management, performance of statutory and internal auditors, adequacy of the internal control systems;
13. Reviewing the adequacy of internal audit function, if any, including the structure of the internal audit department, staffing and seniority of the official heading the department, reporting structure coverage and frequency of internal audit;
14. Discussion with internal auditors of any significant findings and follow up there on;
15. Reviewing the findings of any internal investigations by the internal auditors into matters where there is suspected fraud or irregularity or a failure of internal control systems of a material nature and reporting the matter to the board;
16. Discussion with statutory auditors before the audit commences, about the nature and scope of audit as well as post-audit discussion to ascertain any area of concern;
17. To look into the reasons for substantial defaults in the payment to the depositors, debenture holders, shareholders (in case of non-payment of declared dividends) and creditors;
18. To review the functioning of the whistle blower mechanism;
19. Approval of appointment of chief financial officer after assessing the qualifications, experience and background, etc. of the candidate;
20. Carrying out any other function as is mentioned in the terms of reference of the audit committee.
21. Reviewing the utilization of loans and/or advances from/investment by the holding company in the subsidiary exceeding rupees 100 crore or 10% of the asset size of the subsidiary, whichever is lower including existing loans/advances/investments existing as on the date of coming into force of this provision.

B. The audit committee shall mandatorily review the following information:
   1. Management discussion and analysis of financial condition and results of operations;
   2. Statement of significant related party transactions (as defined by the audit committee), submitted by management;
   3. Management letters/letters of internal control weaknesses issued by the statutory auditors;
   4. Internal audit reports relating to internal control weaknesses; and
   5. The appointment, removal and terms of remuneration of the chief internal auditor shall be subject to review by the audit committee.
   6. Statement of deviations:
      (a) quarterly statement of deviation(s) including report of monitoring agency, if applicable, submitted to stock exchange(s) in terms of Regulation 32(1).
      (b) annual statement of funds utilized for purposes other than those stated in the offer document/prospectus/notice in terms of Regulation 32(7).

PART D—ROLE OF COMMITTEES (OTHER THAN AUDIT COMMITTEE)

[*See* Regulation 19(4) and 20(4)]

A. Role of Nomination and Remuneration Committee: Role of committee shall, *inter-alia*, include the following:

1. Formulation of the criteria for determining qualifications, positive attributes and independence of a director and recommend to the board of directors a policy relating to, the remuneration of the directors, key managerial personnel and other employees;
2. Formulation of criteria for evaluation of performance of independent directors and the board of directors;
3. Devising a policy on diversity of board of directors;
4. Identifying persons who are qualified to become directors and who may be appointed in senior management in accordance with the criteria laid down, and recommend to the board of directors their appointment and removal;
5. Whether to extend or continue the term of appointment of the independent director, on the basis of the report of performance evaluation of independent directors;
6. Recommend to the board, all remuneration, in whatever form, payable to senior management.

B. Stakeholders Relationship Committee

The role of the committee shall *inter-alia* include the following:

1. Resolving the grievances of the security holders of the listed entity including complaints related to transfer/transmission of shares, non-receipt of annual report, non-receipt of declared dividends, issue of new/duplicate certificates, general meetings etc.
2. Review of measures taken for effective exercise of voting rights by shareholders.
3. Review of adherence to the service standards adopted by the listed entity in respect of various services being rendered by the Registrar & Share Transfer Agent.
4. Review of the various measures and initiatives taken by the listed entity for reducing the quantum of unclaimed dividends and ensuring timely receipt of dividend warrants/annual reports/statutory notices by the shareholders of the company

PART E—DISCRETIONARY REQUIREMENTS

[*See* Regulation 27(1)

A. The Board

A non-executive chairperson may be entitled to maintain a chairperson's office at the listed entity's expense and also allowed reimbursement of expenses incurred in performance of his duties.

B. Shareholder Rights

A half-yearly declaration of financial performance including summary of the significant Events in last six months, may be sent to each household of shareholders.

C. Modified opinion(s) in Audit Report

The listed entity may move towards a regime of financial statements with unmodified audit opinion.

D. [omitted].

E. Reporting of Internal Auditor

The internal auditor may report directly to the audit committee.

SCHEDULE V
ANNUAL REPORT

[*See* Regulation 34(3) and 53(f)]

The annual report shall contain the following additional disclosures:

A. Related Party Disclosure

1. The listed entity shall make disclosures in compliance with the Accounting Standard on "Related Party Disclosures".
2. The disclosure requirements shall be as follows:

Sr. no.	In the accounts of	Disclosures of amounts at the year end and the maximum amount of loans/advances/Investments outstanding during the year.
1.	Holding Company	• Loans and advances in the nature of loans to subsidiaries by name and amount. • Loans and advances in the nature of loans to associates by name and amount. • Loans and advances in the nature of loans to firms/ companies in which directors are interested by name and amount.
2.	Subsidiary	Same disclosures as applicable to the parent company in the accounts of subsidiary company.
3.	Holding Company	Investments by the loanee in the shares of parent company and subsidiary company, when the company has made a loan or advance in the nature of loan.

For the purpose of above disclosures directors' interest shall have the same meaning as given in Section 184 of Companies Act, 2013.

(2A) Disclosures of transactions of the listed entity with any person or entity belonging to the promoter/promoter group which hold(s) 10% or more shareholding in the listed entity, in the format prescribed in the relevant accounting standards for annual results.

3. The above disclosures shall be applicable to all listed entities except for listed banks.

B. Management Discussion and Analysis

1. This section shall include discussion on the following matters within the limits set by the listed entity's competitive position:
   (a) Industry structure and developments.
   (b) Opportunities and Threats.
   (c) Segment–wise or product-wise performance.
   (d) Outlook
   (e) Risks and concerns.
   (f) Internal control systems and their adequacy.
   (g) Discussion on financial performance with respect to operational performance.
   (h) Material developments in Human Resources/Industrial Relations front, including number of people employed.
   (i) details of significant changes (i.e. change of 25% or more as compared to the immediately previous financial year) in key financial ratios, along with detailed explanations there for, including:
      (i) Debtors Turnover
      (ii) Inventory Turnover
      (iii) Interest Coverage Ratio
      (iv) Current Ratio
      (v) Debt Equity Ratio
      (vi) Operating Profit Margin (%)
      (vii) Net Profit Margin (%) or sector-specific equivalent ratios, as applicable.
   (j) details of any change in Return on Net Worth as compared to the immediately previous financial year along with a detailed explanation thereof.
2. Disclosure of Accounting Treatment

   Where in the preparation of financial statements, a treatment different from that prescribed in an Accounting Standard has been followed, the fact shall be disclosed in the financial statements, together with the management's explanation as to why it believes such alternative treatment is more representative of the true and fair view of the underlying business transaction.

C. Corporate Governance Report: The following disclosures shall be made in the section on the corporate governance of the annual report.

1. A brief statement on listed entity's philosophy on code of governance.
2. Board of directors:

(a) composition and category of directors (e.g. promoter, executive, non- executive, independent non-executive, nominee director—institution represented and whether as lender or as equity investor);

(b) attendance of each director at the meeting of the board of directors and the last annual general meeting;

(c) number of other board of directors or committees in which a directors is a member or chairperson, and with effect from the Annual Report for the year ended 31st March 2019, including separately the names of the listed entities where the person is a director and the category of directorship;

(d) number of meetings of the board of directors held and dates on which held;

(e) disclosure of relationships between directors inter-se;

(f) number of shares and convertible instruments held by non- executive directors;

(g) web link where details of familiarisation programmes imparted to independent directors is disclosed.

(h) A chart or a matrix setting out the skills/expertise/competence of the board of directors specifying the following:

  (i) With effect from the financial year ending March 31, 2019, the list of core skills/expertise/competencies identified by the board of directors as required in the context of its business(es) and sector(s) for it to function effectively and those actually available with the board; and

  (ii) With effect from the financial year ended March 31, 2020, the names of directors who have such skills/expertise/competence

(i) confirmation that in the opinion of the board, the independent directors fulfill the conditions specified in these regulations and are independent of the management.

(j) detailed reasons for the resignation of an independent director who resigns before the expiry of his tenure along with a confirmation by such director that there are no other material reasons other than those provided.

3. Audit committee:

  (a) brief description of terms of reference;

  (b) composition, name of members and chairperson;

  (c) meetings and attendance during the year.

4. Nomination and Remuneration Committee:

  (a) brief description of terms of reference;

  (b) composition, name of members and chairperson;

  (c) meeting and attendance during the year;

  (d) performance evaluation criteria for independent directors.

5. Remuneration of Directors:

  (a) all pecuniary relationship or transactions of the non-executive directors vis-à-vis the listed entity shall be disclosed in the annual report;

(b) criteria of making payments to non-executive directors. alternatively, this may be disseminated on the listed entity's website and reference drawn thereto in the annual report;

(c) disclosures with respect to remuneration: in addition to disclosures required under the Companies Act, 2013, the following disclosures shall be made:

(i) all elements of remuneration package of individual directors summarized under major groups, such as salary, benefits, bonuses, stock options, pension etc;

(ii) details of fixed component and performance linked incentives, along with the performance criteria;

(iii) service contracts, notice period, severance fees;

(iv) stock option details, if any and whether issued at a discount as well as the period over which accrued and over which exercisable.

6. Stakeholders' grievance committee:

(a) name of non-executive director heading the committee;

(b) name and designation of compliance officer;

(c) number of shareholders' complaints received so far;

(d) number not solved to the satisfaction of shareholders;

(e) number of pending complaints.

7. General body meetings:

(a) location and time, where last three annual general meetings held;

(b) whether any special resolutions passed in the previous three annual general meetings;

(c) whether any special resolution passed last year through postal ballot—details of voting pattern;

(d) person who conducted the postal ballot exercise;

(e) whether any special resolution is proposed to be conducted through postal ballot;

(f) procedure for postal ballot.

8. Means of communication:

(a) quarterly results;

(b) newspapers wherein results normally published;

(c) any website, where displayed;

(d) whether it also displays official news releases; and

(e) presentations made to institutional investors or to the analysts.

9. General shareholder information:

(a) annual general meeting—date, time and venue;

(b) financial year;

(c) dividend payment date;

(d) the name and address of each stock exchange(s) at which the listed entity's securities are listed and a confirmation about payment of annual listing fee to each of such stock exchange(s);

(e) stock code;
(f) market price data–high, low during each month in last financial year;
(g) performance in comparison to broad-based indices such as BSE sensex, CRISIL Index etc;
(h) in case the securities are suspended from trading, the directors report shall explain the reason thereof;
(i) registrar to an issue and share transfer agents;
(j) share transfer system;
(k) distribution of shareholding;
(l) dematerialization of shares and liquidity;
(m) outstanding global depository receipts or american depository receipts or warrants or any convertible instruments, conversion date and likely impact on equity;
(n) commodity price risk or foreign exchange risk and hedging activities;
(o) plant locations;
(p) address for correspondence.
(q) list of all credit ratings obtained by the entity along with any revisions thereto during the relevant financial year, for all debt instruments of such entity or any fixed deposit programme or any scheme or proposal of the listed entity involving mobilization of funds, whether in India or abroad.

10. Other Disclosures:
(a) disclosures on materially significant related party transactions that may have potential conflict with the interests of listed entity at large;
(b) details of non-compliance by the listed entity, penalties, strictures imposed on the listed entity by stock exchange(s) or the board or any statutory authority, on any matter related to capital markets, during the last three years;
(c) details of establishment of vigil mechanism, whistle blower policy, and affirmation that no personnel has been denied access to the audit committee;
(d) details of compliance with mandatory requirements and adoption of the non-mandatory requirements;
(e) web link where policy for determining 'material' subsidiaries is disclosed;
(f) web link where policy on dealing with related party transactions;
(g) disclosure of commodity price risks and commodity hedging activities.
(h) Details of utilization of funds raised through preferential allotment or qualified institutions placement as specified under Regulation 32 (7A).
(i) a certificate from a company secretary in practice that none of the directors on the board of the company have been debarred or disqualified from being appointed or continuing as directors of companies by the Board/Ministry of Corporate Affairs or any such statutory authority.
(j) where the board had not accepted any recommendation of any committee of the board which is mandatorily required, in the relevant financial year, the same to be disclosed along with reasons thereof:

Provided that the clause shall only apply where recommendation of/ submission by the committee is required for the approval of the Board of Directors and shall not apply where prior approval of the relevant committee is required for undertaking any transaction under these Regulations.

(k) total fees for all services paid by the listed entity and its subsidiaries, on a consolidated basis, to the statutory auditor and all entities in the network firm/network entity of which the statutory auditor is a part.

(l) disclosures in relation to the Sexual Harassment of Women at Workplace (Prevention, Prohibition and Redressal) Act, 2013:

   (a) number of complaints filed during the financial year

   (b) number of complaints disposed of during the financial year

   (c) number of complaints pending as on end of the financial year.

11. Non-compliance of any requirement of corporate governance report of sub-paras (2) to (10) above, with reasons thereof shall be disclosed.
12. The corporate governance report shall also disclose the extent to which the discretionary requirements as specified in Part E of Schedule II have been adopted.
13. The disclosures of the compliance with corporate governance requirements specified in regulation 17 to 27 and clauses (b) to (i) of sub-regulation (2) of regulation 46 shall be made in the section on corporate governance of the annual report.

D. Declaration signed by the chief executive officer stating that the members of board of directors and senior management personnel have affirmed compliance with the code of conduct of board of directors and senior management.

E. Compliance certificate from either the auditors or practicing company secretaries regarding compliance of conditions of corporate governance shall be annexed with the directors' report.

F. Disclosures with respect to demat suspense account/unclaimed suspense account

1. The listed entity shall disclose the following details in its annual report, as long as there are shares in the demat suspense account or unclaimed suspense account, as applicable:

   (a) aggregate number of shareholders and the outstanding shares in the suspense account lying at the beginning of the year;

   (b) number of shareholders who approached listed entity for transfer of shares from suspense account during the year;

   (c) number of shareholders to whom shares were transferred from suspense account during the year;

   (d) aggregate number of shareholders and the outstanding shares in the suspense account lying at the end of the year;

   (e) that the voting rights on these shares shall remain frozen till the rightful owner of such shares claims the shares.

10.5 GAPS IN THE SEBI LISTING REGULATIONS AND A FEW SUGGESTIONS FOR MODIFICATION

However, on further analysis of the provisions of the new SEBI (LODR) Regulations, 2015, we have observed certain gaps in the current provisions relating to corporate governance, some of which are highlighted below.

1. *Independent directors [Regulation 16(1)(E)]*

According to the above Regulation, to be qualified as an independent director, the concerned person should not be 'a material supplier, service provider, or customer or a lessor or lessee of the company'. This is a ridiculous and absurd provision unless it is modified forthwith with a provision of appropriate benchmark to be fixed.

2. *Code of conduct [Schedule V, Para D]*

It is not stated clearly what should the code of conduct provide for or what do's and don'ts it should lay down and whether it is a code of best practice. It would be desirable to provide a model code for all board members and senior executives, which the companies may adopt with necessary modifications.

3. *Subsidiary companies [Regulation 24]*

(a) Under sub-rule (1) of this regulation, the compulsion for an independent director to be on the board of a material subsidiary company is very restrictive, oppressive and violation of a fundamental right of an independent person to carry on his vocation freely, particularly without an appropriate safeguard to him in case of default by such subsidiary company.

(b) As per sub-rule (2) of this regulation, the financial statements of the unlisted subsidiary company to be reviewed by the board and the audit committee of the listed holding company without clarifying the end purpose are meaningless.

4. *Disclosures—Related party transactions [Regulation 23]*

This regulation does not spell out as to what type of transactions will be treated as 'related party transactions'. It is suggested that accounting standard on related party disclosures (Ind AS 24) issued by the ICAI should be taken as the basis for compliance with this clause.

5. *Disclosures—Remuneration of directors [Schedule (V), Para C(5)]*

This clause does not spell out clearly whether 'directors' mean all directors, or only executive directors or non-executive directors. There will be an anomaly if it applies in respect of all directors including non-executive directors, or only non-executive directors simply because there cannot be different components of remuneration for non-executive directors as mentioned in Para C (5)(c) (i), (ii), (iii) and (iv). As per the Act, no non-executive directors are paid that kind of remuneration normally except commission on net profits and sitting fees for attending board meetings. Therefore, this clause should be framed properly so that remuneration of non-executive directors can be differentiated from other directors and disclosed accordingly.

6. The most important concern in this country is the issue of the *responsibility of institutional investors.* Most codes agree that these institutions should be encouraged to intervene, should exercise their voting rights, and should state their voting policies. Unfortunately, there is no such recommendation in the SEBI code that the institutions should exercise their voting rights and also state their voting policies. This aspect also needs review and should be incorporated in the SEBI code.

10.6 COMPARISON BETWEEN SEBI LISTING REGULATIONS, 2015 (AS AMENDED ON AND UPTO JULY 2019) AND THE COMPANIES ACT, 2013

The Companies Act, 2013, as we are aware, has endeavoured to overhaul the various provisions relating to corporate governance. The provisions relating to independent directors are the examples that confer greater power and responsibility of the board in the governance of a company. There were no provisions for independent directors under the old Companies Act, 1956. Only Clause 49 of the Listing Agreement did prescribe for the induction of independent directors and made that mandatory for the listed companies. Thereafter, the Ministry of Corporate Affairs introduced the new Companies Act, 2013 (effective from 1st April 2014) after incorporating new provisions and amending old provisions in order to include the requirement of having independent directors on the board of listed companies for the purpose of overseeing corporate governance.

At the same time, the SEBI, the capital market regulator, also introduced amended Clause 49 of the Listing Agreement with effect from 1st October 2014, in order to make the listed companies more transparent as well as to align the provisions of the Listing Agreement with the Companies Act, 2013. Subsequently, several amendments were made both in SEBI Regulations as also the Companies Act in the form of SEBI (LODR) Regulations, 2015 and the Companies (Amendment) Act, 2019 respectively to make these provisions more rational, practical and acceptable.

Though one of the objectives of the SEBI Regulations was to align with the provisions of the Companies Act (as amended), on a closer look and analysis, we have observed some of the *points of difference* still existing between the relevant provisions of SEBI Regulations and the Companies Act, as discussed hereunder.

10.6.1 Applicability

1. The SEBI Listing Regulation is applicable to all listed companies, whereas the provisions relating to independent directors under the Companies Act, 2013 are only applicable to a selective class of unlisted public companies in addition to the listed companies [Section 149(4) of the Companies Act, read with the Rule 4 of the Companies (Appointment and Qualification of Directors) Rules, 2014].

10.6.2 Composition/Number of Independent Directors

The strength of the independent directors in the board under the SEBI Listing Regulations is determined based on the status of the chairman of the board, whereas there are no such parameters under the Companies Act, 2013. Rather the strength of number of independent directors for the prescribed companies has been specified under Section 149(4) read with Rule 4 of the Companies (Appointment and Qualification of Directors) Rules, 2014].

10.6.3 Definition of Independent Director

1. Although the SEBI Listing Regulation is aligned with the definition of independent director as provided in Section 149(6) of the Companies Act, 2013, SEBI Listing Regulations places additional restriction relating to definition of independent director, viz. neither the director herself/himself nor any of her/his relatives shall be material supplier, service provider or customer or a lessor or lessee of the company, and such director shall not be less than 21 years of age.
2. On the contrary, the Companies Act, 2013 places another condition relating to definition of independent director, viz. such person shall possess such other qualifications as may be prescribed under Rule 5 of the Companies (Appointment and Qualification of Directors) Rules, 2014, which provides that an independent director shall possess appropriate skills, experience and knowledge in one or more fields of finance, law, management, sales, marketing, administration, research, corporate governance, technical operations or other disciplines related to the company's business.

10.6.4 Limit on Number of Independent Directorships

Under the SEBI Listing Regulations a person shall not serve as an independent director in more than seven listed companies. Further, any person serving as a whole time director in any listed company shall serve as an independent director in not more than three listed companies. On the contrary, Section 165(1) of the Companies Act, 2013 provides for the maximum limit of 10 public companies. In fact, the Companies Act, 2013 does not provide any separate limit on the number of companies in which a person can be appointed as independent director, but the general limit provided in Section 165(1) of the Act shall be applicable in case of independent director also.

10.6.5 Maximum Tenure of Independent Directors

1. The SEBI Listing Regulation, has been aligned on similar lines of Section 149(10) and (11) of the Companies Act, 2013. The clause provides that an independent director shall hold office for a term up to five consecutive years on the board of a company and shall be eligible for reappointment for another term of five consecutive years on passing of a special resolution by the company. Provided that a person who has already served as an independent director for five years or more in a company as on 1st October 2014 shall be eligible for appointment, on completion of his present term, for one more term up to five years only. The point of difference is that while SEBI Listing Regulation includes the period served before 1st October 2014, the Companies Act, 2013 does not include the period served before the commencement of the Act, i.e., before 1st April 2014.

2. The Companies Act, 2013 provides that the independent director shall not be appointed or associated with a company in any other capacity, directly or indirectly, during the cooling period of three years before which the independent director cannot be considered for reappointment, whereas the SEBI Listing Regulation is silent on this issue.

10.6.6 Manner of Appointment

The SEBI Listing Regulation prescribes the manner of appointment of independent director in the manner prescribed under Section 152 read with Schedule IV of the Act and the Companies (Appointment and Qualification of Directors) Rules, 2014. The point of difference is that under the SEBI Listing Regulations, the letter of appointment along with the detailed profile of independent director shall be disclosed on the websites of the company and the stock exchanges not later than one working day from the date of such appointment. But, under the Companies Act, 2013, terms and conditions of appointment of independent directors shall also be posted on the company's website.

10.6.7 Performance Evaluation of Independent Directors

Under the SEBI Listing Regulations, *Nomination Committee* shall lay down the evaluation criteria for performance evaluation of independent directors. Companies shall disclose the criteria for performance evaluation, as laid down by the Committee in its annual report. But, under Section 149(8) read with Schedule IV Companies Act, 2013, *nomination and remuneration committee* shall identify persons who are qualified to become directors and who may be appointed in senior management in accordance with the criteria laid down, recommend to the board their appointment and removal and shall carry out evaluation of every director's performance.

10.6.8 Training of Independent Directors

The SEBI Listing Regulation stipulates that companies shall provide suitable training to independent directors to familiarize them with the company, their roles, rights, responsibilities in the company, nature of the industry in which the company operates, business model of the company, etc. Details of such training imparted shall be disclosed in the annual report. On the contrary, the Companies Act, 2013 does not contain such provisions. According to Section 149(8) of the Act, companies and independent directors shall abide by the provisions specified in the Schedule IV of the Act, which prescribes the guidelines of professional conduct, roles and functions and duties of the independent directors.

10.6.9 Remuneration of Independent Directors

The SEBI Listing Regulation requires that all fees/compensation paid to independent directors shall be fixed by the board of directors and shall require previous approval of shareholders in general meeting. On the contrary, Section 197(4) of the Companies Act, 2013 requires that remuneration payable to directors (including independent directors) shall be determined in accordance with the articles or if the articles so require, by ordinary/special resolution passed by the company in general meeting.

10.6.10 Liability of Independent Directors

Apart from the provisions contained in Section 149(12) of the Companies Act, 2013 regarding the liability of independent directors, the SEBI Listing Regulation provides another liability clause for independent director in which he has not acted diligently with respect to the provisions contained in the Listing Agreement.

Despite the points of differences as mentioned above, both Companies Act, 2013 (as amended) as well as the SEBI Listing Regulations have empowered independent directors with proper checks and balances so that these powers can be exercised in a rational and judicious manner. These provisions have recognized the role of independent directors as watchdog of corporate governance.

However, there is no denying the fact that SEBI, being a regulatory agency and a subordinate authority, is supposed to ensure the consistency between its own regulations and the company law provisions while dealing with all matters, especially in the matter of corporate governance provided for in the Act. Therefore, with a view to achieving this consistency, there is a need for setting up a formal structure to ensure that Ministry of Corporate Affairs (MCA), which regulates all companies, and SEBI, which regulates only listed companies, act in co-ordination and harmony.

10.7 CONCLUDING OBSERVATION

With the abolition of the office of the Controller of Capital Issues, the Securities and Exchange Board of India (SEBI) was constituted. It was established originally in 1988, but was only given statutory power with the enactment of the SEBI Act in January 1992.

SEBI was empowered to regulate the working of the stock exchanges, monitoring the members of the stock exchanges and all the players of the capital market, including the boards of all listed companies. The bankers and registrars to the issue, merchant bankers, underwriters, portfolio managers, credit rating agencies, Foreign Institutional Investors (FIIs), Venture Capital Funds (VCFs), Mutual Funds (MFs) and Asset Management Companies (AMCs) also came within the purview of SEBI operations. SEBI formulated various rules and regulations for the purpose of regulating the operations of the players of the capital market, which were aimed at promotion of more responsible corporate governance. According to Section 11(1) of the SEBI Act, SEBI has the responsibility to protect the interests of investors in securities and to promote the development of and to regulate the securities markets by way of taking appropriate measures. SEBI has also introduced several regulations, guidelines and schemes since its operations. The chapter mentioned details of SEBI, its functions and powers, regulations, guidelines and schemes.

With the requirements under the Companies Act, 2013 and the rules notified thereunder which would be applicable for every company or a class of companies (both listed and unlisted), SEBI decided to review the provisions of the Listing Agreement, with the objective to align with the provisions of the Companies Act, 2013, adopt best practices on corporate governance and to make the governance framework more effective. Accordingly, SEBI issued a new circular on 17th April 2014, superseding all other earlier circulars on Clause 35B (provision of e-voting facility to the shareholders) and Clause 49 of the Equity Listing Agreement, which have been effective from

1st October 2014. The said Clause 49 has been replaced by SEBI (Listing Obligation and Disclosure) Requirements, 2015.

In between the years 2015 and 2019 there were several amendments of SEBI Listing Regulations. The full text of the relevant portions of SEBI (LODR) Regulations, 2015 as amended on and upto 29th July 2019 has been provided in this chapter for the benefit of the readers.

CASE STUDY–I

Code of Conduct and Ethics in Boeing

INTRODUCTION

The history of Boeing dates back to 1916 when William Boeing and George Westervelt incorporated their airplane manufacturing business as the Pacific Aero Products Company. The company's name was changed to Boeing in the year 1917. Boeing began manufacturing aircrafts for the US military during the First World War. After the Second World War, Boeing shifted its focus from the defence industry to commercial jets. In 1952 Boeing launched its first commercial jet, the Boeing 707. In 1960 Boeing began manufacturing its first jumbo jet, the Boeing 747. In 1962 Boeing manufactured the Air force One, the official air plane of the US President. In late 1969 Boeing entered the spacecraft manufacturing business by contributing to the Apollo Programme.

CODE OF CONDUCT AND ETHICS

Over the years along with engineering excellence, Boeing focused on setting and implementing high standards of conduct and ethics across all its business units. In the year 2012 Boeing's board of directors consisted of 11 directors, of whom 9 were independent directors. Boeing had a comprehensive Code of Conduct and Ethics.

The board of directors of Boeing appointed an ethics and business conduct committee to oversee the implementation of ethical code. The committee comprised the chairman, CEO, chief operating officer, presidents, and vice-presidents of Boeing's business units. It formulated policies and procedures related to conduct and ethics and oversaw the implementation of the ethics programme across all Boeing units.

The committee conducted companywide training programmes to increase awareness among employees about Boeing values and code of conduct and ethics. It was compulsory for all its employees to participate once every year in such a programme. Boeing also set up an ethics helpline by giving toll-free telephone and fax numbers to employees for them to communicate their concerns and to ask questions regarding any ethical issues. Besides, Boeing also appointed business conduct and ethics advisors in all its business units with a view to guiding employees on ethical conduct and behaviour in the workplace, business ethics issues, and the Boeing values.

Boeing values were focused on the issues such as, (a) Leadership, (b) Integrity, (c) Quality, (d) Customer satisfaction, (e) People working together, (f) Diverse and involved team, (g) Good corporate citizenship, and (h) Enhancing shareholder value.

Ethical Lapses in Boeing and Measures Taken

Despite detailed ethical code and implementation of detailed programmes, there were allegations of ethical lapses in the way Boeing conducted its business. Some of these lapses were (a) Accounting lapses, (b) Lockheed controversy, (c) Tanker lease deal controversy etc. What was ironical was that the alleged lapses occurred at the senior executive level rather than in the lower cadres, thereby making a mockery of the Boeing ethics code and values.

After the chairman's resignation, Boeing initiated several measures to regain the confidence of the common public, markets, consumers and over and above the shareholders. In July 2013, Boeing announced that it would be conducting an independent review of its conduct and ethics policies throughout the company. It hired a former Senator to review the company's ethical policies and procedures. Besides, the employees underwent a refresher course in ethics. Boeing established a new ethics office to be headed by the company's senior vice president. The new ethics office would be reporting directly to the CEO and would be responsible for implementation of the ethical code.

Questions for Discussion

1. What are the values on which Boeing management focused and implemented across all its business units?
2. What were the alleged lapses in the way Boeing conducted its business? What measures have taken thereafter, by Boeing to regain the confidence of the common public, markets, consumers and shareholders?

CASE STUDY–II
Whistleblowers Train Guns at Infosys

INTRODUCTION

The IT giant Infosys has recently found embroiled in a fresh corporate governance storm. An anonymous whistleblower group calling itself 'Ethical Employees' of the company, on Monday, the 21st October 2019, brought serious charges against Mr. Salil Parekh, CEO and Mr. Nilanjan Roy, CFO of the company, of inflating profits in recent quarters without recognising some cost items and making questionable assumptions on margins earned by the company from large deals.

Infosys has received whistleblower complaints in the past too, over alleged governance lapses. In the earlier occasion, one such report had alleged wrongdoings by Infosys while buying 'Panaya', an Israeli automation technology firm. Infosys stated that its audit committee investigated into the case and found no evidence supporting the allegations.

CHARGES AGAINST CEO AND CFO

In a letter dated 20th September 2019 addressed by the 'Ethical Employees' to the Infosys board the serious charges were made against Mr. Salil Parekh, CEO who took over the reign of the company in January 2018, and Mr. Nilanjan Roy, CFO who was brought over from Bharti Airtel in March this year. A second letter dated 3rd October 2019 was also made public and sent to 'Washington based Whistleblower Protection Programme (WPP)' stated that 20 enclosures of relevant e-mails and voice recordings claiming to bear substantial charges made against them are being sent to WPP. The alleged charges against Infosys CEO & CFO are mentioned below:

1. The 'Ethical Employees' in their letter to the Infosys board stated that they were asked not to fully recognise costs/expenditures such as those incurred on Visas for the April–June 2019 quarter. They have also said that they have possessed voice recordings to back their claim. The issue was 'postponed' when the auditor 'opposed' it.
2. The letter to the board stated that for the second quarter, i.e. July–September 2019, there was a lot of pressure not to recognise reversals of USD 50 million of upfront payment in FDR contract, which was contrary to the accounting practice. As this would reduce profits for the quarter and would have negative effect for the stock, they (Parekh & Roy) were putting pressure not to take the charge.
3. The letter also reported irregularities in large deal. It stated 'In large contracts like Verizon, Intel, and JVs in Japan, ABN Amro acquisition, revenue recognition matters are forced which are not according to accounting standards'. The ABN Amro acquisition relates to the mortgage services firm Stater which has been acquired by Infosys in March 2019 for ₹1000 crore. The letter disclosed 'We have e-mails and voice recordings and we will share when investigators ask us'.
4. The 'Ethical Employees' also alleged irregularities in large deal approvals by the CEO himself, and accused the CFO of being compliant. The letter to the Infosys board stated 'Large deal approvals have irregularities. CEO is bypassing reviews and approvals and instructing sales not to send mails for approval. He directs them to make wrong assumptions to show the margins. CFO is compliant and he prevents us from showing in board presentations large deal issues'.
5. The letter also referred to the comments made by Parekh on the board members. Parekh had told them ('Ethical Employees') 'no one in the board understands these things, they are happy as long as the share price is up. Those two Madrasis (D. Sundaram and D.N. Prahlad) and Diva (Kiran Mazumdar-Shaw) make silly points, you just nod and ignore them'.
6. Claiming that several billion dollar deals of the last few quarters have 'nil' margin, the whistleblowers urged the board to ask auditors to check deal proposals, margins, undisclosed upfront commitments made and revenue recognition. They stated 'All information is not shared with auditors....... in board meetings, we are told not to present data on large deals and important financial measures as it will get board attention'.
7. They also wrote 'The CEO and CFO are asking us to show more profits in treasury by taking up risks and make changes to policies. This will provide short term profits. They ask us not to make key disclosures in 20F and annual report and to share only good and incomplete information with investors and analysts'.
8. The letter also stated 'whoever disagrees is sidelined and many of them leave. In large deal finance team, important employees are left due to pressure to make deals look good'.
9. The whistleblowers alleged that the company pays the travel expenses for Parekh's weekly personal trips. CEO spends two and half days in a week in E-city and the rest in Mumbai. All his travel expenses are paid by the company for these weekly personal visits.
10. The letter also stated 'He (CEO) is a green card holder and avoids deduction of taxes during his US travel which is non-compliance. Please check and the details will be provided'.

MARKET REACTION

The Infosys stock has come under pressure when trading resumed as the investors reacted negatively to the news of a group of employees making damaging accusations against Infosys CEO and CFO. The impact of the development was already felt in the US markets with the Infosys ADR trading almost 13% lower at USD 9.23 in Nasdaq. The market analysts feel that a major recovery is unlikely, even in the short run till further clarity.

The news of the whistleblower complaints has come just days after the resignation of Mr. Jayesh Sanghrajka, executive vice-president and deputy CFO who spent more than 14 years in this company.

Mr. Harit Shah, the research analyst of Reliance Securities said 'Very serious news indeed. This equates to a corporate governance issue. The deputy CFO has also quit. This in itself is an indirect admission that something is rotten. The stock will now languish 10–15 per cent lower in the near term.' He added that questions would now be raised about the board-level processes at Infosys, which was very disappointing given that when founder Nandan Nilekani was brought back, his specific focus was to ensure high corporate governance standards after the Vishal Sikka fiasco.

Shriram Subramaniun, founder and managing director of proxy advisory firm 'In Govern' stated 'The employees have said they have the evidence of e-mail and voice conversations. The audit committee needs to take urgent action in terms of investigation and presenting a true picture to the investors. As the complaint was made in September to the board, they should have investigated and disclosed the findings by now'.

THE COMPANY'S STATEMENT

Bangalore-based Infosys stated in a statement 'The whistleblower complaint has been placed before the audit committee according to the company's practice and will be dealt with in accordance with the company's whistleblower policy'.

Questions for Discussion

1. Who are called Whistleblowers?
2. Who are involved in the alleged serious charges against Infosys?
3. What are the charges levelled against Infosys CEO and CFO?
4. What are the market reactions on the alleged charges against Infosys?
5. What is the company's statement in regard to these charges?

Test Your Knowledge

1. What are the functions and powers of Securities and Exchange Board of India (SEBI)?
2. What are the rights of the shareholders of a company as per new provisions of SEBI Listing Regulations?

3. What are the roles of stakeholders in corporate governance as per new provisions of SEBI Listing Regulations?
4. What are the provisions of SEBI Listing Regulations on Disclosure and transparency?
5. Enumerate the key functions of the board as per new provisions of SEBI Listing Regulations?
6. What are the provisions of SEBI Listing Regulations on Composition of the Board?
7. Discuss the provisions of SEBI Listing Regulations on Independent Director.
8. What is Code of Conduct? What are the provisions of SEBI Listing Regulations regarding Code of Conduct?
9. Discuss critically the provisions of SEBI Listing Regulations on Audit Committee.
10. What do you mean by Risk Management? What are the provisions of SEBI Listing Regulations regarding Risk Management?
11. What are the provisions of SEBI Listing Regulations on CEO/CFO certification?
12. Give a List of information to be placed before the board of directors of a listed company as required by SEBI Listing Regulations.
13. How do the regulations and guidelines introduced by SEBI help the companies to promote more responsible corporate governance?
14. "There are certain 'gaps' in SEBI Listing Regulations, 2015". Can you highlight some of such gaps and offer a few suggestions for modification?
15. How do you compare between SEBI Listing Regulations, 2015 and the Companies Act, 2013?

CHAPTER 11 Corporate Governance Practice in India: A Case Study of Selected Listed Companies for the Financial Year 2015–2016

Learning Objectives	Key Words
After reading this chapter, the readers will be able to understand: • Corporate Governance Practice in India: A Case Study of Selected Listed Companies (BSE and NSE Nifty) for the Financial Year 2015–2016 • CRISIL Corporate Governance and Value Creation Rating (GVC Rating) • ICRA Corporate Governance Rating (CGR)	• Case Study • Listed Companies • BSE Sensex • NSE Nifty • Annual Report • Board Meetings • Statutory Disclosures • Shareholders' Rights • Audit Qualification • Point Value System • Key Governance Parameters • Private Companies • Public Sector Undertakings • Board Committees • Stakeholders' Interests • Credit Rating

11.1 INTRODUCTION

In the previous chapters we have discussed corporate governance system in India particularly after liberalization of Indian economy in 1991. We also have dealt with the existing gap between the various regulations and enactments made by the new Companies Act, 2013 and Securities and Exchange Board of India (SEBI) and suggested possible improvements in this regard.

In this chapter, we take a case study of some listed companies for the financial year 2015–2016 in order to analyze the structures and processes for corporate governance followed by the Indian corporate houses and their effectiveness in terms of substance and quality of disclosures on corporate governance in the annual reports 2015–2016.

The following issues are framed for the purpose of the empirical study:

I. What are the structure, strength and size of the company's board of directors? Has the requirement of revised Clause 49 of the SEBI Listing Agreement followed by SEBI (Listing Obligations and Disclosure Requirements) Regulations, 2015 in respect of minimum number of independent directors in the boards been maintained?

II. What is the position of chairman and CEO in companies? Is the post of chairman separated from the post of CEO/MD? How many companies did appoint a lead independent director in their boards?

III. How many companies did appoint women directors in their boards? Did they follow the principles of gender diversity in their companies?

IV. How many companies defined 'independent director' and disclosed the selection criterion of board directors including independent directors?

V. Did the companies disclose the retirement policy of directors including their tenure and age limit in the annual report 2015–2016? If so, whether it is in line with the provisions of SEBI (Listing Obligations and Disclosure Requirements) Regulations, 2015?

VI. Are the disclosures of board procedure and information placed before the board? Is there a regular post-meeting follow-up system and compliance reporting to the board?

VII. Are there adequate disclosures of remuneration policy and remuneration of directors in the annual report? Did they fully comply with the provisions of the SEBI Regulations? Did the companies disclose information about formation of statutory board committees? Is the minimum requirement of the number of independent directors and the number of audit committee meetings maintained? Was there any disclosure regarding 'charters' of these committees and the roles played by them?

VIII. Is there adequate information of nature of shareholders' complaints and queries received and disposed—item-wise, in the annual report?

IX. Is there adequate disclosure of minimum requirement of the non-executive directors in remuneration and nomination committee, stakeholders' relationship committee, and risk management committee? Is there disclosure of these committees' charters and reports in the annual report?

X. Are there adequate disclosures of corporate social responsibility discharged by the companies in their annual reports? Did they disclose the CSR policy in the annual reports?

XI. Did the companies comply with all disclosure norms (both statutory and non-mandatory) as required by the SEBI (Listing Obligations and Disclosure Requirements) Regulations, 2015 and also by the new Companies Act, 2013?

XII. Are there adequate disclosure regarding stakeholders' interests and the policies on (a) Environment, Health and Safety (EHS), (b) Human Resource Development (HRD) and Industrial Relation (IR)?

In light of the above-mentioned issues, we have examined the corporate governance practices followed by some selected listed companies as disclosed in their annual reports for the financial year 2015–2016.

11.2 SELECTION OF SAMPLE

Our sample for the study constitutes of the companies, which are considered for computing the Bombay Stock Exchange Sensitive Index, known as BSE Sensex companies, and the National Stock Exchange, known as NSE Nifty companies. Equity shares of 30 companies in BSE Sensex and 50 companies in NSE Nifty are selected for the purpose of computing these indices. This selection is made in such a way that it represents major industries. The main reason for selection of these companies is that their scrips dominate and influence the stock movement of the country. Further these companies represent, as mentioned earlier, different major industries. A list of 30 BSE Sensex companies and 50 NSE Nifty companies is shown in Table 11.1.

TABLE 11.1 List of BSE Sensex Companies and NSE Nifty Companies

	Indian companies listed under BSE Sensex		**Indian companies listed under NSE Nifty**
1.	Adani Ports SEZ Ltd.	1.	Adani Ports SEZ Ltd.
2.	Asian Paints Ltd.	2.	Ambuja Cements Ltd.
3.	Axis Bank Ltd.	3.	Asian Paints Ltd.
4.	Bajaj Auto Ltd.	4.	Associated Cement Companies Ltd. (ACC)
5.	Bharti Airtel Ltd.*	5.	Aurobindo Pharma Ltd.
6.	Bharat Heavy Electricals Ltd.* (BHEL) (PSU)	6.	Axis Bank Ltd.
7.	Cipla Ltd.*	7.	Bajaj Auto Ltd.
8.	Coal India Ltd.* (PSU)	8.	Bank of Baroda (PSB)
9.	Dr. Reddy's Laboratories Ltd. (Dr. Reddy's)	9.	Bharat Petroleum Corpn. Ltd.* (BPCL) (PSU)
10.	GAIL (India) Ltd.* (PSU)	10.	Bharti Airtel Ltd.*
11.	Housing Development Finance Corporation Ltd. (HDFC)	11.	Bharti Infratel Ltd.*
12.	HDFC Bank Ltd.	12.	Bharat Heavy Electricals Ltd.* (BHEL) (PSU)
13.	Hero Motocorp. Ltd.*	13.	Bosch Ltd.
14.	Hindustan Unilever Ltd. (HUL)	14.	Cipla Ltd.*
15.	ICICI Bank Ltd.	15.	Coal India Ltd.* (PSU)
16.	Infosys Technologies Ltd.	16.	Dr. Reddy's Laboratories Ltd. (Dr. Reddy's)
17.	ITC Ltd.	17.	Eicher Motors Ltd.
18.	Larsen & Toubro Ltd.* (L&T)	18.	GAIL (India) Ltd.* (PSU)
19.	Lupin Ltd.	19.	Grasim Industries Ltd.*
20.	Mahindra and Mahindra Ltd.	20.	HCL Technologies Ltd.*
21.	Maruti Suzuki Ltd.*	21.	Housing Development Finance Corpn. Ltd. (HDFC)
22.	NTPC Ltd. (PSU)	22.	HDFC Bank Ltd.
23.	Oil and Natural Gas Corpn. Ltd. (ONGC) (PSU)	23.	Hindalco Industries Ltd.
24.	Reliance Industries Ltd. (RIL)	24.	Hero Motocorp. Ltd.*

TABLE 11.1 List of BSE Sensex Companies and NSE Nifty Companies (*Contd.*)

25.	State Bank of India (SBI) (PSB)	25.	Hindustan Unilever Ltd. (HUL)
26.	Sun Pharmaceuticals Ltd.	26.	ICICI Bank Ltd.
27.	Tata Consultancy Services Ltd. (TCS)	27.	Idea Cellular Ltd.
28.	Tata Steel Ltd.	28.	Infosys Technologies Ltd.
29.	Tata Motors Ltd.	29.	IndusInd Bank Ltd.*
30.	WIPRO Ltd.*	30.	ITC Ltd.
		31.	Kotak Mahindra Bank Ltd.*
		32.	Larsen & Toubro Ltd.* (L&T)
		33.	Lupin Ltd.
		34.	Maruti Suzuki Ltd.*
		35.	Mahindra and Mahindra Ltd.*
		36.	NTPC Ltd. (PSU)
		37.	Oil and Natural Gas Corpn. Ltd (ONGC) (PSU)
		38.	Power Grid Corporation Ltd. (PSU)
		39.	Reliance Industries Ltd. (RIL)
		40.	State Bank of India (SBI) (PSB)
		41.	Sun Pharmaceuticals Ltd.
		42.	Tata Consultancy Services Ltd. (TCS)
		43.	Tata Steel Ltd.
		44.	Tata Motors Ltd.
		45.	Tata Power Ltd.
		46.	Tech Mahindra Ltd.*
		47.	Ultra Tech Cement Ltd.*
		48.	WIPRO Ltd.*
		49.	Yes Bank Ltd.
		50.	Zee Entertainment Ltd.

Note: *Annual Reports 2015–2016 not available.

It may be observed from Table 11.1 that all 30 BSE Sensex companies are included in the list of 50 NSE Nifty companies. Out of these companies listed above, 32 companies' annual reports for the year 2015–2016 were received. The annual reports of the 18 listed companies against which (*) asterisks have been given in the list were not available. Therefore, the study is undertaken on total 32 large cap companies listed under BSE Sensex and NSE Nifty. The final sample of 32 listed companies may now be classified into several industry–groups as shown in Table 11.2.

TABLE 11.2 Classification of Sample Listed Indian Companies—Industrywise

Industry	No. of companies	Name of companies
Automobile	3	1. Bajaj Auto Ltd. 2. Eicher Motors Ltd. 3. Tata Motors Ltd.
Banking	6	1. HDFC Bank Ltd. 2. ICICI Bank Ltd. 3. State Bank of India (PSB) 4. Bank of Baroda (PSB) 5. Axis Bank Ltd. 6. Yes Bank Ltd.
Cement	2	1. ACC Ltd. 2. Ambuja Cements Ltd.
Consumer Products and FMCG	2	1. Hindustan Unilever Ltd. 2. Asian Paints Ltd.
Diversified	1	1. ITC Ltd.
Engineering	1	1. Bosch Ltd.
Entertainment	1	1. Zee Entertainment Enterprises Ltd.
Finance	1	1. HDFC Ltd.
Information Technology	2	1. Infosys Technologies Ltd. 2. Tata Consultancy Services Ltd.
Iron and Steel	1	1. Tata Steel Ltd.
Mining and Metal	1	1. Hindalco Industries Ltd.
Pharmaceuticals	4	1. Dr. Reddy's Laboratories Ltd. 2. Lupin Ltd. 3. Sun Pharmaceuticals Ltd. 4. Aurobindo Pharma Ltd.
Petroleum and Natural Gas	1	1. ONGC Ltd.
Port and SEZ	1	1. Adani Ports & SEZ Ltd.
Power Generation and Distribution	3	1. Tata Power Ltd. 2. Power Grid Corporation Ltd. 3. NTPC Ltd.
Textile, Synthetics and Conglomerate	1	1. Reliance Industries Ltd.
Telecommunication	1	1. Idea Cellular Ltd.
Total	**32**	

11.3 ANALYSIS OF GOVERNANCE STRUCTURES AND PROCESSES AND DISCLOSURES BY SAMPLE COMPANIES ON CORPORATE GOVERNANCE

The study to follow hereunder is based on the statutory and non-mandatory requirements stipulated by the revised new Clause 49 of SEBI Listing Agreement, 2014, followed by SEBI (Listing Obligations and Disclosure Requirements) Regulations, 2015, as applicable for the financial year 2015–2016. All sample companies published corporate governance report as required by the SEBI Regulations that is applicable for the financial year 2015–2016.

We examine the report of each of the sample companies and ascertain the actual position with respect to the following:

1. A statement of company's philosophy on code of governance
2. Board of directors/board issues
   (a) Structure of the board
      (i) Executive versus non-executive
      (ii) Executive versus non-executive (independent)
   (b) Strength of the board
   (c) Size of the board
   (d) Chairman and CEO duality
      (i) Executive chairman/CMD versus non-executive chairman
   (e) Appointment of woman director
   (f) Appointment of nominee director
   (g) Directors' attendance in board meetings
   (h) Disclosure of tenure and age limit of directors
   (i) Disclosure of definition of independent director, and selection criteria of board directors including independent directors
   (j) Board procedure and information placed before the board, post-meeting follow-up system and compliance of the board procedure
   (k) Lead independent director
   (l) Disclosure of other provisions as to the boards and committees
   (m) Disclosure of remuneration policy and remuneration of directors
   (n) Evaluation of non-executive directors
   (o) Training of board members including independent directors
3. Board committees
   (a) Statutory board committees
      (i) Audit committee
      (ii) Remuneration and nomination committee
      (iii) Independent directors' committee
      (iv) Shareholders'/Stakeholders' relationship committee
      (v) Risk management committee
      (vi) Corporate social responsibility committee
   (b) Non-mandatory committees
      (i) Heath, safety and environment committee
      (ii) Fraud monitoring committee
      (iii) Ethics and compliance committee
      (iv) Investment committee
      (v) Share transfer committee
      (vi) Other committees

4. Subsidiary companies
5. Risk management
6. Disclosures and transparency
   (a) Statutory requirements/disclosures
      (i) Significant related party transactions having potential conflicts with the interest of the companies
      (ii) Accounting treatment
      (iii) Remuneration of directors
      (iv) Management discussion and analysis
      (v) Shareholders' information
   (b) Non-mandatory requirements/disclosures
      (i) Entitlement of non-executive chairman to maintain a chairman's office at company's expense
      (ii) Shareholder rights
      (iii) Audit qualification
      (iv) Separate post of chairman and CEO
      (v) Reporting of internal auditor
7. General body meetings
8. Code of conduct and its affirmation
9. CEO/CFO certification
10. Means of communication and general shareholder information
11. Compliance of corporate governance and auditors' certificate

11.3.1 Brief Statement of Company's Philosophy on Code of Governance

All 32 companies had given a brief account on the respective companies' philosophy on code of corporate governance.

11.3.2 Board of Directors

We examine various aspects of the board of directors, namely, board structure, board strength, board size, directors' attendance, and a few others in the following paragraphs under appropriate sub-heads.

Board structure

The board structure of BSE Sensex companies and NSE Nifty companies in 2015–2016 industry-wise is given in Appendix 7.

The analysis of Appendix 7 reveals that:

(a) Large listed companies' boards are generally broad-based. This has been noticed in the board composition of the companies in automobile, banking, diversified, petroleum and natural gas, cement, textile and synthetics, iron and steel, consumer products, finance and telecom sectors. All automobile companies' boards except Eicher Motors and all pharmaceutical companies' boards except Dr. Reddy's and Sun Pharma are broad-based.

(b) All companies/banks, except SBI, Bank of Baroda, ITC, ONGC, Power Grid and NTPC, have greater number of non-executive (outside/part-time) directors than that of the executive (inside/whole-time) directors in the boards, thereby conforming to the SEBI Listing Regulations and the provisions of the Companies Act, 2013.

(c) 10 (31%) listed companies do have chairman/CMDs in the helm of affairs as executive chairman/CMD. The rest 22 (69%) companies do have non-executive chairmen in their boards and are run by the managing directors/CEOs.

(d) 5 companies are headed by the promoter executive chairmen/promoter CMDs, and 5 companies are headed by the non–promoter executive chairmen/non-promoter CMDs.

(e) 4 companies are run by the boards headed by the promoter non-executive chairmen.

(f) 6 companies are headed by the non-executive independent chairmen, and 12 companies are chaired by 'other' non-executive chairmen, including nominated director.

(g) It is interesting to note that the management of these companies decide themselves what would be the status of the chairman/CMD in the board composition within, of course, the limit set by their Articles. Substantial numbers of companies have declared the status of their boards' chairman as independent non-executive, promoter non-executive, and 'other' non-executive to suit their own requirement in line with the minimum statutory number requirement of independent directors in the boards.

(h) It is, however, an open question as to whether a simple majority of independent directors is an indication of board-independence, especially given the fact that minority owners/promoters in India are frequently able to assert over selection of independent board members.

Board strength

The board strength of executive directors, non-executive directors and independent directors of BSE Sensex and NSE Nifty companies in 2015–2016 is given in Appendix 8.

The analysis of Appendix 8 reveals that:

(a) Out of 32 companies studied, 1 private sector company ITC and 5 public sector companies (PSUs)/banks (PSBs) have failed to comply with SEBI Listing Regulations regarding the appointment of independent directors in their boards.

(b) The main reason for non-compliance by these companies, especially the PSUs/PSBs, is that the proportion of independent directors in their boards is less than the minimum requirement of 50% of the total boards, as these companies/banks are chaired by the executive chairman and managing directors (CMDs).

(c) Therefore, the respective ministries of the Government of India should seriously look into the matter and arrange to fill up and increase the required number of independent directors in the boards of these PSUs/PSBs expeditiously in line with the SEBI Regulations.

Board size

The board size of BSE Sensex and NSE Nifty companies in 2015–2016 is shown in Table 11.3.

TABLE 11.3 Board Size of Selected Companies in 2015–2016 (Listed under BSE Sensex and NSE Nifty)

Serial no.	Board size	Nos.	%
A	15 member board	2	7
B	14 member board	3	9
C	13 member board	2	7
D	12 member board	3	9
E	11 member board	9	28
F	10 member board	3	9
G	9 member board	5	16
H	8 member board	3	9
I	7 member board	1	3
J	6 member board	1	3
	Total	**32**	**100**

Source: Annual Reports of Companies, 2015–2016. Results computed.

The analysis shown in Table 11.3 reveals that:

(a) Out of 32 listed companies under study, only 10 companies (31%) have single digit board size ranging from 6 to 9 members. The rest 22 companies (69%) have double digit board size varying from 10 to 15 members.

(b) 9 companies (29%) have the board size of 11 members. Only 2 companies, viz. Bajaj Auto and ITC have the highest 15 members in their boards.

The board size of BSE Sensex and NSE Nifty public sector companies/banks in 2015–2016 is shown in Table 11.4.

TABLE 11.4 Board Size of Selected Public Sector Companies/Banks in 2015–2016 (Listed under BSE Sensex and NSE Nifty)

Serial No.	Name of PSUs/ banks	Board size	Executive directors (EDs)		Non-Executive Directors (NEDs)		Independent Directors (IDs)	
			Nos.	(%)	Nos.	(%)	Nos.	(%)
1.	State Bank of India	14	5 (c)	36	9	64	5	36
2.	ONGC Ltd.	11	6 (c)	55	5	45	3	27
3.	NTPC Ltd.	11	6 (c)	55	5	45	3	27
4.	Bank of Baroda	10	3	30	7 (c)	70	3	30
5.	Power Grid Corpn. Ltd.	7	4 (c)	57	3	43	1	14

Source: Annual Reports of Companies, 2015–2016. Results computed.
Note: (c) denotes Chairman/Chairman and Managing Director in the same category.

An analysis of Table 11.4 indicates that:

(a) Generally, the board size of the Public Sector Undertakings (PSUs) is broad-based and large as compared to that of most of the private sector companies. The boards of the Public Sector Banks (PSBs) especially are large due to induction of directors nominated by the workers, officers of the organizations, the Government of India and Reserve Bank of India, apart from shareholders' directors.

(b) All these PSUs and PSBs are run by the boards headed by the executive chairman/Chairman-cum Managing Director (CMD) except Bank of Baroda which is headed by a non-executive chairman. However, all these chairmen have been appointed by the Government of India as per government policy.

(c) The PSUs and PSBs have not complied with the requirement of Regulation 17 of the SEBI (Listing Obligation and Disclosure Requirement) Regulations in respect of induction of minimum number of independent directors in their boards. Therefore, the Government of India should induct adequate number of independent directors in the boards of all these organizations in order to meet the shortfall of minimum requirement of 50% of the total board members.

Chairman and CEO duality in Indian companies

A statistics of chairman and CEO duality in the selected listed companies for the year 2015–2016 is shown in Table 11.5.

Table 11.5 Chairman and CEO Duality in the Selected Companies in 2015–2016 (Listed under BSE Sensex and NSE Nifty)

Type of organization	Total		Executive chairman/CMD		Non-executive chairman	
	Nos.	%	Nos.	%	Nos.	%
Private sector	27	100	6	22	21	78
Public sector	5	100	4	80	1	20
Total	**32**	**100**	**10**	**31**	**22**	**69**

Source: Annual Reports of Companies, 2015–2016. Results computed.

It is observed from Table 11.5 that:

(a) 78% of the private sector companies have non-executive chairmen in their boards and the day-to-day operations are managed by the CEO/managing directors.

(b) In regard to public sector undertakings and public sector banks, it is observed that 80% of these organizations are headed by single individuals in the name of executive chairman or chairman-cum-managing director. Only 1 PSB, viz. Bank of Baroda has a non-executive chairman in the board.

(c) The position of chairman and CEO/managing director has been segregated in the majority cases in the private sector companies, whereas by contrast, the incidence of chairman–CEO duality remains almost intact in the PSUs due to the government policy.

(d) However, it is an open question as to whether, or to what degree, non-duality is a good indicator of independence, given the fact that the boards can still be effectively controlled by the management or minority owners even without the exercise of duality.

Independent directors and nominee directors in BSE Sensex and NSE Nifty companies in 2015–2016

The position of independent directors and nominee directors in the board of selected listed companies for the year 2015–2016 is shown in Table 11.6.

Table 11.6 Independent Directors and Nominee Directors in the Board of Selected Companies in 2015–2016 (Listed under BSE Sensex and NSE Nifty)

Type of organization	No.	Total directors		Independent directors		Nominee directors	
		Nos.	%	Nos.	%	Nos.	%
Private sector	27	292	100	159	54	11	4
Public sector	5	53	100	14	26	14	26
Total	**32**	**345**	**100**	**173**	**50**	**25**	**7**

Source: Annual Reports of Companies, 2015–2016. Results computed.

An analysis of Table 11.6 reveals that:

(a) Out of 345 directors in the boards of 32 listed companies, 173 directors are independent representing 50% of the total board strength. 25 nominee directors account for 7% of the total board members.

(b) There are 159 independent directors in the boards of 27 private sector companies accounting for 54% of the total board strength of 292 members, thereby complying with the provision of SEBI Listing Regulations and the Companies Act, 2013.

(c) On the contrary, only 14 independent board members are there in 5 public sector companies accounting for 26% of the total board strength of 53 members, thereby failing to comply with the provision of SEBI Listing Regulations and the Companies Act, 2013. Therefore, it is reiterated that the Government of India should induct adequate number of independent directors in the boards of all the PSUs/PSBs in order to meet the shortfall of minimum requirement of 50% of the total board members.

(d) As far as the nominee directors are concerned, PSUs/PSBs account for more number of nominee directors as compared to the private sector companies.

More details on independent directors are available in Chapter 5 and Appendix 8.

Women directors in BSE Sensex and NSE Nifty companies in 2015–2016

As per SEBI Listing Regulations, the board of directors of the company shall have at least one woman director in the board to ensure gender diversity and more effective functioning of the board. Let us see the position of women directors in the board of selected listed companies for the year 2015–2016, shown in Table 11.7.

TABLE 11.7 Position of Women Directors in the Board of Selected Companies for the Year 2015–2016 (Listed under BSE Sensex and NSE Nifty)

Serial No.	Name of companies	Total no. of women directors	Executive directors	Independent directors	Nominee directors	Other non-executive directors
1.	Bajaj Auto Ltd.	1	–	1	–	–
2.	Eicher Motors Ltd.	1	–	1	–	–
3.	Tata Motors Ltd.	1	–	1	–	–
4.	HDFC Bank Ltd.	2	–	1	–	1
5.	ICICI Bank Ltd.	2	2	–	–	–
6.	State Bank of India (PSB)	2	1 (c)	–	1	–
7.	Bank of Baroda (PSB)	2	–	1	1	–
8.	Yes Bank Ltd.	1	–	–	–	1 (c)
9.	Axis Bank Ltd.	3	1	1	1	–
10.	ACC Ltd.	1	–	1	–	–
11.	Ambuja Cements Ltd.	1	–	–	1	–
12.	Asian Paints Ltd.	2	–	1	–	1
13.	Hindustan Unilever Ltd.	1	–	1	–	–
14.	ITC Ltd.	1	–	1	–	–
15.	Bosch Ltd.	1	–	1	–	–
16.	Zee Entertainment Ltd.	1	–	1	–	–
17.	HDFC Ltd.	1	1	–	–	–
18.	Infosys Technologies Ltd.	3	–	3	–	–
19.	Tata Consultancy Services	1	1	–	–	–
20.	Tata Steel Ltd.	1	–	1	–	–
21.	Dr. Reddy's Lab. Ltd.	1	–	1	–	–
22.	Lupin Pharma Ltd.	2	2	–	–	–
23.	Sun Pharma Ltd.	1	–	1	–	–
24.	ONGC Ltd. (PSU)	NIL	NIL	NIL	NIL	NIL
25.	Power Grid Corpn. Ltd. (PSU)	1	–	–	1	–
26.	Tata Power Company Ltd.	NIL	NIL	NIL	NIL	NIL
27.	NTPC Ltd. (PSU)	1	–	1	–	–
28.	Adani Ports & SEZ Ltd.	1	–	1	–	–
29.	Reliance Industries Ltd.	1	–	–	–	1
30.	Idea Cellular Ltd.	3	–	2	–	1
31	Hindalco Industries Ltd.	1	–	–	–	1
32.	Aurobindo Pharma Ltd.	1	–	1	–	–
	Total	**42 (100%)**	**8 (19%)**	**23 (55%)**	**5 (12%)**	**6 (14%)**

Source: Annual Reports of Companies, 2015–2016. Results computed.
Note: (c) denotes Chairman/Chairman and Managing Director in the same category.

It is observed from Table 11.7 that:

(a) Out of 42 women directors representing 12% of the total board strength of 345 directors in 32 listed companies, 23 are independent directors, followed by 8 executive directors, 5 nominee directors and 6 other non-executive directors.

(b) 3 companies/banks, viz. Axis Bank, Infosys and Idea Cellular have 3 women directors in the boards of each of these companies and 6 companies/banks have 2 women directors in each of their respective boards.

(c) Out of 42 women directors, 2 are the chairmen of the 2 banks, viz. State Bank of India (as executive chairman) and Yes Bank (as non-executive chairman).

(d) 2 companies, viz. ONGC and Tata Power have not appointed any woman director in their boards till 31st March 2016, thereby violating the provisions of the Companies Act and SEBI Regulations.

More details on women directors are available in Chapter 6 and Appendix 9.

Directors' attendance in board meetings of the listed companies

Information regarding directors' attendance in the board meetings of selected companies in 2015–2016 is shown in Table 11.8.

TABLE 11.8 Directors' Attendance in the Board Meetings of Selected Companies in 2015–2016 (Listed under BSE Sensex and NSE Nifty)

No. of board meetings attended	Number of directors	Percentage (%)
0	3	1
1	11	3
2	16	5
3	14	4
4	35	10
5	92	26
6	64	18
7	30	9
8	29	8
9	14	4
10	12	4
11	4	1
12	9	3
13	10	3
14	2	1
Total	**345**	**100**

Source: Annual Reports of Companies, 2015–2016. Results computed.

The following points emerge from the information provided in Table 11.8:

(a) Out of 345 directors representing 32 listed companies, 250 (71%) directors have attended 4 to 8 board meetings.

(b) 1 public sector undertaking, Power Grid Corporation held the highest 14 board meetings, followed by 3 PSUs/PSBs, viz. NTPC, ONGC and Bank of Baroda, which held 13 board meetings. SBI held 12 board meetings in the year 2015–2016.

(c) The lowest 4 board meetings were held in 2 listed private sector companies/ banks viz. Lupin and Yes Bank.

(d) Average number of directors attending a board meeting of a BSE Sensex and NSE Nifty company has been 3.

(e) Total number of directors attending the last AGM of these companies has been 276, i.e., 80% of the total board directors in 32 companies.

(f) The maximum time gap between the two board meetings permissible by the SEBI Listing Regulations and the Companies Act, 2013 was not violated by any company.

Disclosure of tenure and age limit of directors in the Annual Report, 2015–2016

The survey reveals that:

(a) Out of 32 listed companies studied, only 5 companies (16%) have clearly disclosed their policy in regard to age limit and tenure of directors. They are: (i) Infosys, (ii) NTPC, (iii) Power Grid, (iv) Tata Motors, and (v) Tata Power.

(b) 2 private sector companies, viz. (i) ITC, and (ii) Tata Steel have not mentioned anything about the tenure and age limit of board directors.

(c) The rest 25 companies/banks (78%) out of 32 companies/banks have disclosed the tenure of directors only in their corporate governance report for the year 2015–2016.

It is also observed that the tenure of service of directors in almost all private sector companies is contractual varying from 3 to 5 years although there is no age limit. On the contrary, the age limit and tenure of directors of PSUs/PSBs are governed by the government through the Department of Public Enterprises (DPE) guidelines.

With a view to discharging the corporate governance functions effectively, particularly for the efficient functioning of the board, the corporate houses should declare a retirement policy of board directors and fix their retirement age maximum at 75 years.

Disclosure of definition of independent director and selection criteria of board directors including independent directors in the Annual Report, 2015–2016

The study reveals that:

(a) Only 4 companies (13%), viz. (i) Infosys, (ii) HUL, (iii) Tata Motors, and (iv) TCS disclosed the definition of 'independent director' in conformity with the SEBI Listing Regulations and the Companies Act, 2013.

(b) 19 companies/banks (59%), viz. (i) Adani Ports, (ii) Asian Paints, (iii) BOB, (iv) Bajaj Auto, (v) Bosch, (vi) HDFC, (vii) Hindalco, (viii) ITC, (ix) Idea Cellular, (x) NTPC, (xi) ONGC, (xii) Power Grid, (xiii) SBI, (xiv) Sun Pharma, (xv) TCS, (xvi) Yes Bank, (xvii) Lupin, (xviii) ZEE, and (xix) Aurobindo Pharma have not disclosed the 'selection criteria' of board directors, including independent directors, in their Annual Reports.

Familiarization programme for independent directors and board evaluation

The survey reveals that:

(a) 5 companies/banks (16%) have not disclosed anything about the familiarization programme for independent directors in their Annual Reports 2015–2016. They are: (i) Adani Ports, (ii) BOB, (iii) ICICI Bank, (iv) SBI, and (v) TCS.

(b) Similarly, 5 public sector companies/banks (16%), viz. (i) BOB, (ii) NTPC, (iii) ONGC, (iv) Power Grid, and (v) SBI have not disclosed how they conduct evaluating their board of directors in their Annual Reports 2015–2016, which is contrary to the SEBI Listing Regulations.

Post-board meeting follow-up system and compliance of board procedure

It has been observed that only 8 companies (26%) out of 31 companies studied, viz. (i) Adani Port, (ii) Ambuja Cement, (iii) Dr. Reddy's, (iv) ITC, (v) ONGC, (vi) Power Grid, (vii) RIL, and (viii) Tata Power have disclosed this item in their Annual Reports 2015–2016.

Lead independent director

The study reveals that only 2 companies (6%), viz. (i) Dr. Reddy's, and (ii) RIL have appointed a lead independent director to represent and act as a spokesperson for independent directors as a group in order to work closely with the chairman and CEO and take a lead role in the board evaluation process, apart from other important board functions. It is considered to be a good governance practice exhibited by these companies at par with the international standard of corporate governance which should be followed by other listed companies also.

Disclosure of other provisions as to the boards and committees

On scrutiny, it has been observed that out of 345 directors on 32 companies' boards, each of 308 persons holds the directorship ranging from 1 to 9 companies. The rest 37 persons hold the office of directorship varying from 10 to 22 companies, including listed, unlisted and private limited companies. It is interesting to note that Mr. K. Satish Reddy and Mr. G.V. Prasad of Dr. Reddy's also hold directorship in 27 and 13 other organizations, respectively, which are not covered under Section 165 of the Companies Act, 2013.

Therefore, several questions naturally arise from the standpoint of corporate governance such as (a) How do these persons manage time to discharge the responsibilities of directors diligently in all these companies? (b) Can they really justify the positions of board directors in properly looking into the affairs of the companies in which boards they sit and take appropriate decisions? (c) Are they able to deliberate in the board meetings effectively and spend sufficient time in discussions before taking crucial decisions? (d) In the present global business uncertainties and stiff competition both inside and outside, how effective they are in taking crucial strategic decisions for survival and growth of each of these companies? (e) Lastly, is it ethical for one person to hold the directorships in so many companies and organizations at a time, particularly when the various stakeholders' fortune are solely dependent on the well-being of these organizations through effective corporate governance, and also, when sufficiently qualified and experienced young professionals are willing to shoulder the responsibility of board directorships as prescribed by the Companies Act, 2013 and SEBI Listing Regulations?

No doubt, there are no ready answers to these questions. It is up to the shareholders of the companies to decide and the legislators to consider whether holding of directorships in so many companies by one individual at a time is justified and reasonable.

So far as the membership in the various board committees is concerned, all 32 companies have disclosed in their corporate governance report that none of their directors were the members in more than 10 committees or the chairman of more than 5 committees individually across all companies. The reports have also disclosed the committee positions occupied by the individual directors in other companies.

Disclosure of remuneration policy and remuneration of directors

Contrary to the requirement of the SEBI Listing Regulations, 13 companies/banks (41%) have not disclosed their remuneration policy in the corporate governance report. They are (i) Asian Paints, (ii) BOB, (iii) Bajaj Auto, (iv) Eicher Motor, (v) Infosys, (vi) NTPC, (vii) ONGC, (viii) Power Grid, (ix) SBI, (x) TCS, (xi) Lupin, (xii) Aurobindo Pharma, and (xiii) Yes Bank.

Out of the above 13 companies/banks, 5 PSUs/PSBs did not publish their policy on the plea that their remuneration policy is determined by the Government of India through DPE and by the RBI/Ministry of Finance. Therefore, the question of adoption of separate policy by these organizations does not arise.

In regard to the disclosure of remuneration of directors, it has been observed that detailed break-up of remuneration of executive/whole time directors has not been furnished by majority of the companies studied.

11.3.3 Board Committees

The study of board committees of all 32 companies/banks listed under BSE Sensex and NSE Nifty, as disclosed in the Annual Reports 2015–2016, reveals the existence and operations of the following committees in companies:

Statutory board committees

1. Audit committee
2. Remuneration and nomination committee
3. Independent directors' committee
4. Shareholders'/stakeholders' relationship committee
5. Corporate social responsibility (CSR) committee
6. Risk management committee

Non-mandatory committees

1. Health, safety and environment committee
2. Ethics and compliance committee
3. Investment committee
4. Share transfer committee
5. Other board committees

Let us discuss in brief about the existence and operations of these committees.

Audit Committee

The study of the various aspects of audit committee reveals that:

(a) There is a lack of transparency in the composition of audit committees of 3 PSUs/PSBs, viz. (i) Power Grid Corporation, (ii) BOB and (iii) SBI, which has caused incompatibility with the provisions of SEBI Listing Regulations.

(b) Lack of minimum requirement of the number of independent directors in the audit committees of 3 PSUs/PSBs, viz. (i) Power Grid Corporation, (ii) BOB and (iii) SBI, has been noticed.

(c) There is a non-disclosure of information about literacy and expertise of the members of the audit committee in finance, accounts, law, etc. by 13 companies (40%), viz. (i) Adani Port, (ii) BOB, (iii) Eicher Motors, (iv) HDFC Bank, (v) Hindalco, (vi) ICICI Bank, (vii) NTPC, (viii) Power Grid, (ix) RIL, (x) Sun Pharma, (xi) TCS, (xii) Yes Bank, and (xiii) Zee Enterprises.

(d) There has been no disclosure of information about participation of head of finance, statutory auditors, internal auditor, in the audit committees by 12 companies (37%), viz. (i) BOB, (ii) Bosch, (iii) HDFC Bank, (iv) HDFC, (v) Hindalco, (vi) ICICI Bank, (vii) Infosys, (viii) Power Grid, (ix) SBI, (x) TCS, (xi) Tata Steel, and (xii) Yes Bank.

(e) 23 companies/banks (72%) have not disclosed audit committee charter in the corporate governance reports. They are (i) ACC, (ii) Asian Paints, (iii) Axis Bank, (iv) Bajaj Auto, (v) Eicher Motor, (vi) HDFC Bank, (vii) HDFC, (viii) Hindalco, (ix) ICICI Bank, (x) Idea Cellular, (xi) NTPC, (xii) ONGC, (xiii) Power Grid, (xiv) RIL, (xv) SBI, (xvi) Sun Pharma, (xvii) TCS, (xviii) Tata Steel, (xix) Tata Power, (xx) Yes Bank, (xxi) Lupin, (xxii) Zee Enterprises and (xxiii) Aurobindo Pharma.

(f) Only 3 companies (10%), viz. (i) Dr. Reddy's, (ii) Infosys, and (iii) Tata Power, have published audit committee reports duly signed and dated by the chairpersons confirming compliance of the roles and responsibilities of the committee members as mandated in the charter/US laws/Indian laws.

(g) All 32 companies/banks, however, have set up audit committee in their organizations as disclosed in the corporate governance report and complied with the statutory requirements in regard to the number of meetings held by the audit committees.

Remuneration and nomination committee

(a) Out of 32 listed companies/banks, only 2 companies/banks (6%) in the public sector, viz. (i) BOB, and (ii) Power Grid Corporation have not set up remuneration and nomination committee, the reason being that remuneration, pay scales, perks, benefits, nomination, etc. of board directors are all determined by the Government of India through the respective ministries. Therefore, these government companies/banks argue that there is no need for setting up this committee.

(b) Only 1 public sector bank, SBI has failed to disclose information about number of committee meetings held during the year 2015–2016.

(c) Similarly, only 1 public sector company, Power Grid Corporation has not disclosed compliance of minimum requirement of the number of non-executive directors in the committee in its corporate governance report.

(d) 3 companies/banks (9%), viz. (i) BOB, (ii) ITC, and (iii) Power Grid Corporation have failed to disclose compliance of the provision of SEBI Listing Regulations on mandatory appointment of independent director as chairman of the committee.

(e) 15 companies/banks (47%) out of 32 studied, have not furnished information about compulsory participation of all members in the committee meetings as required by the SEBI Listing Regulations. They are (i) BOB, (ii) Eicher Motor, (iii) HDFC Bank, (iv) HDFC, (v) Hindalco, (vi) ITC, (vii) Infosys, (viii) Idea Cellular, (ix) Power Grid, (x) SBI, (xi) Sun Pharma, (xii) Tata Motors, (xiii) Tata Steel, (xiv) Lupin and (xv) Zee Entertainment.

(f) 8 companies/banks (25%), viz. (i) ACC Cement, (ii) Bajaj Auto, (iii) Dr. Reddy's, (iv) Power Grid, (v) SBI, (vi) Sun Pharma, (vii) Tata Steel, and (viii) Zee Entertainment have not disclosed both of their nomination policy and terms of reference of the committee in their Annual Report.

(g) Though 23 companies/banks (72%) have furnished the details of terms of reference of the committee, yet they have failed to disclose their nomination policy in the Annual Reports. They are (i) Adani Port, (ii) Ambuja Cement, (iii) Asian Paints, (iv) Axis Bank, (v) BOB, (vi) Eicher Motor, (vii) HUL, (viii) HDFC Bank, (ix) HDFC, (x) Hindalco, (xi) ICICI Bank, (xii) ITC, (xiii) Infosys, (xiv) Idea Cellular, (xv) NTPC, (xvi) ONGC, (xvii) RIL, (xviii) Tata Motors, (xix) TCS, (xx) Tata Power, (xxi) Lupin, (xxii) Yes Bank and (xxiii) Aurobindo Pharma.

(h) Only 1 private sector company, Bosch has disclosed both nomination policy and terms of reference of the committee in its Annual Report.

(i) 4 companies (13%) in the private sector, viz. (i) Dr. Reddy's, (ii) Infosys, (iii) Tata Motors, and (iv) Tata Power have furnished the reports of the committees in their corporate governance reports, duly signed and dated by the chairpersons confirming compliance of the roles and responsibilities of the committee members.

Independent directors' committee

(a) Contrary to the provisions of Regulation 25(3) of the SEBI Listing Regulations, 2015, 6 companies/banks (19%) have failed to hold any meeting of their independent directors during the year 2015–2016. They are (i) BOB, (ii) Bosch, (iii) ICICI Bank, (iv) SBI, (v) ZEE and (vi) Aurobindo Pharma.

(b) 19 companies/banks (59%), viz. (i) ACC, (ii) Adani Port, (iii) Ambuja Cement, (iv) Asian Paints, (v) Axis Bank, (vi) Bajaj Auto, (vii) Eicher Motor, (viii) HDFC Bank, (ix) Hindalco, (x) ITC, (xi) NTPC, (xii) ONGC, (xiii) Power Grid, (xiv) Sun Pharma, (xv) Tata Motors, (xvi) Tata Steel, (xvii) Tata Power, (xviii) Yes Bank, and (xix) Lupin have hold 1 meeting of their independent directors.

(c) 7 companies (22%) in the private sector have hold 2 meetings of independent directors during 2015–2016. They are (i) Dr. Reddy's, (ii) HUL, (iii) HDFC, (iv) Infosys, (v) Idea Cellular, (vi) RIL and (vii) TCS.

Shareholders'/Stakeholders' relationship committee

(a) All 32 companies/banks have formed this committee in line with SEBI Listing Regulations and the Companies Act, 2013. They have also furnished information regarding the number of committee meetings held during the year 2015–2016.

(b) 12 companies/banks (37%) out of 32 studied, have disclosed the nature of various complaints and queries received and disposed—itemwise specifically in the corporate governance report. They are (i) Ambuja Cement, (ii) Dr. Reddy's, (iii) Eicher Motor, (iv) HUL, (v) ITC, (vi) Infosys, (vii) NTPC, (viii) Power Grid, (ix) RIL, (x) SBI, (xi) Tata Motors, and (xii) Zee.

(c) Only 1 private sector company, Tata Power has provided details about action taken on shareholders' survey.

(d) Only 3 companies (9%), viz. (i) Dr. Reddy's, (ii) Infosys, and (iii) Tata Power have disclosed the committee reports duly signed and dated by the chairpersons in the corporate governance report.

Corporate Social Responsibility (CSR) committee

(a) All companies/banks except 2 public sector organizations, viz. (i) BOB, and (ii) ONGC have formed corporate social responsibility (CSR) committee during the year 2015–2016.

(b) 5 companies/banks (16%) have not disclosed the number of committee meetings held in the year 2015–2016. They are (i) BOB, (ii) HDFC Bank, (iii) Lupin, (iv) NTPC and (v) Aurobindo Pharma.

(c) 23 companies/banks (72%) out of 32 companies studied, have not disclosed CSR policy in their Annual Reports 2015–2016.

(d) 9 companies/banks (28%), viz. (i) Adani Ports, (ii) Axis Bank, (iii) BOB, (iv) Bosch, (v) Eicher Motor, (vi) HUL, (vii) Power Grid, (viii) SBI, and (ix) Zee have not disclosed CSR report in their Annual Reports.

Risk management committee

(a) Amongst all 32 companies/banks studied, only 1 private sector company, ITC has not provided any information regarding formation of the committee.

(b) Only 2 out of 32 companies/banks, have disclosed their risk management policy in the Annual Reports. They are: (i) Bosch, and (ii) Tata Steel.

(c) Only 5 companies/banks have provided the committee report in their Annual Reports 2015–2016 and disclosed the manner in which they manage risks in the operations. They are (i) Dr. Reddy's, (ii) Infosys, (iii) SBI, (iv) Tata Power and (v) Aurobindo Pharma.

Health, safety and environment committee

It is observed from the Annual Reports of all 32 companies/banks that most of the listed companies have generally taken health, safety, and environment measures for satisfaction of the stakeholders. However, only 5 companies (16%), viz. (i) ONGC, (ii) RIL, (iii) Tata Motors, (iv) TCS, and (v) Tata Steel have set up a separate committee for this purpose.

Ethics and compliance committee

It is observed that only 4 private sector companies, viz. (i) ACC, (ii) Ambuja Cement, (iii) TCS, and (iv) Tata Steel have formed this committee.

Investment committee

Only 6 listed companies (19%), viz. (i) Dr. Reddy's, (ii) Infosys, (iii) NTPC, (iv) ONGC, (v) Power Grid, and (vi) Tata Steel have set up investment committee to ensure investment and monitoring of the same for best interest of the organizations.

Share transfer committee

9 companies/banks (28%), viz. Adani Port, (ii) Asian Paints, (iii) BOB, (iv) Eicher Motor, (v) HUL, (vi) ITC, (vii) Lupin, (viii) NTPC, and (ix) Power Grid have formed share transfer committee to ensure smooth and expeditious transfer of shares.

Other board committees

Besides the committees mentioned above, many listed companies/banks among 32 studied, have set up various other board committees to look into the different matters important to the respective organizations. For example, all listed banks both in private and public sector have set up **fraud monitoring committee** to ensure prevention of fraudulent activities/transactions and also to monitor fraud cases happened.

11.3.4 Subsidiary Companies

The disclosure of information about subsidiary companies provided by the holding companies in their annual reports are by and large, in line with the requirement of the Listing Agreement and the Companies Act, 1956, particularly in regard to the presentation of consolidated financial statements of the companies including the subsidiary companies.

11.3.5 Disclosures and Transparency

Disclosures and transparency in the report of corporate governance in the Annual Reports of the listed companies/banks during the year 2015–2016, as required by the Companies Act, 2013 and the SEBI Listing (Obligation and Disclosure) Requirements, 2015 have been analyzed under the following heads:

1. Significant related party transactions having potential conflicts with the interest of the company
2. Accounting treatment
3. Management discussion and analysis

4. Shareholders' information
5. Shareholders' rights
6. Audit qualification
7. Vigil mechanism and whistle blower policy

Let us discuss the above chronologically.

Significant related party transactions having potential conflicts with the interest of the company

It is observed that all 32 companies/banks listed under BSE Sensex and NSE Nifty disclosed in the corporate governance report 2015–2016 that there has been no materially significant related party transaction having potential conflict with the interest of the companies/banks.

Accounting treatment

All 32 listed companies/banks have disclosed that the accounting treatment made is no different from that prescribed in the accounting standards. In fact, all of them have disclosed in their 'Directors' Responsibility Statement' in the Annual Report 2015–2016 that in the preparation of annual accounts, the applicable accounting standards have been followed and no material departure has been made from the same.

Management discussion and analysis

The study reveals that except 2 listed companies/banks, viz. (i) BOB, and (ii) Lupin, all other companies/banks have included in their Directors' Report or as an annexure thereto, a Management Discussion and Analysis Report as a part of the Annual Report to the shareholders. This report has included a wide coverage of the items prescribed in the SEBI Listing Regulations.

Shareholders' information

Shareholders' information is generally concentrated on the following items:

(a) Appointment of new directors/re-appointment of retiring directors/resignation of directors
(b) Quarterly results and presentation
(c) Share transfers, and
(d) Directors' responsibility statement

It is observed that all 32 companies/banks have disclosed compliance on the above matters in their corporate governance report 2015–2016.

Shareholders' rights

The scrutiny reveals that all 32 companies/banks have complied with the requirements prescribed by the SEBI Listing Regulations.

Audit qualification

It is observed that all 32 companies/banks have complied with the requirements as disclosed in the corporate governance report.

Vigil mechanism and whistle blower policy

The study reveals that only 5 listed companies (16%) have disclosed both vigil mechanism and their whistle blower policy in the Annual Reports, 2015–2016. They are (i) HUL, (ii) ITC, (iii) Infosys, (iv) Tata Motors, and (v) Tata Steel. The rest 27 companies/banks have disclosed their vigil mechanism only.

11.3.6 General Body Meetings

In regard to reporting of information on the company's general body meetings, following information are to be mandatorily included in the annual report:

(a) Location and time of general meetings held in last three years
(b) Details of special resolution passed in the last three AGMs/EGMs
(c) Details of resolution passed last year through postal ballot including the name of the conducting official and voting pattern/procedure

It is observed that out of 32 listed companies/banks:

1. Only 1 public sector bank, SBI has not disclosed the information under item (a) above in its corporate governance report.
2. 8 listed companies/banks (26%), viz. (i) Adani Port, (ii) Ambuja Cement, (iii) Asian Paints, (iv) HDFC, (v) HDFC Bank, (vi) Hindalco, (vii) SBI, and (viii) ONGC have failed to disclose the details as required under item (b) above.
3. 3 listed companies/banks, viz. (i) Ambuja Cement, (ii) ONGC, and (iii) SBI have not disclosed the details required under item (c) above, in their corporate governance reports 2015–2016.

11.3.7 Code of Conduct and Its Affirmation

All 32 listed companies/banks except the private sector company, HUL have given written affirmation in regard to the code of conduct for all board members and senior management of the companies. The Annual Reports of these companies have contained declaration to this effect duly signed by the CEOs/Managing Directors.

11.3.8 CEO/CFO Certification

It is observed that 14 companies/banks (45%) out of 32 have failed to provide in writing in the Annual Reports, 2015–2016, the CEO/CFO certification confirming absence of materially untrue statement/omission thereof, fraudulent, illegal or violative transactions in the financial statements, and ensuring existence of true and fair view of the companies' affairs, and effective internal control system, etc. The failing companies/banks are (i) Axis Bank, (ii) Bajaj Auto, (iii) Bosch, (iv) HDFC, (v) HDFC Bank, (vi) ICICI Bank, (vii) ONGC, (viii) Power Grid, (ix) SBI, (x) Sun Pharma, (xi) Tata Motors, (xii) TCS, (xiii) Tata Steel, and (xiv) Tata Power.

11.3.9 Means of Communication and General Shareholder Information

All 32 listed companies/banks have provided general shareholder information and adopted various means of communication as prescribed by the SEBI Listing Regulations to be included in the report on corporate governance.

11.3.10 Disclosures on Stakeholders' Interests

We have analyzed the compliance standards of the conditions of corporate governance by 32 companies/banks listed in BSE Sensex and NSE Nifty in terms of the provisions of SEBI Listing Regulations, 2015 and the new Companies Act, 2013. In this section, we focus briefly on the disclosures made by these companies/banks in their Annual Reports, 2015–2016 on various initiatives and measures taken by them in order to meet their commitments on the expectations and interests of stakeholders.

It is observed from the Annual Reports that the companies/banks have deliberated on this issue in five segments:

1. Environment, Health and Safety (EHS) measures
2. Human Resources Development (HRD) initiatives
3. Business Responsibility (BR) reporting
4. Industrial Relations (IR), and
5. Disclosure of Policies on EHS, HRD, and IR

The study reveals that:

(a) Out of 32 companies/banks, 7 companies/banks (23%) have not disclosed EHS measures taken by them in their Annual Reports, 2015–2016. They are (i) BOB, (ii) Bajaj Auto, (iii) Dr. Reddy's, (iv) ICICI Bank, (v) Infosys, (vi) Idea Cellular, and (vii) Zee.

(b) Except Bajaj Auto, all other companies have disclosed various initiatives taken by them for development of human resources in their companies.

(c) 10 listed companies/banks (32%) have failed to report their business responsibility in their organizations in the Annual Reports. These are (i) Axis Bank, (ii) BOB, (iii) Bajaj Auto, (iv) HUL, (v) HDFC, (vi) HDFC Bank, (vii) ICICI Bank, (viii) Sun Pharma, (ix) Tata Steel, and (x) Tata Power.

(d) Only 9 companies/banks (28%), viz. (i) ACC, (ii) Adani Port, (iii) Bajaj Auto, (iv) Bosch, (v) NTPC, (vi) ONGC, (vii) SBI, (viii) Yes Bank, and (ix) Aurobindo Pharma have provided information about industrial relations in their Annual Reports.

(e) No company/bank has disclosed its policy on EHS, HRD, and IR in its Annual Report, 2015–2016.

11.3.11 Compliance of Corporate Governance and Auditors' Certificates

(a) All 32 companies/banks except SBI have published auditors' certificates on compliance with the conditions of corporate governance as stipulated by the SEBI Listing Regulations, 2015 and annexed the same with the Directors' Report for the year 2015–2016.

(b) 28 companies/banks (87%) have obtained the auditors' unqualified certificates, confirming that these companies/banks have complied with the conditions of corporate governance.

(c) 3 listed PSUs (10%), viz. (i) NTPC, (ii) ONGC, and (iii) Power Grid have obtained auditors' certificates with qualifications for non-compliance of one or more conditions of corporate governance such as lack of minimum requirement of the number of independent directors in the boards, and in the audit committees and other statutory committees of these companies.

(d) Only 1 listed PSB, viz. SBI has not disclosed in its Annual Report, 2015–2016, the auditor's certificate on compliance with the conditions of corporate governance as stipulated by the SEBI Listing Regulations, 2015.

11.4 EVALUATION OF GOVERNANCE STANDARD

Having analyzed the governance structures, processes and disclosures made on corporate governance, the questions arise as to what is the standard and quality of governance that has been achieved by the Indian corporate houses? Are there any credit rating agencies in the country, which have evaluated the governance standards of these companies? If so, what are the results of such evaluation? Can we apply the same rating method in this study to pinpoint our findings? If not, what alternative method can we suggest as a 'working method'? Are quality and effectiveness of corporate governance revealed by application of the 'working method'?

Till now, two entities, viz., (a) Credit Rating Information Services of India Limited (CRISIL) and (b) Investment Information and Credit Rating Agency of India (ICRA) have performed such evaluation exercise on a few companies. A glimpse of their activities may be mentioned herein below:

11.4.1 CRISIL Corporate Governance and Value Creation Rating (GVC Rating)

CRISIL addresses the issue of corporate governance by providing an independent assessment of an entity's performance and future expectations on 'balanced value creation through sound corporate governance practices'. CRISIL evaluates two broad aspects to arrive at GVC rating for a company, viz., (i) Value creation and distribution, (ii) Corporate governance and wealth management.

So far as the evaluation of value creation and distribution is considered, CRISIL evaluates value creation and distribution to various stakeholders, e.g., (a) shareholders, (b) debtholders, (c) customers, (d) employees, (e) suppliers, and (f) society.

So far as the evaluation of corporate governance and wealth management is considered, CRISIL uses the broad factors, e.g., (a) assessment of management capabilities, (b) financial transparency and disclosure, (c) influence of majority or large stakeholders, (d) board composition and effectiveness.

The CRISIL process comprises analyzing both confidential as well as public information, discussing with management personnel, board members and key shareholders. The GVC rating is given on a scale of eight levels with detailed write–up of analysis and conclusion. It claims that its rating is a globally unique model which appropriately balances quantitative value creation measures with qualitative evaluation, provides a view on the entity's expected performance in future and addresses all stakeholders more equitably.

11.4.2 ICRA Corporate Governance Rating (CGR)

ICRA addresses the issue of corporate governance by indicating the level to which an entity accepts and follows the codes and guidelines of corporate governance practices. The key variables analyzed while arriving at the CGR for a company are: (a) shareholding structure, (b) governance structure and management process, (c) board structure and processes, (d) stakeholders relationship, (e) transparency and disclosures, and (f) financial discipline.

ICRA states that CGR exercise involves perusal of various corporate documents, viz., board notes, agenda papers, minutes of meetings, statutory returns submitted to the Registrar of Companies (ROC), the stock exchanges, the SEBI, annual reports etc. It also involves, meeting key officials of the corporate being rated, its statutory auditors, directors, and institutional investors. Each of these variables is scored on a set of parameters and a composite score is obtained by using ICRA developed proprietary model. The CGR rating is given on a scale of six levels with detailed analysis and conclusion.

A comparative analysis of CRISIL and ICRA ratings

On a closer look at the credit rating processes adopted by CRISIL and ICRA, it is observed that although the ultimate objective of ratings is the same the methodology adopted for analysis and evaluation are different from one another. The main difference noticed here is that CRISIL has approached the entire exercise in two parts. The first part emphasizes on assessment of maximizing stakeholders' value and their distribution by the corporate entity. The second part of the GVC rating process analyzes and evaluates various factors of corporate governance and wealth management practices followed by the entity. The ICRA, on the other hand, analyzes and evaluates various factors of corporate governance straightway without taking an assessment of stakeholders' value and their distribution separately. However, the analysis of shareholders' value creation and distribution is also considered while evaluating the variables. Therefore, there is no doubt that CRISIL's approach towards corporate governance ratings appears to be logically superior to that of ICRA. Secondly, it is observed that ICRA's coverage of analysis on corporate governance practices being followed by a corporate entity appears to be much wider than that of CRISIL, although the depth of analysis and evaluation processes may be same in both the agencies' rating process. Thirdly, the GVC rating of CRISIL is given on a scale of eight levels, whereas the CGR rating of ICRA is given on a scale of six levels, which means that CRISIL allows more flexibility in its rating process than that of ICRA. However, there is no denying the fact that both these agencies have developed their respective techniques and adopted evaluation methods, which are getting gradual acceptance of the Indian corporate houses.

11.4.3 Suggested Method for Examining the Quality and Effectiveness of Corporate Governance

There are certain genuine difficulties for this author in following similar methodology as that of CRISIL and ICRA for examining the quality and effectiveness of corporate governance in vogue in selected companies. Despite sincere efforts, the required information, particularly the confidential information and documents, viz., board notes, agenda papers, minutes of the meetings, statutory returns submitted to ROC, stock exchanges, SEBI, etc., were not available from the sample corporate houses. Moreover, the rating agencies are shy in sharing many of such information to the author.

Expectedly, they are not willing to part with the 'models' they have developed in this regard. Besides, there was no scope for this author to discuss with key officials of the sample companies being rated, their auditors, directors, and major shareholders. Therefore, it becomes extremely difficult to conduct an in-depth analysis and evaluation of the standard and quality of corporate governance presently practised by the sample companies due to the non-availability of required information.

As an alternative, the author has developed his own model as a **'working method'** as specified below.

The working method applied here for evaluation of the standard and quality of corporate governance practised in the sample companies has considered all the relevant conditions of corporate governance stipulated by SEBI (Listing Obligations and Disclosure Requirements) Regulations, 2015 and the new Companies Act, 2013. In order to ascertain how far these companies are compliant of governance standard, a point value system has been applied, whereby an adequate weightage in terms of points has been provided to these conditions according to their importance. Although this method is subjective having its own limitations, it helps us to pinpoint the quality and effectiveness of corporate governance with points assigned to important parameters of governance. Accordingly, each such company has been awarded points on some parameters, which constitute the governance process in company. These key governance parameters are selected on a 100 point scale as shown in Table 11.9.

TABLE 11.9 Selected Key Governance Parameters

	Key governance parameters	Points assigned
(a)	Statement on company's philosophy on code of governance	2
(b)	Structure and strength of the board	2
(c)	Chairman and CEO duality	5
(d)	Disclosure of tenure and age limit of directors	2
(e)	Disclosure of definition of independent director, appointment of woman director, selection criteria of board members including independent directors, familiarization programme for independent directors and board evaluation	5
(f)	Post-board meeting follow-up system and compliance of the board procedure	2
(g)	Appointment of lead independent director	2
(h)	Disclosure of other provisions as to boards and committees	1
(i)	Disclosure of remuneration policy and remuneration of directors	3
(j)	Board committees	35
(k)	Disclosures and transparency	14
(l)	General body meetings	3
(m)	Code of conduct and its affirmation	2
(n)	CEO/CFO certification	2
(o)	Means of communication and general shareholder information	2
(p)	Disclosure of stakeholders' interests	10
(q)	Compliance of corporate governance and auditors' certificate	8
	Total	**100**

It may be mentioned that out of total 100 points, 67 points have been assigned to four parameters, viz. (i) various board committees (35 points), (ii) disclosure and transparency (14 points), (iii) compliance of corporate governance and auditors' certificate (8 points), and (iv) disclosure of stakeholders' interests (10 points) because these are very important parameters for assessing quality and effectiveness of corporate governance system in a company. Accordingly, these four and many other segments, viz. serial nos. 3, 5, 9, etc. are detailed in Table 11.10 with relative weights. This is followed by justification of assignment of points. After determining total score based on the parameters mentioned in Table 11.10, companies and industry-groups are graded on a five-point scale as stated below:

Score range	Rank
81–100	Excellent
61–80	Very good
41–60	Good
21–40	Average
Below 21	Poor

The position is summed up in Table 11.10

TABLE 11.10 Criterion for Evaluation of Governance Standard of Sample Companies for the Year 2015–2016

	Governance parameters		Points/Scores assigned
1.	**Statement of company's philosophy on code of governance**		**2**
2.	**Structure and strength of the board**		**2**
3.	**Chairman and CEO duality**		**5 (max.)**
	(i) Promoter executive chairman-cum-MD/CEO	1	
	(ii) Non-promoter executive chairman-cum-MD/CEO	2	
	(iii) Promoter non-executive chairman	3	
	(iv) Non-promoter non-executive chairman	4	
	(v) Non-executive independent chairman	5	
4.	**Disclosure of tenure and age limit of directors**		**2**
5.	**Disclosure of**		**5**
	(i) Definition of independent director	1	
	(ii) Appointment of woman director	1	
	(iii) Selection criteria of board of directors including independent directors	1	
	(iv) Familiarization programme for independent directors	1	
	(v) Board evaluation	1	
6.	**Post-board meeting follow-up system and compliance of the board procedure**		**2**
7.	**Appointment of lead independent director**		**2**
8.	**Disclosure of other provisions as to boards and committees**		**1**
9.	**Disclosure of**		**3**
	(i) Remuneration policy	2	
	(ii) Remuneration of directors	1	

TABLE 11.10 Criterion for Evaluation of Governance Standard of Sample Companies for the Year 2015–2016 (*Contd.*)

Governance parameters		Points/Scores assigned
10. **Board committees**		
A. Audit committee		**8**
(i) Transparency in composition of audit committee	1	
(ii) Compliance of minimum requirement of the number of independent directors in the committee	1	
(iii) Compliance of minimum requirement of the number of meetings of the committee	1	
(iv) Information about literacy and expertise of committee members	1	
(v) Information about participation of head of finance, statutory auditor, and chief internal auditor in the committee meeting	1	
(vi) Disclosure of audit committee charter and terms of reference	2	
(vii) Publishing of audit committee report	1	
B. Remuneration and nomination committee		**8**
(i) Formation of the committee	1	
(ii) Information about number of committee meetings	1	
(iii) Compliance of minimum requirement of the number of non-executive directors in the committee	1	
(iv) Compliance of the provision of independent director as chairman of the committee	1	
(v) Information about participation of all members in the committee meeting	1	
(vi) Disclosure of nomination policy and terms of reference	2	
(vii) Publishing of committee report	1	
C. Independent directors' committee		**2 (Max.)**
(i) Information about number of meetings held during the year:		
For 1 meeting during the year:	1	
For more than 1 meeting:	2	
D. Shareholders'/Stakeholders' relationship committee		**5**
(i) Transparency in composition of the committee	1	
(ii) Information about nature of complaints and queries received and disposed—item-wise	1	
(iii) Information about number of committee meetings	1	
(iv) Information about action taken on investors/shareholders' survey	1	
(v) Publishing of committee report	1	
E. Corporate Social Responsibility (CSR) committee		**4**
(i) Formation of the committee	1	
(ii) Information about number of committee meetings	1	
(iii) Disclosure of CSR policy	1	
(iv) Publishing of committee report	1	

TABLE 11.10 Criterion for Evaluation of Governance Standard of Sample Companies for the Year 2015–2016 (*Contd.*)

Governance parameters		Points/Scores assigned
F. Risk management committee		**4**
(i) Formation of the committee	1	
(ii) Disclosure of risk management policy	2	
(iii) Publishing of committee report	1	
G. Health safety and environment committee		**1**
H. Ethics and compliance committee		**1**
I. Investment committee		**1**
J. Share transfer committee		**1**
11. **Disclosure and transparency**		**14**
(a) Significant related party transactions having potential conflicts with the interest of the company	2	
(b) Accounting treatment	2	
(c) Management discussion and analysis	2	
(d) Shareholders' information:		
(i) Appointment of new director/re-appointment of retiring director/resignation of director	1	
(ii) Quarterly results and presentation	1	
(iii) Share transfers	1	
(iv) Directors' responsibility statement	1	
(e) Shareholders' rights	1	
(f) Audit qualification	1	
(g) Vigil mechanism and whistle blower policy	2	
12. **General body meetings**		**3**
(i) Location and time of general meetings held in last three years	1	
(ii) Details of special resolution passed in the last three AGMs/EGMs	1	
(iii) Details of resolution passed last year through postal ballot including the name of conducting official and voting procedure	1	
13. **Code of conduct and its affirmation**		**2**
14. **CEO/CFO certification**		**2**
15. **Means of communication and general shareholder information**		**2**
16. **Disclosure of stakeholders' interests**		**10**
(i) Environment, Health and Safety (EHS) measures	2	
(ii) Human Resource Development (HRD) initiative	2	
(iii) Business responsibility reporting	2	
(iv) Industrial Relation (IR)	2	
(v) Disclosure of policies on EHS, HRD and IR	2	
17. **Compliance of corporate governance and Auditors' certificate**		**8 (max)**
(i) Clean certificate from auditors	8	
(ii) Qualified certificate from auditors	4	
Total		**100**

Justification for assignments of points to major key governance parameters

Chairman and CEO duality (serial no. 3 of Table 11.10)

The corporate governance principles demand that there should be a clear division of responsibilities at the helm of the company, which should ensure a balance of power and authority such that no single individual has unfettered powers of decision. In light of this principle, this segment has been assigned 5 points (Max).

Disclosure of definition of independent director, appointment of woman director, selection criteria of board of directors including independent directors, familiarization programme for independent directors, and board evaluation (serial no. 5 of Table 11.10)

Good corporate governance principles require that majority of the non-executive directors should be independent of management and free from business or other relationship, which could materially interfere with the exercise of their independent judgement. Besides, as per requirement of the new Companies Act, 2013 and Clause 49 of the Listing Agreement, 2014, followed by SEBI (Listing Obligations and Disclosure Requirements) Regulations, 2015, the board of directors must consist of at least one woman director. In light of this principle, it is equally important for every corporate to disclose not only the 'selection criteria' of board members including independent directors but also the definition of 'independent director' and appointment of woman director' in the Annual Report. Moreover, familiarization programme for independent directors and the board evaluation are all essential for enhancing the corporate governance. Therefore, this segment has been assigned 5 points.

Audit committee (serial no. 10 A of Table 11.10)

Audit committee, being one of the mandatory board committees, is the main pillar of corporate governance, the success or failure of which, largely depends upon the effectiveness of the audit committee functioning in the companies. There should be an adequate disclosure of audit committee charter and terms of reference in the annual report. Moreover, there should be clear transparency in composition of audit committee, compliance regarding minimum number of independent directors in the committee, minimum requirement of number of committee meetings, information about literacy, and expertise of committee members etc. The annual report should publish the audit committee report. Therefore, this segment has been assigned total 8 points.

Remuneration and nomination committee (serial no. 10 B of Table 11.10)

Remuneration committee is another very important committee, after audit committee, which deals with all matters relating to remuneration/compensation of board members of a company. Therefore, a good corporate governance principle expects that adequate importance should be given for its formation, compliance of minimum requirement of the number of non-executive directors and appointment of independent director as chairman of the committee etc.

This mandatory committee of the board also deals with all matters relating to selection and nomination of board members of a company. In light of this principle, this segment has been assigned total 8 points.

Independent directors' committee (serial no. 10 C of Table 11.10)

As per the Companies Act, 2013 and also SEBI (Listing Obligations and Disclosure Requirements) Regulations, 2015, the independent directors of the company themselves shall hold minimum one meeting in a year to review the performance of non-independent directors, chairperson and assess the quality, quantity timeliness of flow of information between the management and the board. Considering its importance of the meetings, this segment has been assigned total 2 points.

Stakeholders' and shareholders' relationship committee (serial no. 10 D of Table 11.10)

Shareholders/investors are the owners of the corporates. The stakeholders are their beneficiaries. Therefore, their grievance has to be addressed seriously and sorted out urgently. On this perspective, the corporate governance principle demands that every company must set up a stakeholders' and shareholders' relationship committee as one of the mandatory board committees. Hence, this segment has been assigned total 5 points.

Corporate Social Responsibility (CSR) committee (serial no. 10 E of Table 11.10)

The Companies Act, 2013 and SEBI Listing Regulations, 2015 have mandated formation of a Corporate Social Responsibility (CSR) committee by the companies. As good corporate citizen, the companies are expected to discharge their responsibilities well for welfare of the society to which they belong. Therefore, adequate importance should be given for its formation, framing and disclosure of the company's CSR policy, and monitoring activities on account of CSR, etc. Hence, this segment has been assigned total 4 points.

Risk Management committee (serial no. 10 F of Table 11.10)

Considering the imperative of risk management in the current complicated business scenario, the Companies Act, 2013 and SEBI Listing Regulations, 2015 have mandated formation of a risk management committee by the companies. This segment has been assigned total 4 points.

Disclosures and transparency (serial no. 11 of Table 11.10)

Disclosures and transparency is the uppermost cornerstone of corporate governance in any company. The effectiveness of the corporate governance principles and practices would depend upon strong management information system, active role of board committees, proper internal control systems and procedures, vigilant monitoring and supervisory role of the boards. Therefore, it is imperative for every corporate house to give adequate, full and transparent disclosures of all information relating to business and its performance on a real time basis. In light of this principle, this, being the most important segment, has been attributed total 14 points.

General body meetings (serial no. 12 of Table 11.10)

As a matter of obligation, the corporates are supposed to furnish adequate information regarding general body meetings to the shareholders as these informations are very important to them. Therefore, this segment has been assigned total 3 points.

Code of conduct and its affirmation (serial no. 13 of Table 11.10)

The SEBI Listing Regulations, 2015 have mandated on companies to furnish affirmation in writing by the chief executives on compliance of code of conduct by all senior executives and board members. This, being the important segment, has been assigned 2 points.

CEO/CFO certification (serial no. 14 of Table 11.10)

Regulation 17(8) of SEBI Listing Regulations, 2015 have required both CEO and CFO of the listed companies to certify in writing confirming absence of materially untrue statement/omission thereof, fraudulent, illegal or violative transactions in the financial statements, and ensuring existence of true and fair view of the companies' affairs, and effective internal control system, etc. Considering its importance, this segment has been assigned 2 points.

Means of communication and general shareholder information (serial no. 15 of Table 11.10)

All listed companies/banks are required to provide general shareholder information and adopt various means of communication as prescribed by the SEBI Listing Regulations to be included in the report on corporate governance. Therefore, this segment has been assigned 2 points.

Disclosure of stakeholders' interests (serial no. 16 of Table 11.10)

One of the major principles of corporate governance is the creation of stakeholders' values. A good corporate citizen is expected to take active initiatives and various measures relating to environment, health, safety, human resource development, industrial relations, etc. In light of this principle, this segment, being an important ingredient of the quality of corporate governance, has been attributed total 10 points.

Compliance of corporate governance and auditors' certificate (serial no. 17 of Table 11.10)

A company shall obtain a certificate from its auditors regarding compliance of all requirements of corporate governance as stipulated by the Companies Act, and SEBI regulations. This certificate shall be annexed with the report on corporate governance in the Annual Report and sent to the shareholders of the company annually. Therefore, this certificate is considered to be no less important than the statutory audit report. In light of this principle, this segment, being an important ingredient of the quality of corporate governance, has been attributed total 8 points (maximum).

Disclosure of stakeholders' interests (serial no. 15 of Table 11.10)

One of the major principles of corporate governance is the creation of stakeholders' values. Therefore, a good corporate citizen is expected to take active initiatives and various measures relating to environment, health, safety, human resource development, social responsibility, industrial relations, etc. In light of this principle, this segment, being an important ingredient of the quality of corporate governance, has been attributed total 14 points.

Results

The results of evaluation on corporate governance standards adopted and practised by all 32 BSE and NSE listed companies as disclosed in their Annual Reports are shown in Table 11.11. Table 11.12 shows the grading of the companies based on a five-point scale. The results of evaluation of governance standards attained by 5 listed PSUs/PSBs are shown in Table 11.13. The average points secured by all these listed companies (industry-wise) with respect to the compliance of governance standards are shown in Table 11.14.

TABLE 11.11 Governance Standards Attained (Based on the Assigned Points) by the Sample Companies/Banks for the year 2015–2016

Serial No.	Name of companies/banks	Individual score	Rank	Grade
1.	Infosys	79	1.5	Very good
2.	Dr. Reddy's Laboratories	79	1.5	Very good
3.	Tata Motors	78	3	Very good
4.	ACC Cement	75	4.3	Very good
5.	RIL	75	4.3	Very good
6.	Tata Power	75	4.3	Very good
7.	Ambuja Cement	74	7	Very good
8.	HUL	73	8	Very good
9.	Bosch	72	9	Very good
10.	Aurobindo Pharma	70	10.2	Very good
11.	Eicher Motor	70	10.2	Very good
12.	ITC	70	10.2	Very good
13.	Idea Cellular	70	10.2	Very good
14.	Tata Steel	70	10.2	Very good
15.	Adani Ports & SEZ	69	15.3	Very good
16.	TCS	69	15.3	Very good
17.	Yes Bank	69	15.3	Very good
18.	Asian Paints	68	18	Very good
19.	Axis Bank	65	19.5	Very good
20.	Hindalco	65	19.5	Very good
21.	HDFC Bank	64	21.2	Very good
22.	HDFC	64	21.2	Very good
23.	Lupin	64	21.2	Very good

TABLE 11.11 Governance Standards Attained (Based on the Assigned Points) by the Sample Companies/Banks for the year 2015–2016 (*Contd.*)

Serial No.	Name of companies/banks	Individual score	Rank	Grade
24.	NTPC	64	21.2	Very good
25.	ZEE	64	21.2	Very good
26.	ICICI Bank	63	26.5	Very good
27.	Sun Pharma	63	26.5	Very good
28.	ONGC	61	28	Very good
29.	Bajaj Auto	59	29	Good
30.	Power Grid Corporation	54	30	Good
31.	Bank of Baroda	51	31	Good
32.	State Bank of India	46	32	Good

TABLE 11.12 Grading of the Sample Companies Based on Five-point Scale

Score range	Grade	Number of companies/banks
81–100	Excellent	0
61–80	Very good	28
41–60	Good	4
21–40	Average	0
Below 21	Poor	0
Total		**32**

TABLE 11.13 Governance Standards Attained (Based on the Assigned Points) by the Sample PSEs/PSBs for the Year 2015–2016

Serial No.	Name of companies/ banks	Individual score	Rank	Grade
1.	NTPC	64	21.2	Very good
2.	ONGC	61	28	Very good
3.	Power Grid Corporation	54	30	Good
4.	Bank of Baroda	51	31	Good
5.	State Bank of India	46	32	Good

TABLE 11.14 Governance Standards Attained (Based on the Assigned Points) by the Sample Companies/Banks: Industry-wise Ranks and Grades for the year 2015–2016

Serial No.	Name of the industry	Average score	Ranks	Grade
1.	Textile and synthetics	75	1	Very good
2.	Cement	74.50	2	Very good
3.	Information technology	74	3	Very good
4.	Engineering	72	4	Very good
5.	Consumer products and FMCG	70.50	5	Very good
6.	Diversified	70	6.3	Very good
7.	Iron and steel	70	6.3	Very good
8.	Telecommunication	70	6.3	Very good
9.	Pharmaceuticals	69	9.3	Very good
10.	Port and SEZ	69	9.3	Very good
11.	Automobile	69	9.3	Very good
12.	Mining and metal	65	12	Very good
13.	Power generation and distribution	64.33	13	Very good
14.	Entertainment	64	14.5	Very good
15.	Finance	64	14.5	Very good
16.	Petroleum and natural gas	61	16	Very good
17.	Banking	59.67	17	Good

It may be observed from Table 11.11 that out of 32 sample companies/banks, 28 have obtained rank '*very good*' and 4 have obtained rank '*good*'. The *highest score* obtained by the individual BSE Sensex and NSE Nifty companies are *Infosys* and *Dr. Reddy's Laboratories* jointly, followed by *Tata Motors, ACC, RIL, Tata Power*, etc. The lowest score was obtained by *SBI*, preceded by *Bank of Baroda, Power Grid Corporation*, and *Bajaj Auto*.

It has also been observed that almost all these companies/banks have improved their governance standards substantially over the years, which are evident from the individual scores and also the gap in scores obtained by these companies. So far as the compliance of corporate governance standards in private sector companies/banks is concerned, out of 27 such companies, as many as 26 companies have shown '*very good*' performance and only 1 company has shown '*good*' performance.

Table 11.12 reveals that out of 32 companies, as many as 28 companies/banks are graded '*very good*'. In regard to the compliance of corporate governance standards in PSUs/PSBs, it is observed from Table 11.13 that out of 5 such companies/banks, 2 companies have shown '*very good*' performance, while in case of 3 others, the performance is '*good*'. It is interesting to note that none of the above 32 companies has secured '*excellent*'.

Industry-wise ranking on compliance of corporate governance is, however, different in the sense that the *textile and synthetics sector* ranks first, followed by other sectors, e.g., *cement, information technology, engineering*, etc. Table 11.14 reveals that out of 17 industry groups, only one group, viz. Banking has shown '*good*' performance, whereas other 16 have shown '*very good*' performance.

11.5 CONCLUDING OBSERVATION

From the above microanalysis based on the Annual Reports of 32 large companies/banks listed under BSE Sensex and NSE Nifty for the year 2015–2016, it is quite apparent that the adoption of corporate governance system by these companies is by and large 'very good'. However, their performances do not compare favourably with the international governance standards. The 'box ticking approach' adopted by a few companies/banks (for example, SBI, Bank of Baroda, Power Grid Corporation, Bajaj Auto, etc.) has practically overshadowed the good work done in this area by some sincere, result-oriented and professionally-managed companies.

A good number of companies, especially the companies listed both in Indian and foreign stock exchanges, viz. Infosys, Dr. Reddy's Laboratories, etc. have come up with quality disclosures in compliance with the latest SEBI Listing Regulations, 2015 in their corporate governance reporting of 2015–2016 that can be compared with the international standards. In fact, Infosys report has set a benchmark for the other corporate houses to follow in improving their standards of corporate governance with respect to quality, transparency, full disclosures and in-depth reporting.

The position, however, is different in case of government companies/banks. The main factors responsible for such a position in the public sector may be the non-pragmatic government policy and the government administrative machineries having lackadaisical attitude in implementing the conditions of corporate governance expeditiously. Corporate governance reports of NTPC, ONGC, Power Grid, Bank of Baroda, and SBI bear testimony to this point.

Thus, keeping in view the 'governance requirements' and the 'governance practices' in India as appearing from our case study of 32 listed companies/banks, we venture to make a few suggestions and recommendations in Chapter 13.

CASE STUDY

Price Waterhouse Absolved in Satyam Case

THE CASE

The fraud at Satyam Computer Services dates back to 2009 when Ramalinga Raju, the founder of Satyam Computer, confessed to cooking the company's books of accounts and inflating profits. In January, 2009, Raju admitted an accounting fraud of ₹ 7800 crore. CID arrested two PWC auditors and filed charge sheets against Satyam founder and 8 others. Thereafter Satyam Computer was sold on auction to Tech Mahindra.

SEBI'S PROBE AND PUNISHMENT

In January, 2018, SEBI found the audit firm PW guilty after probe and barred it from auditing or issuing certificates to any listed Indian company for 2 years for its role in the scandal. SEBI also moved on disgorgement of ₹ 13 crore from the auditor along with interest for the wrongful gain.

ICAI'S PROBE AND PUNISHMENT

Following the Satyam Computer scam, the ICAI had cancelled the memberships of the two partners of PW involved in the fraud and imposed a fine of ₹ 5 lakh each against them.

PRICE WATERHOUSE'S CHALLENGE

In January 2018 PW challenged SEBI's Order in Securities Appellate Tribunal (SAT).

SECURITIES APPELLATE TRIBUNAL (SAT)'S VERDICT

In September 2019, after hearing both sides, SAT quashed the 2-year ban that SEBI had imposed on the audit firm Price Waterhouse, the Indian affiliate of accounting giant PWC in the wake of the Satyam Computer fraud in 2009. The SAT however, allowed the disgorgement of ₹ 13 crore from the audit firm along with interest @12% since 2007 for the wrongful gain.

Setting aside the ban SAT ruling stated "There is no shred of evidence that the auditors fabricated, fudged or were in collusion with the management of Satyam Computer Services." It stated that SEBI had no jurisdiction banning an audit firm as that was the sole prerogative of the Institute of Chartered Accountants of India (ICAI). SAT also ruled that negligence cannot amount to misconduct and SEBI action without direct evidence cannot be maintained. If the audit of Satyam was conducted in a careless or reckless manner by the audit firm, then action can only be taken under the Chartered Accountants Act, 1949, by the Institute and not by SEBI. SEBI should not 'encroach' upon territories of other regulators or industry bodies such as the ICAI. If at all, there is a dereliction of duty, only those individuals who did the job can be punished and not their parent organisations.

SAT also stated "Under the existing regulations, the main purpose of SEBI is to protect investors' interests and so its actions must be remedial and not punitive. The 2-year ban of PW and other associated firms violates current regulations. Also to consider the ban as a remedial action is far-fetched and cannot be accepted. SEBI's action of banning PWC was blatantly erroneous."

The fall-out of SAT order is that PWC can continue auditing Indian listed companies. However, SEBI can approach the Supreme Court, said the legal experts.

In 2011 PWC agreed to pay USD 25.5 million to former Satyam investors to settle US litigation and had also paid USD 7.5 million as US penalties after the Securities and Exchange Commission (SEC) and the Public Company Accounting Oversight Board (PCAOB) fined the firm over its auditing work for Satyam.

The SAT order has come at a time when three of the big four audit firms are already under investigation for their role in auditing Infrastructure Leasing and Financial Services (IL&FS) and its subsidiaries. The Serious Fraud Investigation Office (SFIO) and other regulators are already probing the role of affiliate Indian audit firms under the Deloitte, KPMG, and EY umbrellas. In the last few months many auditors have been taking a cautious approach and resigning from some risky accounts in the aftermath of the IL&FS meltdown. The auditors fear being made a scapegoat by regulators and investigating agencies whereas promoters and other stakeholders of fraud-hit companies go scot free.

Robert E. Moritz, the global chairman PWC told to a news agency last year "The firm seemed to have been punished twice for its role as auditor of Satyam. The incident happened nine years ago and clearly, there was a bit of an implied penalty because the market saw the problem then and we lost the opportunity to not only operate in the market place, but also grow in the market place."

Questions for Discussion

1. What was the nature of fraud scam perpetrated in Satyam Computer Services? Who was primarily involved in this accounting fraud?
2. What are punishments given by SEBI after its probe in this scam?
3. What are punishments given by ICAI after its probe in this scam?
4. Do you agree with the verdict delivered by SAT after considering the PW's challenge against the ban of the audit firm imposed by SEBI? Give your points of argument for/against SAT's verdict quashing the ban?

Test Your Knowledge

1. What are your comments on the current status of governance in BSE Sensex and NSE Nifty companies in 2015–2016 as revealed in the case study in respect of:
   (a) Chairman and CEO duality
   (b) the position of Independent Directors and Women Directors
   (c) various aspects of Audit Committee
2. What is the status of 'Disclosures and Transparency' mentioned in the Annual Reports of BSE Sensex and NSE Nifty companies as revealed in the case study?
3. What is your opinion on the standard of corporate governance in vogue in BSE Sensex and NSE Nifty companies in 2015–2016 as revealed in the case study?
4. Write short notes on:
   (a) CRISIL Corporate Governance and Value Creation Rating (GVC Rating)
   (b) ICRA Corporate Governance Rating (CGR)

CHAPTER 12

Corporate Social Responsibility (CSR) and Sustainability

Learning Objectives	Key Words
After reading this chapter, the readers will be able to understand: • Definition of Corporate Social Responsibility (CSR) and its Perspective • Significant factors concerning corporates to recognise CSR • Importance of CSR and formulation of Theories on CSR • Expectations of the society from corporates • Different points of views on the scope of Social Responsibility • Status of Corporate Social Responsibility in India • The concept of Corporate Sustainability and Sustainable Development	• Corporate Social Responsibility (CSR) • Corporate Sustainability • Business Responsibility

12.1 INTRODUCTION

Corporate social responsibility (CSR) is essentially a concept whereby companies integrate social and environmental concerns in their business operations and in the interaction with their stakeholders on a voluntary basis. Through voluntary commitment to CSR, companies send a positive signal of their behaviour to their various stakeholders, viz. shareholders, employees, investors, creditors, suppliers, customers, regulators, government, and the society at large. In doing so, they make an investment towards future and increase their profitability. In fact, corporate governance and corporate responsibility towards society are inextricably interlinked, intertwined and inseparable from each other. If a corporate house is expected to provide good governance to its stakeholders and society at large, it is because it enjoys so much facilities from the society in terms of developed infrastructure, trained workforce, peaceful environment, law and order, etc. that it is only appropriate that the company gives back to the society at least something in return in the form of good governance. Therefore, it is a well-conceived fact that good corporate governance itself is part and parcel of corporate responsibility towards society.

There are certain burning questions in regard to the relationship between corporate social responsibility and corporate governance: (i) What is meant by CSR? (ii) Is there any relationship or congruence between corporate governance and CSR? (iii) Why CSR has been accorded substantial importance in the corporate functioning nowadays? What is the scope of CSR? Can corporate profitability and CSR co-exist and sustain?

In order to find out answers to these questions, we discuss in this chapter the definition of CSR, its different perspectives and importance, and the factors concerning corporates to recognize and adopt CSR in governance practices. The chapter also deliberates on the scope of social responsibility in business, and discharge of such responsibilities by some renowned Indian companies on CSR.

12.2 DEFINITION OF CORPORATE SOCIAL RESPONSIBILITY

It is difficult to define CSR as its definition depends on the perceptions and sensitivity of the analysts. According to Lord Holme and Richard Watts, "CSR is the continuing commitment by business to behave ethically and contribute to economic development while improving the quality of life for the workforce and their families as well as of the local community and society at large."

CSR in the USA has been defined in terms of philanthropic model. The corporates make profits and donate a certain percentage of their profits for charitable causes. In Europe, CSR is more focused on the corporate business activities. The companies operate the core business in a socially responsible manner. They invest in community activities as they believe that social responsibility is an integral part of the wealth creation process, which enhances the competitive capability and maximizes the value of wealth creation for the society.

12.3 PERSPECTIVES ON CSR

The issue of social responsibility of business is not free from the conflicting perspectives or responses from the intellectuals and business community. Economists like Adam Smith and Milton Friedman were of the opinion that the only responsibility of business was to perform its economic functions efficiently and provide goods and services to society and each for itself maximum profit. It was better to leave social functions to other institutions like the government. According to Adam Smith, it is the profit-driven market system and price mechanism that drives business organizations to promote social welfare, though they work for private gain. The organizations employ their capital to ensure greatest value for their products and intend to promote only their own security for their gains rather than to promote public interest. Similarly, according to Friedman, the business has one and only one social responsibility—to make profits as long as it stays within the legal and moral rules of the game established by the society.

But economists like Paul Samuelson, Robert Dahl and Talcott Parsons, while criticizing this highly materialistic viewpoint, advocated that the spirit of responsibility should be an inherent feature of a modern business firm. As business firms are part and parcel of the society, they have to serve primarily its interests, rather than engage themselves in narrow economic gains such as making profits only. Besides, the welfare of the masses should not be the sole responsibility of the government; corporates, being a part of the society, must also play a significant role in this regard. According to Prof. Dahl, it is obligatory for the business organizations to be socially responsible as they primarily exist to benefit the society. Therefore, it is absurd to regard the corporate simply as an organization set up for the sole purpose of churring out profit. After all, corporates are allowed to exist and sustain their development by the society since they continue to benefit it. Therefore, every organization's existence can be justified only if it serves public or social purposes.

12.4 FACTORS CONCERNING CORPORATES TO RECOGNIZE CSR

There are many factors that have compelled the corporates to recognize and attach significant importance to CSR in discharging their day-to-day activities. Some of these are:

(a) New concerns and expectations from various stakeholders in the context of large-scale industrial change due to globalization;

(b) Increased influence of social criteria on the investment decisions of individuals and institutions, both as consumers and as investors;

(c) Increased concern about the damage to the environment caused by economic activity; and

(d) Transparency of business activities brought about by the modern information and communication technologies.

12.5 IMPORTANCE OF CSR—ITS JUSTIFICATION

Social scientists have formulated mainly three theories to justify the importance of CSR to the companies in promoting welfare measures for the society. These theories are as follows:

(i) Trusteeship theory

(ii) Social entity theory

(iii) Pluralistic theory

12.5.1 Trusteeship Theory

The trusteeship theory adopts a realistic perspective of the company as a social institution which has a corporate personality. This theory differs from the agency theory in two respects. First, the fiduciary duty of the trustees is to sustain the company's assets, including the shareholders' wealth, and broader stakeholders' value, such as the expectations of customers and suppliers, skills of employees and the company's reputation in the community. Therefore, the managers and executives, as trustees, are to promote the broader interests of the company as a whole, not only the financial interests of the shareholders. Second, these managers are required to balance the conflicting interests of the present and future stakeholders and develop the corporate's capacities on a long-term basis rather than focus on short-term shareholder gains.

12.5.2 Social Entity Theory

The social entity theory regards the company not as a private association with individual property rights, but as a public association constituted by political and legal processes.

It is a social entity meant for pursuing collective goals with public objectives. In other words, this theory regards the company as a social institution in society based on the grounds of fundamental values and moral order of the community. The executives of the company are the custodians of stakeholders' interests.

12.5.3 Pluralistic Theory

The pluralistic theory advocates the idea of multiple interests of stakeholders. According to this theory, a company should serve and accommodate the broader interests of all stakeholders also in order to make it efficient. It advocates that not only the shareholders, but other stakeholders, such as employees can also claim the ownership rights. The stakeholders making specific investments and contributions to bear risks in the company should have residual claims and should participate in the decision-making process with a view to improve corporate efficiency. The theory asserts that the company's performance in terms of profitability and growth will be increased substantially provided the stakeholders' management is practised by the company.

12.6 EXPECTATIONS OF THE SOCIETY FROM CORPORATES

As we know, companies depend on the society for a number of facilities enjoyed by them, for example, developed infrastructure, peace in the workplace, trained workers and employees. They also depend on the society for the maintenance of law and order in the areas of their operation. Moreover, it should also be remembered that the consumers of the products of companies are the representatives of the society, without whom companies cannot exist. Therefore, when the business firms have drawn so much from the society, it is their responsibility to make adequate contributions towards the welfare of the society. They have to be good corporate citizens and pay their due taxes in time and observe the laws of the land. Business firms must also ensure a healthy and clean environment, maintain standards of operational efficiency, product safety and quality, and assist in conservation of energy and natural resources. Besides, they are also expected to generate employment in all possible manner.

In the present era of intense competition, it is imperative for the corporates to generate and sustain 'goodwill' among their stakeholders and the community at large. Therefore, active participation in various social welfare projects is surely going to improve the corporates' visibility and place them on a pedestal of high public esteem. The business firms should understand the fact that economic goals and social responsibility objectives need not be contradictory to each other. Rather, both can coexist and both can be achieved and sustained as inclusive growth simultaneously.

12.7 SCOPE OF SOCIAL RESPONSIBILITY

The scope of CSR is far and wide. It can be considered from different points of views, some of which may be as enumerated below:

(a) Protecting and promoting interests of various stakeholders;

(b) Addressing social concerns and promoting public welfare programmes;

(c) Engaging in philanthropic activities;
(d) Ensuring good corporate governance in the companies;
(e) Rendering social service;
(f) Sponsoring social and charitable causes, and social welfare activities;
(g) Supplementing the 'government' efforts effectively;
(h) Ensuring ecological balance;
(i) Focusing on human elements; and
(j) Abiding by rules and regulations as good corporate citizen.

Let us discuss each of the above in some detail.

12.7.1 Protecting and Promoting Interests of Various Stakeholders

The stakeholders of a company are generally of two types: (i) insiders and (ii) outsiders. The employees and shareholders are the insiders, and the consumers, suppliers, creditors, competitors, government, and general public are regarded as outsiders. Consumers expect quality goods and services at reasonable prices. Workers and employees expect fair wages and stability of service. Shareholders expect reasonable dividends and fair rate on investments. Executives and managers expect decent salary and perks against the challenging jobs. Government expects regular payment of taxes and duties, etc. on time in order to add to the wealth and welfare of the nation. The general public expects prevention of pollution of the environment and creation of employment opportunities. Therefore, corporates have to consider themselves as the guardians of stakeholders' welfare and render services to various sections of the society.

12.7.2 Addressing Social Concerns and Promoting Public Welfare Programmes

Corporate social responsibility is a way to address social concerns and promote common welfare programmes for the benefits of common public. In fact, there has been occasions where the companies have sponsored advertisements for the promotion of social causes or issues of public concern, for example, smoking, drug addictions, HIV, etc. Sometimes, producers of eye care products, dental products, etc. organize mass clinics or camps free of cost in villages and semi-urban areas, jointly with the hospitals or Lions Club or Rotary Club, in which doctors attend to the medical needs of the poor.

12.7.3 Engaging in Philanthropic Activities

Philanthropic activity is another way of discharging social responsibility. One or two examples can be cited in this regard. During the time of earthquake in Gujarat several years ago, the industrialists, through CII and FICCI, donated large funds and assisted NGOs to adopt a number of villages worst affected by the earthquake. During the time of tsunami in 2004, the corporate houses donated several hundreds of crores of rupees to the Prime Minister's and Chief Ministers' relief funds to help governments rehabilitate the displaced fishermen of South India.

12.7.4 Ensuring Good Corporate Governance in the Companies

As discussed earlier, good corporate governance itself is an ingredient of corporate social responsibility. In fact, corporate governance and CSR are interlinked, intertwined and inseparable from each other.

12.7.5 Rendering Social Service

Some corporates do promote activities that supplement the efforts of public authorities in certain areas of human development. For example, the Tata group contributed substantially to the growth of fundamental and social sciences. They built and nurtured institutions of higher learning. The Birla group also did popularize science among common people through planetariums. Some corporates like ITC, Tata Steel, SAIL, etc. have made contributions in diverse areas such as community development, agriculture, health care, sports, pollution control, etc.

12.7.6 Sponsoring Social and Charitable Causes, and Social Welfare Activities

Some industrialists, in addition to building industrial empires, also contributed individually to certain social and charitable causes. The single contributions of J.R.D. Tata, G.D. Birla, and Jamunalal Bajaj can never be forgotten in this respect.

12.7.7 Supplementing the Government Efforts Effectively

Corporates can supplement several areas of welfare activities to relieve the government that does not have adequate resources to discharge these activities. For example, the companies can run schools and provide quality primary education. They can allocate funds for running family planning clinics, hospitals, adult education programmes, campaigns against smoking, pollution, AIDS, and maintaining public health system.

12.7.8 Ensuring Ecological Balance

Corporates should maintain ecological balance in the areas of their operation. Many companies, such as ITC, TVS and Tata Steel are assisting the local inhabitants to maintain harmony with nature by reducing pollution generated by these organizations.

12.7.9 Focusing on Human Elements

Business organizations can discharge their social responsibility by focusing on human elements, such as ensuring quality of work life, reduction of work hazards, equality in employment opportunities, proper settlement of disputes, assisting employees to adjust themselves in new work environment, etc.

12.7.10 Abiding by Rules and Regulations as Good Corporate Citizen

Needless to say, corporates should abide by the rules and regulations framed by the respective governments, authorities to be good corporate citizens. It demands conformity with and acceptance of the rules, procedures, and interpretations of the business laws.

12.8 STATUS OF CORPORATE SOCIAL RESPONSIBILITY IN INDIA

The CSR, nowadays, is not restricted to philanthropic activity only. Having realized the importance of social responsibility in business, the corporate world is now reaching out to the community at large. Encouraged by their companies, large sections of employees, executives and top managers are doing their best for community causes. They are now deeply involved to give back to the general public who sustain their business. Many more companies have joined hands with NGOs and set up schools and villages to educate the women and small children in slum areas, and have many welfare programmes for various diseases, especially AIDS, cancer, and polio.

While global MNCs like General Motors, General Electric, Ford Motors, Microsoft, McDonalds, etc. have sponsored many social welfare and philanthropic activities, the corporate India is not far behind. Indian companies such as Tata Steel, NTPC, Reliance Industries, ITC, etc. have also been working remarkably on various social service activities. In order to understand the status and extent of corporate social responsibility discharged by the listed large cap corporate houses operating in India in compliance with the new Companies Act, 2013 and Company Rules, 2014, let us focus our attention to Table 12.1.

TABLE 12.1 Expenditure on Corporate Social Responsibility by 32 Listed Large Cap Corporate Houses in India for the Year 2015-2016 (Figures in ₹/Lakh)

Name of the company	Amount to be spent in 2015–16	Amount spent in 2015–16	Cumulative Expenditure upto 31/03/2016	Remarks Short(–)/ Excess(+)
Adani Ports SEZ Ltd.	40.40	40.81	40.81	(+) 0.41
Ambuja Cements Ltd.	34.64	40.98	40.98	(+) 6.34
Asian Paints Ltd.	33.75	34.44	34.44	(+) 0.69
Associated Cement Companies Ltd.	27.90	31.16	31.16	(+) 3.26
Aurobindo Pharma Ltd.	28.22	18.76	18.76	(–) 9.46
Axis Bank Ltd.	163.03	137.41	454.07	(–) 25.62
Bajaj Auto Ltd.	86.46	86.72	100.60	(+) 0.26
Bank of Baroda (PSB)	NA	NA	NA	
Bosch Ltd.	29.24	19.71	29.94	(–) 9.53
Dr. Reddy's Lab. Ltd.	41.89	41.20	41.20	(–) 0.69
Eicher Motors Ltd.	8.36	9.62	9.62	(+) 1.26
Housing Development Finance Corpn. Ltd.	139.26	85.70	92.44	(–) 53.56
HDFC Bank Ltd.	248.00	194.81	313.36	(–) 53.19
Hindalco Industries Ltd.	31.00	34.15	34.15	(+) 3.15
Hindustan Unilever Ltd.	91.94	92.12	92.12	(+) 0.18

TABLE 12.1 Expenditure on Corporate Social Responsibility by 32 Listed Large Cap Corporate Houses in India for the Year 2015-2016 (Figures in ₹/Lakhs) (*Contd.*)

Name of the company	Amount to be spent in 2015–16	Amount spent in 2015–16	Cumulative Expenditure upto 31/03/2016	Remarks Short(–)/ Excess(+)
ICICI Bank Ltd.	212.00	172.00	324.16	(–) 40.00
Idea Cellular Ltd.	54.89	18.47	18.47	(–) 36.42
Infosys Technologies Ltd.	256.01	202.30	202.30	(–) 53.71
ITC Ltd.	246.76	247.50	247.50	(+) 0.74
Lupin Ltd.	54.15	20.51	33.09	(–) 33.64
NTPC Ltd. (PSU)	349.65	491.80	491.80	(+) 142.15
Oil and Natural Gas Corporation Ltd. (PSU)	593.70	419.07	419.07	(–) 174.63
Power Grid Corporation Ltd. (PSU)	121.79	115.78	133.35	(–) 6.01
Reliance Industries Ltd.	557.78	651.57	1412.15	(+) 93.79
State Bank of India (PSB)	NA	*143.92*	NA	
Sun Pharmaceuticals Ltd.	**	11.65	11.96	(+) 11.65
Tata Consultancy Services Ltd.	360.00	294.23	305.82	(–) 65.77
Tata Steel Ltd.	150.36	204.46	204.46	(+) 54.10
Tata Motors Ltd.	**	20.57	20.57	(+) 20.57
Tata Power Ltd.	28.29	29.01	60.14	(+) 0.72
Yes Bank Ltd.	47.75	29.52	45.23	(–) 18.23
Zee Entertainment Ltd.	22.14	22.83	31.00	(+) 0.69
Total	**4059.36**	**3818.86**	**5294.72**	

Source: Annual Reports of Companies, 2015–2016. Results computed.
Note: (**) denotes "Not Applicable" as the concerned companies incurred losses in the preceding year. NA denotes "Figures Not Available" in the Annual Reports.
Total column of the amount spent in 2015–2016 does not include ₹ *143.92* crore spent by SBI as the complete figures are not available.

As mentioned in Chapter 9, Section 135 of the Companies Act, 2013 and Company Rules, 2014 required that every company having a net worth of ₹ 500 crore or more, or turnover of ₹ 1000 crore or more or a net profit of ₹ 5 crore or more during any financial year shall ensure that the company spends, in every financial year, at least 2% of the average net profits made during the three immediately preceding financial years, in pursuance of its Corporate Social Responsibility (CSR) Policy.

In the light of above provision of the Companies Act, let us examine the status and extent of expenditure incurred by the above companies/banks during the year 2015–2016 in discharging the CSR activities in the paragraphs that follow:

1. Out of 32 large cap listed companies/banks, 2 public sector banks SBI, and Bank of Baroda did not publish sufficient information and figures of expenditure on the CSR activities discharged by them in their Annual Reports 2015–2016.
2. Two companies, viz. Sun Pharmaceuticals and Tata Motors incurred losses in the preceding year/immediately preceding year. Therefore, the provision of the Companies Act could not be applied to them. However, Sun Pharmaceuticals and Tata Motors had incurred expenditure of ₹ 11.65 crore and ₹ 20.57 crore, respectively, to discharge their responsibilities on the CSR in 2015–2016.
3. A total sum of ₹ 4059.36 crore was required to be spent in the year 2015–2016 on the CSR activities as per provision of the Companies Act, against which a sum of ₹ 3818.86 crore was spent by these companies, resulting in a shortfall of ₹ 240.50 crore. However, cumulative expenditure upto 31st March 2016 on the CSR activities was ₹ 5294.72 crore, which is quite satisfactory.
4. 16 companies/banks have spent more than the amount required towards discharging various CSR activities. The major contributors are NTPC, Reliance Industries, Tata Steel, etc. In fact, these companies have been discharging their CSR responsibilities much before the mandatory enactment of the Companies Act, 2013 which is evident from the amount of cumulative expenditure incurred by them upto 31st March 2016.
5. 14 companies/banks have spent less than the amount required towards discharging various CSR activities. The major defaulters are ONGC, Axis Bank, HDFC, HDFC Bank, ICICI Bank, Idea Cellular, Infosys, Lupin, TCS, Yes Bank, etc. It is interesting to note that most of these organizations have avoided answering the reasons directly as to why they could not spend the requisite amount towards discharging their responsibilities on this account.

12.9 SUSTAINABILITY AND SUSTAINABLE DEVELOPMENT

As discussed in Chapter 3 (Section 3.9), corporate sustainability is a business approach that creates long-term consumer and employee value by creating a green strategy aimed toward the natural environment and taking into consideration every dimension of how a business operates in the social, cultural, and economic environment. Corporate sustainability can be regarded as the corporate's response to sustainable development represented by strategies and practices that address the key issues for the world's sustainable development. Sustainability requires a company to look internally and externally to understand its environmental and social impacts. Corporate sustainability is a long-term challenge that creates new opportunities and risks that companies must address today to remain competitive tomorrow. The concept of corporate sustainability borrows elements from four more established concepts: (1) sustainable development, (2) corporate social responsibility, (3) stakeholder theory, and (4) corporate accountability theory. These concepts are considered part and parcel of good governance. Therefore, the concept of corporate sustainability is synonymous to the concept of corporate governance.

A company cannot be called a good governed organization unless it has established and well-practised in its organization the concepts of sustainable development, corporate social responsibility, stakeholders' value and corporate accountability.

In this respect, many corporate houses/banks have developed their sustainability framework and disclosed the same in their Annual Reports 2015–2016, some of which deserve mention here.

Hindustan Unilever's sustainable living plan

A. Improving health and well-being

1. Health and hygiene—Target and actual performance
2. Nutrition—Target and Actual Performance

B. Enhancing livelihoods

1. Fairness in the workplace—Target and actual performance
2. Opportunities for women—Target and actual performance
3. Inclusive business—Target and actual performance

C. Reducing environmental impact

1. Greenhouse Gases—Target and actual performance
2. Water—Target and actual performance
3. Waste—Target and actual performance

D. Sustainable sourcing—Target and actual performance

NTPC's sustainable development plan:

A. Waste management

B. Water management

C. Biodiversity

D. Promotion of renewable energy

Activities under the plan:

1. Plantation of trees in and around the plants
2. Installation of rooftop of solar PV on public utilities buildings and on schools
3. Installation of solar powered pump
4. Rainwater harvesting
5. Rehabilitation of water bodies
6. Installation of air quality monitoring system in major cities
7. Studies on impact assessment and carrying capacity river basin

Axis bank's sustainability framework

A. Customers

1. Consistently enhance customer service experience
2. Innovation and quality assurance to deliver superior banking experience

B. Shareholders and providers of capital

1. Actively engage with shareholders and providers of capital to create enduring value

C. People

1. Create and sustain diverse work culture through improving organizational effectiveness.
2. Providing safe and ethical work environment
3. Maintaining stability and sustainability amidst the rapidly changing business environment and growth

D. Environment

1. Promote environmental sustainability and equitable growth through sustainable lending practices
2. Reduce impacts on environment on account of own operations by actively managing environmental footprint and supporting customers to make 'green banking' choices

E. Communities

1. Create and sustain a mechanism that will propagate sustainable livelihoods and contribution back to society across various segments

12.9.1 Corporate Sustainability Reporting

Basically, there are two types of reports the corporates are required to publish exhibiting their sustainability plan and development. These are:

1. Corporate Social Responsibility (CSR) Report
2. Business Responsibility (BR) Report

Corporate Social Responsibility (CSR) Report

The detailed provisions about corporate social responsibility as per Section 135 of the Companies Act, 2013 and Companies (CSR) Policy Rules, 2014, including Annexure showing Format for the Annual Report on CSR activities to be included in the Board's Report, have been discussed and are available in Chapter 9 (Section 9.2.2).

Business Responsibility (BR) Report

In order to exhibit how the companies discharge their total responsibilities towards sustainable development of the companies, the SEBI vide its Regulation 34(2) (f) of the SEBI (Listing Obligations and Disclosure Requirements) Regulations, 2015 mandates inclusion of the Business Responsibility Report (BRR) as part of the Annual Report for top 100 listed corporate houses based on the market capitalization. The details on the aspects required to be disclosed in this Report are available in the Format provided in Appendix 10.

12.10 CONCLUDING OBSERVATION

Corporate Social Responsibility (CSR) is the continuing commitment by business firms to behave ethically and contribute to economic development while improving the quality of life of the employees and their families, as well as of the local community and society at large. We have discussed the definition of CSR, its perspectives, importance and the factors concerning corporates to recognize CSR in governance practices.

Corporate sustainability is a business approach that creates long-term consumer and employee value by creating a *green* strategy aimed towards the natural environment and taking into consideration every dimension of how a business operates in the social, cultural, and economic environment. Corporate sustainability can be regarded as the corporate response to sustainable development represented by strategies and practices that address the key issues for the world's sustainable development. Many corporate houses/banks have developed their sustainability framework and disclosed the same in their Annual Reports 2015–2016, which we have deliberated in this chapter.

CASE STUDY
Corporate Social Responsibility (CSR) of TATA Group

INTRODUCTION

The TATA group was founded by J.N. Tata in the year 1868. It has developed into one of India's largest business conglomerates. TATA Sons was established as a trading company in 1868. It is the promoter of the TATA group. TATA Industries, initially established in 1945 as a managing agency for the businesses promoted by TATA Sons, propelled the group's entry into new and high-tech industries during the early 1980s.

COMMUNITY DEVELOPMENT INITIATIVES

Recognised as pioneers in the field of Corporate Social Responsibility (CSR), the TATA group has played an active role in nation building and socio-economic development since the early 1900s. A survey revealed that TATAs spent ₹ 2.5 billion on community development and social services during the fiscal year 2011–12. It was the highest spending by any corporate house in India at that time. Even while the economic conditions were adverse, as in the late 1990s, the financial commitment of the group towards social activities kept on increasing, from ₹ 670 million in 1997–98 to ₹ 4.36 billion in 2011–12.

From the very inception, the TATA group has taken up a number of initiatives for the development of the society. A unique feature of the group is that 63% of the equity capital of the parent firm–TATA Sons is held by TATA Trusts, which is philanthropic in nature. Over the decades this Trusts has promoted a number of public institutions of national interest, including hospitals, education and research centres, scientific and cultural establishments.

The focus of these efforts in recent decades has been on building self-reliant communities and working towards sustainable development. Adequate grants are provided for community development projects and to organisations undertaking research mainly for medical and educational purposes.

Besides the trust activities, individual group companies took up community development initiatives based on the needs of the local community. For instance, TISCO (now TATA Steel) took up a community health programme to help prevent the spread of AIDS in *Jamshedpur* and its neighbouring areas. Similarly, TELCO (now TATA Motors) set up an institution named *Nav Jagrat Manav Samaj* in Jamshedpur to provide health care for patients suffering from leprosy. Another group company, TATA Consultancy Services (TCS) initiated a project for helping adult illiterates learn using computers.

The TATA group's CSR initiatives had gone beyond community development and aimed at maximising value for its stakeholders. Employee welfare measures were also one of the major focus areas of the group. The TATA's had initiated several labour welfare measures in their group companies even before these were made mandatory by law. For instance, TISCO had in place an 8 hour working day and a welfare department as early as in 1917. In the same way, employee benefits such as, provident fund, accident compensation to workers and maternity benefits were provided to employees long before they became the norm.

Environment protection also figured high on the list of priorities of the TATA group. The ISO 14001 Environmental Standard was given high importance throughout all the group companies. TISCO was the first steel plant in India to be certified with ISO 14001 and was one of the few in the world to have this accreditation in the year 2000. TISCO had an Environmental Management System (EMS) in place, which sought to increase efficiency, and limit adverse environmental effects. The objective of EMS was to analyse and reduce the environmental impact of the company's operations using a set of management systems and procedures. The EMS was used extensively in the TISCO township in Jamshedpur, leading to planned initiatives in areas such as, (i) waste management, (ii) recycling of plastics, (iii) formation of model colonies, and (iv) better sewage disposal and treatment. Jamshedpur became the only city in India with an ISO 14001 certification in late 2002.

Since inception, the TATA group has placed equal importance on maximising financial returns as on fulfilling its social and environmental responsibilities–popularly known as the triple bottom line (TBL). Through this approach, the group aimed at harmonising environmental factors by way of reducing the negative impact of its commercial activities and initiating drives encouraging environmeent-freiendly practices.

In order to build social capital in the community, the group has got its senior management involved in social programmes, and has encouraged employees to share their skills with others, and work with community-based organisations. The group companies are also encouraged to take up fund raising activities.

RECOGNITION

The dedicated CSR endeavours by various TATA group companies have been globally recognised. The different group companies have received several awards for their fulfillment of social responsibility on sustained basis. For instance, TISCO was awarded 'The Energy Research Institute (TERI) award for Corporate Social Responsibility (CSR)' for the year 2002–03 in recognition of its corporate citizenship and sustainability initiatives. TISCO, as the only Indian company that put into practice the global compact principles on human rights, labour, and environment, was conferred ***'The Global Business Coalition Award'*** in 2013 for its commitment in spreading awareness about HIV/AIDS.

Questions for Discussion

1. "*Over the past decades, the TATA group has undertaken several CSR initiatives*". Discuss these initiatives and examine how they have placed the group as a socially responsible and good corporate citizen.
2. "The ultimate aim of business is to make profits". Do you think that companies must be socially responsible but must not undermine the interests of their shareholders? In the light of the above statement, explain the steps taken by the TATA group to make its CSR initiatives sustainable.

Test Your Knowledge

1. Define Corporate Social Responsibility (CSR)? What are the factors concerning corporates to recognise CSR?
2. Explain different theories formulated by social scientists to justify the importance of CSR.
3. What are the expectations of the society from the corporate houses?
4. Discuss the various scopes of social responsibility which should be availed by the corporates in discharging their obligations on CSR.
5. Discuss the present status of corporate social responsibility in India.
6. Define Sustainability and Sustainable Development. Discuss, with examples, how corporate houses/banks have dealt with their sustainability framework and disclosed the same in their Annual Reports.

CHAPTER 13 Suggestions and Conclusions

Learning Objectives	Key Words
After reading this chapter, the readers will be able to understand: • Structural changes in the monitoring system for improvement in the corporate governance standards in Indian corporates • Comprehensive and standard code of corporate governance and disclosure norms etc. • Customisation • Code servicing	• Business Ethics • Monitoring System • Structural Changes • Disclosure Norms • Management Discussion and Analysis • Internal Audit • Subsidiary Company • Environmental Issues • Customisation • Code Servicing

13.1 INTRODUCTION

In the backdrop of our study, this chapter deals with the suggestions and recommendations on various governance issues for bringing about an improvement in the corporate governance system in India. It also presents a comprehensive and standard code of corporate governance and attempts to formulate a standard code of governance practices and disclosure norms on (a) corporate social responsibility and sustainability (b) business ethics, and (c) environmental issues. Evolving a policy for customization and code servicing for corporate governance are also suggested.

In view of our earlier findings, our suggestions and recommendations may be classified under three broad sections, viz.

Section A : Changes in the monitoring system of the Ministry, SEBI and the stock exchanges.

Section B : A comprehensive and standard code of corporate governance and disclosure norms—compulsory and voluntary, for Indian companies.

Section C : A standard code of governance practices and disclosure norms on: (a) social responsibility of business and sustainability, (b) business ethics, and (c) environmental issues.

13.2 SUGGESTIONS AND RECOMMENDATIONS

13.2.1 Section A: Structural Changes

So far as monitoring system of the Ministry, SEBI and the stock exchange authorities are concerned, it is observed that although there are theoretically monitoring cells/departments in all these administrative machineries, but there exists practically no effective machinery to monitor and enforce compliance of the code of corporate governance practices in corporate houses. On the contrary, most of the auditors are also showing lackadaisical attitude in overseeing the compliance of the conditions of corporate governance practices presently followed by their client companies. In this respect, the Institute of Chartered Accountants of India (ICAI) cannot avoid its own responsibility for the alleged casual approach of their practicing members while providing compliance certificates to the client companies. It is therefore suggested that:

(a) All these administrative and regulatory authorities must pull-up their monitoring cells/departments so that a serious vigilance and enforcement pressure could be kept on the companies in the areas of their governance practices.

(b) The Ministry could consider providing absolute judicial powers to SEBI so that it could pronounce punishment orders on the erring companies for repeated non-compliance of the code of corporate governance.

(c) The ICAI must activate its disciplinary committee and take expeditious and exemplary action/punishment against the defaulting practicing members for issuing so called 'clean' certificates to the erring companies.

(d) Joint audits for companies with turnover above a certain threshold should be introduced immediately to ensure more credibility of company accounts.

(e) The Quality Review Board, with members nominated by the ICAI Council and the Centre, should work earnestly to raise the quality of accounting and auditing, including services provided by the internal auditors and accountants.

(f) Ministry of Corporate Affairs needs to take a fresh look whether the existing structure of ICAI and ICSI, really encourage independent and impartial regulation and disciplinary action.

(g) The Ministry should also consider introduction of a penal provision in the Act for suspension of the erring company from trading in the stock exchange, apart from other punitive measures against repeated defaults in compliance.

(h) It is observed that most of the listed public sector companies banks have failed to comply with the conditions of corporate governance. The details of non-compliance and the reasons thereof, are given in Chapter 11. The existing Department of Public Enterprises (DPE) guidelines are not compatible with the SEBI guidelines in many respects. It is imperative that the Government should take a clear and transparent policy decision about the modus operandi of management functioning in these companies. It is, therefore, suggested that all listed public sector companies should be *board managed* and they must fully comply with the SEBI Listing Regulations, 2015 irrespective of the nature of ownership of these companies.

(i) For the unlisted public sector companies, it is suggested that they should also comply with the conditions of corporate governance for which DPE guidelines could be considered for modification expeditiously, wherever necessary. This will facilitate strict monitoring and enforcement of the conditions of governance for compliance by the public sector corporate houses in future.

13.2.2 Section B: Comprehensive and Standard Code of Corporate Governance and Disclosure Norms

In this section, a standard code of corporate governance including disclosure norms—both compulsory and voluntary, have been suggested in the paragraphs that follow for improvement of the corporate governance practices.

Governance issues—Compulsory code

A. The structure for corporate governance

It comprises framework, board of directors, board issues and mandatory board committees as detailed below.

(i) The framework: This code envisages that a good corporate governance would be actualized by a knowledgeable, skillful and well-informed board of directors with a correct blend of expertise and professionalism, independence and involvement focusing and addressing its attention to issues and recommendations, crystallized by a due diligence process followed by its sub-committees as envisaged by this code. It is a basic presumption that the board and its committees shall have free access to relevant expertise within and outside the company. The quality of governance would depend on the adequacy and effectiveness of processes at the corporate level.

(ii) Board of directors and board issues

➤ *Composition and size*

- The board of the company shall have an optimum combination of executive and non-executive directors with not less than 50% of the board comprising non-executive directors to keep a balance, such that no individual or group of individuals can dominate the board's decision-making.
- There shall be at least one woman director in the board of directors of the company.
- In case, a company has a non-executive chairman, at least one-third of the board shall comprise independent directors. In case, a company has an executive chairman, at least 50% of the board should comprise independent directors.
- If the non-executive chairman is a promoter or is related to the promoters or persons occupying management positions at the board level or one level below the board, at least one-half of the board of the company shall consist of independent directors.

➤ *Selection and appointment*

- The appointment of directors shall be made as per provisions of Section 152 and Section 154 of the Companies Act, 2013.
- The managing/whole time/executive directors should be in the whole time employment of only one company at any given time.
- The provision of Section 163 of the Companies Act, 2013 regarding adoption of proportionate representation in the board, should be followed.
- The gap between the exit and entry of independent directors shall not exceed 180 days.

➤ *Tenure and age limit*

- The minimum age for all directors including independent directors shall be 21 years.
- All directors shall be required to submit themselves for re-election at regular intervals. Re-appointment shall not be automatic.
- The non-executive directors shall be appointed for specified terms subject to re-election and the provisions of the Act relating to the removal of a director. They shall be eligible for appointment, maximum for a period of nine years in three terms of three years each.

➤ *Independent director*

- The majority of the non-executive directors shall be independent of management and free from business or other relationship, which could materially interfere with the exercise of their independent judgement.
- The definition and expression of 'independent director' as set out in Regulation 16(b) of the SEBI Listing Regulations, 2019 and the provisions of Section 149(6) of the Companies Act, 2013 is sufficient and should be retained.
- Non-executive independent directors shall be identified in the annual report.
- An independent director shall make a self-declaration at the time of appointment and at the time of change in his status and every year thereafter in the first board meeting that he satisfies the legal conditions for being an independent director.
- The board shall disclose in the 'Directors' Report' that independent directors have given self-declaration and that in the judgement of the board, they are independent and the board shall also disclose the basis for determination.

➤ *Chairman and CEO and Lead independent director*

- A decision to combine the posts of chairman and CEO in one person shall be publicly justified.
- Irrespective of whether the posts are held by different persons or by the same individual, there shall be a strong and independent non-executive element on the board as lead independent director (other than

the chairman), to whom the concerns can be conveyed. It will be the responsibility of the lead independent director to act as a spokesperson for independent directors as a group, work closely with the chairman/CEO, and take a lead role in the board evaluation process, apart from other important board functions.

- The chairman, CEO and the lead independent director shall be identified in the annual report.

➤ *Number of directorships and alternate directors*

- In order to concentrate heavily on day-to-day management for survival and prosperity of the company in the present era of stiff business competition, domestic and international, the number of directorships shall be limited. A person shall not serve as an independent director in more than three listed companies. A serving whole time director in any listed company shall not serve as an independent director in more than one listed company.
- A director shall not be a member in more than three committees or act as chairman in more than two committees across all companies in which he is a director.
- It shall be a mandatory annual requirement for every director to inform the company about the committee positions occupied by him in other companies and notify changes as and when they take place. The same information shall be disclosed in the annual report of the company.
- The maximum tenure of an independent director shall be followed as per provisions of Section 149(10) and (11) of the Companies Act, 2013.

➤ *Remuneration of directors, notice period and compensation*

- The levels of remuneration should be sufficient to attract and retain the directors needed to run the company successfully, but companies shall fix the remuneration of directors within the limit set by the Companies Act. A proportion of executive directors' remuneration shall be structured so as to link rewards to corporate and individual performance.
- The performance related elements of remuneration should form a significant proportion of the total remuneration package of executive directors and should be designed to align their interests with those of shareholders and to give these directors keen incentives to perform at the highest levels.
- No director shall be involved in deciding his or her own remuneration.
- Stock options to directors shall be granted in 'phases' based on 'challenging performance criteria', shall never be issued at a discount and shall not be exercisable for three years from the date of grant. Neither annual bonus nor benefits in kind, should be pensionable.
- The remuneration to directors including the non-executive independent directors shall be approved by the shareholders in the general meeting based on the recommendations of the remuneration committee, through the board within the statutory limits of the Act.

- The present provision relating to stock options, and to the 1% commission on net profits is adequate and does not need any revision. However, limits should be set for the maximum number of stock options that can be granted to the non-executive directors in any financial year and in aggregate.
- All long-term incentive schemes shall be approved by the shareholders.

(iii) Mandatory board committees

➤ *Audit committee*

- *Composition and size*
  - (a) The audit committee shall be comprised solely of independent directors,
  - (b) The audit committee shall be comprised of a minimum of 3 directors, each of who is a financially literate. At least one member of the audit committee shall have accounting or related financial management expertise,
  - (c) The chairman of the audit committee shall be an independent director,
  - (d) The company secretary shall act as secretary to the audit committee.
- *Audit committee procedure*

  The audit committee of each listed company shall adopt a formal written charter approved by the full board of directors. The charter shall be reviewed every three years. The charter shall include the following:

  1. To oversee the financial reporting process, formats and disclosure of the financial information of the company to ensure correctness, sufficiency and credibility of financial statements;
  2. To review the accounting policy of the company;
  3. To review appropriateness of accounting assumptions, in particular the going concern assumption;
  4. To review accounting entries based on an exercise of judgement by the management;
  5. To discuss the qualifications in draft audit report;
  6. To review significant adjustments arising out of audit comments;
  7. To ensure compliance with generally accepted accounting principles;
  8. To ensure compliance with the requirements of governing laws and regulations to the extent they are related to financial statements;
  9. To review related party transactions;
  10. To review draft financial statements before adoption by the board of directors;
  11. To review draft Management Discussion and Analysis (MDA) report;
  12. To review the adequacy of internal control systems;
  13. To review the adequacy and effectiveness of the internal audit function;

14. To review material internal audit findings and follow-up actions;
15. To review all investigations of material nature;
16. To have discussions with external auditors on the nature and scope of audit as well as their significant audit observations;
17. To recommend the appointment and removal of external auditors, fixation of audit fees and payments for any other service to be rendered by the external auditor;
18. To review the removal of the Chief Internal Auditor (CIA) and allocation of resources to the internal audit function;
19. To ensure co-ordination between external and internal auditors;
20. To review the financial and risk management policies;
21. To review the cases of default in meeting financial commitments/obligations;
22. To review the credit rating of the company and credit ratings of financial instruments issued/to be issued by the company;
23. To review quarterly/half yearly results.

- The audit committee shall ensure the receipt of a formal written statement from the external auditor delineating all relationships between the auditor and the company.
- The audit committee chairman shall publish a report in the corporate governance report confirming that:
  (a) Management has reviewed the audited financial statements with the audit committee;
  (b) The outside auditors have discussed with the audit committee the outside auditors' judgements of the quality of accounting principles;
  (c) The members of the audit committee have discussed among themselves without management or the external auditors' presence, the information disclosed to the audit committee, and;
  (d) The audit committee believes that the company's financial statements are fairly presented in conformity with Generally Accepted Accounting Principles (GAAP) in all material respects.

  This disclosure shall also give a succinct but accurate report of the tasks performed by the audit committee, which would also be the audit committee's views on the adequacy of internal control system, perception of risks, and in the event of qualifications, why the audit committee accepted and recommended the financial statements with qualifications.
- The recommendation of the audit committee, if overruled by the board, shall be disclosed in the 'Directors' Report' along with the reasons for overruling.
- The chairman of the audit committee shall be required to attend the AGM of the company to provide clarification on matters relating to audit. If he is unable to attend due to circumstances beyond his control, any other member of the audit committee may be authorized by him to attend AGM on his behalf.

- Meeting and quorum of audit committee
  - (a) The audit committee shall meet at least four times in a year. Not more than four months shall elapse between two meetings. One meeting shall be held before finalization of annual accounts.
  - (b) The quorum shall be either two members or 1/3rd of the audit committee whichever is higher.
  - (c) The audit committee may invite such of the executives, as it considers appropriate (and particularly the head of finance function) to be present at the meetings of audit committee. On occasions, it may also meet without the presence of executives of the company. The finance director, head of internal audit, a representative of the statutory auditor may be present as invitees in the audit committee meetings.
  - (d) The company shall disclose the names of the audit committee members, the dates and the numbers of meetings attended by each member in the corporate governance report.
- Powers of audit committee

  The powers of the audit committee as listed in Regulation 18 with Schedule II Part C of the SEBI Listing Regulations should be retained.
- Role of audit committee

  The role of the audit committee as listed in Regulation 18 with Schedule II Part C of the SEBI Listing Regulations should be retained.
- Review of information by audit committee

  The mandatory review of the information as listed in Regulation 18 with Schedule II Part C of the SEBI Listing Regulations should be retained'.

➤ *Remuneration and nomination committee*

- Composition and size
  - (a) Board of directors shall set up a remuneration and nomination committee to develop policy on remuneration and make recommendations to the board on the company's framework of executive remuneration and its cost and to determine specific remuneration packages for each of the executive directors, including pension rights and any compensation payments. It shall also be responsible for proposing to the board the name of new appointments whether of executive or of non-executive directors in order to make board appointments absolutely clear and transparent.
  - (b) The committee shall have at least three non-executive independent directors as members.
  - (c) The chairman of the committee shall be an independent director.
  - (d) The company secretary shall act as the secretary to the committee.

- Remuneration and nomination committee procedure

  A written charter duly approved by the board shall be as under:

  (a) To recommend broad criteria such as qualifications for identifying individuals suitable for board membership;

  (b) To prepare a panel of experts who may be inducted in the board of directors;

  (c) To review the involvement of non-executive directors in the affairs of the company prior to continuance of their name in the panel.

  (d) To develop a clear policy on executive remuneration of the company and review the structure, design and implementation of the same to ensure fair and competitive remuneration to key personnel of the company;

  (e) To recommend compensation packages for executive directors including pension rights and any compensation payment;

  (f) To recommend compensation packages of the CEO, CFO, CIA, COO and the company secretary;

  (g) To review and evaluate the structure of 'Employees Stock Option Plans' and also to review, on a periodical basis, the effectiveness thereof;

  (h) To review the performance of key personnel.

- The chairman or in his absence due to the circumstance beyond his control, at least one member of remuneration and nomination committee duly authorized, shall be present in the annual general meeting to answer shareholders' queries.
- Meeting and quorum of remuneration and nomination committee

  (a) The committee will meet as and when required, but at least once in a year.

  (b) All the members of the committee shall be present in the meeting.

  (c) The chairman of the board of directors should be present as an invitee.

- The company shall disclose the names of the committee members, the dates and the numbers of meetings attended by each member, in the corporate governance report.
- Powers of remuneration and nomination committee

  The powers of audit committee as listed in Regulation 19 read with Schedule II Part D of the SEBI Listing Regulations shall also be conferred to the remuneration and nomination committee for due discharge of its responsibilities.

➤ *Independent directors' committee*

- In line with the Regulation 25(3) of SEBI Listing Regulations, 2015, the independent directors of the company shall set up a committee and hold at least one meeting in a year, without the attendance of non-independent directors and members of management. All the independent directors shall be present in such meeting.

- In the meeting, the committee members shall, inter alia:
  (a) review the performance of non-independent directors and the board as a whole;
  (b) review the performance of the chairperson of the company, taking into account the views of executive directors and non-executive directors;
  (c) assess the quality, quantity and timeliness of flow of information between the company management and the board that is necessary for the board to perform their duties effectively.

➤ *Shareholders'/Stakeholders' relationship committee*

- Composition and size
  (a) The committee shall have at least three members, all of whom should be non-executive directors.
  (b) The CFO and the compliance officer shall be present as invitees in the meeting.
  (c) The company secretary will act as the secretary to the committee.
- Shareholders'/Stakeholders' relationship committee procedure

  A written charter duly approved by the board shall be as under:
  (a) To review and redress the compliance of laws and regulations governing the company to the extent they relate to shareholders' rights;
  (b) To review and redress the shareholders'/investors' grievance, in particular, complaints, viz. transfer of shares, non-receipt of balance sheet, non-receipt of declared dividends, etc;
  (c) To review shareholders' suggestions and to select them for recommending to the board for consideration;
  (d) To review communications to shareholders in general.
- Meeting and quorum of shareholders'/stakeholders' relationship committee
  (a) The committee shall meet at least four times in a year.
  (b) The quorum shall be, either two members or 1/3rd of the committee whichever is higher.
- The company shall disclose the names of the committee members, the dates and numbers of meetings attended by each member, in the corporate governance report.
- Powers of shareholders'/stakeholders' relationship committee

  The powers of audit committee as listed in Regulation 20 read with Schedule II Part D of the SEBI Listing Regulations shall also be conferred to the shareholders'/stakeholders' relationship committee for due discharge of its responsibilities.

➤ *Risk management committee*

- In line with the Regulation 21 of SEBI (Listing Obligations and Disclosure Requirements) Regulations 2015 as amended upto 2019, the board shall constitute a risk management committee consisting of at least three executive and/or non-executive directors. The chairman of the committee shall be an independent director.
- The board shall define the roles and responsibilities of the risk management committee and delegate monitoring and reviewing of the risk management plan to the committee and such other functions as it may deem fit.
- The committee shall lay down procedures to inform board members about the risk assessment and minimization procedures.
- The committee shall be responsible for framing, implementing and monitoring the risk management plan for the company.
- The risk management policy of the company shall be disclosed in the Annual Report.
- The report of the risk management committee shall be included in the Annual Report of the company every year.

➤ *Corporate Social Responsibility (CSR) committee*

- In line with the provisions of Section 135 of the Companies Act, 2013, the board of a company having net worth of ₹ 500 crore or more, or turnover of ₹ 1000 crore or more or a net profit of ₹ 5 crore or more during any financial year, shall constitute a corporate social responsibility committee of the board consisting of at least 3 or more directors, of which at least 1 director shall be an independent director.
- The CSR committee shall formulate and recommend to the board, a CSR policy indicating the activities to be undertaken by the company in areas or subject, specified in Schedule VII to the Companies Act, 2013.
- The CSR committee shall recommend the amount of expenditure to be incurred on the CSR activities, which shall be approved by the board.
- The CSR policy shall be disclosed in the company's Annual Report every year.
- The CSR committee shall monitor the CSR policy of the company periodically.
- The CSR report shall be disclosed separately in the manner specified in the Companies (Corporate Social Responsibility) Rules, 2014, in the Annual Report of the company every year.

(IV) Other (non-mandatory) committees

➤ *Strategy and investment committee*

- Composition and size
  (a) The committee shall have at least three non-executive directors as members, the majority of whom should be independent.

(b) At least one of the members shall be an accounting/finance professional.

(c) The chairman of the committee shall be an independent director.

- Strategy and investment committee procedure

  A written charter duly approved by the board shall be as follows:

  (a) To formulate and periodically review the company's adherence to its 'Mission' and 'Vision' statements;

  (b) To review the strategic plans of the company;

  (c) To review the technological upgradation plans of the company;

  (d) To review investment proposals to be placed before the board;

  (e) To review the progress of approved investments and projects being implemented;

  (f) To examine post implementation review of completed projects;

  (g) To review restructuring proposals to be placed before the board.

- Meeting and quorum of strategy and investment committee

  (a) The committee shall meet at least once in a year.

  (b) The quorum shall be either two members or 1/3rd of the committee whichever is higher.

  (c) The chairman/CEO and CFO will be present in the meeting as invitees.

  (d) The company secretary shall act as the secretary to the committee.

- The company shall disclose the names of the committee members, the dates and numbers of meetings attended by each member, in the corporate governance report.

- Powers of strategy and investment committee

  The powers of audit committee as listed in Regulation 20 of the SEBI Listing Regulations shall also be conferred to the strategy and investment committee for due discharge of its responsibilities'.

➤ *Share transfer committee*

- Composition and size

  (a) The committee shall have at least three directors as members.

  (b) The company secretary shall act as secretary to the committee.

- Share transfer committee procedure

  A written charter duly approved by the board would be to approve transfer of shares and oversee all related formalities.

- Meeting and quorum of the share transfer committee

  (a) The committee shall meet once in a fortnight.

  (b) The quorum shall be either two members or 1/3rd of the committee, whichever is higher.

- The company shall disclose the names of the committee members, the dates and numbers of the meetings attended by each member, in the corporate governance report.

- Powers of the share transfer committee

  The powers of audit committee as listed in Regulation 20 of the SEBI Listing Regulations shall also be conferred to the share transfer committee for due discharge of its responsibilities.

B. The process for corporate governance

We have covered several important aspects under this head.

(i) Board procedure

➤ *Duty, responsibility and accountability*

- Executive and non-executive directors including independent directors shall have the same duties, responsibility and accountability under the law.
- The board shall fulfill certain important functions, viz.
  - (i) reviewing and guiding corporate strategy, major plan of action, risk policy, annual budget and business plans;
  - (ii) setting performance objectives, monitoring implementation and corporate performance and overseeing major capital expenditures and acquisitions and divestments;
  - (iii) appointing, remunerating, and monitoring key executives' performance;
  - (iv) reviewing the board performance and remuneration;
  - (v) monitoring and managing potential conflicts of interest of management, board members, and shareholders;
  - (vi) ensuring integrity of company's accounting and financial reporting systems;
  - (vii) monitoring the effectiveness of the governance practices;
  - (viii) maintaining appropriate relationship with the company's auditors; and
  - (ix) overseeing the process of disclosure and communication.

➤ *Board meetings and matters to be reserved for board decision*

- The full board shall meet a minimum of six times a year, at an interval of two months. Each meeting should have clear agenda items that require at least one full day's discussion.
- Notice of every board meeting should be given well in advance (say a clear period of seven days) to ensure participation by maximum number of directors.
- Meetings at short notices should be held only to transact emergency business. In such meetings, the presence of at least one independent director is a 'must' in order to ensure that only well-considered decisions are taken. In case even one independent director is not present in the emergency meeting, then decisions taken in such meetings shall be ratified by at least one independent director.

- Meetings of the board by electronic means (i.e. tele-conferencing and video conferencing), should be allowed. The directors participating through electronic means should be marked 'present', be counted and formed part of quorum. Minutes should also be approved/accepted by those directors who attended through teleconferencing/video conferencing by use of digital signature certification.
- While re-appointing the members of the board, the companies should look into the attendance record of the concerned directors. Failure to attend 75% or more of the board meetings in a year (irrespective of absence with or without permission) should be sufficient ground for vacation of office by the concerned directors.
- The names of each individual director attending the board meetings as well as the dates, time and duration of each such meeting shall be disclosed in the section of corporate governance of the annual report.
- The minimum information to be made available to the board and the matters for board decisions as listed in Annexure X of the revised Clause 49 of the Listing Agreement, should be retained. In addition, the following items should be included in the list:
  (a) All documents and records to be placed before the board directors under statutory requirements,
  (b) Strategic plans of the company,
  (c) Any stricture imposed on the company by any stock exchange or SEBI or any other quasi-judicial authority,
  (d) Any material event which might adversely affect the performance of the company,
  (e) Report on compliance with safety norms and staff welfare measures,
  (f) Quarterly report on financial risk exposures, risks management policy and effectiveness of such policy.

➤ *Access of information and consultation*

- The chairman shall ensure that all directors are properly briefed on issues arising at board meetings.

(ii) Orientation and training of directors

- The company shall provide suitable training and orientation to all directors including non-executive/independent directors to familiarize them with the company, their roles, rights and responsibilities in the company, nature of industry in which the company operates, business model of the company etc.
- The details of the training imparted shall be disclosed in the Annual Report of the company.

(iii) Reports of the board of directors

➤ *Directors' Responsibility Statement (DRS)*

- The report shall include a responsibility statement stating that:
  (a) The internal control system and internal audit function are adequate and are operating effectively. The deficiencies (if any), in design or

operation of internal control, as also significant changes in internal control and/or accounting policies (if any) during the year have been disclosed to the auditors and the audit committee.

(b) The board is not contemplating any substantial reduction in the activities of the company and that it will continue its business in the foreseeable future.

(c) The company has complied with generally accepted accounting principles and explained the reasons for deviations, if any.

(d) The board has prepared the financial statements in compliance with statutory requirements and applicable accounting standards and in a manner to provide a true and fair view of the state of affairs of the company.

(e) The board has not taken risk exposure in excess of what is considered reasonable with reference to the size and nature of the business of the company and the company has a well-documented risk management strategy in place.

(f) The related party transactions have been entered into at arm's length and if not, the relationships of the directors in such transactions along with the amount involved have been disclosed as part of the Directors' Report with management justification thereof.

➤ *Management Discussion and Analysis Report (MDA)*

- As part of the Directors' Report or as an addition thereto, a Management Discussion and Analysis Report shall form part of the annual report to the shareholders and shall include a discussion on the following matters:
  (a) Industry structure and developments
  (b) Opportunities and threats
  (c) Segment-wise or product-wise performance
  (d) Outlook
  (e) Risks and concerns
  (f) Technological development
  (g) Internal control system and their adequacy
  (h) Financial performance vis-à-vis operational performance
  (i) Significant development in human resources and industrial relation
  (j) Environment protection initiatives and environmental performance

➤ *Corporate governance report*

- There shall be a separate section on corporate governance in the annual report of the company with a detailed compliance report on the following governance issues:
  (a) A brief statement on company's philosophy on code of governance
  (b) Board of directors including (i) composition and category, viz. promoter, executive, non-executive, independent, and nominee directors, (ii) attendance of each director at the board meeting, and the last

AGM, (iii) number of memberships/chairmanship in other boards or board committees, and (iv) number of board meetings held with dates

(c) Audit committee including (i) brief description of audit committee charter, (ii) composition and names of members and chairperson with adequate disclosure on literacy in finance, accounts laws, etc., (iii) meetings and attendance of each director during the year.

(d) Remuneration and nomination committee including (i) brief description of remuneration and nomination committee charter, (ii) composition and names of members and chairperson, (iii) attendance during the year, (iv) remuneration and nomination policy, and (v) details of all directors' remuneration.

(e) Risk management committee including (i) brief description of risk management committee charter, (ii) composition and names of members and chairperson, (iii) attendance during the year, (iv) risk management policy, and (v) details of action taken to minimize risk.

(f) Corporate social responsibility (CSR) committee including (i) brief description of CSR committee charter, (ii) composition and names of members and chairperson, (iii) attendance during the year, (iv) CSR policy of the company, and (v) details of CSR activities undertaken and also the money spent during the year.

(g) Shareholders'/Stakeholders' relationship committee including (i) brief description of written charter, (ii) composition and names of members and chairperson, (iii) name and designation of compliance officer, (iv) attendance during the year, (v) number of shareholders' complaints/grievances received so far, (vi) number of complaints solved to the satisfaction of shareholders, (vii) number of pending complaints, (viii) shareholders survey on their satisfaction level and other initiatives taken to sort out grievances of shareholders during the year.

(h) Independent directors' committee including (i) brief description of written charter, (ii) composition and names of members and chairperson, (iii) attendance during the year, etc.

(i) Strategy and investment committee including (i) brief description of written charter, (ii) composition and names of members and chairperson, (iii) attendance during the year.

(j) Share transfer committee including (i) brief description of charter, (ii) composition and names of members and chairperson, (iii) attendance particulars during the year.

(k) General body meetings including (i) location and time of holding last three AGMs, (ii) a brief particulars of special resolutions passed in the previous three AGMs, (iii) special resolutions passed during the year through postal ballot including the details of voting pattern, (iv) conducting official of postal ballot exercise and procedure for postal ballot.

(l) Disclosures of all requirements of corporate governance prescribed including (i) significant related party transactions having potential conflict with the interest of the company, (ii) details of non-compliance and the penalties, strictures, censors imposed on the company by the stock exchanges, SEBI or any statutory authority on matters related to capital markets, during the previous three years, (iii) shareholder rights to obtain half-yearly results of company's performance, (iv) training of board members, (v) evaluation of non-executive board members, (vi) whistle blower policy and affirmation of non-denial of access to the audit committee, (vii) maintenance of non-executive chairman's office at company's cost, (viii) tenure of office of directors including non-executive/independent directors.

(m) Means of communication, viz. (i) quarterly results, (ii) newspapers wherein results published, (iii) website information, (iv) official news release, (v) presentation to institutional investors/analysts.

(n) General shareholder information, viz. (i) AGM—date, time and place, (ii) financial year, (iii) date of book closure, (iv) date of dividend payment, (v) listing on stock exchanges, (vi) stock code, (vii) market price data showing high, low during each month in the last financial year, (viii) company's performance vis-à-vis broad-based indices such as SEBI, Sensex, credit rating index, (ix) particulars of registrars and share transfer agents, (x) share transfer system, (xi) shareholding distribution, (xii) dematerialization of shares, (xiii) outstanding GDRs/ADRs/warrants or convertible instruments, date of conversion and its impact on equity, (xiv) plant location, (xv) address for communication.

(iv) Board's performance evaluation

- The board shall undertake a formal and rigorous annual evaluation of their own performance and that of the board committees as also the individual directors. The annual report shall explain how such evaluations have been conducted.
- The independent directors' committee led by the lead independent director, should be responsible for performance evaluation of the chairman, after taking the views of directors.

(v) Disclosure and transparency

- The disclosures of relationships between directors shall be made in documents and filings.
- The company's annual report shall contain a statement of remuneration policy of the company.
- All pecuniary relationship or transactions of the non-executive directors vis-à-vis the company shall be disclosed in the annual report.
- Following disclosures shall be made in the section on corporate governance of the annual report:

(a) All elements of remuneration package of each individual director, i.e., salary, benefits and perks, bonuses, stock options, pensions, etc,

(b) Details of fixed component and performance-linked incentives along with performance criteria,

(c) Service contracts, notice period, severance fees or compensation,

(d) Stock option details, if any, and whether issued at a discount, as well as the period over which accrued and over which exercisable.

- The company shall publish its criteria of making payments to non-executive directors in its annual report, viz. sitting fees, commission, etc.
- The company shall disclose the number of shares and convertible instruments held by non-executive directors in the annual report.
- The non-executive directors shall disclose their shareholdings in the listed company in which they are proposed to be appointed as directors prior to their appointment, which should be disclosed in the notice of the general meeting called for appointment.
- In case of appointment of a new director or re-appointment of a director, the shareholders shall be provided with the following information:

  (a) A brief resume of the director,

  (b) His qualification and nature of his experience in specific functional area, and

  (c) Names of companies in which the person also holds the directorship and membership of committees of the board.

  This information is required to be disclosed in the notice of the general meeting called for appointment. Therefore, it may not be necessary to disclose the same biographical information of such director(s) again in the annual report.
- The company accessing funds through public offers must follow the stringent disclosure norms failing which they shall face adequate and deterrent penalties against wrong disclosures.
- Every director must disclose to the company, the contracts or arrangements with the company in which he/she directly or indirectly, has any interest or concern. The notice of relevant disclosure must be made by the interested director to the board at the meeting in which the transaction is to be discussed. Failure to make disclosure by the concerned director shall be a condition of disqualification to hold office of director of the company.
- Details of transactions of the company with its holding or subsidiary/associated company in the ordinary course of business and transacted on an arm's length basis shall be placed periodically before the board through the audit committee. Details of transactions not in the normal course of business/or not on arm's length basis shall also be placed before the board together with management justification. A summary of such transaction with each party shall form a part of the annual report of the company. Non-compliance of this provision should result in transaction being voidable at the option of the board, apart from penalties etc.

- Every director shall disclose to the company, full information relating to directorship and shareholding in the company and in other companies, including the details of shares or debentures held by him or his relatives, names of companies in which he either singly or with his relatives held not less than a specified percentage (say 2% of the total equity capital) of shareholding, names of other entities in which he has interest as partner, member or key person.
- In addition to disclosures required under generally accepted accounting principles and other statutory provisions every listed company shall disclose information which will be of value to the shareholders. Disclosures shall include:
  (a) A brief resume of each director including the nature of his expertise and names of companies in which he holds the directorship and the membership of committees of the board.
  (b) All elements of the compensation package to all the directors including the terms of appointment.
  (c) Remuneration of senior officers just below the level of directors.
  (d) Movement in stock prices in capital markets where the company's shares are listed.
  (e) Loss/profit arisen out of the company's transactions in future and options.
  (f) Movement of key personnel during the period.
  (g) Summary of financial results as per international accounting standards.

C. Shareholders

Shareholders are the owners of the company. The managers act on behalf of the shareholders to maximize the wealth of the company. So, we suggest a few aspects keeping in view the overall interest of this dominant group.

(i) Shareholders' rights, shareholders' voting, and shareholders' evaluation of governance disclosure

- Shareholders must receive sufficient and timely information about the date, location and agenda of general meetings.
- Shareholders should have the opportunity to ask questions to the board and place items on agenda.
- The rights of minority shareholders shall be protected during meetings of the company. There should be an extensive use of postal ballot including electronic media to enable shareholders to participate in meetings.
- Shareholders shall be invited to approve all new long-term incentive plans, including share option schemes, and existing pay packages.
- The company shall explain to the shareholders, its governance policies, including any circumstances justifying departure from best practice.
- Shareholders' approval must be obtained through a special resolution for the items mentioned in Section 180(I) of the Companies Act, 2013. Shareholders' approval shall also be required for sale of whole or substantially whole of

the undertaking in the financial year. The term 'whole or substantially whole' should mean 20% of the total assets of the company. Shareholders' approval shall also include sale/transfer of investment in equity shares of other bodies corporate, which constitute 20% or more of the total assets of the investing company.

(ii) General meetings

- Except four items of ordinary business, viz. (i) consideration of annual accounts and reports of directors and auditors, (ii) declaration of dividends, (iii) appointment of directors, and (iv) appointment of and fixing remuneration of the auditors, the company should put all resolutions to a postal vote, and announce the results of the ballot at the beginning of the meeting.
- Items of business in respect of which directors/auditors have a right to be heard at the meeting (e.g., in case of a notice for their removal) should not be transacted through voting by postal ballot.
- The company shall count all proxy votes and indicate the level of proxies lodged on each resolution, and the balance for and against the resolution, after it has been dealt with on a show of hands.

(iii) Company's communication with shareholders

- The company shall maintain a website, which should be an interactive communication site, for two-way communication with shareholders. The website must include key information regarding the organization and must be updated regularly.
- The company shall publish quarterly financial reports and should display the same at its website.
- The company shall display on its website (i) the comments of the chairman of the board/CEOs on important reports relating to the company published in important newspapers/journals/electronic media, (ii) number of suggestions received from the shareholders in last three months, (iii) names, e-mail addresses, etc. of key personnel to facilitate communication, (iv) number of grievances received and redressed in last three months and the number of unsettled grievances, and (v) a brief resume of directors.
- The company must send to each household of shareholders the half-yearly financial results including the summary of events in last six months.

D. Stakeholders

- The company shall give stakeholders, who participate in the corporate governance process, access to information necessary to fulfill their responsibilities.

E. Audit and auditors

The importance of audit and the role of auditors hardly need to be emphasized. Some important suggestions are as follows:

- The board must maintain a professional and objective relationship with the auditors of the company.

- The appointment of external auditors shall be made by shareholders of the company taking into account the recommendations of the board, which in turn should be arrived at after obtaining the recommendations of the audit committee. In case, any of the shareholders wish to propose any other auditor in place of retiring auditor, this process shall also necessarily seek the views of the audit committee.
- All non-audit services shall be pre-approved by the audit committee.
- The auditor shall disclose holding in the securities of the company, if any, at the time of appointment.
- The company must take into account strictly the various prohibitions, restrictions etc. prescribed by the Naresh Chandra Committee, while giving an appointment to the external auditors for the audit and non-audit services to the company.
- The company shall provide auditors a direct access to the audit committee members.
- Fees paid to the auditors for non-audit work shall be fully disclosed in the annual report.
- The external auditors should independently report to the shareholders in accordance with statutory and professional requirements and independently assure the board on the discharge of its responsibilities (viz. financial reporting, internal control) in accordance with professional guidance.

F. Accounting standards

- The company shall ensure that the information is prepared, audited, and disclosed in accordance with high standards of accounting, financial, and non-financial accounting, and audit.
- In case, the company has followed a treatment different from that of prescribed in an accounting standard, management shall justify and disclose in the annual report why they believe such alternative treatment is more representative of the underlying business transaction. Also, management must clearly explain the alternative accounting treatment in the footnotes to the financial statements.

G. Internal control and internal audit

- Internal control shall ensure reliability of internal and external reporting and compliance with laws and regulations.
- The board shall set appropriate policies on internal control and assure that the system is functioning effectively, particularly in managing risks.
- The management of the company shall implement the board policies on risk and control and identity and evaluate the risks for consideration by the board and design, operate and monitor a suitable system of internal control to implement the board policy.
- The board shall regularly receive and review reports on internal control. It shall undertake an annual assessment for the purpose of making its public

statement on internal control to ensure that it has considered all significant aspects of internal control for the company, including operational and financial controls.

- The management reports to the board should provide a balanced assessment of the significant risks and effectiveness of the internal control system in managing the risks. Any significant control failure or weaknesses identified should be discussed in the reports, including their impact on the company and the remedial measures taken. There should be an openness of communication by management with the board on matters relating to risk and control.
- The board in its statement shall affirm that there is a continuous process for identifying, evaluating, and managing the significant risks faced by the company, and it is regularly reviewed by the board and accords with the guidance in this document. The disclosure also shall include an acknowledgement of the board's responsibility in this regard.
- Internal controls as mandated by the company with approval of the audit committee shall be certified by the CEO and CFO of the company and included in the Directors' Report.
- The board of a company, which does not have an internal audit function, shall assess the need for such a function annually. Where there is an internal audit function the board shall annually review its scope of work, authority and resources. If the company does not have an internal audit function and the board has not reviewed the need for one, the board must disclose these facts.

H. Financial reporting

- The board shall explain its responsibility for preparing the accounts and there shall be a statement by the auditors about their responsibilities. The directors shall report that the business is a going concern, with supporting assumption, as required.
- The company shall mandatorily consolidate the financial statements of its subsidiaries with it. Presentation of consolidated financial statements by the holding company should be in addition to the mandatory presentation of individual financial statements of that holding company.
- The company shall ensure that financial reporting in respect of each product segment is available to shareholders to obtain a complete financial picture of the company.
- The mandatory provision regarding CEO/CFO certification in Regulation 17(8) read with Schedule II, Part B of SEBI Listing Regulations, 2015 should be retained.

I. Holding company and subsidiary company relationship

- At least one director (executive/non-executive) on the board of directors of the holding company shall be a director on the board of its subsidiary company.
- The audit committee of the holding company shall review the financial statements, particularly the investments made by the unlisted subsidiary company.

- The minutes of the unlisted subsidiary company's board meeting shall be placed at the holding company's board meeting and a statement of all significant transactions entered into by the unlisted subsidiary company shall also be placed there for review and advice, if any.

J. Investor education and protection

- Companies raising money through an Initial Public Offering (IPO) shall disclose to the audit committee, the uses/application of funds by major category (capital expenditure, sales and marketing, working capital etc.), on a quarterly basis.
- On an annual basis, the company shall prepare a statement of funds utilized for purposes other than those stated in the offer document/prospectus. This statement shall be certified by the independent auditors of the company. The audit committee should make appropriate recommendations to the board to take steps in this matter.

K. Code of conduct

- It shall be obligatory for the board of a company to lay down a code of conduct for all its board members and senior management. The code shall be displayed on the website of the company.
- All the board members and senior management personnel (i.e., core management team comprising all members of management one level below the executive directors including all functional heads) shall affirm compliance with the code on annual basis. The annual report of the company shall contain a declaration to this effect signed by the CEO.

L. Protection to whistle blowers

- Personnel who observe an unethical or improper practice (not necessarily a violation of law) should be able to approach the audit committee without necessarily informing their supervisors.
- Companies shall take measures to ensure that this right of access is communicated to all employees through means of internal circulars etc. The employment and other personnel policies of the company shall contain provisions protecting 'whistle blowers' from unfair termination and other unfair prejudicial employment practices.
- Companies shall annually affirm that they have not denied any personnel access to the audit committee of the company (in respect of matters involving alleged misconduct) and that they have provided protection to whistle blowers from unfair termination and other unfair or prejudicial employment practices. Such affirmation shall form a part of the board report on corporate governance.

M. Compliance of corporate governance

- The company shall obtain a detailed report (not merely a certificate) from the auditors of the company regarding compliance of all requirements of corporate governance as stipulated by the Companies Act and SEBI regulations.

This report shall be annexed with the report on corporate governance in the annual report or as an addendum to the main audit report and sent to the shareholders of the company annually.

Governance issues—Voluntary code/code of best practices

We also highlight under this head, some more suggestions, which are voluntary and may be followed by the corporates as the code of best practices of corporate governance.

A. The structure for corporate governance

(i) Board of directors and board issues

➤ *Composition and size*

- Every company should have at least one resident director in India to ensure the availability in case of any issue regarding the accountability of the board.

➤ *Selection and appointment*

- There should be a formal, rigorous and transparent procedure for the appointment of directors to the board with the requisite skills, knowledge, and personal attributes best suited to the role expected of them.

➤ *Tenure and age limit*

- Although the age limit for directors to retire may be decided by the companies, however, the corporate boards should have an adequate mechanism of self-renewal as part of corporate governance best practice.
- As a good practice for directors to retire after a particular age, the companies should fix up the retirement age maximum at 75 years.

➤ *Woman director*

- In order to maintain proper balance in the board functioning and for the purpose of ensuring gender diversity in the board and for its efficient performance it is prudent that the company should have more than one women directors in the board of directors.

➤ *Chairman and CEO and Lead independent director*

- There should be a clear division of responsibilities at the helm of the company, which should ensure a balance of power and authority such that no one individual has unfettered powers of decision.

➤ *Nominee director*

- The nominees of financial institutions, banks and the Government on private and public sector companies' boards should be appointed by the shareholders. They should be subjected to same responsibilities and liabilities as other directors.

➤ *Number of directorships and alternate directors*

- The number of alternate directorships held by an individual should fall within the overall limit of directorships.

- An individual should not be appointed as an alternate director for more than one director in the same company.
- An alternate director may be allowed to be appointed for an independent director. Such alternate director should also be an independent director.

➤ *Remuneration of directors, notice period and compensation*

- Companies should establish a formal and transparent policy on executive remuneration and for fixing the remuneration packages of individual directors based on the principles of fairness, reasonableness and accountability.
- There should be a clear relationship between responsibility and performance vis-à-vis remuneration. The policy underlying directors' remuneration should be articulated, disclosed and understood by the investors/ stakeholders.

(ii) Mandatory board committees

➤ *Audit committee*

- Generally Accepted Auditing Standards (GAAS) require that a company's external auditor discusses with the audit committee the auditor's judgement about quality, not just the acceptability, of the company's accounting principles as applied in its financial reporting.

B. The process for corporate governance

(i) Board procedure

➤ *Duty, responsibility and accountability*

- The board should present a balanced and understandable assessment of the company's position and prospects.
- All directors should bring an independent judgement to bear on issues of strategy, performance, resources, including key appointments and standards of conduct.
- A non-executive/independent director should be held liable only in respect of any contravention of any provision of the Act, which had taken place with his knowledge through board process and where he has not acted diligently or with his consent or connivance. Any follow-up action/dissent of such independent director, upon knowledge of any wrong, should be recorded in the minutes of the board meeting.

➤ *Board meetings and matters to be reserved for board decision*

- If any director has any reservation about the contents of the minutes, he may raise the issue in succeeding meeting and a note of dissent, if any, may be recorded in the minutes of that meeting.

➤ *Access of information and consultation*

- The board should be supplied in a timely manner with information in a form and of a quality appropriate to enable it to discharge its duties.
- In order to discharge its duties properly, there should be a procedure agreed by the board to take independent professional advice, if necessary, at the company's expense.

(ii) Orientation and training of directors

- A company should train every director in the business model of the company as well as the risk profile of the business parameters of the company, his responsibilities as director, and the best ways to discharge them.

(iii) Board's performance evaluation

- The performance evaluation of non-executive directors should be done by a peer group comprising the entire board of directors excluding the director being evaluated. This evaluation should be the mechanism to determine whether to extend/continue the terms of appointment of non-executive directors.

C. Shareholders

(i) Shareholders' rights, shareholders' voting, and shareholders' evaluation of governance disclosure

- The corporate governance framework of the company should protect shareholders' rights.
- Shareholders should have the opportunity to participate effectively and vote in general meetings. They should have access to information about rules, including voting procedures that govern general shareholders' meetings.
- Institutional shareholders should disclose their policies on the use of voting rights. They should have a responsibility to make considered use of their votes.
- Institutional shareholders and companies should be ready to enter into a dialogue with each other where practicable, based on the mutual understanding of objectives.

(ii) General meetings

- The processes and procedures for general shareholders' meetings should allow for equal treatment of all shareholders.
- Board should use the AGM to communicate with private investors and encourage their participation.
- AGM should also be held at a place other than the place of its registered office, provided at least 10% members in number reside at such place (in India only).
- The company should seek independent assessment of the conduct of polls during general meetings of the company.

D. Stakeholders

- Corporate governance framework of the company should recognize the rights of stakeholders as established by law and encourage active co-operation between the company and stakeholders in creating wealth, jobs, and the sustainability of financial soundness of the company. The framework should permit performance-enhancing mechanism for stakeholder communication.

E. Audit and auditors

- A periodic change in the audit partners (not the audit firms) should be arranged by the company to bring a fresh approach to audit.
- Auditors are required to carry out their work with highest standards of excellence and independence within the discipline of legal provisions and accounting standards.
- The auditors should have dual responsibility—the public report to the shareholders on the statutory financial statements and additional private reporting to the directors on operational matters.
- The auditors should provide the shareholders with independent and objective assurance on the reliability of the financial statements and of certain other information provided by the company.

F. Internal control and internal audit

- Directors should exercise judgement in reviewing how the company has implemented the requirements of the code relating to internal control and reporting to shareholders thereon.
- The company's board should adopt a risk-based approach in order to establish a sound system of internal control and review its effectiveness. This should be incorporated by the company within its normal management and governance process.
- Effective financial controls including maintenance of proper accounting records should ensure that the company is not unnecessarily exposed to avoidable financial risks. They should also contribute in safeguarding of assets, detection and prevention of fraud.
- The internal control system should (a) be embedded in the operations of the company, (b) be capable of responding quickly to evolving risks to the business, and (c) include procedure for reporting immediately to the appropriate levels of management about any significant failures or weaknesses in the system for corrective action.
- Should the board become aware at any time of a significant failure or weakness in internal control, it should determine how these failures arose and re-assess the effectiveness of the management's on-going process for designing, operating and monitoring the system of internal control.

G. Financial reporting

- Corporate governance framework of the company should ensure that timely and accurate disclosure is made on all material matters including the financial situation, performance, ownership and governance of the company.

H. Investor education and protection

- Corporate governance ratings are desirable for investor protection. However, it should be left to the management of companies to decide whether they want to be rated or not, on corporate governance.

I. Compliance of corporate governance

- The auditors making the report on compliance of corporate governance should have the same rights and responsibilities as are bestowed on them in respect of annual audit of accounts and statutory audit report of the company.

13.2.3 Section C: A Standard Code of Governance Practices and Disclosure Norms on (a) Social Responsibility of Business and Sustainability, (b) Business Ethics, and (c) Environmental Issues

We venture to make a few suggestions here in respect of:

(a) corporate social responsibility and sustainability,

(b) business ethics, and

(c) environmental issues.

Social responsibility of business and sustainability

The best practices and governance norms towards social responsibility of business or Corporate Social Responsibility (CSR) and sustainability, which need attention and adherence by the companies, are mentioned hereunder:

- While setting the goals and objectives, a company must consider various expectations of the stakeholders into consideration. The values and norms of the society should be properly dealt with so that corporate values and social values do not conflict with one another. Therefore, the companies should formulate such strategies, pursue such policies and take such decisions that promote furtherance of their economic goals as well as satisfy the social values at the same time.
- In order to avoid mismatch and obstacles to development on sustainable basis, there must be reconciliation, integration and harmonization between corporate goals and strategy, and social and community goals and expectations. Also there must be a regular review and evaluation so as to match the corporate goals with the changing expectation of the society.
- There must be a transparent, fair and adequate disclosure of social performance by the companies on regular basis in order to gain confidence and trust of the society and influence community expectations.
- Corporate social performance analysis and reporting should be widespread. Such performance should be rendered more effective and useful for both internal and external purpose provided comprehensive and standardized reporting formats are adopted. Such formats should distinguish between commitments or inputs on the one hand, and outputs or results on the other. In addition, an appropriate comparative information should be provided so that levels of social performance and cost-benefit trade-offs can be better evaluated.
- The corporate governance report should have a separate section wherein various steps and actions taken by the companies towards their commitment of social responsibility are detailed in the form of a CSR report every year as prescribed by the Companies Act, 2013 and Company (CSR) Rules, 2014.

- There is a need for undertaking social audit and sustainability audit of the corporates.

Business ethics

The standard norms of best practice of corporate governance demands setting up of a model of ethical codes by the companies. They should cover the following processes:

- Produce a strategy for integrating the code into the running of business at the time it is issued.
- Make sure that the code is endorsed by the chairman and CEO.
- Send the code to all employees in a readable form and give it to all the employees joining the company.
- Include a short section on how an employee can react if he is faced with potential breach of the code or is in doubt about a course of action involving an ethical choice.
- Give all staff the personal opportunity to respond to the content of the code.
- Make a procedure for managers and supervisors to state regularly that they and their staff understand and apply the provisions of the code and raise matters not covered by it.
- Install a procedure for regular review and updating of the code.
- Make adherence to the code obligatory by including reference to it in all contracts of employees and link it with disciplinary procedures.
- Ask those responsible for company's training programme at all levels to include issues raised by the code in the programme.
- Ensure that the code is translated for use in overseas subsidiaries or other places in the local language for proper understanding of the employees.
- Make copies of the code available to the suppliers, customers and other stakeholders.
- Insert a copy of the code in the annual report so that shareholders and public at large know about the company's position on ethical matters.

While drafting the code of ethics and conduct for corporate governance, the following aspects should be kept in view:

(a) Prescribing of universally acceptable ethical values
(b) Providing for highest standards of board functioning in an impartial and objective manner
(c) Ensuring adequate care, diligence and transparency in corporate functioning
(d) Encouraging discipline throughout the organization
(e) Avoiding conflict of interest
(f) Ensuring confidentiality and respect for each other
(g) Loyalty to the organization
(h) Providing motivation and requisite incentives for efficient and effective functioning

(i) Ensuring no discrimination of gender, caste, creed and religion in employment
(j) Ensuring prevention of child labour employment

Environmental issues

- The companies shall set up Environment, Health and Safety (EHS) standards covering the following items, viz.
  (a) Environment, Health and Safety (EHS) policy
  (b) Management and resources
  (c) Communication and consultation
  (d) Training
  (e) Material hazards
  (f) New plant, equipment and process design
  (g) Modification and changes
  (h) EHS assurance
  (i) EHS processes, e.g., occupation injuries and illness, wellness initiatives, health checkup and nutrition programme, women's health, social consciousness, safety weeks and awareness campaign, HIV/AIDS awareness for contract and sub-contract labours etc.
  (j) Emergency plans
  (k) Risk assessment, disaster recovery and business continuity
  (l) Environmental impact assessment
  (m) Business sustainability assessment
  (n) Resource conservation
  (o) Waste management
  (p) Soil and groundwater protection
  (q) Product stewardship
  (r) EHS performance review and reporting
  (s) Auditing of EHS measures
  (t) Information and documentation as per ISO 14001 and OHSAS 18001 guidelines

Each standard shall be set up in principle and operating unit of the company shall report performance in detail with reference to the specific targets.

- There shall be arrangements to ensure that the safety, health and environment considerations are taken into account prior to the launch of new products and the development of new processes.
- The safety, health and environmental factors associated with any product from conception to the ultimate use and disposal, shall be managed responsibly and ethically.
- The standards shall impose a holistic approach on product management, which shall ensure that all potential risks are identified and considered before a product is launched. Stewardship is essentially about risk management in all its aspects.

- The companies shall monitor environmental standards in the areas of project decisions, including project site selection, project evaluation and choice of alternatives vis-à-vis Environmental Impact Assessment (EIA).
- Day to day monitoring is required of environmental standards and compliance with Environment Acts and Rules.
- There should be a continuous measurement of cost-benefits, environmental assets and liabilities and integration/linking them with corporate accounts.
- An annual audit of Environment Statements by the companies is a 'must' before submission to the pollution control board.
- The companies must report compliance with EHS measures in a separate section in the annual report.

Apart from the above suggestions, some more suggestions and recommendations have been provided specifically in Chapter 9, Section 9.4 as also in Chapter 10, Section 10.4 which should be read while going through this chapter.

13.3 A POLICY FOR CUSTOMIZATION AND CODE SERVICING FOR CORPORATE GOVERNANCE

To evolve a policy for customization and code servicing for corporate governance, a few suggestions are given in this section.

13.3.1 Customization

The code of corporate governance lays emphasis on the fact that while regulatory prescriptions may facilitate good governance practices, achievement of good and effective governance would however, require fine-tuning and customizing in a company specific manner, the governance practices drawing upon the basic ground rules laid down by the code. Accordingly, with a view to installing the best governance model for a company, it would be necessary to go through the following aspects:

(a) A review of present governance practices at the company

(b) Review of the specific nature of activities carried on by the company, the history, stages of development, as also internal and external environment of the company

(c) Prioritizing legitimate expectations of the various stakeholders

(d) Listing of best practices with particular reference to the nature of activities of the company

(e) Setting up of the desired framework and process of corporate governance keeping in view of the above

(f) Firming up the transition period from present practice to recommended best practice and phasing the transition over this period.

The transformation from current practices to recommended best practices, in line with the code for corporate governance requires the process of matured approach to change management and measures to overcome cultural shock and resistance to change.

13.3.2 Code Servicing

The environment the companies operate in, is dynamic, with laws, regulations, practices, concepts and cultures in a constant state of evolution. As a result, any code or framework built thereon must change with the time. Wherever the corporate governance framework has been built on the code of governance, such framework must be serviced time to time to ensure that it reflects appropriate reactions to changing realities.

A one-time installation of a corporate governance system based on the code should not entitle any company to claim, for all times to come, that it has a due process of corporate governance in place. In order to verify whether the substance of the governance process in vogue, meets the expectations of the code of governance it would be imperative for the company to subject themselves to a review every three years and revamp the framework and procedures to the extent required.

Corporate governance extends beyond corporate law. Its fundamental objective is not mere fulfillment of the requirements of law, but to ensure commitment of the board of directors in managing the company in a transparent manner for maximizing long-term shareholders' value. So effectiveness of a system of corporate governance cannot be legislated by law nor can any system of corporate governance remain static. In a dynamic business environment, the corporate governance system needs to continually evolve in accordance with the rapidly changing economic and industrial environment of the country in the new millennium.

13.4 CONCLUDING REMARKS

Apart from the present study, there are many issues on the peripheral areas, which need sustained efforts through separate studies. Nevertheless, the present study is expected to serve as a pointer to the corporate governance practices among the listed Indian companies in particular, and Indian corporate sector in general. This study throws some light on the present corporate governance practice in India and also suggests for its improvement as a road map for the Indian corporate houses for attaining international standards of governance. From these standpoints, the book has its own importance and relevance.

CASE STUDY

IndiGo dogfight over Engine Deal

INTRODUCTION

The battle between Rakesh Gangwal and Rahul Bhatia, the two founders of IndiGo, has erupted over accusations of falling corporate governance standards at the airline—arising mainly from related party transactions between IndiGo and Bhatia's IGE group.

Gangwal, the Florida-based airline executive-turned entrepreneur, has been livid over the manner in which the IndioGo board turned down his request for an extraordinary general meeting of shareholders to discuss a raft of issues, including Bhatia's "unusual controlling rights over IndiGo".

LURKING SUSPICION

But there is a lurking suspicion that Gangwal's accusation of poor corporate governance standards may have more to do with a massive USD 20 billion (₹ 140000 crore) deal that IndiGo has signed at the Paris Air Show on 17th June, 2019 with CFM International for 560 LEAP-1A engines which will be used to power 280 Airbus A320neos and A321neos that the airline has contracted to purchase.

CFM International is owned by General Electric of the US and Saffran of France. It is one of the biggest engine manufacturers for aeroplanes and does compete with Pratt and Whitney of the US. The IndiGo deal was described by CFM as the 'largest ever single engine order in history". In fact the IndiGo deal accounted for almost 40% of the USD 50.2 billion deals that CFM had signed for 1150 engines at the Paris Air Show. The delivery of the first LEAP-1A powered A320neo is scheduled in 2020.

The Airbus planes were ordered a couple of years ago. Pratt and Whitney had been picked as the supplier of engines for the first 150 planes. But last year, IndiGo ran into big trouble when the DGCA grounded several of its Airbus planes fitted with P & W engines in March because of serious glitches. The problem with the P & W engines was not completely sorted out and therefore, some planes had suffered mid-air engine failures this year as well.

The A320neo has to make a straight choice between two new generation engines: the PW1100G-JM from Pratt and Whitney and the LEAP-1A from CFM International. Both engines promise fuel efficiency that can help the airline to reduce its costs. Neither Gangwal nor Bhatia refer to the engine deal with CFM, or when and why the board decided to go for the CFM engine.

Gangwal was a former chief executive at US airways and worked earlier with Air France. He used to oversee the technical aspects and had a big role to play in purchase negotiations. IndiGo has been a CFM customer since 2016. But only 17 A320neos in its fleet of 230 are powered by the CFM56-5B engines, an older version.

In the year 2017, InterGlobe Aviation Ltd., the parent company of IndiGo had come out with a public issue of 33.5 million shares. In the document outlining the share issue, InterGlobe stated: "We have yet to select the engines for 280 of the 430 aircrafts in our A320neos order. There can be no assurance that we will be able to secure engines for these aircrafts on terms comparable to our existing orders."

The purchase of planes and engines involve several negotiations in which the plain manufacturers and engine suppliers do offer a lot of credits to clinch the deal. In that document IndiGo provided a glimpse of how these credits worked and how big they could be. The document mentioned: "We receive non-refundable incentives from manufacturers in connection with our past aircraft and engine orders. The application of these credits to our operating leases results in a net reduction in our aircraft rental expenses which are amortised over the initial terms of the operating leases. As on March 2017, we had unamortised deferred incentives of ₹ 21873.73 million as a result of these credits. Under our A320neos order, we would not receive such credits in the event that the market price of the A320neos was to decrease below the order price."

It is after this that Pratt and Whitney of the US was chosen as its engine supplier. But the latest deal with CFM is considered as one of the biggest switches of engine supplier in aviation history. It is possible that this did not go down well with the RG group.

SCRUTINY OF ALL BOARD MEMBERS

The Government of India wants market regulator SEBI to probe the role of all board members and every entity associated with the two main promoters groups of InterGlobe Aviation and take strict action for all wrongdoings.

According to the officials, there are indication of violations of corporate governance norms, fair market trade and insider trading rules. Therefore, the SEBI needs to probe the role of each and every entity associated with all the board members and promoter-linked entities.

The officials also added that the stock exchanges would collect the data for all suspicious trades over the past one year, especially of those associated with the board members including independent directors, and entities directly or indirectly associated with the two warring promoter groups.

ACTION TAKEN BY SEBI

SEBI has launched a probe a few months ago into suspicious insider trade violations in connection with trading in shares of InterGlobe Aviation. This probe has now been expanded to include alleged violation of corporate governance guidelines, disclosure regulations, and insider trading rules at a much wider level. The regulator has asked the company to reply within 19th July 2019.

Besides, a number of individuals, including executives and board members and promoters of the company would be summoned soon by the regulator as part of the probe. SEBI is looking into allegations of violations of corporate governance norms, and questionable related party transactions by the Rahul Bhatia-led group as alleged by Rakesh Gangwal, who has sent copies of his complaint to the prime minister of India and other ministries.

Questions for Discussion

1. Who are the two warring promoter groups of IndiGo and what is their background?
2. What is the subject matter of disputes between the two promoter groups?
3. Are the allegations of violations of corporate governance norms, and questionable related party transactions by the Rahul Bhatia-led group as alleged by Rakesh Gangwal valid?
4. What actions have been taken so far by the market regulator SEBI as desired by the Government of India?

Test Your Knowledge

1. What are your suggestions concerning Structural Changes in the monitoring system of the Ministry, SEBI and the stock exchanges for improvement in the corporate governance standards in Indian corporates?

2. Can you suggest a comprehensive and standard code of corporate governance and compulsory disclosure norms for Indian companies?
3. Recommend a standard code of corporate governance and compulsory disclosure norms on:
   (a) Board Composition and Size
   (b) Selection and Appointment of directors
   (c) Tenure and Age limit of directors
   (d) Number of directorships and Alternate directors
   (e) Board's Performance Evaluation
   (f) Disclosure and transparency concerning directors
4. What would be your suggestions on improvement of disclosure norms in respect of:
   (a) Directors' Responsibility Statement
   (b) Management Discussion and Analysis Report
   (c) Internal control and Internal audit
   (d) Code of conduct
   (e) Protection to Whistle Blowers
5. Suggest a standard code of governance practices and disclosure norms on:
   (a) Social responsibility of business and sustainability
   (b) Business ethics
   (c) Environmental issues
6. Write short notes on:
   (a) Customisation
   (b) Code servicing

Appendix 1 Self-Test of Effectiveness of a Director in the Board

This self-test is simply a suggestive example of a director's effectiveness in the board proceedings. Judgements will always be different about the attributes or essentiality of quality that a director must have in order to be the ***"most effective"*** *board member because (1) the value systems of individuals on the board; (2) the philosophy, concept and policies of the company; (3) the nature of business of the company; (4) the environment, both external and internal, in which the company operates, etc. are all different. Since the board of a company is not the same as that of the other, it is not possible to standardize the attributes that a director is required to have.*

In this test, the rating of ***"most effective"*** *means the distinction of high effectiveness with which a director serves the board on overall basis. The rating of* ***"effective"*** *signifies that overall the service of the director is satisfactory. The rating of* ***"ineffective"*** *shows that the performance of the director in the boardroom is not satisfactory at all.*

Capability as a Director

Most effective

- He is adequately qualified, vastly experienced and well-respected person.
- He has excellent relationship with peers in the profession, business and with other board members.
- He has excellent communication skills and can differentiate between 'governance' and 'management' of a company.
- He has a clear vision and mission as to the long-term economic goal of the company.
- He is capable of discharging corporate social responsibility and contributes toward sustainability of the company's business.
- He attends board meetings regularly and contributes effectively in the board proceedings by way of giving practical and workable suggestions/solutions to the board problems.

Effective

- He meets most criteria above, but may not be optimal when compared with the most effective person available elsewhere.

Ineffective

- He does not meet most of the criteria mentioned above.
- He does not fit needs of company.

Preparedness and Contributor as a Director

Most effective

- He is thoroughly prepared and understands reports and background materials sent with the board agenda.
- He knows company's history, philosophy, style and strategic plans.
- He understands statutory and fiduciary responsibility of a director.
- He keeps current knowledge on legislative and regulatory matters.
- He is up-to-date on professional and international affairs affecting the company's interest.
- He visits factories and service centres to understand the company's operations.
- He takes keen interest and the responsibility to assist board in making policy and ensures continuing management and company's growth.
- He communicates constructively with chairman and CEO on relevant issues between board meetings or at any time.
- He knows key managers and some of their subordinate officers.
- He exchanges views with others knowledgeable on corporate affairs.
- He is aware of director and officer liability insurance protection and indemnification measures taken by his company for his personal protection.
- He respects confidentiality on company's matters.
- He asks probing questions focused on policy and strategy of the company.
- He insists on and gets information necessary for decision-making.
- He discharges statutory and fiduciary responsibilities.
- He takes active interest in training and education of himself and other board members.
- He is the key resource person to the management and the board.
- He is aware of the risk management policy of the company and takes active interest and offers suggestions to the board to mitigate the risk.
- He has the ability to evaluate CEO, senior management and company performance.

Effective

- He is reasonably up-to-date on company's and industry's problems.
- He is aware of company's philosophy, prospects and problems, but needs to improve upon his own knowledge, experience on the company's business and board functioning.
- He is reasonably able to perform evaluative role.
- He generally participates constructively at meetings and applies prior thought.
- He fulfils statutory and fiduciary responsibilities.

Ineffective

- He has little knowledge of the business philosophy of the company and the nature of the industry.
- He does not exert much beyond attending board meetings.
- He does not prepare himself adequately prior to meetings.
- He does not actively participate and contributes valued inputs in the meetings.
- He is frequently absent from board/committee meetings without legitimate reasons.
- He causes frustration among other board members due to his amateurish performance.
- He cannot truly be considered committed, responsible or interested.
- He is indifferent about the risk management policy of the company and hardly takes interest in discussions of how to minimize the risk.

Independence as a Director

Most effective

- He thinks, speaks and works quite freely and independently with confidence, conviction and courage.
- He takes a free-standing posture where independent decision is important and ignores any conflicts of interest.
- He supports proper, albeit complex, relationships of the board members with the chairman, the CEO and executive management.
- He is willing to take risk and collateral with chairman, board members, and CEO in taking a reasoned, independent stand.
- He prefers relinquishing directorship position in the company rather than be considered captive.
- He is objective when considering trade-offs and consequences in board proceedings.

Effective

- He is generally respected for his independent role in the meetings.
- He generally speaks on critical matters that require objective opinion of the board.
- Generally, he is not captive of the chairman, CEO, or other board member, but he may be influenced at times by their dispositions toward matters.

Ineffective

- He lacks courage to speak and act independently in the meetings.
- He is captive to members of board or outside parties and basically dependent on political pressures.
- He works for other's interest.

Activities as a Board Committee Member

Most effective

- He understands process of committee work, and the relations with executive management.
- He serves usefully on one or more than one board committee.
- He brings in new ideas and takes active part in framing relevant policy of the company to be submitted to the board for consideration and approval.
- He uses abilities and influence constructively in writing committee report for submission to the board for further necessary executive action.
- He is regular in attendance of the committee meeting.

Effective

- He attends meetings normally and takes reasonable interest in committee functioning.
- He is captive to the chairman of the board committee.
- He is generally prepared for working with other board committee members.

Ineffective

- He is irregular in attendance of the committee meetings.
- He is not at all prepared for discussion on urgent matters in the committee meetings.
- He lacks sense of his responsibility towards business in committee meetings and takes a casual approach.
- He does not have new ideas or suggestions to put forward in the meetings nor takes active interest in the proceedings of the meetings.
- He has no contribution in framing relevant policy nor does he have any interest in assisting other committee members in writing committee reports.

Chairman of the Board

Most effective

- He is competent as chairman of the board of directors and in managing group dynamics.
- He commands respect from each member of the board as the most effective leader.
- He understands the significant difference of roles and responsibility of chairman and CEO, irrespective of whether both the posts are held by one person or by separate persons.
- He prepares seriously for board meetings and gives due consideration in making board meetings the most effective use of time of the members present.
- He keeps on discussing major strategic or policy matters in priority in meetings and ensures advance review of presentations when needed.

- He advises the company secretary on keeping major issues in priority while making agenda for the meeting.
- He encourages constructive debate and independent viewpoints to come forward in the meeting and ensures to make each meeting an interesting and rewarding experience for each participant.
- He keeps a proper balance to advocate and adversary views on major issues in the board proceedings.
- He takes active interest in education and training of directors and advises the executive management for necessary action in this regard.
- He believes in succession planning and ensures that the potential candidates are developed for chairman and CEO succession and also for senior management position.

Effective

- He generally earns respect from majority of the board members. But, he is not a dynamic leader.
- He normally prepares well for board meetings and endeavours in making board meetings the effective use of time of the members present.
- He generally encourages constructive debate and independent viewpoints to come forward in the meeting and tries to make each meeting an interesting and rewarding experience for board members.
- He normally tries to keep a proper balance to advocate and adversary views on major issues in the board proceedings.

Ineffective

- He does not meet most of the criteria mentioned above.
- He delegates most governance issues to CEO, if he is a non-executive chairman.
- He hardly exercises leadership in motivating board members and encourages members to contribute in strategy or policy formulation.
- He fumbles and cannot control board members when there is a conflict among them at meetings.
- He does not earn respect from majority of the board members. He is not a dynamic leader.
- He has no positive attitude to lead board members for discussion on critical issues affecting the company's interest.

Corporate Growth Activities

Most effective

- He is fully aware, knowledgeable and updated about the current affairs, both internal and external factors, affecting the growth of the company.
- He makes penetrating suggestions on innovations, strategic directions and planning in the board meetings and also in other fora.

- He recognizes and believes that the company should strive for achieving long-term stakeholders' value for ensuring growth and development of the company.
- He is a strong believer of the concept of corporate social responsibility and sustainability which can bring in corporate prosperity and sustainable growth.
- He tries to ensure that in the development process, governance mechanisms protect shareholder's interests and enhances shareholder's value.
- He is an independent thinker with interest in future directions and economic growth of the company.
- He relates the company to new business opportunities ethically through direct and indirect participation.

Effective

- He normally takes interest in conventional growth prospects of the company and actively participates in strategic directions and planning in the meetings.
- He is not a strong supporter of forward innovative programmes, but does not unduly resist them.

Ineffective

- He does not participate in any financial, commercial, or technical growth activities of the company.
- He resists change and does not keep up with future expectations and trends in the industry, business or geographical areas or company activities.
- He cannot bring or present new ideas or substantive thought nor does he have any interest in working towards all round growth and prosperity of the company.

Appendix 2 Twenty-five Questions for Diagnosing a Board

If you answer "yes" to all 25 questions, you have the most effective board.

1. Is your board the right size (say 8 to 15 members)?
2. Are there at least two outside/independent directors for every executive director?
3. Are there at least two or more women directors in the board?
4. Do the executive directors include the CEO, the COO, and the CFO only?
5. Does the board have one person as the Chairman-cum-Managing Director/CEO or has the post of Chairman been separated from CEO/MD?
6. Does the board take the right measures to build trust among directors?
7. Do your directors regularly speak to senior functional executives who are not represented on the board?
8. Does your audit committee have the authority to approve the appointment of external audit partner in charge of auditing the company?
9. Does your audit committee regularly review highly important matters?
10. Does your audit committee do proper justice to 'whistle blower policy'?
11. Do compensation consultants report to your compensation and nomination committee rather than to the company's human resources department?
12. Do your nomination and remuneration committee rather than the CEO/MD direct the search for new board members and invite candidates to stand for election?
13. Is your remuneration and nomination committee courageous enough to set formulae for CEO and other executive directors' compensation based on long-term results—even if the formulae differ from industry norms?
14. Is the executive board members' pay linked to corporate performance?
15. Has your 'risk management committee' formulated the risk management policy and regularly reports to the board about the on-going as well as emerging risks in business and their mitigation process?
16. Does your 'corporate social responsibility committee', being one of the most important board committees, discharge its responsibility effectively towards solving societal problems and bring in sustainability?

17. Do independent directors formally evaluate your CEO's strengths, weaknesses, objectives, personal plans and performance every year?
18. Is the performance of each of your directors periodically reviewed by the board?
19. Does the board annually review succession plans for senior management?
20. Is your board actively involved in formulating long-range business strategy from the start of the planning cycle?
21. Is there any scope or privilege for outside directors to alter the meeting agenda set by your CEO?
22. Does the company send agenda papers and other important documents to all directors to prepare for meetings, much ahead of the meetings?
23. Is there sufficient meeting time given to the directors for meaningful discussion in addition to management monologue on important and strategic issues?
24. Do the independent directors meet among themselves at least twice a year or more without management/executive directors on a regular basis?
25. Are directors who are no longer pulling their weight discouraged from standing for re-election?

Appendix 3 Sample Diagnostic Questions for Analyzing Board of Directors

Balance membership

1. Is our board composed of ...
   (a) all inside directors?
   (b) one outside director for each inside director?
   (c) two outside directors for each inside director?
   (d) three or more outside directors?
2. Is our board composed of ...
   (a) directors who have experience only in our industry?
   (b) directors who have experience in our industry and related industries?
   (c) directors who have experience in our industry, related industries, and current affairs impacting the economy in general?
3. Is our board composed of ...
   (a) directors within five years of age of each other?
   (b) directors within ten years of age of each other?
   (c) directors within fifteen years of age of each other?

Setting of agenda for meetings

4. Is the agenda for our board....
   (a) set by the CEO/MD?
   (b) set by the CEO/MD with inputs from executive directors only?
   (c) set by the CEO/MD with inputs from all directors?
5. Are the agenda and reading materials for our board circulated ....
   (a) one week prior to our meeting?
   (b) two weeks prior to our meeting?
   (c) three weeks prior to our meeting?
6. Is the board meeting ...
   (a) so constructed that there is virtually no time for discussion?
   (b) structured so that there is time for brief to moderate discussion of each issue?

(c) structured so that there is time for meaningful and thorough discussion of the most important issues?

Policy on the election, re-election to board

7. Is the nomination of a new board member handled ...
   (a) only by the CEO/MD?
   (b) by the CEO/MD who seeks input from all directors?
   (c) by a nomination and remuneration committee with strong input from the CEO/MD?
   (d) by a nomination and remuneration committee with mere input from the CEO/MD?
8. How are board members replaced?
   (a) members serve as long as they desire.
   (b) members who do not attend meetings or otherwise do not participate are asked to resign or are replaced.
   (c) members are formally evaluated each year and replacements are sought as needed duly following the company law provisions.

Operation of board committees

9. How does the audit committee operate?
   (a) it is informed which firm will be the auditor.
   (b) it is involved in selecting the audit firm.
   (c) it recommends to the board which audit firm to use.
   (d) it recommends to the board which audit firm to use and approves the audit partner.
10. How does the audit committee establish an agenda?
   (a) it is informed by the internal auditor which areas to review on an annual basis.
   (b) it decides which areas it wishes to examine.
   (c) it decides which areas it wishes to examine and sets priorities for the study of high exposure areas on a systematic basis.
11. On what does the remuneration and nomination committee base its remuneration recommendations?
   (a) on input from the human resource department.
   (b) on historical trends and industry practices.
   (c) on pre-established standards and a formula-based reward system.

Scoring is done by assigning point values to each answer such as 0 point for (a), 1 point for (b), 2 points for (c), and 3 points for (d). Total scores are evaluated as follows:

0–6: Board is out of control of chairman. Serious problems exist with the board of directors. The board can be considered a liability to the company.

7–14: Board is losing control in its activities. Serious problems exist with the board of directors. But there are immense opportunities to transform the board into a major asset.

15–20: Board is partly in control of chairman. The board is generally doing a good job, but a few areas could be improved by way of taking corrective action.

21–25: The board is in full control of the chairman. The board is a major asset. It is operating effectively.

Appendix 4

List of SEBI Regulations, Guidelines and Schemes

SEBI Regulations

- SEBI (Stock Brokers and Sub Brokers) Regulations, 1992
- SEBI (Prohibition of Insider Trading) Regulations, 1992
- SEBI (Merchant Bankers) Regulations, 1992
- SEBI (Portfolio Managers) Regulations, 1993
- SEBI (Registrars to an Issue and Share Transfer Agents) Regulations, 1993
- SEBI (Underwriters) Regulations, 1993
- SEBI (Debenture Trustees) Regulations, 1993
- SEBI (Bankers to an Issue) Regulations, 1994
- SEBI (Foreign Institutional Investors) Regulations, 1995
- SEBI (Custodian of Securities) Regulations, 1996
- SEBI (Depositories and Participants) Regulations, 1996
- SEBI (Venture Capital Funds) Regulations, 1996
- SEBI (Mutual Funds) Regulations, 1996
- SEBI (Substantial Acquisition of Shares and Takeovers) Regulations, 1997
- SEBI (Buyback of Securities) Regulations, 1998
- SEBI (Credit Rating Agencies) Regulations, 1999
- SEBI (Collective Investment Schemes) Regulations, 1999
- SEBI (Foreign Venture Capital Investors) Regulations, 2000
- SEBI (Procedure for Board Meeting) Regulations, 2001
- SEBI (Issue of Sweat Equity) Regulations, 2002
- SEBI (Procedure for Holding Enquiry by Enquiry Officer and Imposing Penalty) Regulations, 2002
- SEBI (Prohibition of Fraudulent and Unfair Trade Practices relating to Securities Market) Regulations, 2003
- SEBI (Ombudsman) Regulations, 2003
- SEBI (Central Listing Authority) Regulations, 2003
- SEBI (Central Database for Market Participants) Regulations, 2003
- SEBI (Self Regulatory Organizations) Regulations, 2004

- SEBI (Criteria for Fit and Proper Person) Regulations, 2004
- SEBI (Regulatory Fee on Stock Exchanges) Regulations, 2007
- SEBI (Issue and Listing of Debt Securities) Regulations, 2008
- SEBI (Public Offer and Listing of Securitized Debt Instruments) Regulations, 2008
- SEBI (Intermediaries) Regulations, 2008
- SEBI (Delisting of Equity Shares) Regulations, 2009
- SEBI (Issue of Capital and Disclosure Requirements) Regulations, 2009
- SEBI (Investor Protection and Education Fund) Regulations, 2009
- SEBI (KYC Registration Agency) Regulations, 2011
- SEBI (Substantial Acquisition of Shares and Takeovers) Regulations, 2011
- SEBI (Alternative Investment Funds) Regulations, 2012
- SEBI (Stock Exchanges and Clearing Corporations) Regulations, 2012
- SEBI (Investment Advisers) Regulations, 2013
- SEBI (Issue and Listing of Non-convertible Redeemable Preference Shares) Regulations, 2013
- SEBI (Foreign Portfolio Investors) Regulations, 2014
- SEBI (Settlement of Administrative and Civil Proceedings) Regulations, 2014
- SEBI (Real Estate Investment Trusts) Regulations, 2014
- SEBI (Infrastructure Investment Trusts) Regulations, 2014
- SEBI (Prohibition of Insider Trading) Regulations, 2015
- SEBI (Listing Obligations and Disclosure Requirements) Regulations, 2015
- SEBI (Procedure for Search and Seizure Repeal) Regulations, 2015

SEBI Guidelines

- SEBI (Employee Stock Option Scheme and Employee Stock Purchase Scheme) Guidelines, 1999
- SEBI (Disclosure and Investor Protection) Guidelines, 2000
- SEBI (Delisting of Securities) Guidelines, 2003

SEBI Schemes

- Securities Lending Scheme, 1997
- SEBI (Informal Guidance) Scheme, 2003

Appendix 5 Corporate Governance Systems: The USA, The UK, Germany and Japan

Serial No.	Governance issues	Countries			
		USA	UK	Germany	Japan
A.	**Ownership system** **A.1: Cash flow rights**	• More than 50% of the equity shareholding with institutional investors, viz. pension funds, mutual funds, insurance funds, banks, trusts, etc. • About 30% of shareholdings with private shareholders including founders. • Liquid market for holdings and rights of trading of stocks in the market retained.	• 67% of the equity holdings with institutional shareholders including insurance companies, pension funds, unit trusts, etc. • About 20% of shareholdings with the private shareholders (10 million shareholders). • Retention of liquid market and right of trading of stocks freely in the market.	• 40% of the equity holdings of a large company with other large companies followed by institutional investors holding 11%, banks 10% and private shareholders 16%, government and others for the balance. • Smaller companies—family controlled. • Substantial cross holding amongst companies. • No role/limited role of individual investors. • Illiquid holdings. • Strong control by commercial banks via proxy voting (DSVR) on behalf of individual shareholders.	• Corporate cross shareholding (Keiretsu) by affiliated companies and major banks to counter hostile takeovers and spreading of corporate growth throughout the group. • 60%–80% of the shareholdings with institutional investors, e.g., insurance firms, trusts and pension funds and 20%–30% of the shareholdings with the private shareholders. • Shareholders unwilling to trade for short term gains.

Serial No.	Governance issues	Countries			
		USA	**UK**	**Germany**	**Japan**
	A.2: Control rights	• Management and control of operations of corporations delegated to professional managers.	• Management and control of operations delegated to professional managers under governance and supervision of the board.	• Management and control of operations delegated to management board (vorst- and) under governance and supervision of supervisory board (Aufsic-htsrat).	• Control rights by the President and the operating committee or top management committee although decision-making as per "bottom up consensus method".
B.	**Governance rules**	• Single tier majority outside directors' board • One share one vote rule. • Board members including CEO appointed by shareholders. • Audit committee with independent directors setup compulsory as a precondition for listing. • Companies to ensure at least 50% outstanding shares voting at AGM. • Proxy solicitation and proxy voting by mail. • Proportional representation of minorities on boards of directors. • Mechanisms to legally safeguard interest of minority investors. • Pre-emptive rights to the issue of new shares in order to retain proportional holdings.	• Legal framework for corporate governance in the Companies Act extremely sketchy. • Single-tier majority inside directors' board with non-executive chairman. • Board members appointed by shareholders. • Audit committee of at least 3 non-executive directors compulsory as listing requirement. • No requirement of quorum in AGM. • Proxy solicitation not required.	• Two-tier board system: (a) Supervisory board (Aufsichtsrat) discharging all supervisory functions, with equal shareholders' as well as employees/union representatives; and (b) Management board (vorstand) with senior executives discharging functions of direction and management. • Effectiveness of vorstrand functioning monitored by Aufsichtsrat. • Considerable autonomy to management allowed. • Strong protection to creditors' rights. • Auditors' philosophy of "Principle of commercial prudence" rather than "true and fair view" authorized by German law resulting huge accumulation of secret reserves in companies.	• Powerful government interventions by Japanese Ministry of Finance and its strong regulatory control and supervision in every aspect of industrial activity including capital flows. • Protection of both shareholders' rights and creditors' rights. • Single-tier majority of all inside directors' board with employee directors. • Statutory auditors (Kausayaku) appointed by shareholders. • Appointment of 3-member audit committee.

Serial No.	Governance issues	Countries			
		USA	UK	Germany	Japan
C.	**Role of governance**	• Governance system on "market logic". • Dynamism, entrepreneurial drive and accountability largely free and adequate. • Active shareholders' monitoring in the governance process. • Protection of minority shareholders' interests from expropriation by managers. • Proxy voting system most important in the governance process.	• Large influence of institutional shareholders on management of the shareholding companies. • Proxy solicitation and proxy voting not developed. • No employee representation in the board like Germany.	• High standard of performance and higher degree of effectiveness by combination of internal networks and formal structure of governance. • Decisions on all issues including long term issues reached by 'discussion' rather than 'imposition' through a hierarchical structure. • Successful and effective entrepreneurial drive, accountability, well-motivated and trained workforce, technical competence, etc. in vogue. • Strong presence of total voting powers (70%) in general meetings due to the bearer share system. • Overwhelming domination, large influence and control of commercial banks over the German companies due to large proportion of shareholders on behalf of private shareholders (DSVR) along with their own holdings.	• High standard of performance and higher degree of effectiveness by combination of internal networks and formal structure of governance. • Close links and amicable relationship between corporates and government sectors. • Focus on corporate priorities on 'growth' and 'market share', not 'profit' or 'shareholders' returns' except through capital appreciation. • Interlinked concepts of corporate governance: obligation, family and consensus based on community logic. • Insignificant influence of institutional shareholders on management of the company but interested in its overall growth. • Protection of interests of multiple stakeholders primarily holding companies and lenders.

Serial No.	Governance issues	Countries			
		USA	UK	Germany	Japan
				• Strong personal relationship banking with corporates adopted. • Protection of interests of multiple stakeholders primarily lenders and employees.	• As the largest shareholders of the customer companies the banks interested to strengthen their relationship with customers, and hence, no interference from banks.
D.	**Market for corporate control**	• Very strong capital markets and US stock exchange for raising capital. • Role of banks in corporate governance not important. • Management takeover including hostile takeover common.	• Active and strong capital markets and London stock market for raising capital [Market Capitalisation 86% of GDP(1987)]. • UK banks generally not interested to take equity stakes. So their role in corporate governance insignificant. • Mergers and takeover quite strong and very active.	• No market control for corporates by stock exchange and capital markets. • Direct holding of shares by individuals discouraged due to imposition of tax on dividends and exemption of tax on interests. • Increased mergers and acquisitions due to German reunification.	• No market control for corporates. • Friendly mergers and acquisitions not uncommon but minimal hostile take-over activity. • Active stock market but not playing much part in allocation of resources.
E.	**Governance reform**	• Better use of people like Japanese corporations. • More accountability of executives and directors. • More transparency and accuracy of information and disclosures.	• Institutional investors to take a positive interest in the composition of board. • More accountability of company executives and directors.	• Banks reconsidering stakes in companies. • Regulatory measures on: (a) Accounting standards, (b) Insider trading, (c) Restrictive voting structures, (d) Takeover legislation,	• Shift in the public attitudes towards the political, economic and corporate governance system. • Pressure on corporate political links.

Serial No.	Governance issues	Countries			
		USA	UK	Germany	Japan
		• More effective and active monitoring of large shareholders. • More effective monitoring by board of directors.	• Better service to small and minority shareholders through intermediary like banks to cast votes on their behalf as practiced in Germany. • Much stronger link in the chain of corporate governance system between board and its shareholders.	(e) Abolition of shares with enhanced voting rights, (f) More accountability of supervisory boards, (g) Improved standards of financial disclosures.	• Several amendments to the Japanese commercial code involving: (a) Reforms on shareholders' rights, (b) Shareholders law suits, (c) Shareholders' access to the companies' books of accounts, (d) Independent auditors and revamping of audit system, (e) Corporate independence from main bank financing, etc. • Structural changes and changing social attitude and responsibility.

Appendix 6

Impact of International Committees' Recommendations on National Committees' Recommendations and Enactments in India on Corporate Governance

Serial No.	Governance issues recommended	International committees and enactments	National committees	Enactments in India
1.	Composition, strength and size of the board	Cadbury (1992), Hampel (1998), LSE Combined Code (1998), OECD (1999)	CII (1998), KMB (2000), NCC (2002), JJI (2005)	Clause 49 of the Listing Agreement (2000)
2.	Non-executive (Independent) director and related matters	Cadbury (1992), Hampel (1998), LSE Combined Code (1998), OECD (1999)	KMB (2000), NCC (2002), NMC (2003), JJI (2005)	Clause 49 (2000)—Revised Clause 49 (2004)
3.	Orientation and training of directors	Cadbury (1992), Hampel (1998), LSE Combined Code (1998)	NCC (2002), NMC (2003), JJI (2005)	Revised Clause 49 (2004)
4.	Remuneration of directors	Greenbury (1995), Hampel (1998), LSE Combined Code (1998)	KMB (2000), NCC (2002), NMC (2003), JJI (2005)	Clause 49 (2000)—Revised Clause 49 (2004)
5.	Disclosure of remuneration policy, directors' remuneration and biographical information	Cadbury (1992), Greenbury (1995), Hampel (1998), LSE Combined Code (1998), OECD (1999)	KMB (2000), NMC (2003), JJI (2005)	Clause 49 (2000)
6.	Board meetings and matters to be reserved for board decision	Cadbury (1992), LSE Combined Code (1998)	CII (1998), KMB (2000), NCC (2002), JJI (2005)	Clause 49 (2000)
7.	Board's performance evaluation	LSE Combined Code (1998)	NMC (2003)	Revised Clause 49 (2004)

Serial No.	Governance issues recommended	International committees and enactments	National committees	Enactments in India
8.	Audit committee and related matters	Cadbury (1992), Hampel (1998), LSE Combined Code (1998), Blue Ribbon (1999)	CII (1998), KMB (2000), NCC (2002), NMC (2003), JJI (2005)	Clause 49 (2000)—Revised Clause 49 (2004), Companies (Amendment) Act 2000, Section 292 A
9.	Remuneration committee and related matters	Cadbury (1992), Greenbury (1995), Hampel (1998), LSE Combined Code (1998)	KMB (2000), JJI (2005)	Clause 49 (2000)
10.	General body meetings	Cadbury (1992), Hampel (1998), LSE Combined Code (1998), OECD (1999)	KMB (2000), JJI (2005)	Clause 49 (2000)
11.	Auditors	Cadbury (1992), Hampel (1998), OECD (1999)	NCC (2002), JJI (2005)	Companies (Amendment) Act 2000, Section 227
12.	Accounting standards	Cadbury (1992), OECD (1999)	KMB (2000), NMC (2003)	Clause 49 (2000), Companies (Amendment) Act 2000, Section 217(2AA)
13.	Financial reporting	Cadbury (1992), Hampel (1998), LSE Combined Code (1998), OECD (1999)	CII (1998), KMB (2000), NCC (2002), NMC (2003)	Clause 49 (2000)
14.	CEO/CFO certification	Sarbanes Oxley Act (SOX) of USA, (2002)	NCC (2002), NMC (2003)	Revised Clause 49 (2004)
15.	Code of conduct	Sarbanes Oxley Act (SOX) of USA, (2002)	NCC (2002), NMC (2003), JJI (2005)	Revised Clause 49 (2004)
16.	Internal code of ethics including protection to whistle blowers	Sarbanes Oxley Act (SOX) of USA, (2002)	NMC (2003), JJI (2005)	Revised Clause 49 (2004)
17.	Disclosure and transparency	Cadbury (1992), Greenbury (1995), Hampel (1998), LSE Combined Code (1998), OECD (1999)	CII (1998), KMB (2000), NCC (2002), NMC (2003), JJI (2005)	Clause 49 (2000)—Revised Clause 49 (2004)

Note: CII represents Confederation of Indian Industry
KMB represents Kumar Mangalam Birla Committee
NCC represents Naresh Chandra Committee
NMC represents Narayana Murthy Committee
JJI represents J.J. Irani Committee

Appendix 7 Board Structure of Selected Companies in 2015–2016 Industry-wise (Listed under BSE Sensex and NSE Nifty)

Name of companies	Total no. of directors	Number of executive directors		Number of non-executive directors			
		Promoter	Other	Promoter	Independent	Nominee	Other
AUTOMOBILE							
Bajaj Auto Ltd.	15	3 (c)	NIL	3	8	NIL	1
Eicher Motors Ltd.	6	1	NIL	NIL	5 (c)	NIL	NIL
Tata Motors Ltd.	11	NIL	3	NIL	6	NIL	2 (c)
Total	**32**	**4**	**3**	**3**	**19**	**NIL**	**3**
(a) Total no. and % of EDs and NEDs (b) Total no. and % of IDs		**7 (22%)**		**25 (78%) 19 (59%)**			
BANKING							
HDFC Bank Ltd.	11	NIL	3	NIL	5 (c)	NIL	3
ICICI Bank Ltd.	13	NIL	5	NIL	7 (c)	1	NIL
State Bank of India (PSB)	14	NIL	5 (c)	NIL	4	5	NIL
Bank of Baroda (PSB)	10	NIL	3	NIL	3	3	1 (c)
Yes Bank Ltd.	11	1	NIL	NIL	6	NIL	4 (c)
Axis Bank Ltd.	13	NIL	2	NIL	8	3 (c)	NIL
Total	**72**	**1**	**18**	**NIL**	**33**	**12**	**8**
Total no. and % of EDs and NEDs Total no. and % of IDs		**19 (26%)**		**53 (74%) 33 (46%)**			
CEMENT							
ACC Ltd.	12	NIL	1	NIL	7 (c)	NIL	4
Ambuja Cements Ltd.	12	NIL	1	3	5	1	2(c)
Total	**24**	**NIL**	**2**	**3**	**12**	**1**	**6**
Total no. and % of EDs and NEDs Total no. and % of IDs		**2 (8%)**		**22 (92%) 12 (50%)**			

Name of companies	Total no. of directors	Number of executive directors		Number of non-executive directors			
		Promoter	Other	Promoter	Independent	Nominee	Other
CONSUMER PRODUCTS AND FMCG							
Asian Paints Ltd.	14	NIL	1	6 (c)	7	NIL	NIL
Hindustan Unilever Ltd.	9	NIL	3	NIL	5	NIL	1 (c)
Total	**23**	**NIL**	**4**	**6**	**12**	**NIL**	**1**
Total no. and % of EDs and NEDs **Total no. and % of IDs**		**4 (17%)**		**19 (83%)** **12 (52%)**			
DIVERSIFIED							
ITC Ltd.	15	NIL	4 (c)	NIL	7	3	1
Total	**15**	**NIL**	**4**	**NIL**	**7**	**3**	**1**
Total no. and % of EDs and NEDs **Total no. and % of IDs**		**4 (27%)**		**11 (73%)** **7 (47%)**			
ENGINEERING							
Bosch Ltd.	8	NIL	2	NIL	4	NIL	2 (c)
Total	**8**	**NIL**	**2**	**NIL**	**4**	**NIL**	**2**
Total no. and % of EDs and NEDs **Total no. and % of IDs**		**2 (25%)**		**6 (75%)** **4 (50%)**			
ENTERTAINMENT							
Zee Ent. Ltd.	8	NIL	1	3 (c)	4	NIL	NIL
Total	**8**	**NIL**	**1**	**3**	**4**	**NIL**	**NIL**
Total no. and % of EDs and NEDs **Total no. and % of IDs**		**1 (12%)**		**7 (88%)** **4 (50%)**			
FINANCE							
HDFC Ltd.	11	NIL	3	NIL	6	1	1 (c)
Total	**11**	**NIL**	**3**	**NIL**	**6**	**1**	**1**
Total no. and % of EDs and NEDs **Total no. and % of IDs**		**3 (27%)**		**8 (73%)** **6 (55%)**			
INFORMATION TECHNOLOGY							
Infosys Tech. Ltd.	9	NIL	2	NIL	7 (c)	NIL	NIL
Tata Consultancy Services Ltd.	11	NIL	2	NIL	6	NIL	3 (c)
Total	**20**	**NIL**	**4**	**NIL**	**13**	**NIL**	**3**
Total no. and % of EDs and NEDs **Total no. and % of IDs**		**4 (20%)**		**16 (80%)** **13 (65%)**			
IRON AND STEEL							
Tata Steel Ltd.	11	NIL	2	NIL	6	NIL	3 (c)
Total	**11**	**NIL**	**2**	**NIL**	**6**	**NIL**	**3**
Total no. and % of EDs and NEDs **Total no. and % of IDs**		**2 (18%)**		**9 (82%)** **6 (55%)**			

Name of companies	Total no. of directors	Number of executive directors		Number of non-executive directors			
		Promoter	Other	Promoter	Independent	Nominee	Other
MINING AND METAL							
Hindalco Industries Ltd.	10	NIL	2	2 (c)	5	NIL	1
Total	**10**	**NIL**	**2**	**2**	**5**	**NIL**	**1**
Total no. and % of EDs and NEDs **Total no. and % of IDs**		**2 (20%)**		**8 (80%)** **5 (50%)**			
PHARMACEUTICALS							
Lupin Ltd.	12	4 (c)	2	NIL	6	NIL	NIL
Dr. Reddy's Laboratories Ltd.	9	2 (c)	NIL	NIL	7	NIL	NIL
Sun Pharma Industries Ltd.	9	1	2	NIL	5	NIL	1 (c)
Aurobindo Pharma Ltd.	10	1	3	2	4	NIL	NIL
Total	**40**	**8**	**7**	**2**	**22**	**NIL**	**1**
Total no. and % of EDs and NEDs **Total no. and % of IDs**		**15 (37%)**		**25 (63%)** **22 (55%)**			
PETROLEUM AND NATURAL GAS							
ONGC Ltd. (PSU)	11	NIL	6 (c)	NIL	3	2	NIL
Total	**11**	**NIL**	**6**	**NIL**	**3**	**2**	**NIL**
Total no. and % of EDs and NEDs **Total no. and % of IDs**		**6 (55%)**		**5 (45%)** **3 (27%)**			
POWER GENERATION AND DISTRIBUTION							
Power Grid Corpn. Ltd. (PSU)	7	NIL	4 (c)	NIL	1	2	NIL
Tata Power Ltd.	9	NIL	2	NIL	5	1	1 (c)
NTPC Ltd. (PSU)	11	NIL	6 (c)	NIL	3	2	NIL
Total	**27**	**NIL**	**12**	**NIL**	**9**	**5**	**1**
Total no. and % of EDs and NEDs **Total no. and % of IDs**		**12 (44%)**		**15 (56%)** **9 (33%)**			
TEXTILE, SYNTHETICS AND CONGLOMERATE							
Reliance Ind. Ltd.	14	1 (c)	4	1	8	NIL	NIL
Total	**14**	**1**	**4**	**1**	**8**	**NIL**	**NIL**
Total no. and % of EDs and NEDs **Total no. and % of IDs**		**5 (36%)**		**9 (64%)** **8 (57%)**			
TELECOMMUNICATION							
Idea Cellular Ltd.	11	NIL	1	2 (c)	6	NIL	2
Total	**11**	**NIL**	**1**	**2**	**6**	**NIL**	**2**
Total no. and % of EDs and NEDs **Total no. and % of IDs**		**1 (9%)**		**10 (91%)** **6 (55%)**			

Name of companies	Total no. of directors	Number of executive directors		Number of non-executive directors			
		Promoter	Other	Promoter	Independent	Nominee	Other
PORTS AND SEZ							
Adani Ports and SEZ Ltd.	8	1 (c)	1	1	4	1	NIL
Total	**8**	**1**	**1**	**1**	**4**	**1**	**NIL**
Total no. and % of EDs and NEDs		**2 (25%)**		**6 (75%)**			
Total no. and % of IDs				**4 (50%)**			

Source: Annual Reports of Companies, 2015–2016. Results computed.

Note: (c) denotes Chairman/Chairman and Managing Director in the same category.

Appendix 8

Board Strength of Executive Directors, Non-Executive Directors and Independent Directors of Selected Listed Companies in 2015–2016

Serial No.	Name of companies	Executive Directors (EDs)		Non-Executive Directors (NEDs)		Independent Directors (IDs)	
		Nos.	(%)	Nos.	(%)	Nos.	(%)
A.	**15-member board**						
1.	Bajaj Auto Ltd.	3	20	12	80	8	53
2.	ITC Ltd.	4	27	11	73	7	47
B.	**14-member board**						
1.	State Bank of India (PSB)	5	36	9	64	4	29
2.	Asian Paints Ltd.	1	7	13	93	7	50
3.	Reliance Industries Ltd.	5	36	9	64	8	57
C.	**13-member board**						
1.	ICICI Bank Ltd.	5	38	8	62	7	54
2.	Axis Bank Ltd.	2	15	11	85	8	62
D.	**12-member board**						
1.	ACC Ltd.	1	8	11	92	7	58
2.	Ambuja Cements Ltd.	1	8	11	92	5	42
3.	Lupin Ltd.	6	50	6	50	6	50
E.	**11-member board**						
1.	Tata Motors Ltd.	3	27	8	73	6	55
2.	HDFC Bank Ltd.	3	27	8	73	5	45
3.	Yes Bank Ltd.	1	9	10	91	6	55
4.	HDFC Ltd.	3	27	8	73	6	55
5.	Tata Consultancy Services Ltd.	2	18	9	82	6	55
6.	Tata Steel Ltd.	2	18	9	82	6	55

Serial No.	Name of companies	Executive Directors (EDs)		Non-Executive Directors (NEDs)		Independent Directors (IDs)	
		Nos.	(%)	Nos.	(%)	Nos.	(%)
7.	ONGC Ltd. (PSU)	6	55	5	45	3	27
8.	NTPC Ltd. (PSU)	6	55	5	45	3	27
9.	Idea Cellular Ltd.	1	9	10	91	6	55
F.	**10-member board**						
1.	Bank of Baroda (PSB)	3	30	7	70	3	30
2.	Hindalco Industries Ltd.	2	20	8	80	5	50
3.	Aurobindo Pharma Ltd.	4	40	6	60	4	40
G.	**9 member board**						
1.	Hindustan Unilever Ltd.	3	33	6	67	5	56
2.	Infosys Technologies Ltd.	2	22	7	78	7	78
3.	Dr. Reddy's Laboratories Ltd.	2	22	7	78	7	78
4.	Sun Pharmaceuticals Ltd.	3	33	6	67	5	56
5.	Tata Power Company Ltd.	2	22	7	78	5	56
H.	**8-member board**						
1.	Bosch Ltd.	2	25	6	75	4	50
2.	Zee Entertainment Enterprises Ltd.	1	13	7	87	4	50
3.	Adani Ports & SEZ Ltd.	2	25	6	75	4	50
I.	**7-member board**						
1.	Power Grid Corporation Ltd. (PSU)	4	57	3	43	1	14
J.	**6-member board**						
1.	Eicher Motors Ltd.	1	17	5	83	5	83
	Total = 345 (100%)	**91**	**(26%)**	**254**	**(74%)**	**173**	**(50%)**

Source: Annual Reports of Companies, 2015–2016. Results computed.

Note: % has been calculated on the respective total number of directors in the board.

Appendix 9

Women Directors in Selected Companies in 2015–2016 (Listed under BSE Sensex and NSE Nifty)

S. No.	Name of companies	Total no. of directors	Total no. of executive directors	Total no. of non-executive directors	Total no. of women directors	Status of women directors
1.	Bajaj Auto Ltd.	15	3 (c)	12	1 (7%)	Independent director
2.	Eicher Motors Ltd.	6	1	5	1 (17%)	Independent director
3.	Tata Motors Ltd.	11	3	8	1 (9%)	Independent director
4.	HDFC Bank Ltd.	11	3	8	2 (18%)	Independent director: 1 Non-executive director: 1
5.	ICICI Bank Ltd.	13	5	8	2 (15%)	Executive directors
6.	State Bank of India (PSB)	14	5	9	2 (14%)	Executive director and chairman: 1 Nominee director: 1
7.	Bank of Baroda (PSB)	10	3	7	2 (20%)	Nominated director: 1 Independent director: 1
8.	Yes Bank Ltd.	11	1	10	1 (9%)	Non-executive director and chairman
9.	Axis Bank Ltd.	13	2	11	3 (23%)	Executive director:1 Independent director: 1 Nominated director: 1
10.	ACC Ltd.	12	1	11	1 (8%)	Independent director
11.	Ambuja Cements Ltd.	12	1	11	1 (8%)	Nominated director
12.	Asian Paints Ltd.	14	1	13	2 (14%)	Independent director: 1 Non-executive director: 1
13.	Hindustan Unilever Ltd.	9	3	6	1 (11%)	Independent director
14.	ITC Ltd.	15	4	11	1 (7%)	Independent director
15.	Bosch Ltd.	8	2	6	1 (12%)	Independent director
16.	Zee Entertainment Ltd.	8	1	7	1 (12%)	Independent director

S. No.	Name of companies	Total no. of directors	Total no. of executive directors	Total no. of non-executive directors	Total no. of women directors	Status of women directors
17.	HDFC Ltd.	11	3	8	1 (9%)	Executive director
18.	Infosys Technologies Ltd.	9	2	7	3 (33%)	Independent directors
19.	Tata Consultancy Services	11	2	9	1 (9%)	Executive director
20.	Tata Steel Ltd.	11	2	9	1 (9%)	Independent director
21.	Dr. Reddy's Lab. Ltd.	9	2	7	1 (11%)	Independent director
22.	Lupin Pharma Ltd.	12	6	6	2 (17%)	Prom. executive directors
23.	Sun Pharma Ltd.	9	3	6	1 (11%)	Independent director
24.	ONGC Ltd.	11	6	5	Nil (0%)	Nil
25.	Power Grid Corpn. Ltd.	7	4	3	1 (14%)	Nominee director
26.	Tata Power Company Ltd.	9	2	7	Nil (0%)	Nil
27.	NTPC Ltd.	11	6	5	1 (9%)	Independent director
28.	Adani Ports & SEZ Ltd.	8	2	6	1 (12%)	Independent director
29.	Reliance Industries Ltd.	14	5	9	1 (7%)	Prom. non-executive director
30.	Idea Cellular Ltd.	11	1	10	3 (27%)	Prom. non-executive director: 1 Independent directors: 2
31.	Hindalco Industries Ltd.	10	2	8	1 (10%)	Prom. non-executive director
32.	Aurobindo Pharma Ltd.	10	4	6	1 (10%)	Independent director
	Total (%)	**345 (100)**	**91 (26%)**	**254 (74%)**	**42 (12%)**	

Source: Annual Reports of Companies, 2015–2016. Results computed.

Note: (%) of women directors shown has been calculated on the total board strength of the respective companies.

Appendix 10 Format of Business Responsibility Report (BRR)

Section A: General Information about the Company

1. Corporate Identity Number (CIN):
2. Name of the company:
3. Address of the registered office:
4. Website:
5. E-mail id:
6. Financial year reported:
7. Sector(s) that the company is engaged in (industrial activity code-wise):
8. List three products/services that the company manufactures/provides (as in balance sheet):
   (i) Locations where business activities are undertaken by the company:
   (ii) Number of international locations
9. Number of national locations
10. Markets served by the company:

Section B: Financial Details of the Company

1. Paid-up capital:
2. Total turnover:
3. Total profit after taxes:
4. Total spending on Corporate Social Responsibility (CSR): As percentage of profit after tax:
5. List of CSR activities in which expenditure has been incurred:

Section C: Other Details

1. Does the company have any subsidiary company/companies?
2. Does the subsidiary company/companies participate in the BR initiatives of the parent company? If yes, then indicate the number of such subsidiary company(s):
3. Do any other entity/entities (e.g. suppliers, distributors, etc.) that the company does business with participate in the BR initiatives of the company?

If yes, then indicate the percentage of such entity/entities?
[Less than 30%, 30–60%, more than 60%]

Section D: BR Information

1. Details of the director/directors responsible for implementation of the BR policy/policies

   Director Identification Number (DIN):
   Name:
   Designation:
   Telephone number:
   E-mail id:

2. Principle-wise (as per NVGs) BR policy/policies (Reply in Y/N)

   The national voluntary guidelines (NVGs) on social, environmental and economic responsibilities of business released by the Ministry of Corporate Affairs has adopted nine areas of business responsibility. These are briefly as under:

   P 1: Businesses should conduct and govern themselves with ethics, transparency and accountability.

   P 2: Businesses should provide goods and services that are safe and contribute to sustainability throughout their life cycle.

   P 3: Businesses should promote the well-being of all employees.

   P 4: Businesses should respect the interests of, and be responsive towards all stakeholders, especially those who are disadvantaged, vulnerable and marginalized.

   P 5: Businesses should respect and promote human rights.

   P 6: Businesses should respect, protect and make efforts to restore the environment.

   P 7: Businesses, when engaged in influencing public and regulatory policy, should do so in a responsible manner.

   P 8: Businesses should support inclusive growth and equitable development.

   P 9: Businesses should engage with and provide value to their customers and consumers in a responsible manner.

S. No.	Questions	Business ethics	Product responsibility	Well-being of employees	Stakeholder engagement	Human rights	Environment	Public policy	CSR	Customer relation
		P 1	P 2	P 3	P 4	P 5	P 6	P 7	P 8	P 9
1.	Do you have a policy/ policies for.....									

S. No.	Questions	Business ethics	Product responsibility	Wellbeing of employees	Stakeholder engagement	Human rights	Environment	Public policy	CSR	Customer relation
		P 1	P 2	P 3	P 4	P 5	P 6	P 7	P 8	P 9
2.	Has the policy being formulated in consultation with the relevant stakeholders?									
3.	Does the policy conform to any national/international standards? If yes, specify?									
4.	Has the policy been approved by the board? If yes, has it been signed by MD/owner/CEO/appropriate board director?									
5.	Does the company have a specified committee of the board/director/official to oversee the implementation of the policy?									
6.	Indicate the link for the policy to be viewed on-line.									
7.	Has the policy been formally communicated to all relevant internal and external stakeholders?									
8.	Does the company have in-house structure to implement the policy/policies?									
9.	Does the company have a grievance redressal mechanism related to the policy/policies to address stakeholders' grievance related to the policy/policies?									
10.	Has the company carried out independent audit/evaluation of the working of this policy by an internal or external agency?									

2.(a) If answer to Serial No. against any of the Principle is 'No', please explain why: (Tick upto 2 options)

S. No.	Questions	Business ethics	Product responsibility	Wellbeing of employees	Stakeholder engagement	Human rights	Environment	Public policy	CSR	Customer relation
		P 1	P 2	P 3	P 4	P 5	P 6	P 7	P 8	P 9
1.	The company has not understood the principle.									
2.	The company is not at a stage where it finds itself in a position to formulate and implement the policies on specified principles.									
3.	The company does not have financial or manpower resources available for the task.									
4.	It is planned to be done within next 6 months.									
5.	It is planned to be done within next 1 year.									
6.	Any other reason (please specify)									

3. Governance related to BR
   - Indicate the frequency with which the board of directors, committee of the board or CEO to assess the BR performance of the company: within 3 months, 3–6 months, annually, more than 1 year.
   - Does the company publish a BR or a sustainability report? What is the hyperlink for viewing this report?

Section E: Principle-wise Performance

Principle 1: Business should conduct and govern itself with ethics, transparency and accountability

1. Does the policy relating to ethics, bribery and corruption cover only the company? Yes or No.

   Does it extend to the group/joint ventures/suppliers/contractors/NGOs/others?
2. How many stakeholder complaints have been received in the past financial year and what percentage was satisfactorily resolved by the management? If so, provide details thereof in about 50 words or so.

Principle 2: Business should provide goods and services that are safe and contribute to sustainability throughout their life cycle

1. List upto 3 of your products or services whose design has incorporated social or environmental concerns, risks and/or opportunities.
2. For each such product, provide the details in respect of resource use (energy, water, raw materials etc.) per unit of product (optional).
3. Does the company have procedures in place for sustainable sourcing (including transportation)? If yes, what percentage of your inputs was sourced sustainably? Also, provide details thereof in about 50 words or so.
4. Has the company taken any steps to procure goods and services from local and small producers, including communities surrounding their place of work? If yes, what steps have been taken to improve their capacity and capability of local and small vendors?
5. Does the company have a mechanism to recycle products and waste? If yes, what is the percentage of recycling of products and waste (separately as < 5%, 5–10%, > 10%). Also, provide details thereof in about 50 words or so.

Principle 3: Business should promote the well-being of all employees.

1. Please indicate the total number of employees (category-wise).
2. Please indicate the total number of employees hired on temporary/contractual/ casual basis.
3. Please indicate the number of permanent women employees.
4. Please indicate the number of permanent employees with disabilities.
5. Do you have an employee association that is recognized by management?
6. What percentage of your permanent employees are members of this recognized employee association?
7. Please indicate the number of complaints relating to child labour, forced labour, involuntary labour, sexual harassment in the last financial year and pending, as on the end of the financial year.
8. What percentages of your under-mentioned employees were given safety and skill upgradation training in the last year?
   A. Permanent employees
   B. Permanent women employees
   C. Casual/temporary/contractual employees
   D. Employees with disabilities

Principle 4: Business should respect the interests of, and be responsive towards all stakeholders, especially those who are disadvantaged, vulnerable and marginalized.

1. Has the company mapped its internal and external stakeholders? Yes/No.
2. Out of the above, has the company identified the disadvantaged, vulnerable and marginalized stakeholders?
3. Are there any special initiatives taken by the company to engage with the disadvantaged, vulnerable and marginalized stakeholders? If so, provide details thereof, in about 50 words or so.

Principle 5: Businesses should respect and promote human rights.

1. Does the policy of the company on human rights cover only the company or extend to the Group/Joint Ventures/Suppliers/Contractors/NGOs/Others?
2. How many stakeholder complaints have been received in the past financial year and what percent was satisfactorily resolved by the management?

Principle 6: Businesses should respect, protect and make efforts to restore the environment.

1. Does the policy related to Principle 6 cover only the company or extend to the group/joint ventures/suppliers/contractors/NGOs/others?
2. Does the company have strategies/initiatives to address global environmental issues such as climate change, global warming, etc.? Yes/No. If yes, please give hyperlink for web page, etc.
3. Does the company identify and assess potential environmental risks? Yes/No.
4. Does the company have any project related to clean development mechanism? If so, provide details thereof in about 50 words or so. Also, if yes, whether any environmental compliance report is filed?
5. Has the company undertaken any other initiatives on clean technology, energy efficiency, renewable energy, etc.? Yes/No. If yes, please give hyperlink for web page, etc.
6. Are the emissions/waste generated by the company within the permissible limits given by CPCB/SPCB for the financial year being reported?
7. Number of show cause/legal notices received from CPCB/SPCB which are pending (i.e., not resolved to satisfaction) as on end of the financial year.

Principle 7: Businesses, when engaged in influencing public and regulatory policy, should do so in a responsible manner.

1. Is your company a member of any trade and chamber or associations? If yes, name only those major ones that your business deals with.
2. Have you advocated/lobbied through above associations for the advancement or improvement of public good? Yes/No. If yes, specify the broad areas (drop box: Governance and administration, economic reforms, inclusive development policies, energy security, water, food security, sustainable business principles, others).

Principle 8: Businesses should support inclusive growth and equitable development.

1. Does the company have specified programmes/initiatives/projects in pursuit of the policy related to Principle 8? If yes, give details thereof.
2. Are the programmes/projects undertaken through in-house team/own foundation/ external NGO/government structures/any other organization?
3. Have you done any impact assessment of your initiative?
4. What is your company's direct contribution to community development projects and the details of the projects undertaken?
5. Have you taken steps to ensure that this community development initiative is successfully adopted by the community?

Principle 9: Businesses should engage with and provide value to their customers and consumers in a responsible manner.

1. What percentage of customer complaints/consumer cases are pending as on the end of the financial year?
2. Does the company display product information on the product label, over and above what is mandated as per local laws? Yes/No/N.A./Remarks (additional information).
3. Is there any case filed by any stakeholder against the company regarding unfair trade practices, irresponsible advertising, and/or anti-competitive behaviour during the last five years and pending as on the end of the financial year? If so, provide details thereof in about 50 words or so.
4. Did your company carry out any consumer survey/consumer satisfaction trends?

Source: SEBI (Listing Obligations and Disclosure Requirements) Regulations, 2015.

Glossary

Advisory Group (RBI) on Corporate Governance: An Advisory Group on corporate governance was constituted by a Standing Committee of Reserve Bank of India in 2000 for evolving sound standards of corporate governance based on recognised best practices and for adopting transparency while adhering to the codes.

Agency Theory: Agency Theory is the theory which advocates checks and balance mechanism on corporate directors as they cannot be trusted to act in the public welfare in general and in the interest of shareholders in particular. The directors need to be monitored and controlled to ensure compliance.

All-Executive Board: All-Executive Board is the board which consists of all directors holding management positions in the company. In the all-executive board there is really no separation between ownership and management as the management is dominated by the owners/promoters of the company (example, Japanese board).

Anglo-American System (1992 and Onwards): Anglo-American System is the system introduced by the Government of India in 1992 after adoption of economic liberalisation and opening up of the economy since 1991 as the replacement of the Promoter System. This system strongly relies on capital markets as a disciplinary tool and a single-tier board structure in which representation is limited to directors elected by the shareholders.

Arm's Length Transaction: Arm's Length Transaction, as per Section 188 of the Companies Act, 2013, means a transaction between two related parties that is conducted as if they were unrelated so that there is no conflict of interest.

Audit Committee: An Audit Committee is one of the most important board committees that is formally set up by the board, usually consisting of independent board members and reporting to the board. It acts as a link between the board and the outside auditors. The major roles of the audit committee are to discuss the scope of the audit, explore matter that the auditors raise about management systems and controls, resolve any disagreement in the matter of form and content of the published financial accounts, recommend audit fees and/or reappointment or change of auditors etc.

Audit committee is mandated for the corporates under Section 177 of the Companies Act, 2013 as also Regulation 18 read with Schedule II, Part C of SEBI (LODR) Regulations, 2015.

Board of Directors or Board: As per Section 2 (10) of the Companies Act 2013, Board of Directors or Board in relation to a company means the collective body of the directors of the company.

Board Review: Board Review involves a comprehensive look at the board and its activities, the aim of which is to explore board processes, structure and style in the light of corporate needs, to highlight potential problems for the future and to provide the basis for measuring effectiveness.

Board Structure: Board Structure is a foundation for an effective board, focusing on the background interests, affiliations and positions of board members. It is concerned with the balances of power and is at the heart of board's performance and accountability.

Board Style: Board Style is the way in which the members of the board work together, both inside and outside the boardroom. Generally four types of board style are observed viz. (i) Country club board, (ii) Rubber stamp board, (iii) Representative board, and (iv) Professional board.

Board's Performance Evaluation: Board's Performance Evaluation is considered as an integral part of the overall board's planning process which should be flexible, dynamic and non-confrontational. It includes the act of setting goals and standards of performance which should be measurable and achievable and should allow regular evaluation of these criteria for each director and the board as a whole.

BSE Sensex: BSE Sensex means Bombay Stock Exchange Sensitive Index.

Business Responsibility Report: The SEBI vide its Regulation 34 (2) of the SEBI (LODR) Regulations, 2015 mandates inclusion of the Business Responsibility Report as part of the annual report for top 100 listed corporate houses based on the market capitalisation in order to exhibit how the companies discharge their total responsibilities towards sustainable development of the companies.

Chairman: Chairman is the leader of the board of directors who is appointed by the board members from among them. The contribution of the chairman ultimately determines the effectiveness of the board.

CII Code: For the first time in the history of corporate governance in India the Confederation of Indian Industry framed in the year 1998, a voluntary code of corporate governance for the listed companies known as CII Code of desirable corporate governance.

Code for Independent Directors: The Code for Independent Directors is a guide to professional conduct for independent directors. Adherence to these standards by independent directors and fulfillment of their responsibilities in a professional and faithful manner should promote confidence of the investment community, particularly minority shareholders, regulators and companies in the institution of independent directors.

Code of Conduct: Code of Conduct is the code which is designed to reflect the intention of highest standards of integrity to be followed by the corporate board of directors and senior management in practice.

Conformance Roles: Conformance Roles are the roles played by the board of directors in which the board ensures that the company is conforming to the policies, procedures and plans laid down by the board and being properly accountable for its activities.

Core Values: Core Values are the desirable and auditable values which are in-built in the system of governance so that boundaries for performance of each player viz. directors, auditors, shareholders and other stakeholders are well defined. They facilitate in laying down the responsibility and accountability in ensuring proper governance.

Corporate Governance: Corporate Governance is a system of structuring, operating, and controlling a company with a view to achieving long-term strategic goals to satisfy its shareholders, creditors, employees, customers and suppliers. It prescribes a Code of Corporate Conduct in relation to all the stakeholders.

Corporate Policy: Corporate Policy is an articulated document prepared and adopted by the board of directors that is of utmost importance for its implementation by the corporate management. The policy documents translate the corporate vision, mission and goals in writing and set parameters for governing the course of conduct of business.

Corporate Social Responsibility (CSR): Corporate Social Responsibility (CSR) is essentially a concept whereby companies integrate social and environmental concerns in their business operations and in the interaction with their stakeholders on a voluntary basis. Corporate responsibility towards society and corporate governance are inextricably interlinked, intertwined, and inseparable from each other.

Corporate Social Responsibility Committee: A Corporate Social Responsibility Committee is one of the most important board committees that is formally set up by the board, consisting of 3 or more directors out of which at least 1 director shall be an independent director. Main role of this committee is to discharge various responsibilities of the corporates for the society.

Corporate Social Responsibility committee is mandated for the corporates under Section 135 of the Companies Act, 2013, CSR Policy 2014, and Schedule VII to the Companies Act.

Corporate Social Responsibility Report: As per Section 135 of the Companies Act, 2013 and Companies (CSR) Policy Rules, 2014 a company is required to submit a report on the social responsibilities discharged by it as per its CSR policy which shall be included in the Board's report of the annual report every year.

Corporate Sustainability: Corporate Sustainability is a business approach that creates long term consumer and employee value by creating a green strategy aimed towards the natural environment and taking into consideration every dimension of how a business operates in the social, cultural, and economic environment. In other words, Corporate Sustainability is a business approach that creates long-term shareholder value by embracing opportunities and managing risks deriving from economic, environmental and social developments.

Credit Rating Information Services of India Ltd. (CRISIL): Credit Rating Information Services of India Ltd. (CRISIL) is a renowned credit rating agency in India which addresses the issue of corporate governance by providing an independent assessment of an entity's performance and future expectations on 'balanced value creation through sound corporate governance practices'. CRISIL evaluates two broad aspects to arriving at GVC rating for a company, viz. (i) value creation and distribution, and (ii) corporate governance and wealth management.

Customisation and Code Servicing: Customisation is a process of fine-tuning in a company specific manner, the governance practices drawing upon the basic ground rules laid down by the code. Wherever the corporate governance framework has been built on the code of governance, such framework must be serviced time to time to ensure that it reflects appropriate reactions to changing realities.

Depositories Act, 1996: Depositories Act, 1996 is the legal provisions enacted by the Government of India in order to bring in the concept of holding equity shares into electronic form from the physical form.

Director: Section 2 (34) of the Companies Act 2013 defines a Director as a director appointed to the Board of a company.

Ethical Principles: Ethical Principles are the rules of conduct that are derived from ethical values, known as six pillars, viz. (i) trustworthiness, (ii) respect, (iii) responsibility, (iv) fairness, (v) caring, and (vi) citizenship. These values are inseparable from one another and are closely interwoven and interlinked with each other.

Ethics: Ethics owes its origin to Greek word 'ethos' which means a system of moral principles, the basis for deciding right and wrong actions, and implies customs, habits, noble traits in character, discipline, culture, and disposition.

Executive Director: Executive Director is the director in the board who holds management position in the company.

Financially Literate: The term Financially Literate means the ability to read and understand basic financial statements (i.e. Balance Sheet, Profit & Loss Account, and Statement of Cash Flows).

Gap Analysis: Gap Analysis is the analysis undertaken to examine the gap of men and women's participation in corporate boards of various countries of the world.

Gender Diversity: Gender Diversity is the way to create diversity in the boards of corporate houses in order to improve the structure of corporate governance and bring in gender quality and balance in the board's activities.

Section 149(1) of the Companies Act 2013 and Rule 3 of the Companies (Appointment and Qualification of Directors) Rules 2014 as well as SEBI (LODR) Regulations 2015 require certain companies to appoint at least one woman director on the board.

Independent Director: Independent Director is a non-executive director in the board who is genuinely independent of the company's affairs, other than holding his board appointment and receiving sitting fees only. Independent directors do not have any other pecuniary relationship or transaction with the company, its promoters, management or subsidiaries, which in the judgement of the board may affect their independence of judgement.

Industrial Policy Resolution, 1948: Industrial Policy Resolution, 1948 is the first major policy statement announced by the Government of India in 1948 which affirmed the complimentary roles of both 'state' and the 'private sector' for development of the economy.

Industrial Policy Resolution, 1956: Industrial Policy Resolution, 1956 is the policy statement announced by the Government of India in 1956 in pursuit of a socialist pattern of society as the principal objective of all economic and social policy.

Industries (Development and Regulation) Act, 1951: Industries (Development and Regulation) Act, 1951 is one of the most significant of all legislations of the Government of India in 1951 which provided the legal basis for industrial licensing scheme.

Insider Trading: Insider Trading, as per Section 195 of the Companies Act, 2013, means (i) an act of subscribing, buying, selling, dealing or agreeing to subscribe, buy, sell, or deal in any securities by any director or key managerial personnel or any other officer of a company either as principal or agent if such director or key managerial personnel or any other officer of the company is reasonably accepted to have access to any non-public price sensitive information in respect of securities of company; or (ii) an act of counselling about procurement or communicating directly or indirectly any non-public price sensitive information to any person.

Institutional Investors: Institutional Investors is a broad umbrella which covers mutual funds, unit trusts, investment trusts, foundations, endowments, trustee departments of banks, insurance companies, private as well as public pension funds. All these bodies invest funds on behalf of others and so have a fiduciary role. They play an active role in monitoring portfolio companies.

Internal Financial Controls: Internal Financial Controls, as per Section 134 (5) of the Companies Act, 2013, means the policies and procedures adopted by the company for ensuring the orderly and efficient conduct of its business, including adherence to company's policies, the safeguarding of its assets, the prevention and detection of frauds and errors, the accuracy and completeness of the accounting records, and the timely preparation of reliable financial information.

Investment Information and Credit Rating Agency of India (ICRA): Investment Information and Credit Rating Agency of India (ICRA) is a renowned credit rating agency in India which addresses the issue of corporate governance by indicating the level to which an entity accepts and follows the codes and guidelines of corporate governance practices. The key variables analysed by ICRA to arrive at CGR for a company are: (i) shareholding structure, (ii) governance structure and management process, (iii) board structure and processes, (iv)stakeholders relationship, (v) transparency and disclosures, and (vi) financial discipline.

J.J. Irani Committee: J.J. Irani Committee was constituted by the Government of India in December 2004 to evaluate the comments and suggestions received on 'concept paper' and to provide recommendations to the government in making a simplified modern company law.

K.M. Birla Committee: K.M. Birla Committee was set up by SEBI in the year 2000. Most of the committee's recommendations on corporate governance were accepted by SEBI and included in its new Clause 49 of the Listing Agreement in 2000.

Lead Independent Director: Lead Independent Director is a strong and independent non-executive element on the board to whom concerns can be conveyed and whose responsibility is to work closely with the Chairman/CEO and a take a lead role in the board evaluation process, to act as a spokesperson for independent directors as a group, apart from other important board functions.

Majority Executive Board: Majority Executive Board is the board in which the non-executive directors are appointed in small proportions, say 2 or 3 in the board. In majority executive board there is a danger of domination of board affairs by the executive members (example, boards in the UK and India).

Majority Outside Board: Majority Outside Board is the board in which the non-executive directors form the majority on the board, particularly the independent majority. Majority outside board can emphasise checks and balances and keep close supervision of management performance (example, boards in the USA and Australia).

Managing Agency System (1850–1955): The Managing Agency System is an age-old system of governing companies in India initially by the British merchants, which began in 1850 and was in vogue till 1955. This system played a key role in the industrialisation of India in the pre-independence period.

N.R. Narayana Murthy Committee: N.R. Narayana Murthy Committee was constituted by SEBI in 2003 and mandated to review the performance of corporate governance in India and make appropriate recommendations.

Naresh Chandra Committee: Naresh Chandra Committee was set up by the Government of India in 2002 to examine and recommend drastic amendments to the law pertaining to auditor-client relationships and the role of independent directors.

New Economic Policy: New Economic Policy is the economic policy adopted by the Government of India consequent to liberalisation and opening up of the economy since 1991.

Nomination Committee: A Nomination Committee is one of the most important board committees that is formally set up by the board, usually consisting of independent board members and reporting to the board. It is the vehicle by which new non-executive directors are brought for selection.

Nomination committee is mandated for the corporates under Section 178 of the Companies Act, 2013 as also Regulation 19 read with Schedule II, Part D of SEBI (LODR) Regulations, 2015.

Nominee Director: Nominee Director is a director in the board who is appointed by a financial institution, bank, or government appointee representing government shareholding. Nominee director represents specific interests of these institutions and hence, cannot be termed as independent director.

Non-Executive Director: Non-Executive Director is the director in the board who does not hold management position in the company.

Non-Executive Non-independent Director: Non-Executive Non-independent Director is the director in the board whose position might bring his objectivity and independence into questions.

NSE Nifty: NSE Nifty means National Stock Exchange 50 companies.

Performance Roles: Performance Roles are the roles played by the board of directors in which the board focuses on strategic and policy issues for the future of the company, sets the corporate direction and contributes to the performance of the business.

Pluralistic Theory: Pluralistic Theory is the theory that advocates the idea of multiple interests of stakeholders. This theory asserts that the company's performance in terms of profitability and growth will be increased substantially provided the stakeholders' management is practised by the company.

Policy: Policy is defined as a course or principle of action adopted or proposed by an individual or an organisation.

Price-sensitive Information: According to Section 195 of the Companies Act, 2013, Price-sensitive Information means any information which relates directly or indirectly, to a company and which, if published, is likely to materially affect the price of securities of the company.

Principles of Corporate Governance: Principles of Corporate Governance are the cornerstones which revolve around the basic interrelated segments viz. (i) integrity and fairness, (ii) transparency and disclosures, and (iii) accountability and responsibility.

Promoter System (1956–1991): The Promoter System is an old system of governing companies in India by the leading Indian managing agents, which began in 1956 and was in vogue till 1991.

Related Party: As per SEBI Listing Regulation 23, a Related Party is a person or entity that is related to the company. Parties are considered to be related if one party has the ability to control the other party or exercise significant influence over the other party, directly or indirectly, in making financial and/or operating decisions.

Related Party Transaction: Related Party Transaction is a transfer of resources, services or obligations between a company and a related party, regardless of whether a price is charged.

Remuneration Committee: A Remuneration Committee is one of the most important board committees that is formally set up by the board, usually consisting of independent board members and reporting to the board. The main role of remuneration committee is to have an appropriate reward policy that can attract, retain, and motivate directors to achieve the long-term goals of the company.

Remuneration committee is mandated for the corporates under Section 178 of the Companies Act, 2013 as also Regulation 19 read with Schedule II, Part D of SEBI (LODR) Regulations, 2015.

Risk Management Committee: A Risk Management Committee is one of the most important board committees that is formally set up by the board and reporting to the board. The main role of this committee is to manage risks of the company successfully in order to survive and sustain profitability in the competitive market.

Risk management committee is mandated for the corporates under Regulation 21 of SEBI (LODR) Regulations, 2015.

Securities and Exchange Board of India (SEBI): Securities and Exchange Board of India (SEBI) was constituted and established by the Government of India in the year 1988 after abolition of the office of the Controller of Capital issues. It was given statutory and regulatory powers in 1992 in order to pursue its goals of *investor protection* and *market development.* It formulated various rules and regulations for the purpose of regulating the operations of the players of the capital market aimed at promotion of more responsible governance in companies.

Securities Contracts (Regulation) Act, 1956: Securities Contracts (Regulation) Act, 1956 is the legal provisions enacted by the Government of India in 1956 in order to regulate the transactions in securities and check speculation in the securities.

Senior Management: As per Section 178 of the Companies Act, 2013 the expression 'Senior Management' means personnel of the company who are members of its core management team excluding board of directors comprising all members of management one level below the executive directors, including the functional heads.

Single-tier Board Structure: Single-tier Board Structure is the board structure of a company which is characterised by election of directors by the shareholders, various shareholders' rights and restrictions (example, Anglo-American model).

Small Shareholder: As per Section 151 of the Companies Act, 2013, Small Shareholder means a shareholder holding shares of nominal value of not more than ₹ 20,000 or such other sum as may be prescribed.

Social Entity Theory: Social Entity Theory is the theory that regards the company as a social institution in society based on the grounds of fundamental values and moral order of the community. This theory requires the managers and executives to work as the custodians of stakeholders' interests.

Stakeholders: Stakeholders are the parties/agencies that have direct or indirect relationship with the company for their welfare and fulfilment of their expectations from the company. They include (a) shareholders (including institutional shareholders), (b) employees, (c) customers, (d) competitors, (e) creditors, (f) government, (g) community, and (h) public at large.

Stakeholders' Relationship Committee: Stakeholders' Relationship Committee is one of the most important board committees that is formally set up by the board for resolving the grievances of security holders of the company. The committee shall consist of a chairperson who shall be a non-executive director and such other members as may be decided by the board.

Stakeholders' relationship committee is mandated for the corporates under Section 178 of the Companies Act, 2013 as also Regulation 20 read with Schedule II, Part D of SEBI (LODR) Regulations, 2015.

Statutory Auditors: Statutory Auditors are the auditors appointed by the shareholders of the company in annual general meeting every year to audit the accounts and financial statements and express their opinion on them, which are placed before the members in annual general meeting. The statutory auditors are also supposed to certify on the compliance by the board on the code of corporate governance since it has become mandatory by the Companies Act as also by the Listing Agreements, on the companies for compliance all over the corporate world.

Stewardship Theory: Stewardship Theory is the theory based on the assumption that man is essentially trustworthy, able to act in good faith in the interest of others with integrity and honesty. This is implicit in the fiduciary relationship required of directors. This theory is based on the belief that stewardship would be exercised by the directors to whom the shareholders have delegated responsibility and authority, while requiring appropriate accountability.

Strategy Formulation: Strategy Formulation is the process through which each member of the board appreciates the competitive situation in which the business exists and moves towards a shared vision of the future that the board holds for the company.

The Blue Ribbon Committee: The Blue Ribbon Committee was set up in October 1998 by the Securities and Exchange Commission, the New York Stock Exchange and the National Association of Securities Dealers to address the effectiveness of corporate audit committees. The committee submitted its report in 1999 recommending guiding principles for best practices for the audit committees of the US companies.

The Cadbury Committee: The Cadbury Committee was set up in May 1991 by the Financial Reporting Council, the London Stock Exchange and the accounting profession to address the financial aspects of corporate governance consequent to a number of scams and failures in the corporate sector in the late 1980s and the early 1990s.

The Combined Code, Principles of Good Governance and Code of Best Practice: The Committee of Combined Code was set up in 1998 by the London Stock Exchange to examine the reports and recommendations of Cadbury and Greenbury, and to suggest to the London Stock Exchange a set of principles of good governance and codes of best practice for the UK companies finally for implementation.

The Companies Act, 1956: The Companies Act, 1956 is the legal provisions introduced by the Government of India in the year 1956 in order to stop abuses to shareholders and the common public prevailing in the Managing Agency System and to lay the basis for a socialist pattern of society.

The Greenbury Committee: The Greenbury Committee was set up in January 1995 by the Confederation of British Industry to study executive pay issues and provide recommendations for governance reform in British corporates.

The Hampel Committee: The Hampel Committee was set up in November 1995 by the Confederation of British Industry, the London Stock Exchange, the Institute of Directors, the Consultative Committee of Accountancy Bodies, the National Association of Pension Funds and the Association of British Insurers to assess progress of implementation of Cadbury and Greenbury recommendations on corporate governance.

The Organisation for Economic Co-operation and Development (OECD) Principles on Corporate Governance: The Organisation for Economic Co-operation and Development (OECD) is an inter-governmental organisation of the industrially developed nations of the world. OECD has come out with a set of clearly defined principles to assist both its member governments as also non-member governments to bring about suitable improvements in their legal, institutional and regulatory framework for facilitating good corporate governance regimes. The main objective of these principles is to safeguard the interests of shareholders and other stakeholders. The OECD principles of corporate governance were released in late 1999 and these have been accepted as an international benchmark.

Trusteeship Theory: Trusteeship Theory is the theory that adopts a realistic perspective of the company as a social institution which has a corporate personality. This concept requires the managers and executives to work as trustees of the organisation, promote the broader interests of the company as a whole, balance the conflicting interests of the stakeholders and develop the company's capacities on a long term basis.

Two-tier Board Structure: Two-tier Board Structure of a company consists of a Supervisory Board and a Management Board. In the supervisory board workers are allocated 50% of the seats and the major banks, financial institutions are also represented there (example, German model).

Two-tier Supervisory Board: Two-tier Supervisory Board is the board in which the ultimate separation of the executive management from the non-executive direction is found. It recognises the difference in the position of executive and non-executive directors. Two-tier supervisory board can monitor the decisions of the management board and ensure that these decisions are in the best interests of the shareholders (example, German board).

Value Creation: Value Creation means governing the companies in an effective and ethical manner that should ultimately result in transparency and best practices on the one hand and a healthy bottom line on consistent basis for all the stakeholders on the other.

Whistle Blowers: Whistle Blowers are the individuals or employees who report concerns about unethical behaviour, actual or suspected fraud or violation of the company's code of conduct or ethics policy. As per Listing Regulation 22 a company shall establish a vigil mechanism for the whistle blowers to safeguard them adequately against the victimisation of the whistle blowers who avail of this mechanism.

Bibliography

Adams, R.B. and Ferreira, D., "Women in the Boardroom and Their Impact on Governance and Performance", *Journal of Financial Economics*, Vol. 94, 2009.

Adler, N.J., "Global Leadership: Women Leaders", *Management International Review*, Vol. 37, 1997.

Agarwal, S., "Corporate Governance and Audit Committee", *Chartered Secretary*, October, 2003.

Allen, W.T., "Redefining the Role of Outside Directors", in Monks, R.A.G. and Minow, N. (Eds.), *Corporate Governance,* Blackwell Publishers, Massachusetts, USA, 1995.

Annual Reports of Companies Listed in BSE Sensex and NSE Nifty, 2015–2016.

Arfken, D.E., Bellar S.L., and Helms, M.M., "The Ultimate Glass Ceiling Revisited: The Presence of Women on Corporate Boards", *Journal of Business Ethics*, Vol. 50, 2004.

Bain, N. and Band, D., *Winning Ways Through Corporate Governance*, Macmillan Press Limited, London, 1996.

Bergen, V.C.W. and Massey, J., "Workforce Diversity and Organisational Performance", *Equal Opportunities International*, Vol. 24, 2005.

Bhojani, S.H., "FICCI Seminar on Independent Director", New Delhi, December 2–4, 2002.

Brammer, S., Millington, A., and Pavelin, S., "Corporate Reputation and Women on the Board", *British Journal of Management*, Vol. 20, 2009.

Canadian Institute of Chartered Accountants, *Governance Processes for Control*, November 1995.

Carson, C.M., Mosley, D.C., and Boyar, S.L., "Performance Gains through Diverse Top Management Teams", *Team Performance Management*, Vol. 10, 2004.

Carter, D.A., Simkins, B.J., and Simpson, W.G., "Corporate Governance, Board Diversity and Firm Value", *Financial Review*, Vol. 38, No. 3, 2003.

Catalyst Census of Women Board Directors of the Fortune 1000, New York, 2004.

Catalyst Census: Fortune 500 Women Board Directors, New York, 2011.

Catalyst Information Centre, "India: The Case for Gender Diversity", January, 2012.

Charkham, J.P., *Keeping Good Company, A Study of Corporate Governance in Five Countries*, Oxford University Press, New York, 1995.

Chitayat, G., "Working Relationship between the Chairman of BOD and the CEO", in Tricker, R. (Ed.), *International Corporate Governance*, Prentice-Hall International (UK) Ltd., London, 1994.

Cochrun, P. and Wartick, S.L., "Corporate Governance—A Review of the Literature", in Tricker, R.I. (Ed.), *International Corporate Governance*, Prentice-Hall International (UK) Ltd., London, 1994.

Chandratre, K.R., "Corporate Governance vis-à-vis The Listing Agreement–II", *Chartered Secretary*, October, 2003.

"Corporate Governance in Listed Entities—Amendments to Clauses 35B and 49 of the Equity Listing Agreement" vide SEBI Circular no. CIR/CFD/POLICY CELL/2/2014 dated April 17, 2014.

Dalton, D.R. and Dalton, C.M., "Women and Corporate Boards of Directors: The Promise of Increased and Substantive Participation in the Post Sarbanes-Oxley Era", *Business Horizons*, Vol. 53, 2010.

Das, S.C., "Corporate Governance in France", *The Management Accountant*, November, 2004.

Das, S.C., "Corporate Governance in Japan", *The Management Accountant*, December, 2004.

Das, S.C., "Corporate Governance in Australasian Countries", *The Management Accountant*, April, 2005.

Das, S.C., "Corporate Governance in Germany", *The ICFAI Journal of Corporate Governance*, April, 2005.

Das, S.C., "Corporate Governance in United Kingdom (UK)", *The Management Accountant*, May, 2005.

Das, S.C., "Corporate Governance in the USA", *The ICWAI Research Bulletin*, July, 2005.

Das, S.C., "Sarbanes—Oxley Act (SOX) and its influence on Naresh Chandra Committee recommendations towards good corporate governance in Indian corporates", *The Management Accountant*, July, 2005.

Das, S.C., "Company Law Concept Paper (2004) Related to Corporate Governance," *The Management Accountant*, August, 2005.

Das, S.C., "J.J. Irani Committee Report on Company Law Related to Corporate Governance," *The Management Accountant*, September, 2005.

Das, S.C., "Ethics in Governance Practices in Corporates—Some Issues and Implications," *The Management Accountant*, April, 2006.

Davies, A., *A Strategic Approach to Corporate Governance,* Grower Publishing Ltd., England, 1999.

Desirable Corporate Governance—Code by CII, 1998.

Dimsdale, N.H., "A Postscript on the Draft Report of the Cadbury Committee", in Dimsdale, N. and Prevezer, M. (Eds.), *Capital Markets and Corporate Governance*, Oxford University Press, New York, 1994.

Dimsdale, N. and Prevezer, M., *Capital Markets and Corporate Governance*, Oxford University Press, New York, 1994.

Dwyer, S., Richard, O.C., and Chadwick, K., "Gender Diversity in Management and Firm Performance: The Influence of Growth Orientation and Organisational Culture", *Journal of Business Research*, Vol. 56, 2003.

Erchardt, N.L., Werbel, J.D., and Shrader, C.B., "Board of Director Diversity and Firm Financial Performance", *Corporate Governance*, Vol. 11, 2003.

Fairfax, L.M., "The Bottom Line on Board Diversity: A Cost-Benefit Analysis of the Business Rationales for Diversity on Corporate Boards", *Wisconsin Law Review*, Vol. 795, 2005.

FICCI Conference, on "Models and Dimensions of Corporate Governance: Discussion Paper", New Delhi, December 2–4, 2002.

Gopalsamy, N., *Corporate Governance*, A.H. Wheeler and Co. Ltd., New Delhi, 1998.

Hart, O., "Mechanisms for Controlling Management—Some Theories and Implications", in Keasy, K., Thomsom, S., and Wright, M. (Eds.), *Corporate Governance,* Edward Elgar Publishing Ltd., Cheltanham, UK, 1999.

Indian Companies Act, 2013 and Company Rules, 2014.

International Labour Organization (ILO), "Global Employment Trends for Women", Geneva, 2004.

Joshi, V., "Institutional Investors and Corporate Governance", *The Management Accountant,* November, 2002.

Knight, A., "The Aims and Objectives of Corporate Bodies", in Midgley, K. (Ed.), *Management Accountability and Corporate Governance*, The Macmillan Press Ltd., London, 1982.

Kumar, S., *Corporate Governance—A Question of Ethics*, Galgotia Publishing Co., New Delhi, 2002.

Lahiri, A., "The Essence of Good Corporate Governance", *Chartered Secretary*, January, 2004.

Lee, H.U. and Park, J.H., "Top Team Diversity, Internationalisation and the Mediating Effect of International Alliances", *British Journal of Management*, Vol. 17(3), 2006.

Lusch, R.F. and Harvey, M.G., "The Case for an Off-Balance Sheet Controller", *Sloan Management Review*, Winter, 1994.

Mahajan, R., "Blowing the Whistle", *Chartered Accountant*, June, 2001.

Miller, T. and Triana M. del C., "Demographic Diversity in the Boardroom: Mediators of the Board Diversity—Firm Performance Relationship", *Journal of Management Studies*, Vol. 46, No. 5, 2009.

Mittal, K.M., *Social Responsibilities of Business: Concepts, Areas and Practices*, Chanakya Publications, Delhi, 1988.

Monks, R.A.G. and Minow, N., *Corporate Governance,* Blackwell Publishers, Massachusetts, USA, 1995.

Mueller, R.K., *A Director's Performance Appraisal, Directors and Boards*, Spring, 1993.

Mukherjee, R., "The Ultimate Result of Corporate Governance, Value Management", *Chartered Secretary*, August, 2003.

Mukherjee, Reed, A. and Reed, D., "Corporate Governance in India , Three Historical Models and Their Development Impact", in Reed, D. and Mukherjee, S. (Eds.), *Corporate Governance, Economic Reforms, and Development,* Oxford University Press, New Delhi, 2004.

Pandey, T.N., "Ethics in Corporate Governance", *Chartered Secretary*, January, 2004.

Prahalad, C.K., "Corporate Governance or Corporate Value Added?", in Chew, D.H. (Ed.), *Studies in International Corporate Finance and Governance Systems—A Comparison of the US, Japan and Europe*, Oxford University Press, New York, 1997.

Prahlada Rao, D.K., "The Companies (Amendment) Bill, 2003—A Trend Setter", Chartered Secretary, October, 2003.

Reed, D., *Three Historical Models of Corporate Governance: An Examination of Corporate Economic Responsibilities*, Indian Institute of Management, Calcutta, 1998.

Report of The Cadbury Committee, Appendix 1.1, in Gopalsamy, N., *Corporate Governance*, A.H. Wheeler and Co. Ltd., New Delhi, 1998.

Report of the Expert (J.J. Irani) Committee on Company Law, 2005.

Report of the Kumar Mangalam Birla Committee on Corporate Governance, 2000.

Report of the Committee on Corporate Audit and Governance—Naresh Chandra Committee, 2002.

Report of the SEBI Committee on Corporate Governance—Narayana Murthy Committee, 2003.

"Revised Clause 49 of The Listing Agreement by SEBI", *Chartered Secretary*, November, 2004.

Revised Clause 49 of The Listing Agreement by SEBI, 2014.

Roberson, Q.M. and Park, H.J., "Examining the Link between Diversity and Firm Performance: The Effects of Diversity Reputation and Leader Racial Diversity", *Group and Organisation Management*, Vol. 32, 2007.

Salmon, W.J., "Crisis Prevention: How to Gear Up Your Board", *Harvard Business Review*, January/February, 1993.

Sarker, J. and Sarker, S., "Corporate Governance Reforms and Corporate Sector Development in India", in Reed, D., and Mukherjee, S. (Eds.), *Corporate Governance, Economic Reforms, and Development,* Oxford University Press, New Delhi, 2004.

SEBI (Listing Obligations and Disclosure Requirements) Regulations, 2015.

Seth, A., "Corporate Governance System: An Integrative Model and Implication for India" in Munshi, S. and Abraham, B.P. (Eds.), *Good Governance, Democratic Societies and Globalisation,* Sage Publications, New Delhi, 2004.

Shah, H.N., Lakhani, D.V., and Juthani, P.S., *Corporate Governance*, Bombay Chartered Accountants' Society, Mumbai, 2000.

Sherman, Howard, D., "Corporate Governance Changes Make Inroads in Europe", in Chew, D.H. (Ed.), *Studies in International Corporate Finance and Governance Systems—A Comparison of the US, Japan and Europe,* Oxford University Press, New York, 1997.

Sisodiya, A.S., "Corporate Governance—Lessons from the East India Company", *Effective Executive*, October, 2003.

Sinha, A., "Economic Reforms, Corporate Philosophy, and Development" in Reed, D. and Mukherjee, S. (Eds.), *Corporate Governance, Economic Reforms, and Development,* Oxford University Press, New Delhi, 2004.

Standing Committee on Internal Financial Standards and Codes, Report of the Advisory Group on Corporate Governance, The Director, Division of Reports, Reviews and Publications, Department of Economic Analysis and Policy, Reserve Bank of India, Mumbai, 2001.

Sundararaman, S., "Accountability—The Global View", *The Chartered Accountant*, August, 2000.

Taxmann's SEBI Manual, 2005.

The Blue Ribbon Committee on Corporate Governance, Report and Recommendations of The Blue Ribbon Committee on Improving the Effectiveness of Corporate Audit Committees.

The Cadbury Committee of Corporate Governance, The Report of the Committee on The Financial Aspects of Corporate Governance: The Code of Best Practice, Gee and Co. Ltd. (UK), December, 1992.

The Combined Code, Principles of Good Governance and Code of Best Practice, Committee on Corporate Governance, London Stock Exchange, June, 1998.

The Companies (Amendment) Bill, 2003", *Chartered Secretary*, June, 2003.

The Economic Times dated 2 July, 2019, 10 September, 2019.

The Hampel Committee on Corporate Governance—Final Report, January, 1998.

The Organization for Economic Cooperation and Development (OECD) Principles on Corporate Governance, 1999.

The Telegraph dated 1 July, 2019; 2 July, 2019; 12 July, 2019, 10 September, 22 November, 2019.

Tricker, R.I., *Corporate Governance*, Gower Publishing Co. Ltd., Aldershot, England, 1984.

Tricker, R.I., *International Corporate Governance*, Prentice-Hall International Ltd. (UK), London, 1994.

Vyas, A.K., "Companies (Amendment) Bill, 2003 Poised to Set New Horizons", *Chartered Secretary*, July, 2003.

www.sebi.com

www.crisil.com

www.icraratings.com

Index